CAPE BRETON

LONDON: PRINTED BY
SPOTTISWOODE AND CO., NEW-STREET SQUARE
AND PARLIAMENT STREET

A HISTORY

OF

THE ISLAND OF CAPE BRETON

WITH SOME ACCOUNT OF THE

DISCOVERY AND SETTLEMENT

OF

CANADA, NOVA SCOTIA, AND NEWFOUNDLAND

BY

RICHARD BROWN, F.G.S. F.R.G.S.

LONDON
SAMPSON LOW, SON, AND MARSTON
CROWN BUILDINGS, 188 FLEET STREET
1869

DEDICATORY EPISTLE

TO THE

YOUTH OF CAPE BRETON.

I DEDICATE and address to you, my dear friends, this volume of letters upon the History of Cape Breton—compiled and written for your special use—for the following reasons :—

When I first visited the island, more than forty years ago, my professional duties led me into various districts, at that time quite destitute of inns and the ordinary means of locomotion. Thus I was frequently compelled to ask from the inhabitants both shelter and subsistence, as well as aid in moving from place to place. I need hardly say that in the comfortable houses of the merchants and the farmers—in the log huts of the new settlers—in the wigwams of the wandering Indians—in short, everywhere I received a hearty and hospitable welcome. In later years, during a long residence at one locality, I had the happiness of enjoying the friendship of a wide circle of neighbours of all ranks. And lastly, when failing health and advancing age obliged me to return to my native land, I received so many proofs of the affection and regard of my numerous friends, that I felt bound to express my acknowledgments in some more substantial shape than even the warmest thanks for their kind adieux and good wishes.

Having often had occasion to regret the want of a history of the island, it occurred to me that, if I could supply this want, I might thereby be enabled to give proof of the sincerity of my grateful recollections, and at the same time render you an acceptable service. I am aware that you will find, in some recent histories of Canada and Nova Scotia, short accounts of the island, and narratives of the two celebrated sieges of Louisbourg; but in your case much more than these is required. There are also in many books, both ancient and modern, in European libraries, scattered fragments of Cape Breton history, and in the rich stores of the State Paper Office many valuable documents relating to the island; but as all these are inaccessible to you, I concluded that I could not occupy my leisure time in a more profitable way than in collecting, from all the sources within my reach, every scrap of intelligence that would be interesting to you, and in arranging it in chronological order. Having had little experience in writing for the press, especially with the precision indispensable in historical works, I determined to address you in familiar letters—a form to which I have been more accustomed—feeling assured that I could in that way make myself better understood.

As my object was to write a history of Cape Breton *only*, I endeavoured in the first instance to treat of matters relating to the discovery, settlement, and progress of the island *exclusively*; but I soon found it was so closely connected, both geographically and politically, with the neighbouring provinces, that it was impossible to give a clear and intelligible account of its history without at the same time submitting contemporary sketches of the discovery and settlement of Canada, Nova Scotia, and Newfoundland. My work has in consequence been considerably increased in bulk; but as some of you may not have histories of these provinces to refer to, I trust the short sketches given in the following letters may prove useful. My aim all through has been to submit the information obtained from old books and official documents, wherever it was possible, in the form of extracts from the originals, in the exact words and orthography of the writers. You will see at a glance that my letters, in a literary point of view, have no claims upon your attention. I have tried 'to tell the story as 'twas told to me.' If I have succeeded in making it intelligible and useful, my object has been fully accomplished. I have industriously sought for information wherever there was the slightest prospect of finding it; and having pointed out the sources from whence it was obtained, I hope future historians may derive some benefit from my labour and researches.

For the great bulk of the most important matter embodied in the following letters, I am under great obligations to Sir Roderick Murchison for free access to the extensive library of the British Museum, and to his Grace the Duke of Buckingham and Chandos for permission to examine and make extracts from the voluminous colonial documents in the Public Record Office. To the courteous and obliging officers of both these truly noble national institutions I beg to tender my sincere thanks for their valuable aid in guiding me in my researches.

I must not forget also to thank my Cape Breton friends —the Honourable John Bourinot, Consul of France, his Honour Mr. Justice Dodd, and James P. Ward and Henry W. Crawley, Esquires, for the perusal of some valuable documents in their possession.

In bidding you farewell, I can say, with all truthfulness, it will ever be to me a cause of much gratification that my destiny led me in my younger days to your highly favoured island, where I spent so many years of a happy, and I trust, not altogether useless life. The recollection of those bygone years will last as long as life and memory endure; and I shall ever hope and pray that you, my young friends, may live to see your country attain the high rank to which it is justly entitled by its geographical position and vast natural resources.

Ever faithfully yours,

RICHARD BROWN.

LONDON: *May*, 1869.

CONTENTS.

LETTER I.

LETTER II.

LETTER III.

LETTER IV.

LETTER V.

LETTER VI.

LETTER VII.

LETTER VIII.

LETTER IX.

LETTER X.

LETTER XI.

LETTER XII.

LETTER XIII.

LETTER XIV.

LETTER XV.

LETTER XVI.

LETTER XVII.

LETTER XVIII.

LETTER XIX.

LETTER XX.

LETTER XXVI.

LETTER XXVII.

LIST OF MAPS AND ILLUSTRATIONS.

HISTORY
OF
CAPE BRETON
ETC.

LETTER I.

TO THE YOUTH OF CAPE BRETON.

I AM AWARE, my dear friends, that you, who have the happiness of calling Cape Breton your home, are well acquainted with its vast natural resources; but as there are many persons, both in England and the United States, deeply interested in their successful development, I hope you will not consider that I am neglecting the special object of these Letters in here giving a short account of the physical geography of the island for their information. I am the more inclined to adopt this course, because I hope it will be the means of dispelling some very erroneous notions which have been widely circulated respecting the soil, climate, and capabilities of your highly-favoured island.

If you refer to a map of North America, you will observe that the island lies between the parallels of 45° 27′ and 47° 3′ north, and the meridians of 59° 47′ and 61° 32′ west; and is bounded on the north-east and south-east by the Atlantic Ocean, on the south-west by George's Bay and the Gut of Canso, and on the north-west by the Gulf of St. Lawrence. Its length from north to south is 110 miles, and its width from east to west 87 miles. On the south it is separated from Nova Scotia by the Gut of Canso—a navigable strait 15 miles in length, and about 1 mile in width. Cape St. Lawrence—its most northern extremity—is about 70 miles from Cape Ray in Newfoundland.

The whole circuit of the island, with the exception of the north-west coast, is indented by deep bays and inlets, often terminating in excellent harbours. A great portion of the interior is occupied by an estuary, or arm of the sea, called the Bras d'Or Lakes, which communicates with the ocean by means of two narrow channels opening into Spanish Bay on the north-east coast. These lakes divide the island into two unequal parts, or peninsulas, united by an isthmus less than half a mile in width.

Few countries of the same limited extent present such varied natural features as the island of Cape Breton. In the western division, the great promontory extending from Margarie and St. Ann's to Cape St. Lawrence, covering an area of 1,100 square miles, is one vast plateau or table-land, elevated in some places more than 1,200 feet above the level of the sea. It is bounded on three of its sides by a coast line of bold rugged bluffs and lofty precipices, furrowed by deep clefts and gorges, partially covered by scrubby spruce and pine. Three ranges of hills, as you will observe by referring to the map at the end of this volume, branch off from the fourth side of the table-land in a southerly direction. The first range extends from St. Ann's to Great Baddeck, being bounded on the east by the Baddeck river, and on the west by the Wagamatcook; the second or middle range extends from the source of the east branch of the Margarie river to Why-co-comah; and the third from Margarie river to Mabou, between Lake Ainslie and the sea-coast.

Neither the middle nor the western range is continuous, the first being separated from the table-land by the Margarie river, and the second by a deep gorge or ravine running at right angles with the course of the Wagamatcook, from near its source to the Forks of the north and south branches of the Margarie.

Another large tract of highlands lies between St. George's Bay and Why-co-comah, which throws off two branches, one running easterly, between the basin of the river Denys and the West Bay, the other southerly, between the Gut of Canso and the valley of the river Inhabitants. Proceeding easterly, we find a detached range of elevated land, about ten miles in length, between St. Patrick's Channel and the Straits of Barra; and still farther, in the same direction, a lofty range, between St. Ann's Harbour and the great entrance of the Bras d'Or Lakes, which terminates in the rocky promontory of Cape Dauphin.

All the high lands in the western division, except the southern end of the range lying between the Gut of Canso and the valley of the river Inhabitants, consist of syenite, gneiss, mica slate, and other metamorphic rocks of old date. A coarse conglomerate, the basis of the carboniferous system, rests upon the flanks of many of the hills, which in some places attain an elevation of 600 feet. Between Port Hood and Margarie, the upper beds of the carboniferous system, containing some workable seams of bituminous coal, occur in the cliffs, being the eastern margin of an extensive coal field lying under the waters of the Gulf of St. Lawrence. Similar beds of coal also occur in the low country, between the Gut of Canso and St. Peter's, but they are of small economic importance. The valleys, and the low country generally, intervening between the hills above mentioned, consist chiefly of sandstones, shales, limestone, and gypsum, of the lower carboniferous system.

In the eastern division of Cape Breton there are only two ranges of hills of considerable elevation: one running parallel and near to the shore of Bras d'Or Lake, from St. Peter's to the head of the East Bay; the other from Long Island, nearly to the Straits of Barra. These hills consist chiefly of syenite, granite, and metamorphic rocks. From St. Peter's to Scatari the coast-line is generally low, with occasional bluffs of clay and gravel, and small lakes at frequent intervals, separated from the sea by barriers of sand and shingle. The land on this coast rises gradually from the sea towards the interior, presenting a swelling and undulating outline, but it nowhere reaches a greater elevation than 300 feet, except at the head of Gabarus Bay. A low but uneven tract of great extent occupies the interior between these undulating hills and the range bordering on the East Bay, through which flow the Grand, the Salmon, and the Mirá rivers. The low hills on the coast consist chiefly of metamorphosed Devonian and upper Silurian rocks—the low country in the interior, of sandstones, shales, and limestones, of the carboniferous system.

From Scatari to the great entrance of the Bras d'Or Lakes, the numerous bays and harbours which indent the coast are bounded by cliffs varying from 20 to 100 feet in height, with here and there long beaches or dunes of sand produced by the abrading action of the ocean. The land rises very gradually from the coast towards the interior, to a height rarely exceeding 250 feet. The cliffs, composed of sandstones and shales of the upper carboniferous formation, exhibit in many places valuable seams of bituminous coal. They constitute the northern land boundary of the Sydney coal field, which occupies an area of 250 square miles. As the general dip of the strata is north-east or seaward, this great area of productive coal measures is in all probability the segment of a vastly greater area extending under the sea.

The country occupied by the upper and lower members of the carboniferous system rarely attains an elevation of more than 300 feet; so that if the whole island were depressed to that depth, there would remain only an archipelago mostly composed of long narrow islands of igneous and metamorphic rocks.

The principal rivers of Cape Breton are the Denys, the Baddeck, and the Wagamatcook, which flow into the Bras d'Or lakes; the Margarie, the Mabou, the Inhabitants, the Grand, and the Mirá, which discharge their waters into the sea. Small freshwater lakes are very numerous, both in the lowlands and the great plateau at the northern end of the island; the largest is Lake Ainslie, the source of the southern branch of the Margarie river, which covers an area of twenty-five square miles.

Excellent harbours abound on the north-east, the south-east, and the south-west coast; the harbours of St. Ann's, the great entrance of the Bras d'Or, Sydney, Louisbourg, Arichat, Hawkesbury, and Port Hood, are navigable by ships of large burden; those of the little entrance of the Bras d'Or, Lingan, Menadou, Baleine, Fourché, L'Ardoise, Inhabitants, Mabou, and Margarie, are only suitable for vessels of a light draught.

The most remarkable feature in the physical geography of Cape Breton is the Mediterranean Sea, called the Great and Little Bras d'Or Lakes, which occupies an area of 450 square miles in the very heart of the island. These two lakes are united by a narrow channel—the Strait of Barra—and communicate, as has already been mentioned, with the ocean by two entrances, one of which has sufficient depth of water for ships of large burthen. All the basins, creeks, and inlets of the lakes, can be navigated by vessels of a similar class. In the middle of the Little Bras d'Or, between Boisdale and Boulardarie, there is a depth of 114 fathoms, showing that the lake bottom at that spot is depressed just as much below the surface of the water as the opposite hills of syenite are elevated above it. The scenery of the lakes is exceedingly striking and diversified. Long rocky cliffs and escarpments rise in some places abruptly from the water's edge; in others, undulating or rolling hills predominate, fringed on the shores by low white cliffs of gypsum or red conglomerate; whilst the deep basins and channels, which branch off in all directions from the central expanse of waters, studded with innumerable islets covered with a rich luxuriant growth of spruce and hemlock, present views the most picturesque and diversified imaginable.

The scenery on the southern coast, from Port Hood to Scatari, and on the north-east coast, from Scatari to the Bird islands, is generally tame and uninteresting; but a sudden change occurs when we reach the rugged promontory of Cape Dauphin. From hence to Cape North, the coast-line exhibits steep ascents covered with scrubby spruce and pine, and rocky precipices rising abruptly from the sea to heights varying from 600 to 1,200 feet. Grand and very beautiful are the rocky gorges and ravines which furrow these hills and precipices between St. Ann's and Ingonish, when first the golden rays of the rising sun light up their deep recesses, and in an instant make all clear and distinct, which just before was hid in the dark shades of twilight. Equally grand and picturesque is the red Syenitic escarpment of Smoky Cape, capped with the cloud from which it derives its name, with many a lofty headland in the background, and the peak of the Sugarloaf mountain just peeping above the far distant horizon. On the western coast, from Cape St. Lawrence to Margarie, scenery of a similar character occurs; but it is the setting, not the rising sun, which reveals all its hidden beauties.

Cape Breton comprises an area of 2,650,000 acres, exclusive of the lakes in the interior. About one-half of this area is supposed to be fit for cultivation, which, before the island was settled, was covered by dense forests of pine, spruce, hemlock, birch, maple, and ash, with a few oaks and elms. The great northern plateau, and the hills composed of igneous and altered rocks, were then, as now, partially covered with a stunted vegetation of spruce, rock maple, and birch. The soil of the first region is generally good, yielding abundant crops of grass, wheat, barley, oats, potatoes, stone fruits, and garden vegetables. On the banks of some of the larger rivers there are extensive tracts of rich alluvial soil of great fertility.

Although lying within the temperate zone, the climate of Cape Breton is marked by wide extremes of heat and cold; but, owing to its insular character, and its proximity to the Gulf Stream, the cold of winter is not so intense, nor the frost so continuous, as in Canada. During the summer the mercury has occasionally been observed as high as 92°, but it does not often exceed 75°. In winter it has only once fallen, in the course of the last forty years, to 30°, but it has frequently been seen as low as 20° below zero. Snow lies upon the ground from December to April, but the atmosphere during that period is generally bright and clear. In the spring the drift ice, in its passage from the Gulf of St. Lawrence to the ocean, is often driven upon the north-east coast by the easterly winds which prevail at that season, chilling the atmosphere and retarding the operations of the farmer, but it generally clears off before the middle of April, although it sometimes does not leave the coast until the first week in May. The summers of Cape Breton, say from May to October, may challenge comparison with those of any country within the temperate regions of the world. During all that time there are perhaps not more than ten foggy days in any part of the island, except along the southern coast, between the Gut of Canso and Scatari. Bright sunny days, with balmy westerly winds, follow each other in succession, week after week, whilst the mid-day heats are often tempered by cool refreshing sea breezes. Of rain there is seldom enough; the growing crops more often suffer from too little than too much. The rainy season, which sets in upon the breaking up of the summer, is of brief duration, seldom extending beyond the middle of November; and even this, the most disagreeable season of the year, is often shortened by an intervening week or two of warm balmy weather, known by the name of 'the Indian Summer.'

The discovery of Cape Breton now demands our attention. Owing to the prominent position of the island, it may reasonably be inferred that it was discovered quite as soon, if not sooner, than any of the other countries bordering on the Atlantic. According to certain ancient Icelandic manuscripts, or Saga (as they are called), the whole of the eastern coast of America, from Greenland to Nantucket, was discovered by Norweigan rovers in the tenth century, soon after the settlement of Iceland and Greenland. The country called Helluland, or Slateland in the Saga, was evidently Newfoundland; that called Markland, or Woodland, was Nova Scotia and Cape Breton.[1] It is stated in the Saga that frequent voyages were made during the eleventh and twelfth centuries to various parts of the newly-discovered countries, and that, in 1347, a vessel returning from Markland with a cargo of wood was wrecked on the coast of Iceland. As Cape Breton is the nearest country to Iceland which produces any wood, we may reasonably conclude, if the Saga are worthy of credit, that the island was well known and visited by the Northmen at least 500 years ago. Some modern writers pronounce the Saga mere fables. Bancroft says, 'They rest on narratives mythological in form and obscure in meaning; ancient yet not contemporary.'[2] On the other hand, many learned men, who

[1] Torfæus, in his *Vinlandia Antiqua.*

[2] In his *History of the United States.*

have devoted much time and labour to a careful study of the Saga, have arrived at a very different conclusion.[1] It has even been surmised by some writers that Columbus himself first obtained information of the existence of a great continent beyond the Atlantic, on his visit to Iceland in 1477, from intelligent natives of that island.[2] It is, however, quite certain that the Saga were not known in Europe in the time of Columbus; so that, after all, wherever he imbibed the idea, to him alone must be assigned the honour of making a discovery which 'caused great talk in all the court of King Henry VII., insomuch that all men, with great admiration, affirmed it to be a thing more divine than human.'[3]

This unlooked-for discovery of the West Indies by Columbus soon brought other adventurous spirits into the field, anxious to embark in similar enterprises; or, as Purchas quaintly says, 'Columbus, his fortunes awakened others' industry, amongst the rest John Cabot, a Venetian,' &c.[4] As either John Cabot, or his son Sebastian, beyond all doubt, coasted along the shores of Cape Breton, I must give you a short account of their celebrated voyages, although, I dare say, many of you are already well acquainted with all that is known about them.

John Cabot, a Venetian merchant, residing at Bristol, applied to king Henry VII. in the year 1494, for permission to make a voyage to the north-west, for the purpose of discovering a shorter route to India or Cathay (China); and, in the year 1496, the king granted to him and his three sons, Lewis, Sebastian, and Santius, 'full and free authoritie, leaue, and power, to sayle to all partes, countreys, and seas, of the east, of the west, and of the north, under our banners and ensignes, with fiue ships of what burden or quantitie soeuer they be; and as many mariners or men as they will haue with them in the said ships, upon their own proper costes and charges, to seeke out, discouer, and finde, whatsoeuer iles, countreys,

[1] The most eminent of these is Professor Rafn, of Copenhagen, the author of the *Antiquitates Americanæ*, who has recently published the manuscripts, with a translation in Latin.

[2] Washington Irving mentions this visit in his *Life of Columbus*.

[3] Hakluyt's *Collection of Voyages*, &c.

[4] Purchas, *His Pilgrims*.

regions, or prouinces, of the heathen and infidelles, whatsoeuer they bee, and in what part of the world soeuer they be, whiche before this time haue been vnknowen to christians. . . . And that the foresaid John and his sonnes . . . may subdue, occupie, and possesse, all such townes, cities, castles, and yles, of them founde, which they can subdue occupie, and possesse, as our vassales and lieutenants, getting unto us the rule, title, and jurisdiction. . . . Yet, so that the foresaid John and his sonnes and heires and their deputies, bee holden and bounden of all the fruites, gaines, and commodities, growing of such nauigation . . . to pay vnto vs in wares or money, the fifth parte of the capitall gaine so gotten, &c.'[1]

Armed with these ample powers, John Cabot, accompanied by his son Sebastian, sailed in the beginning of May, 1497, in a vessel called the 'Mathew' of Bristol, and discovered the continent of North America; but strange to say, only one or two authentic notices of this voyage can now be found. One of these is an ancient Bristol manuscript in the possession of Mr. Barrett, of that city, in which the following passage occurs: 'In the year 1497, the 24 June, St. John's day, was Newfoundland found by Bristol men, in a ship called the Mathew.'[2] The second is an inscription copied by Hakluyt from an old map dated 1549, drawn by Sebastian Cabot, and engraved by Clement Adams, which he states 'was to be seen [in 1589] in Her Majesty's Privy Gallery at Westminster, and in many other ancient merchants' houses.' This inscription, as given by Tytler, runs as follows: 'In the year of our Lord 1497, John Cabot, a Venetian, and his son Sebastian, discovered that country, which no one before his time had ventured to approach, on the 24th June, about 5 o'clock in the morning. He called the land Terra Primum Visa, because, as I conjecture, this was the place that first met his eyes in looking from the sea. On the contrary, the island which lies opposite the land he called the island of St. John—as I suppose because it was discovered on the festival of St. John the Baptist. The inha-

[1] Hakluyt's *Divers Voyages touching the Discoverie of America.* Original in Latin in Rymer's *Fœdera Angliæ.*

[2] Quoted by Mr. Biddle in his *Memoir of Sebastian Cabot.*

bitants wear beasts' skins and the intestines of animals for clothing, esteeming them as highly as we do our most precious garments. In war their weapons are the bow and arrow, spears, darts, slings, and wooden clubs. The country is sterile and uncultivated, producing no fruit; from which circumstance it happens that it is crowded with white bears and stags of an unusual height and size. It yields plenty of fish, and these very large, such as seals and salmon; there are soles also above an ell in length; but especially great abundance of that kind of fish called in the vulgar tongue baccalaos. In the same island also breed hawks, so black in their colour that they wonderfully resemble ravens; besides which, there are partridges, and eagles of dark plumage.'[1]

This account, as you will observe, was written more than fifty years after the date of the voyage, and, if it was written by Sebastian Cabot, may contain information respecting the inhabitants, acquired by him (Sebastian) on his second voyage. It is remarkable that we are indebted to a foreigner, residing in England when John Cabot returned from America, for more trustworthy intelligence, who must have been personally acquainted with his countryman. In a letter written by Lorenzo Pasqualigo on the 23rd August, 1497, (a few days probably after Cabot's return), to his brothers Aloise and Francisco, in Venice, we read:—'This Venetian of ours, who went in a ship from Bristol in quest of new islands, is returned, and says, that 700 leagues hence he discovered "Terra Firma," which is the territory of the Grand Cham; he coasted for 300 leagues, and landed; he saw no human being whatever, but he has brought hither to the king certain snares, which had been set to catch game, and a needle for making nets; he also found some felled trees: wherefore he supposed there were inhabitants, and returned to his ship in alarm. He was three months on the voyage; and coming back, he saw two islands to starboard, but would not land, time being precious, as he was short of provisions. The king is much pleased with this intelligence. He says that the tides are slack, and do not flow as they do here.

[1] *Historical View of the Progress of Discovery on the More Northern Coasts of America.* By Patrick Frazer Tytler. Edinburgh: 1855.

The king has promised that in the spring he shall have ten ships, armed according to his own fancy; and at his request he has conceded him all the prisoners, except such as are confined for high treason, to man them with. He has also given him money wherewith to amuse himself until then, and he is now at Bristol with his wife, who is a Venetian woman, and with his sons; his name is Zuan Cabot, and they call him the great admiral. Vast honour is paid him, and he dresses in silk; and these English run after him like mad people, so that he can enlist as many of them as he pleases, and a number of our own rogues besides. The discoverer of these places planted on his new-found land a large cross, with one flag of England, and another of St. Mark, by reason of his being a Venetian; so that our banner has floated very far afield.'[1]

According to this and the previous account, the land seen by John Cabot must have been the coast of Labrador, and the island just opposite, that part of Newfoundland near the northern end of the Straits of Belle Isle. In his coasting voyage, Cabot must have sailed all along the southern shore of Cape Breton and Nova Scotia to Cape Sable, which is just 300 leagues from Belle Isle. Observing the land at Cape Sable to trend suddenly to the northward, and being short of provisions, with an unknown sea before him, he wisely bore up for England. The two islands seen on his return were most probably some of the higher hummocky sand-hills of Sable Island, which, viewed from a distance, may easily be mistaken for separate islands. If, therefore, Cape Breton was not discovered by the Northmen, we have every reason to believe that it was seen and perhaps visited by John Cabot in 1497, more than a year before Columbus first reached the mainland of South America.[2]

On the 3rd of February, 1498, the king granted a new patent to John Cabot, authorising him to sail with six ships 'to the londe and isles of late founde by the said John in oure

[1] Collections of the Philobiblion Society, quoted by Dr. Asher in his Introduction to Hudson's *Voyages*, published by the Hakluyt Society.

[2] Columbus discovered the West Indies on October 12, 1492, but did not touch any part of the continent of America until August 1498.

name and by oure commaundement,' and ordering 'all and every oure officers, ministers, and subjects . . . to succour the said John, his deputy, &c. . . .'[1] This appears to have been merely a supplementary commission, as it does not revoke or modify any of the privileges conferred by the first patent. For reasons which cannot be ascertained, John Cabot did not go out with this expedition. The sole conduct of the enterprise was entrusted to his son Sebastian, a youth of not more than twenty-three years of age. There are various brief accounts of this voyage, but they all seem to have been based upon information given by Sebastian Cabot to his friend and contemporary, Peter Martyr of Angleria, who first published a narrative of the principal incidents of the voyage in 1516. A translation of Peter Martyr's book was published in England in 1555, from which I make the following extracts:—'The weste of the lande of Baccalaos is a greate tracte; and the greatest altitude thereof is 68 degrees and a halfe. Sebastian Cabot was the fyrst that brought any knowledge of this lande. For beinge in Englande in the dayes of Kyng Henry the Seventh, he furnysshed twoo shippes at his owne charges, or (as sum say) at the kynges, whom he persuaded that a passage might bee fownde to Cathay by the north seas, and that spices might bee brought from thense soner by that way, then by the vyage the Portugales use by the sea of Sur. He went also to knowe what maner of landes these Indies were to inhabite. He had with him three hundreth men, and directed his course by the tracte of Island [Iceland] uppon the Cape of Labrador at 58 degrees: affyrminge that in the monethe of July there was such could and heapes of Ise that he durst passe no further; also that the dayes were very longe and in maner without nyghte, and the nyghtes very cleare. Certyne it is, that at the 60 degrees, the longest day is of 18 houres. But consyderynge the could and the strangeness of the unknowne lande, he turned his course from thence to the Weste, folowynge the coaste of the lande of Baccalaos unto the 38 degrees,

[1] This document was discovered by Mr. Biddle in the Rolls Chapel, and published in his *Memoir of Sebastian Cabot* in 1831.

from whense he returned to Englande.'[1] Gomara, a Spanish author of the same period, says:—'Cabot, yielding to the cold and the strangeness of the land, turned towards the west, and refitting at the Baccalaos,[2] he ran along the coast as far as 38 degrees, &c.'[3] As Sebastian Cabot must have observed, on his former voyage with his father, that Cape Breton was the nearest country that produced timber of any value, it may fairly be inferred that he 'refitted' his vessels at some port in your island before completing that memorable voyage which secured for England, by the right of discovery, a claim to the whole coast of America, from the burning sands of Florida to the ice-bound shores of Hudson's Bay.

It is said, in some accounts of this voyage, that Sebastian Cabot first gave the name of Baccalaos to the countries adjacent to the fishing grounds. Peter Martyr, generally allowed to be the best authority, as quoted by Tytler,[4] says, 'Sebastian Cabot himself named these lands Baccalaos, because in the seas thereabouts he found such an immense multitude of large fish like tunnies, called Baccalaos by the natives, that they actually impeded the navigation of his ships.'[5] This, if correctly copied, must be a mistake of Peter Martyr's, for the natives do not call codfish 'baccalaos,' nor is it likely that Cabot, who was born in England of Venetian parents, would apply a Basque name to the countries he discovered. Fournier, in his remarks on this subject, says: 'It cannot be doubted this name was given by the Basques, who alone in Europe call that fish Bacalaos, or Bacallos; the aborigines term them Apagé.'[6] In confirmation of this I may mention that the Indians of Cape Breton call a codfish 'Pahshoo' at this day. The Basques began to fish on the coasts of Cape Breton and

[1] *The Decades of the Newe Worlde or West India.* By Peter Martyr of Angleria, translated into English by Rycharde Eden. London: 1555.

[2] In the original, 'y rehaziendo se en los Baccalaos.'

[3] Lopez de Gomara's *La Historia general de las Indias.* Anvers: 1554.

[4] In his *Historical View of the Progress of Discovery in the more Northern Coasts of America.*

[5] I could not find this passage in the black letter copy of Eden's translation of P. Martyr's book in the Library of the British Museum.

[6] *Hydrographie.* Par le Père Georges Fournier, de la Compagnie de Jésus. 2nd edition. Paris: 1667.

Newfoundland in 1504,[1] and first gave the name of Baccalaos to those countries—a name which was consequently in use many years before Peter Martyr published his 'Decades of the New World.'

Peter Martyr does not give a very pleasing account of the manners and customs of the natives of Cape Breton in 1516. He says: 'Of these landes Jacobus Bastaldus wryteth thus: The newe lande of Baccalaos is a coulde region, whose inhabytantes are Idolatours and praye to the sonne and moone and dyuers Idoles. They are whyte people and very rustical, for they eate flesshe and fysshe and all other thynges rawe. Sumtymes also they eate man's flesshe priuily, so that their Cacique have no knowledge thereof. The apparell, both of the men and women, is made of beares skynnes, although they have sables and marternes, not greatly estemed because they are lyttle. Sum of them go naked in sommer and weare apparell only in wynter. The Brytons [Bretons] and Frenche men are accustomed to take fysshe in the coastes of these landes, where is fownd great plenty of Tunnies which the inhabytauntes caul Baccalaos, whereof the lande was so named. . . . In all this newe lande is neyther citie or castell, but they live in companies lyke heardes of beastes.'[2]

Although the fishing grounds and the adjacent countries were first discovered by English navigators, English merchants and fishermen were the last to profit by them, because at that time they carried on a lucrative fishery on the coasts of Iceland,[3] so much nearer home. There was, however, another reason for this apparent indifference of the English merchants. They received so little encouragement from their Government, at the instigation, it was supposed, of the King of Spain, to embark in such enterprises, that the newly-discovered fishing grounds were entirely in the hands of foreigners. A letter has

[1] 'In the year 1504, as appears by the history of Nifiet and Magin, the Basques, Normans, and Bretons went on the coast of the Cod, called the Grand Bank, towards Cape Breton.'—Père Fournier's *Hydrographie.*

[2] Eden's Translation. London: 1555.

[3] In 1518 there were 360 English traders in the harbour of Hafne Fiord alone. See 'Iceland, Greenland, and the Faroe Islands,' in the *Edinburgh Family Library.*

very recently been discovered by an English antiquary in the Spanish archives at Simancas, which clearly proves with what jealousy and suspicion the discoveries of the Cabots were regarded by the Spanish Court. It is dated at London, July 25, 1498, and is addressed to Ferdinand and Isabella of Spain, by Don Pedro de Ayala, their ambassador at St. James's. Ayala tells their Majesties that the King of England had equipped and sent out five ships, under a Genoese, to discover certain continents and islands which some people from Bristol had seen the year before; that the King of England had often spoken to him on the subject; and that he had told His Majesty the land was already possessed by the King of Spain, and had given him reasons with which he did not seem well pleased. In answer to this letter Ferdinand wrote back: 'Henry might be aware of such men, who are sent by the King of France in order to distract him from more serious business.'[1] There is every reason to believe that this answer produced the desired effect, as no further English expeditions were sent to the north-west during the remainder of the reign of Henry VII.

Immediately after the discovery of the Baccalaos, which embraced Nova Scotia, Cape Breton, and Newfoundland, the fishermen of Normandy, Brittany, and the Basque Provinces, began to frequent the coasts to take cod. It is generally supposed, and apparently with good reason, that the Basque fishermen first gave the name of Cape Breton[2] to the eastern promontory of your island, after 'Cap Breton,' near Bayonne, in remembrance of their home. De la Marre[3] states, on the authority of the Flemish geographers, Corneille Niflet and Antoine Magin, that the Basques crossed the Atlantic in pursuit of whales, discovered and named the island of Cape Breton, and even penetrated the Gulf of St. Lawrence, 100 years before Columbus discovered America; but as no authority is given for this statement, it is not entitled to credit. I think,

[1] See a letter from Simancas in the *Athenæum* of December 29, 1860.

[2] The Indian name of Cape Breton Island, according to the late Dr. Gesner, was 'Oonumahghee.'

[3] In his *Traité de la Policé.*

however, we may safely conclude, from a careful consideration of the routes pursued by John Cabot and his son Sebastian, after touching the mainland of Labrador, that both of those celebrated navigators coasted along, if they did not actually land upon, the shores of Cape Breton in 1497 and 1498, and that, consequently, your island was one of the first countries discovered on the Atlantic coast of America.

LETTER II.

1500–1548.

CAPE BRETON, as I have already stated, was regularly visited by the European fishermen soon after its discovery; but there are so few authentic materials for compiling a connected narrative of its history during the 16th century, that I must content myself with submitting to you, in chronological order, some extracts from the records of the voyages made to your part of the world, in which you will find frequent mention made of the island.

In the year 1500, the King of Portugal sent out Gaspar Cortoreal in command of two ships, on the track of the Cabots. Cortoreal first made the land on the coast of Labrador, where he kidnapped fifty of the natives, whom he carried off to Portugal. It is supposed he first gave the name of Labrador to the country, under the expectation of obtaining from thence a supply of labourers or slaves for the king, his master. Encouraged by the king, he made a second voyage for that nefarious purpose, but was never heard of again, having, it is supposed, fallen a victim to the just vengeance of the natives.[1] In some old maps, Labrador is called 'Terra Cortorealis.'

In the year 1506, Jean Denys, of Harfleur, published a map of the Baccalaos country (not now extant); and in 1508, Thomas Aubert, a pilot of Dieppe, in command of a ship called the 'Pensée,' excited great curiosity in France by bringing home two natives of the New World.[2] Warburton supposes they were brought from Cape Breton.[3]

[1] Damiano Goes, *Chronica do Rey Dom Manuel.*
[2] Ramusio's *Terzo Volume delle Navigationi.* Venice, 1565.
[3] Warburton's *Conquest of Canada.*

The first attempt to establish a settlement in this part of America was made by the Baron de Lery, in 1518. He took out a number of cattle and pigs; but having been a long time at sea, and having in consequence arrived too late upon the coast to put his people under shelter before winter set in, he landed part of his live stock at Campseau (Canso), and the remainder at Sable Island, on his way back to France. The first died during the winter; but the latter, owing to the mildness of the climate and the abundance of herbage, multiplied exceedingly, and proved of great service to the people left there by the Marquis de la Roche in 1591.[1]

You are, of course, aware that, immediately after the discovery of America by Columbus, Pope Alexander VII. by a Bull dated May 4, 1493, granted the whole of the New World and the East Indies to Spain and Portugal, at that time the two chief maritime nations of Europe. Louis XII. of France and Henry VII. of England seem to have paid due respect, in the later years of their reigns, to the Pope's decree; but their respective successors, Francis I. and Henry VIII.—both enterprising and ambitious monarchs—determined that Spain and Portugal should not monopolise all the glory and advantage of acquiring new territory in America. Accordingly, they refused to acknowledge the validity of the Papal decree which conferred such magnificent and undefined gifts upon their rivals. 'What!' said Francis, 'shall the Kings of Spain and Portugal divide all America between them, without suffering me to take a share as a brother? I would fain see the article in Adam's will that bequeaths that vast inheritance to them.'[2] As neither of his royal brothers could satisfy Francis on this point, he determined to send out an expedition to explore the coasts of America. Four ships were accordingly equipped, which left France in December 1523, under the command of Giovanni Verazano, a Florentine navigator. Three of the ships sustained so much damage in a gale that Verazano sent them back and continued his voyage in the 'Dolphin' alone. On March 7, 1524, he first made land, supposed to have been

[1] Père Fournier's *Hydrographie*.

[2] From the *French Encyclopædia*.

the coast of Carolina. Thence he proceeded along the shore to the northward, frequently going into harbours, in some of which he remained several days, until he arrived on the coast of Cape Breton. Having spent nearly all his provisions, he took in a supply of wood and water, and returned to France.[1] Under the pretext of priority of discovery, founded on this voyage, France, at a later period, set up a claim to the countries visited by Verazano, 'all which, and much more,' says Purchas, 'had long before bene discouered by Sir Sebastian Cabot for the King of England, who was the first that set foote on the American continent in behalf of any Christian Prince, anno 1496, or, as others, 1497; and therefore the French reckoning falleth short, some of which nation, upon Verazano's discouerie, challenge I know not what right to all that coast, and make their New France neere as great as all Europe.'[2]

Henry VIII. was not far behind his brother of France in sending out an expedition in the same direction, of which Hakluyt gives us the following account in the third volume of his 'Collection of Voyages:'—'Master Robert Thorne of Bristoll, a notable member and ornament of his country, as wel for his learning as great charity to the poore, in a letter of his to King Henry VIII. and a large discourse to Doctor Leigh, his ambassadour to Charles the Emperour (which both are to be seene almost in the beginning of the first volume of this my work), exhorteth the aforesayd King with very waighty and substantial reasons, to set forth a discouerie euen to the North Pole. And that it may be knowne that this his motion took present effect, I thought it good herewithall to put down the testimonies of two of our chroniclers, M. Hall and M. Grafton, who both write in this sort:—This same moneth (they say) King Henrie VIII. sent two faire ships wel manned and victualled, having in them diuers cunning men to seeke strange regions, and so they set forth out of the Thames the 20th day of May in the 19th yeere of his reigne, which was the year of Our Lord 1527. And whereas Master Hall and

[1] From Hakluyt's *Diverse Voyages to America.*

[2] Purchas, *His Pilgrims.*

Master Grafton say, that in those ships there were diuers cunning men, I have made great enquirie of such as by their yeeres and delight in nauigation might giue me any light to know who those cunning men should be, which were the directors in the aforesayd voyage. And it hath bene tolde me by Sir Martin Frobisher, and M. Richard Allen, a Knight of the Sepulchre, that a Canon of St. Paul in London, which was a great mathematician, and a man indued with wealth, did much aduance the action, and went therein himselfe in person; but what his name was I cannot learne of any. And further they told me that one of the ships was called The Dominus Vobiscum, which is a name likely to be giuen by a religious man in those dayes: and that sayling very farre northwestward, one of the ships was cast away as it entered into a dangerous gulph, about the great opening between the north parts of Newfoundland and the country lately called by Her Meaistie Meta Incognita.[1] Whereupon the other ship, shaping her course towards Cape Briton and the coastes of Arambec [the name by which Nova Scotia and the country adjacent was known in Queen Elizabeth's time], and oftentimes putting their men on land to search the state of those unknown regions, returned home about the beginning of October of the year aforesayd. And thus much (by reason of the great negligence of the writers of those times, who should haue vsed more care in preseruing of the memories of the worthy actes of our nation) is all that hitherto I can learne or find out of this voyage.'

As the surviving ship was several months on the coasts of Nova Scotia, Cape Breton, and Newfoundland, we have good reason for lamenting, with Hakluyt, the negligence of the writers of those days. There is, however, one document in existence relating to this voyage, which I will now give you entire, as it affords some valuable information concerning the fisheries of Newfoundland at that period (1527). This is a letter from the master of the surviving ship to King Henry VIII., which I have copied from Purchas 'His Pilgrims.'

[1] This name was applied to the Labrador coast in the reign of Queen Elizabeth.

Purchas says, 'King Henry VIII. set forth two ships for discouerie, one of which perished in the north parts of New-foundland. The master of the other, John Rut, writ this letter to King Henrie, in bad English and worse writing. Ouer it was this superscription:—

'"Master Grubes two ships departed from Plymouth the 10 day of June, and arriued in the Newfoundland, the 21 day of July: and after we had left the sight of Selle, we had neuer sight of any land, till we had sight of Cape de Bas.

'"Pleasing your Honorable Grace to heare of your seruant John Rut, with all his Company here, in good health, thanks be to God and your Graceship. The Mary of Gilford with all her [here three or four words are obliterated] thanks be to God. And if it please your Honorable Grace, we ranne in our course to the northward, till we came into 53 degrees, and there wee found many great Ilands of Ice and deepe water; we found no sounding, and then we durst not go no further to the northward for feare of more Ice, and then we cast about to the southward, and within foure dayes after we had one hundred and sixtie fathom, and then wee came into 52 degrees and fell with the mayne land, and within ten leagues of the mayne land we met with a great Iland of Ice, and came hard by her, for it was standing in deepe water, and so went in with Cape de Bas, a good harbour, and many small Ilands, and a great fresh riuer going up farre into the mayne land, and the mayne land all wildernesse and mountaines and woodes, and no naturall ground but all mosse, and no inhabitation nor no people in these parts: and in the woodes wee found footing of diuers great beastes, but we saw none not in ten leagues. And please your Grace, the Sampson and wee kept company all the way till within two days before we met with all the Ilands of Ice: that was the first day of July, at night; and there arose a great and a maruailous great storme, and much foul weather. I trust in Almightie Jesu to heare good newes of her. And please your Grace, we were considering and a writing of all our order, how we would wash (sic) us and what course we would draw, and when God doe send foule weather, that with the Cape de Sper shee should goe, and he that come first should tarry the space of sixe weekes one for another, and watered at Cape de Bas [illegible] of your Grace and fishing, and so departed to the southward to seeke our fellowe; the third day of August we entered into a good harbour, called Saint John, and there we found eleuen saile of Normans and one Brittaine [Breton] and two Portugall Barks, and all a fishing, and so we are readie to depart toward Cape de Bas, and that is twentie fiue leagues, as shortly as we haue fished, and so along the coaste till we may meete with our fellowe, and so with all diligence that lyes in me toward parts to that Ilands that we are commanded at our departing: And thus Jesu saue and keepe your Honorable Grace, and all your honorable Reuer.

'"In the hauen of St. John the third day of August, written in haste, 1527.

'"By your seruant John Rut, to his vttermost of his power.'

It appears from this letter that Hakluyt had been misinformed respecting the name of one of these vessels, which he says was 'The Dominus Vobiscum,' as Rut, the commander of the 'Mary of Gilford,' distinctly says the other was called the 'Sampson.' Rut probably received intelligence of the loss of the 'Sampson' before he left St. Johns, and, consequently, instead of returning to the northward to meet her, 'shaped his course,' as Hakluyt says, 'towards Cape Breton and the coastes of Arambec.'

This voyage, as I mentioned at page 19, was undertaken at the suggestion of 'Master Robert Thorne of Bristoll, a notable member and ornament of his country,' then residing at Seville in Spain, who sent thereon 'a large discourse to Doctor Leigh,' accompanied by 'a little Mappe or Carte of the Worlde' to illustrate his views. This map is such a curiosity, that I give you a copy of a part of it to show the imperfect knowledge of the geography of the Atlantic coast of North America at that period (1527). Neither Newfoundland nor Cape Breton, which were both well known at that time, is marked upon the map. The deep estuary or bay adjoining the 'Nova terra laboratorum dicta' (Labrador), was probably intended to

Nº 1. to face p. 22.

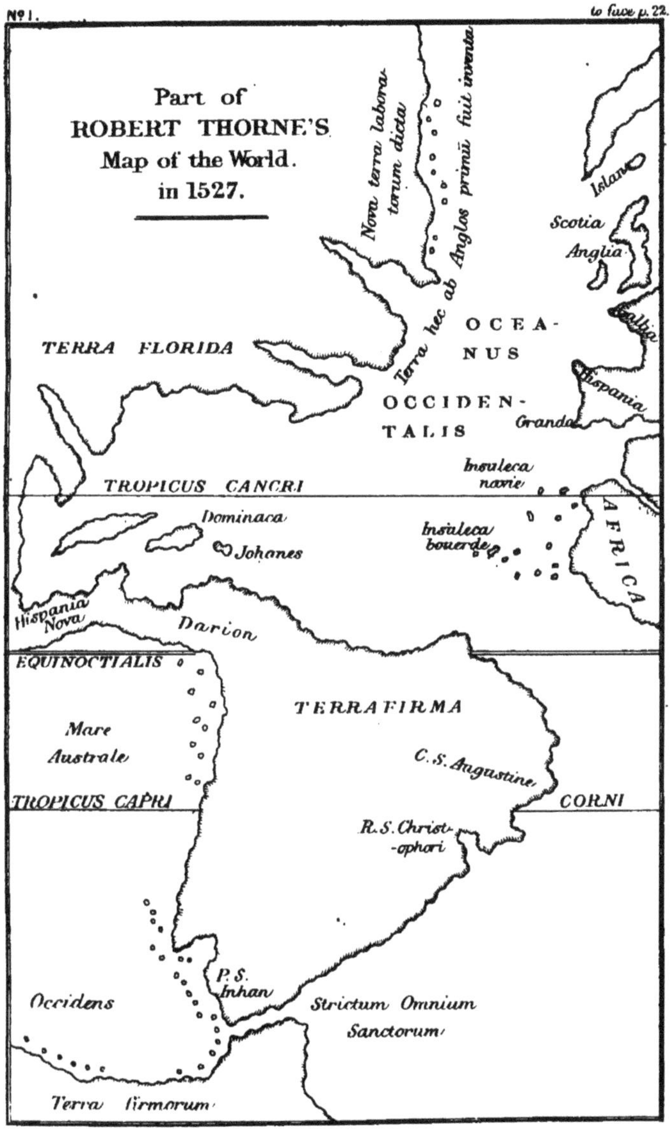

represent the Gulf of St. Lawrence, and the promontory at the southern side of the Gulf, Cape Breton.[1]

The next English voyage to Newfoundland and Cape Breton was undertaken in 1536 by a party of lawyers and private gentlemen, which, as might have been expected, ended most disastrously. It does not furnish us with much information respecting Cape Breton or Newfoundland, but it gives us a graphic account of the dangers and sufferings to which men 'desirous of seeing the strange things of the world' were exposed at that period, when so little was known of the geography of the New World. The narrative, which I copy from Hakluyt's general 'Collection,' is rather long; but I feel assured you will agree with me, that such a curious chronicle of the olden time could not be condensed into smaller compass without robbing it of its chief interest:—

'The voyage of M. Hore and diuers other Gentlemen to Newfoundland and Cape Briton, in the yere 1536 and in the 28 yere of King Henry the 8.

'Master Hore of London, a man of goodly stature and of great courage, and giuen to the study of Cosmographie, in the 28 yere of King Henry the 8 and in the yere of Our Lord 1536 encouraged diuers Gentlemen and others, being assisted by the king's fauor and good countenance, to accompany him in a voyage of discouerie upon the north-west parts of America; wherein his perswasions tooke such effect, that within short space many gentlemen of the Innes of Court, and of the Chancerie, and diuers others of good worship, desirous to see the strange things of the world, very willingly entered into the action with him, some of whose names were as followeth: M. Weekes, a gentleman of the West Countrey, of fiue hundred

[1] A map of older date has recently (1866) been found in the Queen's Library at Windsor among a collection of papers in the handwriting of Leonardo da Vinci, in which the whole of North America is represented by two large islands called Florida and Bacalar. Mr. Major, of the British Museum, supposes it was constructed about the year 1513.

In another map of still older date (1508), in the Library of the Royal Geographical Society, Terra Nova or Newfoundland is laid down as part of the continent of North America; it shows no trace whatever of Nova Scotia or Cape Breton, although the Cape itself was well known at that time.

markes by the yeere liuing; M. Tucke, a gentleman of Kent; M. Tuckfield; M. Thomas Buts, the sonne of Sir Wm Buts, knight, of Norfolk, which was lately liuing, and from whose mouth I wrote most of this relation; M. Hardie; M. Biron; M. Carter; M. Wright; M. Rastall, Serieant Rastall's brother; M. Redley; and diuers other, which all were in the Admyrall called The Trinitie, a ship of seuen score tunnes, wherein M. Hore himselfe was embarked. In the other ship, whose name was the Minion, went a very learned and virtuous gentleman, one M. Armigil Wade, afterwards Clerke of the Counsailes of King Henry the 8 and King Edward the sixth, father to the most worshipfull M. William Wade, now Clerke of the Priuy Council; M. Oliuer Dawbeney, marchant, of London; M. Joy, afterward gentleman of the King's Chapell with diuers others of good account. The whole number that went in the two tall ships aforesaid,' to wit, the Trinitie and the Minion, were about fiue score persons, whereof thirty were gentlemen, which all were mustered in warlike maner at Grauesend, and after the receiuing of the Sacrament, they embarked themselues in the ende of April 1536.

'From the time of their setting out from Grauesend, they were very long at sea, to witte, aboue two moneths, and neuer touched any land untill they came to part of the West Indies about Cape Briton, shaping their course thence northeastwardes untill they came to the Island of Penguin, which is very full of rockes and stones; whereon they went and found it full of great foules white and gray, as big as geese, and they saw infinite numbers of their egges. They draue a great number of the foules into their boates upon their sayles, and took up many of their egges; the foules they flead, and their skinnes were very like honey combes full of holes being flead off: they dressed and eate them and found them to be very good and nourishing meat. They saw also store of beares both blacke and white, of whome they killed some, and tooke them for no bad foode.

'M. Oliuer Dawbeney which (as it is before mentioned), was in this voyage, and in the Minion, told M. Richard Hakluyt, of the Middle Temple, these things following: to wit,

That after their arriuall in Newfoundland, and haueing bene there certaine dayes at ancre, and not hauing yet seene any of the naturall people of the countrey, the same Dawbeney, walking one day on the hatches, spied a boate with Sauages of those parts, rowing down the bay towards them, to gaze upon the ship and our people, and, taking vewe of their coming aloofe, hee called to such as were under the hatches, and willed them to come up if they would see the naturall people of the countrey, that they had so long desired so much to see: whereupon they came up, and tooke viewe of the Sauages rowing toward them and their ship, and vpon the viewe they manned out a ship boate to meet them and to take them. But they, spying our ship boat making towards them, returned with maine force and fled into an island that lay up in the bay or riuer there, and our men pursued them into the island, and the Sauages fled and escaped; but our men found a fire, and the side of a beare on a wooden spit, left at the same by the Sauages that were fled. There in the same place they found a boote of leather, garnished on the outward side of the calfe with certaine braue trailes, as it were of rawe silke, and also founde a certaine great warme mitten; and, these caryed with them, they returned to their shippe, not finding the Sauages, nor seeing anything else besides the soyle, and the things growing in the same, which chiefly were store of firre and pine trees.

'And further the said M. Dawbeney told him, that, lying there, they grew into great want of victuals, and that there they found small reliefe, more than that they had from the nest of an Osprey, that brought hourely to her young great plenty of diuers sortes of fishes. But such was the famine that increased among them from day to day, that they were forced to seeke to relieue themselves of raw herbes and rootes that they sought on the maine; but the famine increasing, and the reliefe of herbes being to little purpose to satisfie their insatiable hunger, in the fieldes and deserts here and there, the fellowe killed his mate while he stooped to take up a roote for his reliefe, and cutting out pieces of his body whom he had murthered, broyled the same on the coles and greedily deuoured them.

'By this meane the company decreased, and the officers knew not what was become of them; and it fortuned that one of the company, driuen with hunger to seeke abroad for reliefe, found out in the fieldes the sauour of broyled flesh, and fell out with one for that he would suffer him and his fellowes to sterue, enioying plenty, as he thought: and this matter growing to cruell speaches, he that had the broyled meate, burst out into these wordes: "If thou wouldst needs know, the broyled meate that I had was a piece of such a man's buttocke." The Report of this, brought to the ship, the captain found what became of those that were missing, it was perswaded that some of them were neither deuoured with wilde beastes, nor yet destroyed with Sauages: and hereupon he stood up and made a notable oration, containing, Howe much these dealings offended the Almightie, and vouched the Scriptures from first to last, what God had in cases of distresse done for them that called upon him; and told them that the power of the Almighty was then ne lesse, then in al former times it had bene. And added, that if it had not pleased God to haue holpen them in that distresse, that it had bene better to haue perished in body, and to haue liued euerlastingly, than to haue relieued for a poore time their mortal bodyes, and to be condemned euerlastingly both body and soule to the vnquenchable fire of hell. And thus haueing ended to that effect, he began to exhort to repentance, and besought all the company to pray that it might please God to looke upon their miserable present state, and for his owne mercie to relieue the same. The famine increasing, and the inconuenience of the men that were missing being found, they agreed amongst themselues that rather than that all should perish, to cast lots who should be killed: And such was the mercie of God, that in the same night there arriued a French ship in that port, well furnished with vittaile, and such was the policie of the English that they became masters of the same, and changing ships and vittailing them, they set sayle to come into England.

'In their journey they were so far northwards that they saw mighty islands of yce in the sommer season, on which were hawkes and other foules to rest themselues, being weary of flying ouer farre from the maine. They saw also certaine great white foules with red bils and red legs, somewhat bigger than herons, which they supposed to be storks. They arriued at S. Iues in Cornwall about the ende of October. From thence they departed vnto a certaine castle belonging to Sir John Luttrell, where M. Thomas Buts and M. Rastall, and other gentlemen of the voyage, were very friendly entertained; after that they came to the Earle of Bathe at Bathe, and thence to Bristoll, so to London. M. Buts was so changed in the voyage, with hunger and miserie, that Sir William his father, and my Lady his mother, knew him not to be their sonne untill they found a secret marke, which was a warte, upon one of his knees, as hee told me Richard Hakluyt of Oxford himselfe, to whom I rode 200 miles onely to learne the whole truth of this voyage from his own mouth, as being the onely man now aliue that was in this discouerie.

'Certaine moneths after, those Frenchmen came into England, and made a complaint to King Henry the 8th: the King causing the master to be examined, and finding the great distresse of his subjects, and the causes of the dealing so with the French, was so moued with pitie, that he punished not his subjects, but of his owne purse made full and royall recompence unto the French.

'In this distresse of famine, the English did somewhat relieue their vitall spirits, by drinking at the springs the fresh water out of certaine wooden cups, out of which they had drunke their "aqua composita" before.'

The mishaps attending Master Hore's ill-conducted enterprise seem to have deterred English adventurers from making any further voyages to the Baccalaos for many years; but the King of France, at the suggestion of his chief admiral, Chabot, determined to follow up the discoveries so auspiciously begun by Verazano, and to explore the countries beyond the fishing-grounds. Accordingly, two ships of about sixty tons each were fitted out and placed under the command of Jaques Cartier, an able and experienced pilot of St. Malo, who had probably been engaged in the fisheries, and had obtained some knowledge of the geography of that part of the Ne

Cartier made three voyages, of which there are long and interesting accounts in 'Hakluyt's Collection.' To give them at length would occupy more space than I can spare; but as they led to one of the most important events of those days, namely, the discovery of Canada, I will endeavour to lay before you a summary of the leading incidents of Cartier's voyages. Sailing from St. Malo on April 20, 1534, Cartier first made the land at Cape Buonavista, on the east coast of Newfoundland, on May 10. Following the coast to the northward, and touching at various harbours, he reached a river, which he named St. James, in latitude 51°, 55′. He remarks, 'that if the soyle were as good as the harboroughes are, it were a great commoditie; but it is not to be called the new found land, but rather stones and cragges and a place fit for wilde beastes.... In short, I believe this was the land allotted to Caine.' Passing through the Straits of Belle Isle, he ran down the coast to the latitude of 48°, 30′, but finding no harbour, he stood out to sea, and discovered three islands, one of which he named Brions Island—the name which it still bears. It here occurred to him, 'that there be some passage between Newfoundland and Brions Island. If so it were, it would be a great shortning, as wel of the time as of the way, if any perfection could be found in it.' Sailing to the westward, and sighting several islands and capes, he made the coast of the mainland in 47½ degrees. Here he met with a great number of the natives, with whom he trafficked, giving knives, beads, &c., in exchange for whatever they had to dispose of, including even their clothing, such as it was. 'They gave us whatsoeuer they had, not keeping anything, so that they were constrained to go backe again naked.' Continuing his voyage to the northward, he entered a large bay, which he called the Baye du Chaleur, on account of the great heat. Being satisfied that there was no opening to the westward out of this bay, Cartier resumed his voyage to the northward, and fell in with a cape on July 24, upon which he erected a large cross with the inscription 'Vive le Roy de France' engraved upon it. This is supposed to have been Cape Gaspé. Observing the land trending to the westward, with a wide expanse of water before him, and no land in sight to the northward, Cartier concluded that he had found a passage leading into the Pacific Ocean. The season being now far advanced, Cartier persuaded two young savages to return with him to France, and started on his homeward voyage on August 5. In four days, with a strong south-west wind, he reached the coast of Newfoundland, passed through the Straits of Belle Isle, and arrived at St. Malo on September 5.

These great discoveries produced a great sensation at the French Court, and induced the King to send out another expedition in the following spring, to take possession of the country, and to explore the great gulf or river whose mouth only had been seen by Cartier in the preceding year. Cartier accordingly left St. Malo on May 15, 1535, with three ships, and, passing through the Straits of Belle Isle, then supposed to be the only entrance into the gulf, shaped his course towards Cape Gaspé. On August 15 he discovered a large island, called by the natives Natiscottee (Antiscosti), and on September 1 entered the St. Lawrence, up which he proceeded 120 leagues from the sea, where he discovered an island, which he named the Isle d'Orleans. Here he met with a number of natives, who received their visitors with much kindness and courtesy. Leaving his ships at the Isle d'Orleans, he ascended the river in his boats to a place called Hochelaga, a large fortified village at the foot of a hill, which he called Mont Royal, the site of the present city of Montreal. Returning to his ships, he spent the winter on the banks of a small river, which he called the St. Croix, since named the Jacques Cartier. During the winter a number of his people were attacked by a loathsome disease, which carried off twenty-five and left the others in a very weak condition. This proved to be the scurvy, a disease at that time unknown in Europe. Grieved at the loss of so many of his people, and disappointed with the climate, Cartier prepared to return to France as soon as the ice broke up in the river. 'On May 3, being Holyroode Day, he caused a goodly fayre crosse of thirty-five foote in height to bee set up, under the crosset of which he caused a shield to be hanged, wherein were the armes of France, and ouer them was written in antique letters, "*Franciscus primus Dei gratia*

Francorum Rex regnat."' Cartier sailed on the 16th for France, carrying with him the native king, Donnacona, whom he induced to go on board just before he sailed. He arrived at St. Malo on July 6, 1536. Instead of returning through the Straits of Belle Isle, after reaching Brion's Island he shaped his course to the eastward, and discovered a promontory in 47½ degrees, which he named Cape Loreine (Cape Ray), and another on the starboard, which he named St. Paul's (Cape North, in Cape Breton). Sailing south-easterly along the coast, he next made St. Peter's Island, and then Cape Race. There is every reason to believe that the Basque and Breton fishermen, who came out every spring to St. Peter's, had long ere this sailed to the westward of Cape Ray; but Cartier was the first to make known the existence of a passage between Cape North and Cape Ray into the Gulf of St. Lawrence. He says also, 'Whilst wee were in the sayd St. Peter's Islands we met with many ships of France and Britaine' (Brittany.)

Cartier's account of the severity of the climate seems to have caused much disappointment in France, as no further attempt was made to form a settlement in Canada until 1540, when Sieur Jean Francis de la Roche, Seigneur de Roberval, applied to Francis I. for permission to equip an expedition for that purpose, at his own expense. This was readily granted, and a commission issued, appointing Roberval viceroy of all the territories bordering on the river and Gulf of St. Lawrence, which was called 'New France.' Cartier was made chief pilot and captain-general of the expedition. He went out with five ships in the spring of 1541, and arrived in the St. Lawrence in August, where he built a fort on the north side of the river, near the present site of Quebec, which he called Charlesbourg. The conduct of the Indians during the long and dreary winter which followed, as might have been expected, was very different from what it had been on the last occasion. They could not forgive the French for carrying off their king, who had, unfortunately, died in France. Open hostilities broke out, and lives were lost on both sides. Cartier, disappointed at the non-arrival of Roberval, who was to have followed him in the preceding spring, disheartened by the severe cold, and harassed by the Indians, now his bitter enemies, determined to return to France as soon as the ice would permit. In the meantime, Roberval, who had not been able to complete his equipment in the preceding year, 'sailed from Rochelle on the 16 April, 1542, furnished with three tall ships, chiefly at the king's cost, carrying out 200 persons, as well men as women, with divers gentlemen of quality.' Owing to contrary winds, he did not reach the coast of Newfoundland until the 7th June. Next day he entered the harbour of St. John's, where he 'found 17 ships of Fishers.' Whilst he 'made a somewhat long abode here,' Jacques Cartier and his people, returning from Canada, arrived in the same harbour. Cartier presented specimens of diamonds and gold ore to Roberval, which he had obtained in Canada. The ore was tried in a furnace, and found to be good. He told Roberval that he could not, with his small company, withstand the savages, which was the cause of his leaving Canada. Roberval, being furnished with plenty of men, commanded Cartier to go back with him; but Cartier, with all his people, sailed next night and returned to France, 'moved with ambition, it is said, and jealous of being deprived of the glory of the discovery of these parts.'

Roberval spent great part of June at St. John's, and then sailed through the Straits of Belle Isle to the St. Lawrence. Having anchored his ships near Cap Rouge, he landed his company, built a large house to accommodate all his people, and erected a fort which he called 'France Roy.' On the 14th September, he sent back to France two ships, which had brought out his furniture, to carry an account of his proceedings to the king, and to return in the spring with provisions. As a late writer observes, 'Experience and forecast had alike been wanting. There were storehouses, but no stores; mills, but no grist; an ample oven, and a woful dearth of bread. It was only when two of the ships had sailed for France that they took account of their provision, and discovered its lamentable shortcoming.'[1] Fifty of his people died of famine and disease

[1] Parkman, in his *Pioneers of France in the New World*. Boston: 1865.

during the winter. In the spring he embarked with all his company, and returned to France. The narrative of Roberval's voyage,[1] from which I have made these extracts, is very short and imperfect. There is no record of his proceedings after he left the St. Lawrence. Some writers say that he went out again to Canada, accompanied by his brother, and, as he was never heard of again, it was supposed he was wrecked on the coast of Labrador; but Thevet, who was a personal friend of his, says that he was assassinated at night in the streets of Paris.[2]

Charlevoix, and some other French authors, say that Roberval built a fort in Cape Breton. The oldest work in which this is mentioned is Fournier's 'Hydrographie,' published in 1667. Fournier says:—'In the year 1540 Jean-Francis de la Roque, Sieur de Roberval, a gentleman of Picardy, returned to Canada with Cartier, in the capacity of Lieutenant of the King: they fortified Cape Breton; but grave affairs caused him to be recalled. In the year 1543 the same Roberval returned with the Pilot Jean Alphonse Xantoignes.'

According to Hakluyt, as you will have observed, Cartier went alone in 1541, and began a fort at Cap Rouge on the St. Lawrence. Roberval went thither in 1542, after Cartier had left, and built a fort at the same place. I am inclined to think the error originated in a misprint of Cap Breton for Cap Rouge, in Fournier's book, which has been copied by later writers. If he had said '*they* fortified Cap Rouge,' it would have been strictly in accordance with the other accounts. Cape Breton, therefore, I fear, cannot claim the honour of having been fortified at such an early period.

The repeated failures, and, in many instances, the disastrous terminations of the voyages undertaken for discovery and settlement on the eastern coasts of America, which I have briefly related, for a long time damped the ardour and ambition both of the French and English governments. Roberval's expedition was soon forgotten in the distracted state of France during the religious wars in which her people were then

[1] In Hakluyt's *Collection*.

[2] Thevet's *Cosmographie universelle*. Paris: 1575.

unhappily engaged; but even these important events did not check the enterprise and energy of the fishermen of Normandy and Brittany, who continued to follow their vocation on the coasts of Newfoundland and Cape Breton, and began to engage in the whale fishery which Cartier's discoveries had first brought into notice. The English also, about this time, seem to have directed more attention than heretofore to the Newfoundland fisheries, as we find that in the second year of the reign of Edward VI. (in 1548) an Act was passed imposing heavy penalties upon officers of the Admiralty for 'exacting sums of money, doles or shares of fish, for licenses to traffic in Newfoundland, to the great discouragement and hindrance of the merchants and fishermen, and to no little damage of the whole common wealth, and thereof also great complaints have been made and informations thereof to the King's Majesty's most honorable Council.'

If this Act, proving that the English frequented the coasts of Newfoundland about the beginning of the reign of Edward VI., had not been passed, we should literally not have had a single record of the existence of this branch of commerce, as there are no accounts extant of any voyages to Newfoundland and Cape Breton during the next forty years. Hakluyt, who was a most diligent collector of such records, having, as he informs us, upon one occasion travelled more than 200 miles[1] to obtain an account of M. Hore's voyage, from the only survivor of that unfortunate expedition, had good reason 'to marvel, that by the negligence of our men, the country in all this time had not been better searched.' To his zeal and diligence in all matters relating to cosmography and maritime discovery, we are indebted for accounts of several voyages to America, which would otherwise have been lost and forgotten. In my next, I purpose giving you extracts from some of these voyages, undertaken in the latter years of the sixteenth century.

[1] *Ante*, p. 27.

LETTER III.

1548–1599.

THE long blank of forty years, dating from the Act of Edward VI., referred to near the end of my last letter, is followed, in Hakluyt's 'Collection,' by a letter from Anthony Parkhurst, a merchant of Bristol, dated November 13, 1578, to M. Richard Hakluyt, of the Middle Temple,[1] in reply to some enquiries made by the latter 'about the state and commodities of Newfoundland.' The document is too long for insertion here; so you must be satisfied with a few extracts relating to Cape Breton, and the state of the fisheries, at that period. Parkhurst first gives an interesting account of the soil, climate, and productions of Newfoundland; rather highly coloured, it is true (unless the country has changed for the worse since his day), but nevertheless abounding in valuable information. He says he had made four voyages to Newfoundland, and 'had searched the harbours, creeks, and lands more than any other Englishman.' That there were generally more than 100 sail of Spaniards taking cod, and from twenty to thirty killing whales; fifty sail of Portuguese; 150 sail of French and Bretons, mostly very small; but of English only fifty sail. He accounts for the small proportion of English by the fact of a large trade being still carried on with Iceland. 'Nevertheless,' he adds, 'the Englishmen are commonly lords of the harbours where they fish, and use all strangers help in fishing, if need require, according to an old custom of the country; which thing they do willingly, so that you take nothing from them more than a boat or two of salt, in respect

[1] M. Richard Hakluyt, of the Middle Temple, was a cousin of the author of the *Collection of Voyages*, from which I have drawn so largely.

of your protection of them against rovers or other violent intruders, who do often put them from good harbours.'

After enumerating the various kinds of fish in Newfoundland, he tells us (which I dare say will be quite new to you), 'that the mussels all contain pearls, and that he had heard of a Portugal that found one worth 300 ducats. . . . That in half a day he could take as many lobsters as would find 300 men with a day's meat.' Speaking of the trees of Newfoundland, 'The timber is most Fir, yet plenty of Pineapple trees; few of these two kinds meet to mast a ship of three score and ten tons; But near Cape Breton and to the southward, big and sufficient for any ship. . . . I could find in my heart to make proof whether it be true or no that I have read and heard, of Frenchmen and Portugals to be in that river [the St. Lawrence] and about Cape Breton. If I had not been deceived by the vile Portugals, descending of the Jews and Judas kind, I had not failed to have searched that river, and all the coast of Cape Breton, what might have been found to have benefited our country.' He adds, 'In conclusion, if you and your friend shall think me a man sufficient and of credit to seek the Isle of St. John, or the river of Canada, with any part of the firm land of Cape Breton, I shall give my diligence for the true and perfect discovery, and leave some part of mine own business to further the same.' We have much reason to lament, that, in the first place, Parkhurst was persuaded against visiting Cape Breton by the 'vile Portugals,' who probably, as reported by some later writers,[1] had made a temporary settlement in the island, and were carrying on a lucrative trade, which they wished to keep to themselves; and in the second, that he did not obtain sufficient encouragement from M. Richard Hakluyt, of the Middle Temple, and his friend, to seek the firm land of Cape Breton. In either case, we should have undoubtedly had a curious and interesting account of the 'state and commodities' of the island at that early period, from the pen of an intelligent and observant traveller.

Before the accession of Queen Elizabeth, in 1558, no Eng-

[1] See *post*, p. 61.

lishman of note had engaged in maritime adventure, but under her wise and energetic rule, a host of naval heroes, following the example of Sir John Hawkins, embarked in these enterprises. Sir Walter Raleigh sent various expeditions to the coasts of America; Sir Francis Drake, passing through the Straits of Magellan, unfurled the flag of England in the Pacific Ocean; others of less note explored the West Indies and the coasts of the Spanish Main, more for the sake of plunder than legitimate trade; but Sir Humphrey Gilbert, step-brother of Raleigh, was the first Englishman who attempted to establish a settlement in the neighbourhood of Cape Breton. This brave and enterprising hero, who had rendered himself conspicuous by his military exploits under the celebrated Huguenot admiral, Coligny, in the French civil wars, readily obtained a liberal patent from the Queen, dated June 11, 1578, granting him permission to form settlements in any part of North America, with 'free liberty and licence from time to time, and at all times for ever, to discover, find, search out and view, such remote heathen and barbarous lands, not actually possessed of any Christian Prince or people, as to him, his heirs and assigns, or to every or any of them, shall seem good, and the same to have, hold, occupy and enjoy for ever.' It was further stipulated that no other persons should be allowed to form settlements within 200 leagues of any place Sir Humphrey Gilbert and his associates should take and occupy, during the space of six years.

As the whole coast, from Florida to Hudson's Straits, was at that time unoccupied, Gilbert's object in sailing first towards Cape Breton and Newfoundland was evidently to secure possession of the best lands in the neighbourhood of the fisheries. The following extracts from Captain Hayes's journal of the voyage are taken from Hakluyt's 'Collection.' The little fleet comprised five vessels, viz. 'The Delight' of 120 tons, Admiral, in which went the General; the 'Raleigh' of 200 tons, M. Butler, captain; the 'Golden Hind,' of forty tons, Edward Hayes, captain; the 'Swallow,' forty tons, Maurice Browne, captain; and the 'Squirrel,' of ten tons, Wm. Andrews, captain. 'We were in number in all about 260 men; among whom we had of euery faculty good choice, as Shipwrights, Masons, Carpenters, Smithes, and such like, requisite to such an action; also Minerall men and Refiners. Besides, for solace of our people and allurement of the Sauages, we were prouided of Musike in good variety; not omitting the least toyes, as Morris dancers, Hobby horse, and Maylike conceits to delight the Sauage people, whom we intended to winne by all faire meanes possible.' The fleet sailed from Plymouth on June 11, 1583, for Cape Race, in Newfoundland, having been instructed that if they should not happen to meet there, 'then the place of rendezvous was to be at Cape Briton, or the nearest harbour unto the westward of Cape Briton.' On the 13th a contagious fever broke out on board the 'Raleigh,' in consequence of which she put back to Plymouth. On July 20, the 'Swallow' and the 'Squirrel' separated from the other ships in a fog. On July 30, the 'Delight' and 'Golden Hind' first got sight of land in latitude 51°, from whence they steered to the southward to the small island of Baccalaos, on the north side of Conception Bay, where they met the 'Swallow.' Many of the crew of this vessel, men of bad character, who had been pirates, having obtained leave from the captain—'a good religious man'—to go on board a homeward-bound ship they fell in with, 'to borrow such provisions as could be spared,' plundered the 'Newlander of tackle, sails, cable, victuals, and the men of their apparell.' Some of them were drowned in returning to the 'Swallow.' Holding on their course to the southward, 'vntill we came against the harbour called St. John, about fiue leagues from Cape St. Francis, we found also the Frigate or Squirrel lying at anchor before the entrance into the harbour, whom the English merchants would not permit to enter into the harbour. Glad of so happy a meeting both of the Swallow and Frigate in one day (being the 3d August) we made readie our fights, and prepared to enter the harbour, any resistance to the contrarie notwithstanding, there being within, of all nations, to the number of 36 sailes. But first the Generall despatched a boat to giue them knowledge of his coming for no ill intent, haueing Commission from her Maiestie for his voyage he had in hand.' No resistance being now made, they entered the harbour, where they were liberally supplied by all the ships in port, foreign as well as English, with all the necessaries they required, as well as many luxuries, which 'were enjoyed the more by how much the same were unexpected in that desolate corner of the world.' These good things were furnished, probably, not so much from motives of generosity, as from 'their not being able to match us, suffer us not to be hunger starved.' On August 5, Sir Humphrey, having summoned the masters of all the vessels in port, in their presence took formal possession of the island in the name of his Sovereign, and proclaimed that, by virtue of his grant, he held a circuit of 200 leagues in every direction. These limits included Nova Scotia and New Brunswick, pa-t of Labrador, and the islands of Newfoundland, St. John's, and Cape Breton.

Having despatched the 'Swallow' to England with the sick, Sir Humphrey left St. John's on August 20, shaping his course for Cape Breton, with the intention, if the weather would permit, of touching at Sable Island for a supply of cattle and swine, which a Portuguese in St. John's had informed him could be procured there. 'The distance between Cape Race and Cape Briton is 87 leagues. In which nauigation we spent 8 dayes, haueing many times the wind indifferent good; yet could wee neuer attaine sight of any land all that time, seeing we were hindered by the current. At last we fell into such flats and dangers, that hardly any of us escaped; where neuertheless we lost our Admiral,[1] with all the men and prouision, not knowing certainly the place.' According to a reckoning kept by the master of the 'Golden Hind,' of the courses and the distances run from Cape Race towards Cape Breton, the 'Delight' must have struck upon one of the dangerous flats which lie off the western end of Sable Island. No help could be given by the other ships, which, seeing the sad fate of their consort, hauled their wind and escaped, 'the sea going mightily and high.' They beat about all that day and the next, but

[1] The principal ship of a fleet was then called the 'Admiral.' The commander of the fleet was called the 'General.'

could learn nothing of the fate of the crew of the 'Hind,' all of whom, nearly 100 in number, perished,[1] except sixteen who got into a small pinnace with only one oar and without a drop of water. These men, after being six days at sea, were driven by a southerly gale upon the coast of Newfoundland, where they subsisted for eight days upon berries and wild peas, until they were rescued by a Spanish ship which carried them to Passages in Biscay.

The crews of the 'Hind' and 'Squirrel' were 'so sorely depressed' by this misfortune, that Sir Humphrey abandoned his design of going to Cape Breton, and on August 31 bore up for England. When they left St. John's, Sir Humphrey 'made choise to go in his Frigat, the Squirrel, the same being most conuenient to discouer upon the coast, and to search into every harbour or creeke, which a great ship could not do.' Twice, on their homeward voyage across the Atlantic, he went on board the 'Hind,' but would not listen to the entreaties of her officers to remain in her, saying, 'I will not forsake my little company going homeward, with whom I haue passed so many storms and perils.' On September 9, they passed the Azores, when 'the Squirrel was neere cast away, oppressed by waues, yet at that time recouered; and, giuing forth signs of joy, the Generall, sitting abafte with a booke in his hand, cried out vnto us in the Hind (so oft as we did approach within hearing), "We are as neere to Heaven by sea as by land."' These memorable words, which have cheered many a hardy British seaman in storm and danger, were the last they heard from the gallant knight on board the 'Hind,' for, 'aboute twelue of the clocke, or not long after, on the same night, the Frigat being ahead of vs in the Golden Hind, suddenly her lights were out, whereof as it were, in a moment, we lost the sight, and with all our watch cryed, "the Generall was cast away," which was too true. For in that moment the Frigat was deuoured and swallowed vp of the sea.' Thus perished the brave leader of this unfortunate expedition—the victim of an

[1] Amongst these were Parmenius, who was to have been the historian of the expedition, the Saxon Refiner, and Captain Maurice Browne, 'a vertuous, honest, and discreete gentleman.'

idle report which had gone through the little fleet, 'that he was afraid of the sea,' which he resolved to disprove by rashly exposing his life to the risks of an autumnal voyage across the Atlantic in a frail bark of scarce ten tons burthen, 'preferring,' as Captain Hayes remarks, 'the winde of a vaine report to the weight of his own life.' Well might Sir Humphrey have treated such reports with contempt; his character was above suspicion. 'He was one of those,' observes Hakluyt, 'who alike despised fickleness and fear; danger never turned him aside from the pursuit of honour or the service of his Sovereign; for he knew that death is inevitable and the fame of virtue immortal.' Owing to the disastrous intelligence of the issue of Gilbert's voyage, brought to England by the 'Golden Hind,' Sir Walter Raleigh and his friends, who had an interest in the enterprise, gave up all idea of forming a settlement in that part of America, and directed their attention to the more genial climates of the South; so that we are indebted to captains in the merchant service for the only accounts extant of further voyages made to the fishing-grounds before the close of the sixteenth century. Hakluyt and Purchas have rescued many of these from oblivion; but I purpose giving you extracts from the journals of Captains Strong and Leigh only, as they alone contain any references to Cape Breton.

The 'Marigold,' of seventy tons burthen, Richard Strong master, sailed from Falmouth on June 1, 1593, for the island of Ramea, on the southern coast of Newfoundland, to kill morse, or sea-oxen; 'in which isle are so great abundance of the huge and mightie sea-oxen with great teeth in the moneths of April, May and June, that there haue beene fifteene hundreth killed there by one small barke in the yeere 1591.' The 'Marigold' reached Cape St. Francis on July 11, whence she sailed round Cape Race in search of Ramea Island (which you may see upon any good map.) 'We beat about a very long time, and yet missed it, and at length overshot it, and fell in with Cape Briton. . . . Heere diuers of our men went on land vpon the very cape, where, at their arriuall they found the spittes of oke of the Sauages which had roasted meate a little before. And as they viewed the countrey they saw diuers beastes and foules, as blacke foxes, deeres, otters, great foules with redde legges, penguins, and certaine others. And, haueing found no people here at this our first landing, wee went againe on shipboorde, and sayled farther foure leagues to the west of Cape Briton, where wee saw many seales. And here, haueing neede of fresh water, we went againe on shore, and, passing somewhat more into the lande, wee founde certain round pondes artificially made by the Sauages to keepe fish in, with certaine weares in them to take fish. To these pondes wee repayred to fill our caske with water. Wee had not bene long here, but there came one Sauage with blacke long hayre hanging about his shoulders, who called vnto vs, weaving his hands downwardes towards his bellie, vsing these wordes, "Calitogh, calitogh;" as wee drew towardes him one of our mens muskets vnawares shot off; wherevpon hee fell downe, and rising vp suddenly againe hee cryed thrise with a loude voyce, "Chiogh, chiogh, chiogh;" Thereupon nine or tenne of his fellowes running right vp ouer the bushes with great agilitie and swiftnesse came towardes vs with white staues in their handes like half pikes, and their dogges of colour blacke, not so bigge as a greyhounde, followed them at the heeles; but wee retired vnto our boate without any hurt at all receiued. Howbeit one of them brake a hogshead which wee had filled with fresh water, with a great branche of a tree which lay on the ground. Vpon which occasion wee bestowed halfe a dozen muskets shotte vpon them, which they auoyded by falling flatte to the earth, and afterwarde retired themselues to the woodes. One of the Sauages, which seemed to be their captaine, wore a long mantle of beastes skinnes hanging on one of his shoulders. The rest were all naked except their priuities, which were couered with a skinne tyed behinde. After they had escaped our shotte they made a great fire on the shore, belike to giue their fellowes warning of vs. . . . The kinde of trees that wee noted to bee here, were goodly Okes, Firre trees of a great height, a kinde of tree called of vs Quickbeame, and diuerse other kindes to vs vnknowne, because wee stayed not long with diligence to obserue them; and there is great shewe of rosen, pitch and tarre. Wee found in both the places where wee went on land abundance of Raspeses, Strawberries, Hurtes, and herbes of good smell, and diuers good for the skuruie, and grass very ranke and of great length. Wee sawe fiue or six boates sayling to the southwardes of Cape Briton, which wee judged to bee Christians, which had some trade that way. Wee sawe also, while wee were on shore, the manner of their hanging vp their fish and flesh with withes to dry in the ayre; they also lay them vpon raftes and hurdles and make a smoake vnder them, or a softe fire, and so drie them as the Sauages vse to doe in Virginia.' Hence they sailed along the coast to the south-west as far as the latitude of 44½°, and in their course 'sawe exceeding great store of Seales and abundance of Porposes, whereof we killed eleuen. We sawe Whales also of all sortes as well small as great; and here our men took many berded Codde with one teate vnderneath, which are like to the North East Cods, and better than those of Newfoundland.' On September 28 they left the coast and steered for England, which they reached on December 22.

The place where the 'Marigold's' boat's crew landed to obtain fresh water was evidently the point of land upon which Louisbourg was afterwards built, the distance from the Cape being exactly four leagues.

Captain Leigh's voyage, to which I have already alluded (p. 40), was made in 1597. He sailed from Gravesend on April 11, in command of the 'Hopewell,' of 120 tons, accompanied by the 'Chancewell,' Captain Van Herwick, of 70 tons, on a fishing and trading expedition to the St. Lawrence. Both ships arrived in safety on the coast of Newfoundland on May 20, but parted company in a fog off Placentia Bay on June 5. Captain Leigh, from whose journal I make the following extracts, informs me, that on June 11, 'at sunsetting, we had sight of Cape Breton. . . . On the 12th, by reason of contrary winds they cast anchor under the north-east end of the island of Menego, to the north of Cape Breton . . . and on the 14th came to the two islands of Birds.' After visiting Brion's Island, they gave up the idea of going to the St. Lawrence without their consort, and returned to the eastward in search of her. On his arrival at the Isle of Ramea, finding four French vessels in the port, Leigh coolly ordered the masters to deliver up their munitions and powder to him, promising to return them on his departure. This demand was resisted by the fishermen, who called in a number of men from the other harbours near, and prepared to attack the 'Hopewell' with three pieces of ordnance planted on the shore. Finding the Frenchmen too strong for him, Leigh prudently left the port on the 21st, and sailed for Isle Blanch, two leagues distant; but he was not allowed to remain long, his white flag having been answered 'by a bullet out of a great piece of ordnance.' By the advice of his sailing master, Leigh now shaped his course for the river of Cape Breton [Syndey?], supposed to be 40 leagues distant. 'The 24 June we sent our boate on shore in a great Bay vpon the Isle of Cape Briton, for water. The 25 we arriued on the west side of the isle of Menego, where we left some caske on shore in a sandy bay, but could not tary for foule weather. The 26 we cast anker in another Bay vpon the maine of Cape Briton. The 27, about tenne of the clocke in the morning, we met with eight men of the Chancewell, our consort, in a shallope, who told us that their ship was cast away vpon the maine of Cape Briton, within a great bay eighteene leagues within the Cape, and vpon a rocke within a mile of the shore, vpon the 23 of this moneth, about one of the clocke in the afternoone; and that they had cleered the ship from the rocke: but being bilged and full of water, they presently did run her vp into a sandy bay, where she was no sooner come on ground, but presently after there came aboord many shallops with store of French men, who robbed and spoyled all they could lay hands on, pillaging the poore men euen to their very shirts, and vsing them in sauage maner; whereas they should rather as Christians haue aided them in that distresse. Which newes, when we heard, we blessed God, who by his diuine providence and vnspeakable mercy had not onely preserued all the men, but brought us thither so miraculously to ayd and comfort them. So presently we put into the road where the Chancewell lay; where also was one ship of Sibiburo, whose men that holpe to pillage the Chancewell were runne away into the woods. But the master thereof, which had done very honestly with our men, stayed in his ship, and came aboord of vs; whom we vsed well, not taking from him any thing that was his, but onely such things as we could finde of our owne. And when we had dispatched our businesse, we gave him one good cable, one olde cable and an anker, one shallop with mast, sailes and other furniture, and other things which belonged to the ship. In recompense whereof he gaue vs two hogsheads of sider, one barrel of peaze, and 25 score of fish.

'The 29, betimes in the morning we departed from that road [St. Ann's?] toward a great Biscaine some 7 leagues off, of 300 tuns, whose men dealt most doggedly with the Chancewell's company. The same night we ankered at the mouth of the harborow where the Biskaine was. The 30, betimes in the morning we put into the harborow, and, approached nere their stage, we saw it uncouered, and so suspected the ship to be gone; whereupon we sent our pinesse on shore with a dozen men, who, when they came, found great store of fish on shore, but all the men were fled; neither could they perceiue whether the ship could be gone, but, as they thought, to sea. This day, about twelue of the clocke, we took a sauage boate which our men pursued; but all the Sauages ran away into the woods, and our men brought their boat on boord. The same day, in the afternoon, we brought our ship to an anker in the harborow: and the same we tooke three hogsheads and an halfe of traine, and some 300 of greene fish. Also in the euening three of the Sauages, whose boat we had, came vnto vs for their boat; to whom we gaue coats and kniues, and restored them their boat againe. The next day, being the first of July, the rest of the Sauages came vnto vs, among whom was their king, whose name was Itary, and their queene, to whom also we gaue coats and kniues and other trifles. These Sauages called the harborow Cibo [Sydney]. In this place are the greatest multitude of lobsters that euer we heard of; for we caught at one hawle with a little draw net above 140.

'The fourth of July, in the morning we departed from Cibo. And the fifth we cast anker in a reasonable good harbour called New Port [Puerto Novo or Baleine] some eight leagues from

Cibo, and within three leagues from the English Port (Louisbourg). At this place, in pursuing certain shallops of a ship of Rochel, one of them came aboord, who told vs that the Biskainer whom we sought was in the English Port, with two Biskainers more and two ships of Rochel. Thereupon we sent one of our men in the Rochellers shallop to parle with the Admiral [1] and others our friends in the English Port, requesting them ayd for the recouery of our things, which the other ship, called the Santa Maria, of St. Vincent (whereof was master Johannes de Harte, and pilot Adam de Lauandote), had robbed from the Chancewell. To which they answered, that if we would come in vnto them in peace, they would assist vs what they might. This answer we had the sixt day.

'On the seuenth, in the forenoon, we arrived in the English Port, and cast anker aloofe from the other ships; which done, I went aboord the Admirall to desire the performance of his promise; who sent for Johannes de Harte, who was contented to restore most of our things againe: whereupon I went aboord his ship to haue them restored. This day and the eight I spent in procuring such things as they had robbed; but yet in the end we wanted a great part thereof. Then we were briefe with them, and willed them either to restore vs the rest of our things which they had, or els enforce them to do it, and also haue satisfaction for our victuals and merchandises, which by their means were lost in the Chancewell. The ninth, in the morning, wee prepared our ship to goe neere vnto them. Whereupon their Admirall sent his boat aboord and desired to speak with mee; then I went vnto him, and desired to haue our things with peace and quietnesse, proffering to make him and the masters of the two ships of Rochel our vmpires, and what they should aduise I would stand vnto. Heereupon we went aboord the other ship to make peace, but they would heare no reason, neither yet condescend to restore any thing

[1] It was customary in the fishing ports for the master of the first ship that arrived to act as admiral until another came in, when the last comer became admiral, and so on in succession. Any disputes or difficulties that arose were referred to the admiral for settlement. The admiral, upon coming into office, gave a feast to all the masters of vessels in port.

els which they had of ours. Then I desired that, as I came in peace vnto them, they would so set me aboord my ship againe; which they denied to doe, but most uniustly detained me and Stephen van Herwicke [master of the Chancewell], who was with me. A while after, our shallop came with foure men to know how I did, and to fetch me aboord; but so soone as she came to the Admirall's ship's side, his men entered, and tooke her away, detaining our men also as prisoners with vs. Then presently all the three Biscainers made toward our ship, which was not carelesse to get the winde of them all; and hauing then by the mercy of God obtained the same, shee then stayed for them; but when they sawe they had lost their advantage, they presently turned their course, making as great haste in againe as they did out before. Afterwards I attempted twise to goe aboord, but was still enforced backe by the two other Biscainers, who sought our liues, so that in the end the master of the Admirall was enforced to man his great boat to waft vs; and yet, notwithstanding, they bent a piece of great ordinance at vs; for we were to passe by them vnto our ship; but we rescued our shallop under our master's great boat; and by that means passed in safety. The next morning, being the tenth of the moneth, we purposed, if the winde had serued our turn, to haue made them repent their euill doing, and to restore vs our owne againe, or els to haue suncke their ships if we could. But the winde serued not our turne for that purpose, but carried vs to sea; so that the same morning we tooke our course toward the Bay of St. Lawrence, in Newfoundland, where we hoped to finde a Spanish ship, which we had intelligence did fish at that place.'

On his arrival at St. Lawrence Bay, learning that there was a Spanish ship in Little St. Lawrence, not far distant, he sent an officer and sixteen men to seize her. This was easily effected; but another Spanish ship, which arrived a day or two after on the scene of action, recaptured her consort, and made prisoners of the prize crew. Finding himself overmatched, Leigh was glad to exchange the Spanish prisoners in his hands for the prize crew, and hasten his departure from such a dangerous neighbourhood. On the 24th, he reached the harbour of Cape St. Mary, where he found a French ship of Belle Isle, 200 tons burthen, with a crew of forty men. Disappointed in his views upon the Spaniard, Leigh attacked, and, after a sharp fight, captured the unoffending Frenchman, who had nothing whatever to do with the robbery of the 'Chancewell.' Having thus satisfied his desire for revenge, Leigh sailed with his prize for England, and on August 31 made Lundy Island, in the Bristol Channel.

In 'certaine observations,' at the end of his 'Journal,' Leigh says:—'The island of Menego [probably St. Paul's] is scant two leagues long, and very narrow. In the midst of it, a great way within the wood, is a very large poolc. . . . The land of Cape Briton we found to be somewhat like the New-foundland, but rather better. Here, toward the west end of it, we saw the clouds lie lower than the hils; as we did also at Cape Laurence in Newfoundland. The easterly end of the island of Cape Briton is nothing so high land as the west. We went on sho: e vpon it in fiue places: 1. At the bay where the Chancewell was cast away; 2. At Cibo; 3. At a little island between Cibo and Newport; 4. At the Newport; and 5. At Port Inglese, or the English Port.'

Captain Leigh is the first navigator that calls Cape Breton an *island*.[1] All the other writers whom I have quoted in the preceding pages, seem to have been of opinion that the Cape itself was the eastern extremity of Nova Scotia, or, as it was then called, Norumbega, or Arambec—the name applied upon the old maps to all the territory to the eastward of the Hudson river. They speak of the Cape, the country adjacent to or about the C pe, or the firm or mainland of Cape Breton, but never make any allusion to its insular character. The Cape, from its prominent position, naturally became the land-fall anxiously looked for by the fishermen coming out from Europe in the spring, as well as their point of departure on their home-

[1] Since the above passage was written, my attention has been directed to a voyage (recorded in Hakluyt's 'Collection') made by Master Rice Jones, in the 'Grace' of Bristol, in 1594, to the island of Anticosti, in pursuit of whales, in which Master Jones says that on his return 'he had sight of the *island* of Cape Breton.' This was three years before Leigh's voyage.

ward voyages, and was known by its present name so far back as the year 1504 (p. 14).

I have not been able to ascertain when the Gut of Canso was first discovered. The oldest map on which it is delineated is that constructed by the celebrated geographer Gerard Mercator, published at Duisbourg in 1569, of which you have a copy annexed. Mercator must have derived his information from an authentic source—probably from some intelligent fisherman who frequented that part of the coast—as the position and direction of the Gut is laid down with tolerable accuracy.[1] Neither Hakluyt nor Michael Lok could have seen Mercator's map, when the former published Lok's map in the 'Divers Voyages to America,' in 1582, as Cape Breton is laid down as the eastern extremity of Norumbega. This is the more extraordinary, as, according to Hakluyt, 'Michael Lok was a man, for his knowledge in divers languages, and especially in cosmographie, able to do his country good.'

During the latter years of the sixteenth century, although England, France, and Spain were at constant warfare, it is gratifying to learn that the coasts of Cape Breton were considered neutral ground by the European fishermen, who frequented the same harbours and followed their vocation in peace and amity. It was only when such an outrage as the plundering of the 'Chancewell' occurred, that the smouldering embers of national animosity burst into a flame. In other parts of the world, this commendable conduct was not, unhappily, pursued. Every sea traversed by the argosies of Spain, laden with the treasures of Mexico and Peru, was closely watched by bold English rovers, ever ready to pounce upon their prey. To these men it was a matter of indifference whether England and Spain were at peace or war. If they fell in with a Spanish galleon, they never wanted an excuse for attacking her; and if the Spanish Ambassador complained of the outrage at the English Court, Elizabeth, it is said,

[1] Lescarbot says that a Frenchman, Savalette, began to fish at a harbour four leagues to the westward of Cape Canso, in 1563. Savalette must of course have been well aware of the existence of the strait which separates Cape Breton from Nova Scotia. See Lescarbot's *Histoire de la Nouvelle-France.*

No. 2.

to face p. 48

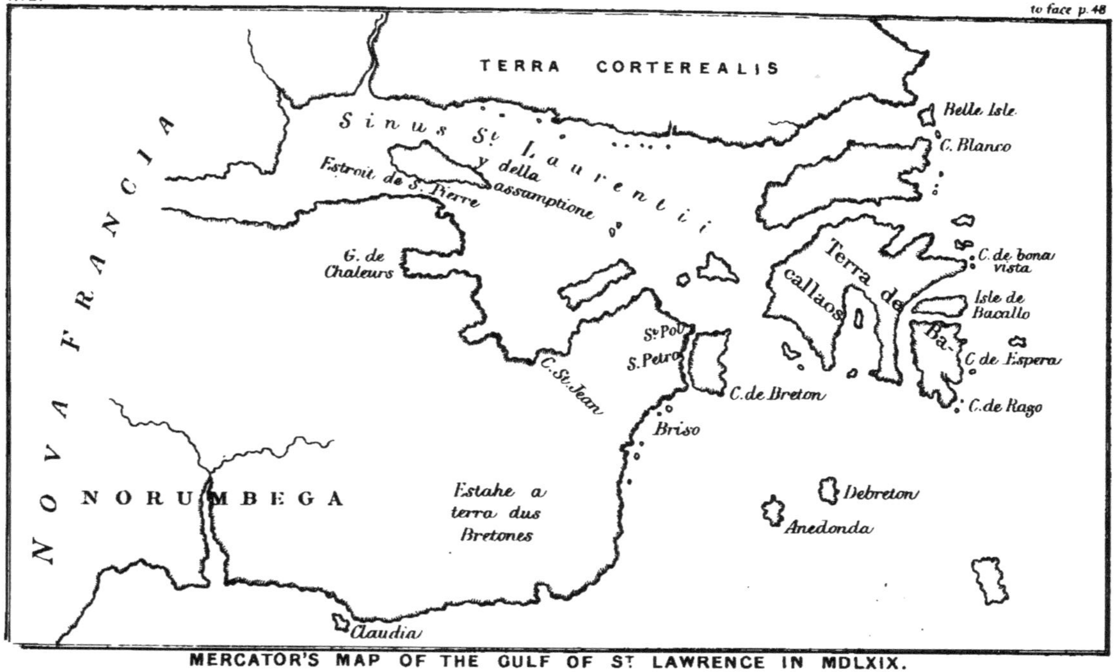

MERCATOR'S MAP OF THE GULF OF ST. LAWRENCE IN MDLXIX.

'reproved the offenders with smiles, and occasionally condescended to share in the plunder.' Fortunately for the Spanish fishermen, the small value of their cargoes offered no temptation to such men as Hawkins, Drake, and Grenville; and hundreds of cargoes of salt cod and train oil annually reached Spain without molestation. Although the ports of Cape Breton were open to all nations, St. Anne's was the favourite resort of the French, Port Inglese (Louisbourg), of the English, and Baie des Espagnols (Sydney), of the Spanish fishermen. Before the close of Elizabeth's reign (1603), more than 200 English vessels were engaged in the fisheries of Newfoundland and Cape Breton.[1]

After the failure of Baron de Lery to make a settlement in America in 1518, no attempts were made by the French to take actual possession of any part of the country bordering on the Gulf of St. Lawrence until the year 1598, when the Marquis de la Roche took out a number of persons, amongst whom were forty convicts, to establish a colony in New France. On his arrival at the Isle of Sable, the Marquis put the convicts on shore, with the intention of leaving them there until he had explored the coasts of the mainland in search of a suitable place for settlement. Whilst engaged in this duty, the Marquis was overtaken by a tempest, driven off the coast, and obliged to return to France. The unfortunate convicts, abandoned to their fate on a desolate island, built a house with materials obtained from the wrecks of some Spanish vessels which had been cast away on their way to Cape Breton, with the intention of making a settlement there.[2] Seven years afterwards, a vessel was sent out by the king of France to look after the miserable outcasts, when only twelve were found alive, who had subsisted principally upon the progeny of the cattle left there by the Baron de Lery in 1518.[3]

In the year 1599, the Sieur Chauvin, a captain in the French navy, who had some influence at Court, by the advice of Captain Pontgrave of St. Malo, who had made a voyage up the

[1] Lord Bury's *Exodus of the Western Nations.*
[2] Charlevoix's *Histoire et Description de la Nouvelle-France.*
[3] See p. 18.

St. Lawrence, obtained a patent from the king, granting him the exclusive right of trading upon that river, on condition of colonising the country. Chauvin and Pontgrave, accompanied by M. de Monts, who went out to see the country, arrived at Tadoussac, an Indian village at the confluence of the rivers Saguenay and St. Lawrence, where they established a post for trading with the natives. Pontgrave and De Monts strongly advised Chauvin to go farther up the St. Lawrence; but the latter, ignoring the conditions of his patent, and thinking of nothing but enriching himself by the collection of furs, left sixteen men at Tadoussac for that purpose, and returned with his friends to France. In the following spring, Chauvin again went out to Tadoussac, where he found that several of his men had died of cold and hunger during the winter, and that the survivors owed their lives to the kindness of the Indians. Taking his men to France, he was busily engaged in preparations for another expedition upon a larger scale, when he died suddenly, and the scheme was consequently abandoned.[1]

Equally unfortunate was the result of an enterprise undertaken soon after the death of Chauvin by the Sieur Aymer de Chastes, Governor of Dieppe, who obtained a commission from Henry IV. to establish a colony in Canada. De Chastes sent out Captain du Pontgrave and Samuel Champlain to examine the country, for the purpose of selecting a place for settlement, who, after completing that service, returned to France, where, to their great grief, they found that De Chastes had died during their absence. This, of course, put an end to the enterprise.

The attempts of Sir Walter Raleigh and his friends to establish an English colony in the more genial climate of North Carolina were equally unsuccessful. Having obtained a patent from Queen Elizabeth, Raleigh sent out an expedition in 1585, which, owing to the gross mismanagement of its leader, proved a disastrous failure. Most of the settlers died of hunger and disease; the few survivors were fortunately rescued from a similar fate by Sir Francis Drake, who visited the settlement in 1586, on his return from Carthagena. A

[1] Champlain's *Voyages de la Nouvelle-France.*

second band of settlers, who went out in 1587, 120 in number, was supposed to have perished in hostilities with the Indians. Not a single soul was left to tell the sad story of their fate. In the short space of a dozen years almost every trace of the City of Raleigh, on the island of Roanoke, was obliterated.

Thus you see that up to the year 1600—103 years after the discovery of the continent of North America by Cabot—every attempt to establish a permanent settlement on the long line of coast stretching from Florida to Labrador had signally failed; not a single European was then known to be living within those limits, save the few miserable outcasts left by De la Roche on the desolate Isle of Sable.

LETTER IV.

1600—1613.

The dawn of the seventeenth century was distinguished by an event of no small importance in connection with our story—namely, the first settlement of Nova Scotia. This, too, was immediately followed by another attempt to establish a colony in Canada, which happily proved more successful than those which I briefly noticed in my last letter. If the simple colonisation of those countries had been the only object in view, the failures I have recorded would most likely have discouraged others from undertaking similar enterprises; but a new branch of commerce—the fur trade—had been gradually growing up, which yielded such profitable returns, that the moment one adventurer disappeared, another was ready to step into his place. The Norman and Breton fishermen, who had occasionally visited the Gulf and River St. Lawrence in the pursuit of whales, ever since the time of Jacques Cartier, were the first who began this traffic. Finding that the savages readily exchanged the glossy beaver skins with which they were clothed for the merest trifles, the fishermen brought out knives, beads, and other worthless trinkets, and in the course of time established a regular trade with the savages, who flocked to the shore every spring with the fruits of their winter's hunting. This lucrative traffic was not confined to the banks of the St. Lawrence. The fishermen who frequented the coasts of Nova Scotia and Cape Breton were not long in discovering that the traffic in furs was a much more profitable, and at the same time a less laborious occupation than catching and curing codfish. Many abandoned their old vocation, and, being supplied by the merchants of St. Malo, Rouen, &c., with abundant stocks of such commodities as were most eagerly purchased by the Indians, penetrated every harbour and creek upon the coasts of the Gulf and the Atlantic in search of customers. Cape Breton, owing to its position, and the facilities afforded by its internal water communication, soon became a favourite resort of the fur traders.[1]

The mortal remains of M. de Chastes, the worthy governor of Dieppe, had scarcely been deposited in their last resting-place, when a new candidate for the honour of colonising New France, and at the same time of enriching himself in the lucrative fur trade, appeared in the person of Pierre du Gast, Sieur de Monts, a gentleman of great influence at the court of Henry IV., who in the year 1603 obtained a grant from that monarch of all the territory included between the fortieth and forty-sixth degrees of north latitude. This territory, which was called La Cadié or Acadié in his commission, extended from Pennsylvania on the south, to the St. Lawrence on the north, including therein the present British provinces of Nova Scotia and New Brunswick, to which in later times, the name Acadié was restricted. De Monts, by his grant, enjoyed a monopoly of the soil, and the exclusive right of trading in furs with the Indians; but the rights of the fishermen to follow their vocation on the coasts without interruption were strictly reserved. This reservation, however, did not satisfy either the fishermen or the merchants of the French fishing ports, who had for a long time been deriving great profits from the fur trade. A great outcry was raised against the monopoly by all parties

[1] It is evident the Cape Breton Indians were regularly engaged in this trade in the year 1594, and ready to dispose of their furs to any chance vessel that arrived on the coast; for Henry May, who visited the island on his way from Bermuda (where he had been shipwrecked) to Newfoundland, in search of a passage to England, says: 'On the 20th May (1594) we fell with the land near to Cape Briton, where we ran into a fresh-water river, whereof there be many, and tooke in wood, water, and ballast. And here the people of the countrey came unto us, being clothed all in furs, with the furred side unto their skins, and brought with them furres of sundry sorts to sell, besides great store [illegible]ks; so some of our company, having saved some small beads, bough[illegible]ks. Here we stayed not above foure houres, and so departe[illegible]me to be a very good countrey. And we saw very fine ch[illegible]woods.'—*Hakluyt.*

interested in the old state of affairs, which De Monts could only appease by following the example of his predecessor De Chastes, who had been obliged to give the malcontents a share in his exclusive rights.

De Monts and his partners lost no time in taking possession of their territory. In the spring of 1604, they fitted out two vessels, in which they embarked a motley company, comprised of gentlemen volunteers, Catholic priests, Huguenot ministers, agriculturists, artisans, soldiers, and some persons of less reputable character, taken from the gaols and galleys.

De Monts sailed from Havre de Grace on April 7, 1604, in the first ship, commanded by Captain Timothy, accompanied by his friend Jean de Biencourt; Baron de Poutrincourt, who went out to see the country for the purpose of fixing upon a suitable place to settle his family; Samuel Champlain, chief pilot of the expedition, of whom I shall have to say more anon; and M. d'Orville, M. de Champdoré, and 'other men of reckoning.' De Monts and many of his associates being Protestants, were allowed the free exercise of their religion upon condition of taking out a certain number of priests to instruct the aborigines in the dogmas of the Roman Catholic faith. This condition he faithfully carried out, much to his own discomfort. They had not been many days at sea when the priests and ministers began to discuss the tenets of their respective creeds, which led to unseemly quarrels, sometimes ending in blows. Champlain says he does not know which had the best of it, but that he heard the minister of what he calls 'the pretended reformed religion,' complain to De Monts that he had been beaten by the priest.

Captain Pontgrave, a merchant of St. Malo, who had often been up the St. Lawrence, and was said to have realised a fortune in the fur trade, embarked in the second ship, commanded by Captain Morell, and sailed from Havre de Grace a few days after De Monts, having previously arranged to meet him at Campseau.

De Monts had a favourable voyage, but overshot his destined port, making the land at Cape La Héve, sixty leagues to the westward of Campseau; whilst Pontgrave, on the other hand, fell short of it, first making the land at Havre à l'Anglois (Louisbourg). From Cape La Héve De Monts coasted along to the westward, and entered a harbour which he named Port-Rossignol (Liverpool), after the captain of a ship which he seized there, 'who did trucke for skins with the savages.' Proceeding further west, he reached a harbour which he called Port Mouton (the name which it still bears), in consequence of one of his sheep having leaped overboard whilst at anchor there. Here he waited a month for Pontgrave's ship, but receiving no tidings of her, he engaged a party of Indians to go along the coast to the eastward in search of her. The missing ship was found at La Baie des Isles, having been detained, as Lescarbot[1] says, 'for two causes: the one, that, wanting a cocke-boate, they imploied their time in building one, on the land where they arrived first, which was the English Port (Louisbourg). The other, that, being come at Campseau Port, they founde there foure ships of Baskes, or men of St. John de Luz, that did trucke with the Savages, contrarie to the said inhibitions [De Mont's Patent], from whom they took their goods, and brought the masters to the said M. de Monts, who used them very gently.'

Pontgrave then 'returned backe towards the great river of Canada (the St. Lawrence) for the trade of skinnes or furres;' but De Monts, who had been in Canada with Chauvin, and had noticed the rigour of the climate, determined to seek for a suitable place for his settlement in a more genial climate to the southward. Doubling Cape Sable, he discovered the Bay of Fundy, which he called 'La Baie Françoise,' and a narrow channel on the starboard leading into a beautiful basin of great extent, surrounded by undulating wooded hills, to which he gave the name of Port Royal (Annapolis). Poutrincourt was so enchanted with this beautiful harbour, that he obtained from De Monts a grant of the country bordering upon it, with the intention of bringing out his family and forming a settle-

[1] Both Lescarbot and Champlain were engaged with de Monts in the settlement of Acadié. My hasty sketch has been chiefly compiled from Erondelle's Translation of Lescarbot's *History of New France*, published in London in 1610, and Champlain's *Voyages de la Nouvelle-France*. Paris edition of 1632.

ment. Proceeding up the bay, De Monts discovered the basin of Minas, the river St. John, and the Bay of Passamaquoddy, where he decided upon establishing his settlement upon a small island near the mouth of the river St. Croix. Here he erected a fort and suitable buildings, in which he and his company spent a miserable winter, after the departure of Poutrincourt, who had returned to France in the preceding autumn. Of seventy-nine persons who remained with De Monts on the island, thirty-five died of scurvy before spring. As soon as the weather would permit, Champlain and De Monts embarked in a small craft of fifteen tons burthen to complete the survey of the coast to the westward, which they had commenced in the previous autumn. They proceeded as far as Cape Cod, but finding the natives generally fierce and hostile, or, as Lescarbot calls them, 'traitours and theefes whom one had neede to take heede of,' they returned to St. Croix in the beginning of August. Despairing of receiving the expected succours, they were preparing to go to Newfoundland, in the hope of meeting with a vessel to take them to France, when Pontgrave arrived, bringing with him abundant supplies and a reinforcement of forty men, 'to the great joy of all.' By the advice of Pontgrave, De Monts now decided upon crossing the bay and forming a settlement at Port Royal. Having carried over all their stores and utensils, and such portions of the buildings as could be removed, they at once set to work to clear the land, and to erect houses and a fort, on a point at the mouth of the Equille River (Annapolis River). As soon as the people were all comfortably housed, De Monts returned to France, leaving Pontgrave in charge of the settlement, and Champlain and Champdoré to explore the country.

In the spring of 1606, De Monts and Poutrincourt engaged a ship called the 'Jonas' to take out mechanics, labourers, and supplies to Port Royal. Poutrincourt sailed from Rochelle in the 'Jonas,' accompanied by his friend Marc Lescarbot, 'avocat en Parlement,' who wished to see the country. We are indebted to Lescarbot for the first, as well as the best account of the settlement of Acadié. They had a rough and tedious voyage. On the 4th July they made the Isles of St. Peter's, on the coast of Newfoundland; and on the 7th, 'discovered on the larboard a coast of land, high raised up, appearing unto us as long as one's sight could stretch out, which gave us greater cause of joy than yet we had had; wherein God did greatly shew his merciful favour unto us, making this discovery in fair calm weather. Being yet far from it, the boldest of the company went up to the main top, to the end to see it better, so much were all of us desirous to see this land, true and most delightful habitation of man. M. de Poutrincourt went up thither, and myself also, which we had not yet done. Even our dogs did thrust their noses out of the ship, better to draw and smell the sweet air of the land, not being able to contain themselves from witnessing by their gestures the joy they had of it. We drew within a league near unto it, and (the sails being let down) we fell a fishing of Cod, the fishing of the Bank beginning to fail. They which had before us made voyages in those parts, did judge us to be at Cape Breton. The night drawing on, we stood off to the seaward; the next day following drew near to the Bay of Campseau.'

Having called at several places on the coast, they did not reach Port Royal until the 27th July, when they found that Pontgrave and all his people, save two men in charge of the fort, had left the place a few days before in boats, in quest of a fishing vessel bound for France. Meeting with a boat sent to explore some harbours on the coast by Poutrincourt, Pontgrave immediately returned to Port Royal, and having seen all parties comfortably settled, proceeded in the 'Jonas' along the coast towards Cape Breton in search of contraband traders, and then sailed for France. Champlain and Poutrincourt then set out in a little bark of fifteen tons, to survey the coast to the southward, leaving Lescarbot busily occupied in superintending the completion of the fort and magazines, clearing land, laying out fields and gardens, erecting a water mill, and making all needful preparations for the coming winter.

Having received an abundant supply of wine and other creature comforts by the 'Jonas,' and having from the first wisely established most friendly relations with the Indians, who brought in a profusion of fish, game, and venison, the little band of settlers seem to have had a jolly time of it during the winter. They accompanied the Indians in their hunting expeditions, encamped with them in the forest, invited the chiefs to their table, and regaled the squaws and children with bread and biscuit. On the return of spring, all hands, including even Poutrincourt and Lescarbot, set to work to prepare the soil for cultivation; they dug, planted, and sowed their little fields, with the hope of receiving an abundant return for their labour. Whilst they were thus employed, 400 Indian warriors, from various parts of the country, rendezvoused at Port Royal, under the command of an aged Sagamore called Memberton, a firm friend of the French, on their way to attack a tribe called Armouchiquois, who dwelt on the coast of Maine. The professed object of assembling at Port Royal was to gratify their French friends; the real object, probably, was to make a demonstration of their power. If the truth were known, the departure of the fleet of war canoes was to the French the most pleasing part of the spectacle.

Spring was fast slipping away, and the colonists were anxiously looking for the arrival of De Monts with supplies from France, when a vessel entered the harbour, bringing the unwelcome intelligence of the revocation of De Monts's charter, in consequence of the complaints of the Basque and Breton fishermen, who alleged that their property had been unjustly confiscated, and their business ruined, by De Monts's cruisers. Champlain says this was effected by the intrigues of influential persons about the Court, who were jealous of the great privileges granted to De Monts; and that the fishermen, notwithstanding their great outcry, had been able to give a heavy bribe to 'a certain person' to persuade the king to cancel the commission.

Thus, at the very time when their hopes were brightest—when all seemed full of promise and success—the noble enterprise in which De Monts had embarked was brought to an abrupt and disastrous termination by the intrigues of the favourites of a corrupt Court. Under these circumstances the colonists had no choice; they were obliged to abandon Port Royal, and immediately set about making preparations for that purpose. In the month of August, 1607, Poutrincourt and all his people, with heavy hearts left the fort and buildings of Port Royal, together with the growing crops, to their friends the Indians, who had just returned victorious from their raid against the Armouchiquois, and proceeded to Campseau to join the other vessels belonging to De Monts and his associates.

The French, by their kind and courteous conduct, had so completely won the affection and esteem of the Indians, that on their departure from Port Royal 'the shore resounded with lamentation.' 'It was piteous,' says Lescarbot, 'to see at his (Poutrincourt's) departing, those poor people weep, who had always been kept in hope that some of ours should always tarry with them. In the end, promise was made unto them that the year following households and families should be sent thither, wholly to inhabit their land, and teach them trades for to make them live as we do, which promise did somewhat comfort them.' It is a painful task to contrast the conduct of our own countrymen and other Europeans with that of the French towards the Indians. I will only mention two instances. In this same year (1607), the crew of a Dutch vessel, which had put into Campseau harbour, plundered the graves of the Indians of the beaver skins in which it was their custom to wrap the bodies of the dead. And two years later, the celebrated navigator, Henry Hudson, on his voyage along the coast of Acadié, entered a port to repair his ship, where the Indians received him with great kindness, giving all the aid in their power, and offering valuable beaver skins in exchange for common 'redde gownes;' and how do you suppose he repaid them? He shall answer for himself: 'In the morning wee manned our scute with foure muskets, and sixe men, and tooke one of their shallops, and brought it aboord. Then wee manned our boate and scute with twelve men and muskets, and two stone pieces, or murderers, and drave the sauages from their houses, and tooke the spoyle of them, as they would have done of us.'[1]

[1] Hudson's *Voyages*, published by the Hakluyt Society.

Leaving these painful subjects, let us note the progress of our friends from Port Royal to Campseau. Coasting along shore, they at length arrived at a port four leagues to the westward of Campseau, where they found an old French captain who had been fishing on the coast of Acadié for more than forty years. As Lescarbot's relation throws some light upon the way the fishery was carried on at that time on the coasts of Acadié and Cape Breton, I must give it in full:—'In the end we arrived within foure leagues of Campseau, at a port, where a good old man of St. John de Luz, called Captain Savalet,[1] received us with all the kindness in the world. And for as much as this port (which is little but very faire) hath no name, I have qualified it, in my geographical map, with the name of Savalet. This good honest man told us that the same voyage was the 42 voyage that he had made into these parts, and neverthelesse the Newfoundland men do but make one in a yeare. He was marvellously pleased with his fishing, and tolde us moreover that he tooke every day fiftie crownes worth of fish, and that his voyage would be worth 1000 pounds. He paid wages to 16 men, and his vessell was of 80 tunnes, which could carry 100,000 dry fishes. He was sometimes vexed with the savages that did cabine there, who too boldly and impudently went into his ship and carried away from him what they liked.' Next day they arrived at Campseau, where they were soon after joined by Poutrincourt and Champlain, who had made the voyage from Port Royal, a distance of 120 leagues, in an open boat. The whole party then sailed for France.

Poutrincourt and Lescarbot do not seem to have visited Cape Breton during their residence in Acadié, but Champlain, who was employed in surveying the coast and harbours of New France, gives in his work a short description of the island, which I will give at length, as it is the first on record. It is accompanied by a quaint old map, of which I annex a copy, for the purpose of showing how little was then known of the geography of the island, even by a person professionally engaged in maritime surveying. The harbour of Sydney, one of the

[1] This is the person mentioned at p. 48.

No 3.

to face p. 60.

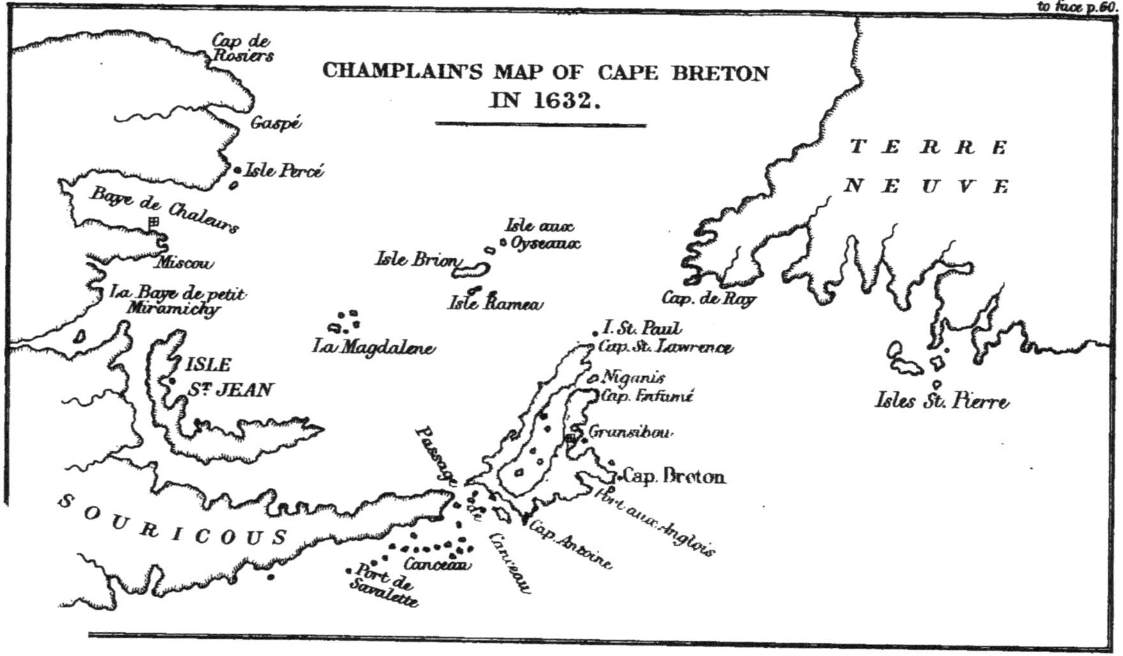

best and most conspicuous on the Atlantic coast, which had been long known, you will observe, is not shown at all, whilst the Bras d'Or Lakes are represented as communicating with the ocean by means of a channel opening into Ingonish Bay. Having described the principal harbours between Cape Sable and Canceau,[1] he goes on to say, 'Between Canceau and Cape Breton there is a great bay which runs nine or ten leagues inland and forms a passage between the island and the mainland. It communicates with the great Bay of St. Lawrence, leading up to the fisheries at Gaspé and Isle Percée. The passage is exceedingly narrow. Large ships cannot pass through it, although there is sufficient depth of water, on account of the changing tides and rapid currents. For this reason we have named it "Le Passage Courant." It lies in the latitude of 43¾ degrees. Cape Breton Island is of a triangular form, eighty leagues in circuit, and is generally mountainous, nevertheless in some parts very pleasant. In the midst of the island there is a kind of lake communicating with the sea on the north-east and south-east. In the lake there are a number of islands abounding in game; shell-fish of various kinds are found, including oysters of poor flavour. In this island there are several harbours and fishing places—namely, Port aux Anglois (Louisbourg), about three or four leagues from the Cape, and Niganis (Ingonish), eighteen or twenty leagues further north. The Portuguese formerly made a settlement on this island, but the cold and rigorous climate compelled them to abandon it.'[2]

For the present you must be satisfied with this short account of your island. I shall have more interesting intelligence to communicate by and by; but we must first trace the fortunes of Poutrincourt to their bitter end. Undaunted by the losses he had sustained, charmed with the salubrity of the climate and fertility of the soil about Port Royal, and ambitious of becoming the father of New France, Poutrincourt, on his

[1] I now adopt Champlain's orthography of this name. Lescarbot always spells it 'Campseau.'

[2] There is a description of Cape Breton in Joan de Laet's *Novus Orbis*, published at Leyden in 1633, but it differs so little from Champlain's account, from which it was probably compiled, that I did not consider it worth while to transfer it to these pages.

return to France, readily obtained a ratification of De Mont's grant from the King, upon condition of carrying out certain Jesuit missionaries to convert the savages. The King himself, who had abjured the Protestant faith on his accession to the throne—quite indifferent about religious matters—was easily persuaded to insist upon this condition by the Queen and the Jesuits—then all-powerful at Court; but Poutrincourt, a zealous Catholic of the national Church, and consequently an enemy of the Jesuits, managed to evade it, by leaving the missionaries waiting for him at Bourdeaux, whilst he embarked at Dieppe, taking with him a Catholic priest named Josué Fléche, in their place. On his arrival at Port Royal in the spring of 1610, desirous of showing that the Jesuits were not required to christianize the savages, Poutrincourt and La Fléche immediately entered upon the task of converting them. The old chief, Memberton, and his family were the first proselytes. These, with the rest of his followers, were baptized on St. John's Day, in the presence of all the colonists. The sincerity of their conversion is very questionable. The cunning old chief saw that the conversion of himself and followers was ardently desired by Poutrincourt, and therefore complied with his wishes, in the hope of thereby receiving more substantial advantages. The Jesuit Biard, who arrived at Port Royal in 1611, says, that when the priest was teaching Memberton to repeat the Lord's Prayer, the latter came to a full stop when he was told to say, 'Give us this day our daily bread,' and eagerly inquired whether, 'if he asked for bread alone, he would not get any fish or moose meat.'[1]

Elated with his success, Poutrincourt sent his son Biencourt to France, to obtain supplies much needed by the colony, and to deliver to the King a register of the baptisms, with the view, probably, of showing that the services of the Jesuits were not wanted. This ruse, however, did not succeed. In the meantime, Henry IV. had been assassinated, and the Jesuits had obtained a powerful ally at court in the person of the Marchioness de Guercheville, lady of honour to the Queen,

[1] Biard's Letter of January 21, 1612, to Belthazar, the R. P. Provincial à Paris.

who entered with such zeal upon the task of christianizing the benighted savages of Acadié, that Charlevoix, himself a Jesuit, says it was almost impossible to confine it within reasonable limits. Young Biencourt, when he sailed in the spring of 1611, was compelled, sadly against his wishes, to take out two Jesuit fathers, Pierre Biard and Enemonde Masse, to Port Royal. Their coming out caused great annoyance to Poutrincourt, who was obliged, by the terms of his grant from the King, to receive them. Both Poutrincourt and his son, who shortly succeeded his father as governor, on the return of the latter to France, contrived to make the residence of the fathers at Port Royal so uncomfortable, that they were glad to avail themselves of the offer of M. de Saussaye to take them to the Isle of Mount Desert, on the coast of Maine, in the year 1613. This De Saussaye had been sent out by the Marchioness de Guercheville with forty-eight emigrants, including two Jesuit fathers, to form a settlement at the mouth of the Penobscot River, and, luckily for Biard and Masse, had called at Port Royal on his way thither.

Biencourt and his friends were glad beyond measure when the obnoxious Jesuits left Port Royal; but they never dreamed that their departure would in the end bring upon them such disastrous consequences as their own dispersion and the total ruin of the settlement. That you may clearly understand how this happened, we must leave Port Royal for a while, to note the doings of another and more fortunate band of colonists, who had settled on the coast far to the southward of Acadié. In the year 1606, James I. of England granted to Sir John Popham, and several other influential persons, all the territory on the eastern coast of America, between the thirty-fourth and forty-fifth degrees of north latitude. These limits included nearly the whole of Acadié; but as England and France both claimed the whole of that part of America, no respect was paid by the Government of either country to grants or concessions made by the other. Two associations, composed of leading men in London and the West of England, styling themselves respectively, the 'London' and the 'Plymouth' Companies, undertook to settle the country. The

London Company sent out a body of emigrants without delay, to form a settlement upon the island of Roanoke, the site of Sir Walter Raleigh's unfortunate city of Raleigh. The ships having been driven far to the northward of Roanoke by a heavy gale, ran into the mouth of Chesapeake Bay for shelter. Sailing up the bay, a large river was discovered, upon the banks of which the leading men of the expedition decided upon building a city, to be called Jamestown, in honour of the King. Serious dangers and difficulties were encountered, but the enterprise was successful. In the year 1613, the population of Virginia, as the new colony was named, exceeded 700 souls.

The Plymouth Company having failed to take possession of their territory to the northward, the London Company claimed jurisdiction over the whole of the King's grant up to the forty-fifth parallel, and the colonists began to fish on the coast far to the northward. In the summer of 1613, the captain of an illicit trading vessel, called Samuel Argall, set out on a fishing expedition from Jamestown in an armed vessel mounting fourteen guns, and arrived on the coast of Acadié soon after M. de Saussaye and his party anchored in the channel on the east side of Mount Desert. Having learned from some Indians who visited his ship, that a party of Frenchmen were making a settlement at Mount Desert, Argall determined at once to drive them off, a task of no great difficulty with a ship of fourteen guns and a crew of sixty men.[1] A few of the bravest Frenchmen made some resistance on board De Saussaye's vessel, but the most of them ran off into the woods. One of the Jesuit fathers, Du Thet, was killed by a musket-ball on board the vessel. The ruthless Argall demolished all their tents, threw down the cross which they had just erected, and made prisoners of the whole party. Fifteen of the prisoners, including De Saussaye and Father Masse, were put on board an open boat and left to find their way to Cape Sable, which they fortunately succeeded in doing, and also in meeting with a vessel which took them to France. The rest, including Father Biard, were carried by Argall to Jamestown. Sir

[1] Champlain.

Thomas Gates, the governor of Virginia, not only approved of Argall's unjustifiable conduct (England and France being then at peace), but learning from the prisoners that the French had made a settlement and erected a fort at Port Royal, despatched Argall in command of three armed vessels to destroy the fort and drive away the people. The Jesuit Biard, it is said, to gratify his revenge on his old enemy Biencourt, not only gave information concerning the settlement, but also piloted the ships into Port Royal. Of course the little fort, with a handful of men, could make no resistance; it was surrendered to Argall, and together with all the surrounding buildings demolished. Many of the inhabitants were made prisoners, but Biencourt, who with some of his followers fled to the forests, was kindly received and supported by the Indians.

In the following spring, Poutrincourt came out to Port Royal, where he found all his property destroyed, and his unfortunate son wandering in the forest, with no shelter but an Indian wigwam. Utterly disheartened, and giving up all hopes of succeeding in his enterprise, he abandoned Port Royal for ever, and returned to France, where he entered the king's service, and fell, in the moment of victory, in the attack upon Méry sur Seine, in the month of December, 1615.

The destruction of the French settlement in Acadié does not seem to have excited much attention in the mother country. The French Ambassador, it is true, complained to the British Government of the unjustifiable conduct of the Virginian authorities in a time of peace; but no redress was obtained, and the outrage was soon forgotten. After the departure of Argall, Biencourt and his followers left their hiding places and returned to Port Royal, which they partially rebuilt; the fishermen and fur traders were allowed to pursue their respective callings on the shores of Acadié without molestation. Champlain says he received intelligence in Quebec that Biencourt, who had lived many years with the Indians, died in Acadié in 1624.

LETTER V.

1613–1629.

I MUST crave your forbearance a little longer, to conduct you up the St. Lawrence, to note the commencement and progress of an enterprise undertaken in that quarter, which, as our story proceeds, you will find exercised a commanding influence upon the destinies of Cape Breton. Various unsuccessful attempts, as I have before told you, had been made to establish settlements in Canada; but for Champlain was reserved the honour of planting the first European colony on the beautiful and fertile banks of the St. Lawrence.

Champlain was introduced to you in my last letter; but I am sure you will like to know something more of the antecedents of the man who laid the foundation of England's greatest colony in North America.

Samuel Champlain, a captain in the Royal Navy, born at Brouage, on the Bay of Biscay, in 1567, had been employed in various important duties, and was highly esteemed by his sovereign for his skill in navigation, and general knowledge of military affairs. Charlevoix says he was reported to be a brave, capable, and experienced officer. He had been three or four years engaged in surveying the coasts of Acadié and Cape Breton, and had ascended the St. Lawrence as far as the rapids at Sault St. Louis, in the service of De Chastes. When, therefore, his friend De Monts obtained permission from the king, in 1608, to trade with the Indians, and to establish a settlement on the St. Lawrence, as a recompense for the great loss he had sustained by the revocation of his grant of Acadié in the previous year, Champlain was selected to conduct the enterprise. Two ships were sent out by De

Monts, from Honfleur, in the spring of 1608; one, commanded by Captain Pontgrave, to trade with the Indians; the other, by Champlain, to select a site for a settlement on the St. Lawrence. Champlain arrived at the Isle of Orleans on July 3, and, having carefully explored the river, decided upon planting his settlement upon a picturesque wooded hill, called by the natives 'Kebec,' about five miles above that island.

Having cleared some land, erected huts for his people, and provided a supply of fuel, he spent the first winter in exploring the country, and in receiving visits from the Indians, who treated the little band of Frenchmen with great kindness. In the following spring, Champlain was induced by the Algonquins to join them in an expedition against the Iroquois. In a battle which ensued, the destructive powers of Champlain's musketry secured a decisive victory for the Algonquins, which so irritated the Iroquois that, from that time, they became inveterate enemies of the French, and whenever their services were required, invariably took the part of the English, in the long wars waged between those nations for the possession of the country bordering on the Great Lakes.

Champlain had been only two years in Canada when he learned that De Monts, who held a monopoly of the fur trade, and had, in consequence, provoked the enmity of the Basques, Bretons, and Normans, had again been deprived of his commission.

Nevertheless, De Monts determined to proceed with his enterprise, and, having gained the ear of Madame de Guercheville, through her influence managed to form a company, upon condition of establishing a Jesuit mission in the colony. It would occupy far more time and space than I can afford, to give you even a slight outline of all that occurred on the banks of the St. Lawrence during the next ten years. Champlain, as chief of the colony, honestly and laboriously exerted himself to carry out the conditions which the promoters had engaged to perform, but he was thwarted and obstructed on all sides by their selfish views, which were entirely confined to making all the profit they could out of the fur trade. Of this no better proof can be given than the fact, that there were only sixty inhabitants, including men, women and children, in the whole colony when the Duke de Montmorency was appointed Viceroy and Lieutenant-General of New France in 1620.

The appointment of a Viceroy, whose commission covered all that part of North America extending from Labrador to Florida in one direction, and from Newfoundland to Lake Superior in the other, shows that the French Government had begun to recognise the importance of their transatlantic territory. Champlain, who was appointed Lieutenant of the Viceroy, had now a wider field for the exercise of his administrative abilities, and, at the same time, more power to carry out his views, than when acting in the capacity of chief of a trading company.

On his arrival at Quebec, in 1620, armed with ample powers, he immediately put into order the neglected fields and gardens, and repaired the ruined houses which had been suffered to fall into decay. The fort, which had been commenced upon the heights on which the Castle of St. Louis now stands, was also completed; and every endeavour was made to improve his relations with the Indian tribes, over whom he had gained a commanding influence. On more than one occasion, Champlain had reconciled the differences of tribes just on the point of breaking out into open hostilities. He clearly saw that it was his interest to preserve tranquillity, and that a state of war in his vicinity would involve him on one side or the other, which would compromise the safety of the colony. One of the most striking proofs of his tact and skill in such affairs was the admirable manner in which he contrived to maintain friendly relations, over a period of nearly twenty years, with the surrounding tribes of savages, who, by uniting together, could at any moment have driven him and his handful of men into the St. Lawrence.

Leaving Champlain busily engaged in these laudable pursuits, we must now return to Acadié. After the expulsion of the French from Port Royal by Captain Argall, in 1613, no steps were taken by the English Government to secure possession of that country until the year 1621, when Sir William Alexander, Secretary of State for Scotland, obtained a grant from James I. of all the vacant territory to the northward of that held by the Virginia and Plymouth Companies. As this led to the first British settlement of Cape Breton, I must give you a description of the boundaries of Sir William Alexander's grant, which, you will observe, utterly ignored the right and title of France to the lands lying south of the St. Lawrence:—

'To commence at Cape Sable, and thence follow the coast of Acadié to St. Mary's Bay; thence to cross the Bay of Fundy to the mouth of the St. Croix river; thence to run northerly to the great river of Canada; thence along the said river to Gaspé; thence south-easterly through the Gulf of St. Lawrence to the Isle of Baccalaos, or Cape Breton, leaving the same on the right hand, and Newfoundland on the left; thence to the promontory called Cape Breton; and thence along the coast of Cape Breton and Acadié to the starting-point of Cape Sable.' It was provided by the patent that this immense territory, which included the whole of the present provinces of Nova Scotia and New Brunswick, the islands of Cape Breton and Prince Edward's, and part of Lower Canada, should in all future time be called 'Nova Scotia, in America.'

Sir William Alexander has furnished us with an interesting account of his first attempt to take possession of Nova Scotia, in a little work which he published in 1625.[1] He says that he hired a ship in London, in March 1622, to carry out a party of emigrants to settle in Acadié, but that, owing to innumerable delays in getting men and provisions, she did not sail until August. In the middle of September they discovered St. Peter's Islands, 'and were near to Cape Breton,' when they were driven back far to the eastward by a heavy gale. They then put into St. John's, Newfoundland, where they concluded to stay all winter, having sent the ship home for 'a supply of needful things.' In the spring of 1623, he sent out the ship again, but she did not arrive at St. John's until June 5, when it was found that half of his people, doubting of her coming out, had engaged themselves to the fishermen. Several of the men had also died, including the minister and

[1] *An Encouragement to Colonies.* Published in London in 1625.

the smith, 'both, for spiritual and temporal respects, the two most necessary members;' therefore, seeing no hope 'of planting' that year, ten of the principal persons concluded to go along with the ship to New Scotland, 'to discover the country and make choice of a place for a habitation against the next year.' On June 23, they sailed from St. John's, and 'saw the most part of Cape Breton on the 8 July.' They then sailed along the coast to Port Mouton, and 'discovered three very pleasant harbours and went ashore in one of them, which, after the ship's name, they called Luke's Bay, where they found, a great way up, a very pleasant river, being three fathoms deep at the entry thereof, and on every side of the same they did see very delicate meadows, having Roses white and red growing thereon with a kind of white Lily, which had a dainty smell.' Proceeding farther to the west, they discovered another river, two leagues from the preceding, which they thought 'a very fit place for a Plantation, both in regard that it was naturally apt to be fortified, and that all the ground between the two rivers was without wood, and very good fat earth, having several sorts of berries growing thereon, as Gooseberries, Strawberries, Hindberries, Raspberries, and a kind of Wine Berry; as also some sorts of Grain, as Pease, some ears of Wheat, Barley, and Rye growing there wild.' From this place (Port Jolly), they sailed to Port Negro, and found the coast all along of the 'same pleasant' character. 'They found likewise in every river abundance of Lobsters, Cockles, and other Shellfish.' 'And all along the coast, numbers of several sorts of wild fowl, as Wild Geese, Black Duck, Woodcock, Crane, Heron, Pidgeon, and many other sorts which they knew not.' 'Also great store of Cod, with several other sorts of great fishes. The country is full of woods not very thick, and the most part Oak, the rest are Fir, Spruce, Birch, with some Sycamores and Fishes.' 'Having discovered this part of the country,' they resolved to go back to Newfoundland, 'where their ship was to receive her loading of fishes.' Touching at Port Mouton, they sailed from thence on July 20, and arrived at St. John's on the 27th. From thence they coasted along to Conception Bay, where they left their ship to take in her cargo, and took passage in some ships belonging to the West of England.[1]

Although such flattering accounts of the soil and productions of Acadié had been brought home, no further steps were taken towards its colonisation until the year 1627, when the war broke out with France. In the meantime, Sir William Alexander had not been unmindful of his interests, for he had obtained from Charles I., soon after his accession to the throne, in 1625, not only a confirmation of his extensive grant, but an additional tract extending from the St. Lawrence to the Gulf of California. Sir William's ambition was great, but unfortunately his purse was small, so he was obliged to associate with himself some wealthy and enterprising persons, to enable him to carry out his views. These were Gervase Kirke and his sons Louis and Thomas, William Berkley, Robert Charlton, John Love, Thomas Wade, and some others, who styled themselves 'The Merchant Adventurers of Canada.' David Kirke, or, as he is commonly called, Sir David Kirke, 'was sent out to plant and trade there in 1627.' There are no records of the locality of the first plantation in Nova Scotia. From such scattered notices as I have met with, I am inclined to believe that it was on this occasion Sir William Alexander's son went out with a party of Scotch emigrants to settle at Port Royal, where they built the fort still known in 1827, as Haliburton informs us, by the name of the 'Scotch Fort.' Having landed young Alexander, who acted as governor in behalf of his father, and the emigrants, Sir David Kirke sailed up the St. Lawrence, but finding he had not sufficient force to take possession of the country, returned to England to obtain assistance.[2] Upon his arrival in England, the Company peti-

[1] Haliburton, in his *History of Nova Scotia*, says they returned to England because they found the country in occupation of the French; but it is evident from Sir William's narrative, published only two years after the voyage, that his people had no design of making a settlement, but went specially to 'make choice of a place for habitation against the next year.' See p. 70.

[2] Champlain says that when a detachment of Kirke's force landed at Cape Tourmente on July 9, 1628, on being asked who they were, they replied, 'Do you not recollect us? We were here last year.' From this it may be fairly inferred Kirke was up the St. Lawrence after leaving Port Royal in 1627.

tioned the King to grant him a commission to equip an armed squadron for that purpose.[1] This petition being granted, Kirke sailed in the spring of 1628 with six ships for the Gulf of St. Lawrence, where he seized the settlement of Miscou, with all the boats engaged in the fisheries, and then proceeded to Tadoussac, where he anchored, and despatched a courteous letter by the crew of a Basque fishing vessel which he had captured, to Champlain, the governor of Quebec, informing him that he had been commissioned by the King of Great Britain to take possession of Canada and Acadié, and requesting him to surrender the fort, promising at the same time kind and honourable treatment.

Champlain was ill prepared for resistance, being almost destitute of gunpowder and provisions, but concluding, as he says, that if Kirke wished to meet him he had better make his appearance before Quebec, he informed him, in reply to his summons, 'that he was well supplied with provisions, and could not think of surrendering his charge without having first made trial of the English guns and batteries.' This bold answer had the desired effect. Kirke gave up his intention of reducing Quebec, and sent his cruisers to look out for vessels expected from France with supplies for the colony.

Kirke's little squadron had not to wait long at Tadoussac for their expected prey. Champlain had only just despatched his answer of defiance, when a messenger arrived, bringing news of the arrival at Gaspé of the Sieur de Roquemont, with a fleet of eighteen transports, laden with provisions and munitions of war, including 134 cannon for the forts of Port Royal and Quebec. These vessels had been sent out by a new company, organised under the auspices of Cardinal Richelieu, styled the 'Company of One Hundred Associates,' which in the previous year had obtained a grant of the whole coast of America, from Florida to Newfoundland. Hearing that Kirke's squadron was at Tadoussac, De Roquemont, instead of proceeding direct to Quebec to relieve the starving settlement, determined to risk an attack. This unwise resolution produced the most calamitous results; the whole of his ships,

[1] State Papers in Her Majesty's Record Office.

after a sharp engagement, were captured by Kirke; the crews were sent to France in one of the vessels; and the commander of the fleet, with some persons of distinction who were on their way to Quebec, were kept as prisoners of war.

The sufferings of Champlain and his people, in consequence of this mishap, during the ensuing winter, may easily be imagined. They were reduced to such straits before the spring, that they would have hailed the appearance of the English with delight. But even in this they were for some time disappointed, and were just on the point of abandoning Quebec, and embarking in a small vessel of ten tons—the only one which they possessed—to look for relief from the traders who came to Gaspé in the spring, when intelligence was brought by an Indian that Kirke's squadron had returned, and was at anchor behind Point Levy, about a league below Quebec.[1] On July 19, a summons was sent to Champlain to surrender, by Louis and Thomas Kirke, Sir David having remained at Tadoussac. This was immediately agreed to; and the preliminaries having been arranged, and the articles of capitulation duly signed, the cross of St. George was hoisted, on July 20, 1629, upon the mouldering walls of Port St. Louis. Sir David Kirke, having soon after come up to Quebec, and arranged everything to his satisfaction, left his son Louis in charge of the fort, with a garrison of 150 men. Such of the inhabitants as wished to remain, were permitted to do so, and were abundantly supplied with all the necessaries they required by their new governor, who treated them with the greatest kindness and courtesy. Champlain, and some of the principal inhabitants, both lay and clerical, were carried by Kirke to England. On their arrival at Plymouth on November 20, Champlain, to whom I am principally indebted for the leading points in my brief sketch of the fall of Quebec, says that the 'General' was greatly disappointed to find that hostilities had been suspended, and that the two nations were

[1] Kirke's squadron, consisting of six ships and two pinnaces, left Gravesend on March 26, 1629, arrived at Gaspé on June 15, and Tadoussac on July 3.—*From Deposition of David and Thomas Kirke before the Judge of the Admiralty, in State Papers in Record Office.*

engaged in settling the terms of peace, as his company would most likely have to give up the peltry they had taken at Quebec. Champlain, being now free, after visiting the French Ambassador in London, crossed the channel to Dieppe, where he met Captain Daniel, who gave him a narrative of his voyage to Cape Breton, and of his proceedings there.

Before I submit a copy of Captain Daniel's curious narrative, I must inform you that when Sir William Alexander obtained his grant of the territory designated 'Nova Scotia' (see p. 68), he received permission from the king 'to divide it into 100 parcels, and to dispose of them, with the title of Baronet, to purchasers, for their encouragement to improve the Colony.' As each purchaser had to pay 200*l.* sterling to Sir William Alexander, very few persons seem to have applied for allotments; but amongst these few was a Scotch nobleman, Lord Ochiltree, son of the Earl of Arran. This gentleman, who was better known by the name of Sir James Stewart, of Killieth, purchased the title and lordship of Ochiltree from his cousin Andrew, the third Lord Ochiltree, General of the Ordnance, and Governor of Edinburgh Castle in the time of James VI., in 1615.[1] Lord Ochiltree equipped two small vessels, and went out with sixty emigrants, 'to seat a Colony' in Cape Breton, in the spring of 1629. He arrived on the coast, and entered the little harbour of Baleine, two leagues to the eastward of Louisbourg, on July 1, where he began without delay to clear some land, and to construct a fort for the protection of his people. Although his chief object, as he says, was 'to seat a Colony,' he sent one of his vessels to collect tribute from the foreign fishermen, and, in consequence, got into serious trouble, as will appear from the narrative of Captain Daniel, of which the following is a translation from the original, in Champlain's 'Voyages to New France.'

Narrative of the Voyage undertaken by Captain Daniel, from Dieppe to New France, in 1629.

'On April 22, 1629, I took my departure from Dieppe by leave of Monseigneur the Cardinal de Richelieu, Grand Master,

[1] Sir Robert Douglas's *Peerage of Scotland.* Edinburgh: 1813.

Chief and Superintendent-General of the Navigation and Commerce of France, in charge of the ships called the "Great St. Andrew" and the "Marguerite," for the purpose (pursuant to the order of Messieurs the Intendants and Directors of the Company of New France) of meeting the Commandant de Rasilly either at Brouage or Rochelle, and of thence proceeding under his escort to succour and carry provisions to M. de Champlain and the French who were in possession of the Fort and Settlement of Quebec in New France. On May 17, the day following our arrival at Ché de Boys, it was announced that peace had been made with the King of Great Britain. After remaining in the above named place for the space of thirty nine days, waiting for M. de Rasilly, but finding that he was not prepared to leave, and that the season was advancing for the undertaking of the said voyage: By the advice of the above named Directors, and without waiting any longer for M. de Rasilly, I took my departure from the roads of Ché de Boys on June 26, with four vessels and a barque belonging to the Company, and, pursuing my voyage as far as the Grand Bank, I encountered such stormy and foggy weather that I lost sight of my other vessels and was compelled to continue my voyage alone, until, being within about two leagues of the land, I perceived a ship with English colours hoisted, which ship, seeing that I carried no cannon, approached me within reach of pistol-shot, thinking that I was completely unprovided with ammunition. I then ordered the deck ports to be opened and a battery of sixteen cannon prepared for action. The Englishman becoming aware of this circumstance, endeavoured to escape, and I to pursue him, until, having approached him, I ordered him to haul down his colours whilst lying off coasts appertaining to the King of France, and to show me his commission, in order to ascertain if he was not a Pirate. Upon his refusal I ordered a few cannon shot to be fired, and boarded him. Having discovered that he was proceeding towards Cape Mallebarre with cattle and other things for some of his countrymen settled there, I informed him that as peace had been concluded between the two Crowns, he had nothing to fear, and might continue his voyage.

'On August 28, I entered the river called by the Savages Great Cibou, and on the following day despatched a boat with ten men along the coast, to discover some Savages and learn from them the condition of the Settlement of Quebec. On their arriving off Port Baleines, they found there a vessel from Bordeaux, the master of which was named Chambreau, who informed them that James Stewart, a Scotch Lord, had come there about two months previously with two large ships and an English cutter; that he had met in the said place Michael Dihourse of St. Jean de Luz engaged in fishing and drying Cod; that the said Scotch Lord had seized Dihourse's ship and cargo and had permitted his men to pillage the crew. Also that shortly after the said Lord had sent his two largest ships, with that taken from Michael Dihourse, to found a settlement at Port Royal,[1] and had with part of his men constructed a fort at Port aux Baleines. Further, that Stewart had given him a document signed with his own hand, purporting that he would not grant permission to him or any other Frenchmen to fish in future on the said coast or to traffic with the Savages, unless the tenth part of the profits were paid over to him; and that his Commission from the King of Great Britain authorised him to confiscate all vessels attempting to proceed to the above named places without his permission. These matters being reported to me, I considered that it was my duty to prevent the said Lord from usurping the country belonging to the King my master, and from exacting tributes from his subjects, which he intended to appropriate to himself. I therefore ordered 53 of my men to be well armed, and provided myself with ladders and other necessary materials for the siege and escalade of the said Fort. Having arrived on September 18 at Port Baleines, I landed at about two in the afternoon and ordered my men to advance towards the Fort according to the instructions I had given them, which were to attack on several sides with hand and pot grenades and other combustibles.

'Notwithstanding the resistance made by the enemy, with the aid of musketry, after a time finding themselves closely

[1] More probably with supplies and reinforcements for Sir William Alexander the younger, who settled at Port Royal in 1627.

pressed, they took alarm, and appeared on the parapets displaying a white flag and imploring for life and quarter from my lieutenant, whilst I made my way towards the gates of the Fort, which I promptly forced open, and, closely followed by my men, I entered and seized the above named Lord, whom I found armed with sword and pistol, surrounded by all his men, fifteen of whom were clothed in armour, each carrying a musket, the remainder armed with muskets and pikes only. Having disarmed these, I gave orders that the Banner of the King of England should be taken down and replaced by that of the King my master. I then searched the Fort, and there discovered a Frenchman, a native of Brest, whose name was Réné Cochoan, detained prisoner until his Captain (who had arrived two days previously at a port two leagues distant from Port Baleines) should bring a cannon which he had on board, and should pay the tenth of the fish he had taken.

'On the following day I ordered a Spanish Caravel, which had run aground before the said Port, to be equipped and laden with the provisions and ammunition found in the Fort, which I caused to be razed to the ground, and the whole to be transported to the river of the Great Cibou,[1] where I ordered 50 of my men and 20 Englishmen to work with the greatest diligence at the construction of an intrenchment or fort at the entrance of the above named river, so as to prevent the enemy from entering it.

'I left as a garrison 40 men, including the Reverend Fathers Vimond and Vieupont, Jesuits, 8 pieces of cannon, 1,800 pounds of Powder, 600 matches, 40 muskets, 18 pikes, cannon and musket balls, provisions and all other things necessary, besides all that which had been found in the before named Fort of the

[1] The river of Great Cibou was undoubtedly St. Anne's Harbour. In Champlain's map, at page 60, you will observe that Grand Cibou occupies the exact position of St. Anne's; and in many modern maps the Bird Islands, as they are now called, at the mouth of the bay, are styled the 'Ciboux Islands.' Captain Leigh, it is true, says in his journal (p. 44) that the savages called Sydney Harbour 'Cibo,' but this may have been a mistake; or, perhaps there were two harbours of that name—Cibou and Grand Cibou. Captain Daniel was probably the person who gave the name of St. Anne to Grand Cibou—the name which it retained until 1713, when the French called it Port Dauphin.

English. Having hoisted the arms of the King and of Monseigneur the Cardinal, erected a house, chapel, and magazine, and having taken an oath of fidelity from the Sieur Claude, a native of Beauvais, whom I left there in command of the Fort and Settlement for the service of the King, and also the same oath from the men left in the above named place, I left on November 5 and brought with me the said Englishmen, women, and children, 42 of whom I landed near Falmouth, a seaport in England, with their clothes; the rest, 18 or 20, I brought to France, waiting the orders of Monseigneur the Cardinal. Which narrative I certify to be true, and to which I have appended my signature.

'Paris, December 12, 1629.'

Such is Captain Daniel's story. To form a correct judgment, however, you must hear both sides of the question. The following is a verbatim copy of a Memorial upon the subject, presented by Lord Ochiltree to King James I., now in the Public Record Office in London:—

'*The Barbarous and perfidious cariage off the Frenche towards the Lord Wchiltrie in the Ile off Cap britaine proved in the Court off Admiralty off Deepe:*

'Aboutt the tent of Sep[r] or thereby on Captaine Daniell Induellar in Deepe accompanyed with three score soiours and ane certane number off Savages in six schallops cumis to the coast off Cap britane and surprysit too shallops and six fishermen in them who were at fishing for the intertinement off the sayd Lo. Wchiltrie his Colony in that part seattilt by wertew off the King off Brittane his commissione, having surprysed the schallops he seased upon the fishermen, and enclosed them in ane West Ile withoutt meatt drink fyr houses or any schelter from the rayne or cold. Therafter with his soiours and six schallops enterid the harborye the said Lo. Wchiltrie and the greatestt pertt off his men being abroad at bissiness.

'The said Lo. Wchiltrie persaving them enterid his Forthe and with the few that wair in it esteming the said Captan Danyell and his people to have been Savages caused discharge sum muskattis att the schallops to mak them discover who they wer which did so fall furthe for they did immediatly approche the forthe and the said Lo. Wchiltrie finding by thayr apparell that they wer not savages did demand them who they wer they answered they were Frenche, he said the Frenche and they were freeinds because off the peace betwix the two kingis they replyed thatt they wer Frenche and thatt they did know the peace and wer thair freeinds then he said in theiar hearine they wer welcum how soone they did enter (expecting no wrong usage after the words which hayd past) they did seas on us all disarmed them entromittit with all thair goods expulsit the poor people outt off the forth and exposed them withoutt schelter or cover or clothis to the mercy off the rayne and cold wind which did exceed att that tym so yat the poor people (whereof ane greatt number of them wer old men and wemen with chyld and young childrein att thair breasts) they I say were forced to turne doune the face off ane old schallope and to creepe in under itt to save thayr lyffis from the bitterness off the cold and rayne which was most extreem in thatt place.

'Therefter the said Captane Danyell and his people did enter the flea boatt which the said Lo. Wchiltrie hayd thayr seased upon all the goodis and immediately they did lavishly drink outt three hogsheads off wyne, too hogsheadis of strong ceadar and the whole beer which sould have served the people and did nocht reserve so muche as to save the sayd Lo. Wchiltrie and his people lyff in thayr jorney to France so that they wer all forced to drink stincking water to the Lo. Wchiltrie his greatt distemper by seckness and the loss off the lyffis of many of the people his Majesties subjecties.

'They did take outt off the sayd Lo. Wchiltries schipe his Majesties collors and throw thayme under foott and did sett up the king off France collors with so much disdayne that the lyke hes nether beein seine nor red off in the tym of ane standing peace betwix two kings Efter some few dayis they did send away the most pertt of the said Lo. Wchiltrie his people in shallops some thretty league by sea to Schibo when the said captane Danyell his schipe did lye and all this thretty league did cause the poor people work at oareis as they hayd been slaves having no thing all this tym to live upone bott bread and water and many off them nocht having clothes nather to cover thair nackednes nor schelter them from the cold whatt greatter barbaryty could the Turke have used to Christians.

'Efter some few dayes the said Lo. Wchiltrie with some too or thrie Ingliss gentlemen and thair wyffis wer caryed away in schalloups to the said Schiboa and for the tempestes of weather being forced to sett to the land at nycht they did ly upon the cold ground without schelter the rayne pouring downe upon them throche which unusuall distemper the said Lo. Wchiltrie did contract ane flux of blood which did continew with him for the space of fyve monthes which he is nocht yet lykely to scheack off.

'Then he arrived at Schibo and howsoone Captaine Danyell cam to his schipe he did sett up the Kyng of Bretains collors on his schipe as a pryss ane actt unusuall in the tym of pace.

'At Schibo for the space off sax or sevin weekis all the poor people wer compelled as slaves to work and labor upon bread and water only and many of them naked and without clothes so yatt for pitie of the poor people the sayd Lo. Wchiltrie was constrayned to give them his bed clothes to cover thair nackednes and saiff them in some measure from the extremitie of the cold and to tear the very lininge of his bed. When the said Lo. Wchiltrie and his people had indured this wrong and miserie for the space of two monthis, they were all imbarked in the said Captaine Danyells ship fyty men women and childrein being inclosed in the hold of the schipe in so little bound that they wer forced to ly upon other as they hayd beein so mony fisshes lying in thair awin filthe and fed upon bread and water That by famine and the pestiferus smell of thair awin filth many of them wer throwin in the sea throu famin the mothers losing thair milk the poor souking childrein lost thair lyffe and wer throwin in the sea.

'In this tym the said Lo. Wchiltrie distempered of ane flux of blood was for the compleaning of the people's usage threattnit to have his throatt cutt and to be pistolled his servant who did attend him in his seaknes discharged to cum to him to gitt him ane drink of water, his coffers where his clothes and his papers being only left unriffillid and unseasit upon till that tym wer taken and openit and his accuttances of great sowms of money wche he hayd payed obligationes of sowmis securities of his freinds lands wer taken by the said Captan Danyell and throwen in the sea.

'And to crown the rest of the said Captn Danyells insolences before the Serjeant Major of Deepe Monsieur Schobneaw he did call the King of Britain ane usurpater.

'In this action the said Lo. Wchiltrie hathe proven that pertly by the goods takin from him his lossis in his voyage and his loss by his accutances and wry-this which wer throwin in the sea he is losser above twenty thousand pounds starling.

'This wholl relation the said Lo. Wchiltrie did prove before the Court of Admyraltie at Deepe procurit sentence upon itt and being keepit closs prisoner in Deepe for ane monthe by the means off his Majesties imbassador he was brocht to his he.:ring his offences against the King of France objected to him he defended himself by his Majesties Commission which he proved yat he navyr contrived nor transgressed and having no more to say against him he was delyvered to his Majesties imbassador he did present to the Consell his relation off his injuries and losses with the verification thereoff in the Court off Admiralty off Deepe the Judges sentence interposit thereto bot nether can he have his wronges repaired his lossis repayit nor the offender punished bot bi the contrarye the said Captan Danyell is imployed in new comission to go to America with on of the Kinge of France's shipis and to others to make good his possession of Cap Britan and the Ile of Cap Britan giving to him for his injuries done to the King of Britan and his subjects. Yea which is most barbarous and unjust the sentence of the Court of Admiraltie which he did present to the Consell of France is denyed to be given back to him it being so ordered as itt shamefull it suld be upon record so that the Lo. Wchiltrie is forced to have his recours to his Majestie whois humble desyr is "That his Majestie may be pleasit to tak his wrongis and losses to his princely and royall consideration and to be pleasit to provyd suche remead thereunto as in his Majesties unquestionable judgement will be found most fealt and for the truth of his relation he is content to answer it upon his lyff and in the mean tym doeth remitt the proff of it to the relation of Captane Constance Ferrer, Louietennant Tho. Maie Stewart, Hary Pew Gentleman and such others as theaie will find out who are witnissis in the said action and that his Majestie may be graciously pleasit to cause call them for the verification of theas relations in testimony of the treuth whereof the said Lo. Wchiltrie hath signed theas presentes."

'J. L. WCHILTRIE.'

Comparing these two statements, and making some allowance for palpable exaggerations on both sides, any impartial reader will, I think, admit that Lord Ochiltree had good reason to complain of the treatment he received from a French officer, after peace, according to Captain Daniel's own narrative, 'had been made with the King of Great Britain.'

Lord Ochiltree's party, sixty persons in all, including old men, women, and children, was clearly no match for Captain Daniel's sixty fighting men, especially after the latter had been admitted into the fort as friends; even if this had not been the case, it is not likely that the fort was a very formidable structure, seeing that its occupants had been there only two months. So that, after all, Captain Daniel had as little reason to boast of his doings as a recent American writer had to designate the capture of the little fort 'a signal exploit.'[1]

In the Public Record Office there is also a petition, dated December, 1629, from Captain Constance Ferrar (above mentioned) to the King, in which the petitioner states that he agreed with Lord Ochiltree to go out with his wife and family 'to plant at Cape Breton,' where they arrived on July 1, and that on September 10 they were treacherously surprised and taken prisoners by Captain Daniel, who landed them in England, but that Lord Ochiltree and seventeen others were taken

[1] Parkman's *Pioneers of France in the New World.* Boston: 1865.

prisoners to France. He prays that the French ambassador may be instructed to apply for their release and for restitution of above 10,000*l.* damages.

It does not appear that either Lord Ochiltree or Captain Ferrar ever obtained any redress for their wrongs and losses; but in a despatch from Paris, dated January 22, 1630, in the foreign correspondence in the Record Office, Sir Thomas Edmondes says that he had complained of Captain Daniel's cruel usage of Lord Ochiltree, who had been set at liberty by the Council of Marine, as they could find no cause for his longer detention. Sir Thomas Edmondes adds, that Captain Daniel, in justification of his conduct, alleged that he had a special order from the Cardinal to recover for the French all the plantations between the fortieth and forty-sixth degrees of latitude.

Lord Ochiltree had scarcely regained his liberty, when he involved himself in a much more serious misfortune than the loss of his plantation in Cape Breton, by bringing charges against the Marquis of Hamilton, which he could not substantiate. 'The hereditary enmity of the family against the house of Hamilton induced Lord Ochiltree, in 1631, to prefer a charge against the Marquis of Hamilton, as intending to employ the troops raised by him for the service of Gustavus Adolphus, King of Sweden, to seize upon the throne of Scotland for himself. His Lordship having failed in his proof, was tried for leasing making, and, being found guilty, was sentenced to be imprisoned for life in Blackness Castle. He remained there till 1652, when he was released by the English after the battle of Worcester, in 1659.'[1]

[1] Sir Robert Douglas's *Peerage of Scotland.* Edinburgh: 1813.

LETTER VI.

1629—1654.

The little garrison at St. Anne's, which Captain Daniel left well supplied with ample provision for their bodily and spiritual wants, as related at p. 77, did not pass such a comfortable winter as might have been expected. The Indians, who came in great numbers to the fort on the arrival of the French, finding that the latter had not brought any goods to exchange for furs, venison, or other products of the chase, soon discontinued their visits, so that the men, obliged to live all winter upon salt provisions, were attacked towards spring by that terrible disease, the scurvy, which carried off nearly one-third of the garrison.

Fortunately for the two Jesuits, they were ordered to proceed to Quebec by the Rev. Father Provincial, where, of course, they did not give a very flattering account of St. Anne's, which they said was neither 'pleasant nor agreeable,' but nevertheless well adapted for the prosecution of the cod fishery.

The Directors of the French company, however, did not forget their first settlement in Cape Breton. In the spring of 1630, they sent out a vessel with supplies, and another in the following year, under the command of Captain Daniel. On his arrival at St. Anne's, on June 24, Captain Daniel found the settlement in a state of great agitation, on account of a tragical event which had occurred about a month previously, viz.—the assassination of Lieutenant Martell by Captain Gaude, the Commandant of the garrison. Gaude and his subaltern had for some time been upon very bad terms, so much so, that the Directors of the Company had instructed Captain Daniel to take Martell with him to France, and to appoint some other person in his place, selected either from the men then at St. Anne's, or from the settlers that had embarked with him on this voyage.

Upon enquiry, Captain Daniel learned that on the day after Whitsunday, Gaude and Martell having supped together, and the hour for mounting guard having arrived, the former gave the watchword to Martell and then entered the fort, where he loaded a carbine with three balls, and fired through a loop-hole at Martell, who was playing at skittles outside. All the balls struck the unfortunate Martell, one passing directly through his heart. The men of the settlement seized Gaude and kept him in close confinement, but he managed to escape soon after Daniel's arrival. Champlain justly observes, 'This deed, so basely perpetrated, is not to be excused in Gaude on the mere ground of incompatibility of temper, for, if he wished to punish Martell, he should have put him under arrest until the arrival of a vessel from France. Thus he would have had lawful revenge on his enemy, without committing a desperate deed which could only bring shame and trouble upon himself, at the risk even of his own life, if he had not found means to escape into the country.'

We have no further account of the fortunes of the settlers at St. Anne's. Ferland[1] says a Jesuit mission was established there in 1634, but this, and the garrison also, seem to have been withdrawn before Nicholas Denys obtained a grant of Cape Breton and established a fishery at St. Anne's a few years afterwards, as will be related in its proper place.

Although negotiations had been commenced in 1629, peace was not fully established between England and France until March 29, 1632. According to this treaty, Great Britain having restored to France all the places which had been occupied by her subjects in New France, including the ports of Port Royal, Quebec, and Cape Breton, Champlain again returned to Quebec, in the capacity of Lieutenant-Governor, to the great satisfaction, both of the colonists and the natives. During the next two years he administered the government of

[1] *History of Canada*. Quebec: 1861.

the colony with great wisdom and firmness, and before his death, which occurred in 1635, the country began to show signs of advancement in wealth and population. For thirty years, amidst difficulties and discouragements which would have disheartened a man of less energy and enterprise, he had succeeded in establishing the foundations of a great French colony on the banks of the St. Lawrence; had penetrated the remote regions occupied by the Hurons and Algonquins; had explored the country in all directions, even so far as the ice-bound shores of Hudson's Bay; and upon all occasions had given his valuable aid to the missionaries, in endeavouring to promulgate Christianity amongst the savage tribes which surrounded him. As the historian Bancroft observes, 'He possessed a clear and penetrating understanding, with a spirit of cautious enquiry; untiring perseverance, with great mobility; indefatigable activity, with fearless courage.' If Champlain's plans had not been thwarted by the short-sighted, grasping policy of the trading companies he represented, 'New France in 1632,' as remarked by Charlevoix, 'would have consisted of more than an establishment in the island of Cape Breton, the fort of Quebec surrounded by a few miserable huts, two or three cabins on the Isle of Orleans, as many more perhaps at Tadoussac and some other places on the St. Lawrence, for the convenience of trade and the fisheries, a few habitations at Three Rivers, and the ruins of Port Royal—the only fruits of the discoveries of Verrazano, Jacques Cartier, Roberval and Champlain, and of the great expenditures of La Roche, De Monts, and many other Frenchmen.'

The old companies neither sent out emigrants nor cleared any extent of land worth naming. Their attention was chiefly directed to the fur trade, from which they derived great profits without any risk of loss. Before the arrival of Europeans on the coasts of North America, the natives had only killed as many of the fur-bearing animals as were necessary to supply their scant wardrobes; but when the skins of the beaver, the fox, the marten, &c., were so eagerly purchased by the traders, they brought them for sale in such abundance, that they were offered at prices far below their real value. Even so late as the year 1760, the fixed price of a pound of beaver skin in Nova Scotia was only 14 lbs. of pork.[1]

Let us now return to Acadié. The restoration of New France, according to the third Article of the Treaty of St. Germains, seems to have been unexpected, even by the French themselves. Charlevoix says:—'The facility with which the English restored all Acadié to France, was doubtless owing to the fact that it was urgent they should securely establish themselves in New England before embarking in new enterprises.' But this could not have been the reason, because the English were then firmly established in their southern colonies. In Virginia, for instance, where there were only 700 inhabitants in 1613, the population had increased so rapidly, that in 1626 a colonial legislature was convoked, to which eleven thriving towns sent their representatives. And in New England, the small band of Puritans which landed on Plymouth Rock in 1620, had been reinforced by so many arrivals, that their settlements had spread over Massachusetts, New Hampshire, and Maine, as far as the trading-post of Pemaquid on the Kennebec, close to the confines of Acadié. Besides, so far from 'not embarking in any new enterprise,' expeditions under the auspices of Sir William Alexander had been sent out to take possession of Quebec, Cape Breton, and Port Royal, before the suspension of arms agreed to at Suza.

At all events, the French Government considered the restitution of New France a matter of the greatest importance; for immediately after the signing of the treaty of St. Germains, Isaac de Razilly, a commander in the Royal Navy, was appointed Lieutenant-Governor of Acadié, and sent out to occupy it for the Company of 'One Hundred Associates.' Razilly was accompanied by a relative, the Sieur d'Aulnay de Charnisay, Charles Etienne la Tour (the son of one of the first settlers in Acadié), and Nicholas Denys, Sieur de Fronsac. Razilly, Charnisay, and La Tour seem to have divided

[1] From an affidavit in the Public Record Office respecting Sir David Kirke's refusal to give up the furs seized by him at Quebec to the French claimants, it appears that the price of beaver skins in Paris in 1630 was twenty-five shillings sterling per pound.

the western part of Acadié amongst themselves for trading purposes; but so many exchanges and disputes took place concerning their claims, that I cannot pretend to give you the real boundaries of their respective portions. This, however, is not of much consequence, as our business lies with M. Denys, who subsequently obtained a concession, fortunately not mixed up with the others.

Denys appears to have gone to Acadié for the purpose of embarking in the fisheries. In the first instance, he established a 'pesche sédentaire,' or shore fishery, at Port Rossignol, in partnership with Razilly and M. d'Auray, a merchant of Brittany. This enterprise proved so successful, that they purchased a ship of 200 tons burthen to carry their fish to market; but having despatched her to Portugal with a cargo just after the war broke out between Spain and that country, she was seized and taken into a Portuguese port. The French ambassador endeavoured to obtain her release, but Denys says 'they never got anything but fair promises.'[1] This misfortune was soon followed by another of more serious import—the death of Razilly, which occurred in 1636. Razilly's property fell, by inheritance, into the hands of his brother Claude, who sold all his interest in Acadié to Charnisay, who contrived by all sorts of petty annoyances to make Denys's residence at Port Rossignol so uncomfortable, that he abandoned his shore fishery in disgust.

Charlevoix says that when Denys first went out to Acadié he was appointed Governor of all the eastern coast, from Canceau to Gaspé; but it is singular that Denys himself does not mention this in his book. It is probable, therefore, after leaving Port Rossignol, that he retired within the limits of his government, and began to establish those settlements which afterwards excited the envy of his covetous neighbours. Whilst Charnisay and La Tour were squabbling on the west coast, Denys was industriously occupied in clearing land, erecting little forts for the protection of his people, trading with the denizens of the forest, and gathering a rich harvest

[1] Denys's *Description géographique et historique des Costes de l'Amérique Septentrionale.* Paris: 1672.

from the teeming depths of the ocean. His settlement at Chedabouctou, at the head of the large bay of that name, where Guysborough now stands, seems to have been his principal station. Here he had large warehouses, with a fort for their protection, and employed about 120 men erecting buildings and working on his land, of which he had 30 arpents or acres under cultivation.

At St. Peter's, in Cape Breton, he had a large establishment defended by a fort mounted with cannon, erected upon the rocky point on the right hand of the cove near the narrow isthmus which separates the head waters of the Bras d'Or Lake from the sea. Across this isthmus he made a road, over which he hauled his boats, to avoid the long circuitous voyage around the island. He cleared nearly the whole of the hill behind his fort, and had eighty arpents of arable land under cultivation.

At St. Anne's he also had a fort near the entrance of the harbour, several fields under cultivation, and a fine orchard of apple trees. His visits to St. Anne's made him of course well acquainted with the Bras d'Or Lakes. It was probably upon one of these visits that he discovered the beautiful river and basin which still bear his name.

His establishment at the isle of Miscou, at the entrance of Baye des Chaleurs, was situated in the very centre of the most valuable fishing grounds in the Gulf of St. Lawrence.

A glance at the map of British North America will clearly show that Denys had displayed great judgment in the selection of his fishing and trading posts. Miscou and Chedabouctou possessed every advantage for carrying on the fisheries; St. Peter's and St. Anne's for trading with the Indians. The great lakes in the middle of the island, with their numerous bays and channels, ramifying in all directions, being admirably adapted for canoe navigation, gave the Indians residing in remote districts an easy means of communicating with the trading posts at St. Peter's and St. Anne's. Denys had been some years engaged in directing and superintending these establishments, when his tranquillity was rudely invaded by one Le Borgne, who had come into possession of Charnisay's property in Acadié. To place this before you in a clear light, I must go back to the year 1636, and endeavour to explain how Le Borgne acquired a pretended right to interfere with M. Denys. After the death of Razilly, his successors, Charnisay and La Tour, who together occupied the whole of western Acadié, became rivals in the fur trade. The boundaries of their respective districts being not clearly defined, each, in his eagerness to monopolise the custom of the savages, often encroached upon the territory of the other; and as each chief had his fort or citadel, surrounded by a band of retainers ready to embark in any expedition that held out a prospect of plunder or profit, collisions often occurred, which terminated in bloodshed. All legitimate trade was paralysed, and little progress made in the cultivation of the soil—the real foundation of wealth and prosperity, especially in a new country. It would lead me too far from my object to attempt to give you a mere outline of the history of the unhappy contentions of the rival Seigneurs of Acadié, between 1636 and 1647; if you feel disposed to pursue the subject, I must refer you to Murdoch's 'History of Nova Scotia.' In 1647, the quarrel was brought to a crisis by the capture of La Tour's fort on the St. John River. The fort was, however, defended with such gallantry and heroism by Madame La Tour, in the absence of her husband, that Charnisay, with a vastly superior force, after a siege of four days only succeeded in his object by the treachery of one of the garrison.

Charnisay did not long enjoy the fruits of his triumph. He died in 1650, when La Tour immediately went to France and obtained a commission from the King, conferring upon him the appointment of Governor of Acadié.

In 1653, La Tour married the widow of his old and inveterate enemy, Charnisay, hoping thereby to neutralise any claims that might arise from that quarter. He soon, however, found out his mistake; for Charnisay, or his widow, had contracted a debt of large amount with Emmanuel Le Borgne, a merchant of Rochelle, who had obtained a judgment or decree of the Parliament of Paris, authorising him to take possession of Charnisay's property in Acadié, in liquidation of the debt.

This brings back our story to M. Denys, who, you will recollect, had held undisturbed possession for many years of all the country to the eastward of Canceau, and, to make good his title, had obtained in 1653 a grant thereof from the Company of New France. Six years before this grant (in 1647) Charnisay, it seems, had been appointed by the King, Governor and Lieutenant-General of all Acadié, from its western confines to the St. Lawrence, which of course included all M. Denys's settlements.

Le Borgne, armed with his authority, lost no time in taking possession of Acadié. Having arrived at Canceau with an armed ship, he first despatched an officer with sixty men to seize Denys's fort at St. Peter's, where a ship had just come into the harbour with a cargo of merchandise, and a number of men to cultivate his lands. The commander of Le Borgne's detachment, finding that Denys was absent, immediately made prisoners of all his people, and sent out twenty-five men to lie in ambush on the road by which Denys was expected to return from St. Anne's. Denys, accompanied only by three unarmed men, and perfectly unconscious of any danger in his path, was seized and made prisoner just before he reached his home. Le Borgne, having been informed of what had occurred, sent a party to take charge of St.-Peter's, and carried off Denys and all his people, as well as the ship and merchandise, valued at 53,000 livres, to Port Royal. Not satisfied with seizing his property and breaking up his settlement at St. Peter's, the ruthless Le Borgne cast Denys into prison, and put him in irons on his arrival at Port Royal; but fearing, probably, upon reflection, that he had rather exceeded his authority, he soon after set Denys at liberty. Failing to obtain any redress from Le Borgne for the wrongs he had suffered, Denys went by the first opportunity to France to make his complaints to the proper authorities.

The Company of New France, satisfied with the justice of Denys's complaints, granted him a new commission, as already mentioned (p. 87), which was confirmed by Letters Patent from the King, re-establishing him in all his rights, and clothing him with most ample powers.

The careless and reckless manner in which these Patents were issued led to endless confusion, and often to bloodshed, as we have seen in the case of La Tour and Charnisay. They were lavished with an unsparing hand from time to time, evidently without enquiring whether the rights they so freely conferred had not already been bestowed upon others. For instance, the territory which Denys had held for ten years was in 1647 given to Charnisay, and then, without revoking Charnisay's Patent, it was again granted to Denys.

As you may, perhaps, wish to see one of these documents, I now submit a translation of the Patent which invested Denys with unlimited sway over the destinies of Cape Breton for many long years.

'*Patent, dated January 30, 1654, of the Sieur Nicholas Denys, as Governor and Lieutenant-General in Canada, defining and designating the Limits and extent of his Government.*[1]

'Louis, by the grace of God, King of France and Navarre. To all present and to come. Having been informed and assured of the laudable and commendable affection, care and diligence of the Sieur Nicholas Denys, who was heretofore appointed and established by the Company of New France, Governor of the great bay of St. Lawrence and of the adjacent islands extending from Cape Canceau to Cape Rosiers in New France, and who has for the space of nine or ten years usefully employed himself in the conversion of the Savages of the said country to the Christian faith and religion, as well as in the establishment of our authority throughout the extent of the said country, having constructed two Forts and contributed to the utmost of his power to the maintenance of several Ecclesiastics for the instruction of the children of the said Savages, and having worked at the clearing of untilled land, on which he had built several habitations and would have continued so

[1] It was usual about this time to speak of the coasts of the Gulf of St. Lawrence and the islands therein, as parts of Canada, and of the country to the west of the ocean as Acadié, although, when the country was first granted to De Monts, in 1603, all the region to the south of the forty-sixth parallel of latitude was called Acadié.

to do, had he not been prevented by Charles de Menou, Sieur d'Aulnay Charnisay, who without any right, by means of an armed force, on his own private authority expelled him from the said forts and seized his victuals and merchandise and destroyed the above-named habitations, without making any compensation whatever: And whereas, in order to restore the place and to re-establish it in its original state and condition, capable of receiving the settlers who had begun to establish themselves there by means of the habitations and forts which had been made and constructed, of which the said Charnisay took possession, it is necessary to send there a man well acquainted with the said places and faithful in our service, in order to repair the said forts or to construct others and to bring the said country again under our dominion, and to restore to the said Company all the rights specified in the proclamation of its establishment; and for the defence of the said country, to furnish and hold the said forts, and those which shall be constructed, with a sufficient number of men-at-arms and other equipments, for which it will be necessary to go to great expense; and to render us a service of this importance, being assured of the zeal, care, industry, courage, worth, good and wise conduct of the said Sieur Denys who has been named and presented to us by the said Company: We have of our certain knowledge, full power and Royal authority, confirmed and do confirm, appoint and establish, by these presents, signed with our own hand, the said Sieur Denys Governor and our Lieutenant-General, representing our person throughout the country, territory, coasts and borders of the great bay of St. Lawrence from Cape Canceau up to Cape Rosiers, Newfoundland, Cape Breton, St. John and other adjacent islands, in order to re-establish our dominion and the rights of the said Company of New France, to cause our name, power and authority to be recognised, to overcome, subject and render obedient the people who inhabit there, and have them instructed in the knowledge of the true God and in the light of the Christian faith and religion, and to command there both by sea and by land: to order and cause to be executed all that he may consider necessary for maintaining and preserving the above named places under our authority, with power to appoint and establish all officers, both for war and justice, for the present and henceforth, name and present them to us in order to furnish and give them our letters necessary for this purpose; and according to the occurrence of affairs, with the advice and counsel of the most prudent and capable persons, to establish laws, statutes and ordinances as much as possible similar to ours; to treat for and contract peace, alliance and confederation with the said people or others having power or command over them; to go to open war with them in order to establish and preserve our authority and liberty of traffic and trade between them and our subjects, and other things which we may think proper to enjoy and grant to our subjects who shall reside and trade in the said country, and also to the natives of the same, favours, privileges and honours according to their qualities and merits, at our good pleasure: We will and do intend that the said Sieur Denys shall reserve and appropriate to himself, and enjoy fully and peaceably, all the lands before granted to him by the Company of New France, both for himself and those belonging to him, and that he may give and part with such portions thereof as he may choose, either to our said subjects residing there or to the aborigines, as he may think best, according to their qualities, merits and services: to cause a careful search to be made for Mines of Gold, Silver, Copper and other Metals, and to have them worked and converted to use as prescribed in our ordinances, reserving for ourselves only one tenth of the profit which shall be derived from Mines of Gold and Silver, leaving to him whatever appertains unto us of the other metals and minerals, in order to aid him in bearing the other expenses which the said service will create: We will that the said Sieur Denys, before all others, shall enjoy the privilege, power and right of trafficking and carrying on the trade in skins with the Savages throughout the whole extent of the said country, both on the mainland and coasts of the Gulf of St. Lawrence, Newfoundland, Cape Breton and other adjacent islands, in order that he and those whom he may appoint may have the enjoyment of all the things before mentioned, and that satisfaction shall be made to him by the widow of the said d'Aulnay Charnisay and his heirs, for all the losses and damages which he has suffered through the said Charnisay: Moreover, We have given and do give, attributed and do attribute, to the said Sieur Denys the right, power and privilege of forming a Stationary Company for the fishing of Cod, Salmon, Mackerel, Herring, Sardines, Sea Wolves, Sea Cows and other fish which are to be found throughout the extent of the said country and coast of Acadié and the islands adjacent towards Virginia, in which Company all the inhabitants of the country shall have whatever share they may wish to take, each participating in the profits according to the amount embarked therein; and to prohibit all persons of whatever quality and rank from encroaching upon the said Company in carrying on the said Stationary Fishery in all the extent of the country; with the exception, nevertheless, of our subjects, whom we will and intend shall be allowed to go everywhere in the said country of New France with ships, into such ports and harbours as may please them best, in order to carry on fresh and dry fishing in the usual manner, without being troubled in any way by the said Company; making express inhibition and prohibition to all Merchants, Masters and Captains of vessels and others our ordinary subjects of the said country, of whatever rank and condition they may be, to carry on the traffic in Skins with the Savages of the said country, or the said stationary fishery, without his express order and permission, under pain of disobedience and entire confiscation of their ships, arms, ammunition and merchandise to the benefit of the above named Sieur Denys, and of a penalty of ten thousand francs. We hereby authorize the said Sieur Denys to stop and arrest all those who act contrary to our orders, their vessels, arms and provisions, to give them up into the hands of justice and to prosecute the persons and goods of the disobedient; and in order that this our intention and will be made known, and that none may pretend ignorance thereof, We send to and command all our officers of justice whom it may concern, that on the petition of the said Sieur Denys they shall cause these presents to be read, published and registered, and what is contained therein to be punctually kept and observed, causing them to be posted up in the ports, harbours and other places of our kingdom, countries and lands under our sway, and, if necessary, an abridgment of their contents, commanding that, to the copies which shall be duly collated by our friends and faithful Counsellors, Secretary or Royal Notary, at their request, as much faith shall be given as to the present decree: For such is our pleasure. As Witness to which we have caused our Privy Seal to be affixed hereto. Given at Paris, the Thirtieth of January One thousand Six hundred and fifty-four, and in the Eleventh year of our reign.

'Signed with the Great Seal of green wax, in strings of red and green silk.

'LOUIS.

'Par le Roi.
'De Lomenie.'

Provided with the ample legal powers which this document conferred, Denys immediately returned to his settlement at St. Peter's, which was at once surrendered by the officer left in charge by Le Borgne. He then despatched a messenger to Le Borgne at Port Royal, with a copy of his commission, and to notify him that he had taken possession of St. Peter's, as therein authorised. When the messenger arrived at Port Royal, he found that Le Borgne had just sailed for the St. John's river to take La Tour's fort by surprise, under the pretence of carrying a supply of provisions to his starving neighbour. As soon, however, as Le Borgne heard of the arrival of Denys's messenger, he gave up his intention of attacking La Tour, and immediately returned to Port Royal with the design of seizing the messenger—pretending ignorance of the despatches—and of falling upon Denys, whom he expected to find quite unprepared to resist him. This wicked and unscrupulous scheme was, however, happily frustrated by an unlooked-for event, which justly brought upon Le Borgne the very calamity which he intended to inflict upon Denys. Early in the spring of 1654, Oliver Cromwell sent out three or four ships with a small body of soldiers, to reduce the Dutch colony of Manhattan, with instructions to the Governor of Massachusetts to give all the aid in his power. A force of 500 volunteers was soon raised and placed under the command of Major Sedgwick; but there was no occasion for their services in that direction, as peace was made with Holland before the ships, which had a long passage from England, arrived at Boston. England and France were at that time at peace; but Sedgwick, who, it is supposed, had secret orders from Cromwell, 'turned his forces, with those raised in Massachusetts, another way, and dislodged the French from Penobscot, St. John, &c., where they met with no great resistance.'[1] Having then taken the posts of La Hêve and Cape Sable, Sedgwick unexpectedly made his appearance before Port Royal, just at the time that Le Borgne was preparing to carry into execution his audacious design of attacking M. Denys at Chedabouctou. Although Le Borgne occupied a strongly-fortified post, defended by a numerous garrison, and abundantly supplied with ammunition and provisions, he surrendered the place to Sedgwick after a slight show of resistance. Fortunately for Denys, the English did not visit either Chedabouctou or St. Peter's, but returned to Boston, carrying off Le Borgne prisoner.

Relieved from all fears of a visit from Le Borgne, Denys soon repaired his forts and buildings, and was able to give shelter and support to the children of Charnisay after their expulsion from Acadié. 'His establishment at Chedabouctou,' he says, 'served not only for the maintenance of my own family, but of theirs also, for nearly a year, during their time of need, as well as for the support of all those who had persecuted me.'

It might have been reasonably expected that, after all these troubles, M. Denys would have been allowed to enjoy the fruits of his laudable exertions in peace, his title being secured by grant from the Company of New France, confirmed by the king's patent; but it did not prove to be the case, for a person named La Giraudiere, who had been residing many years on the St. Mary's river, twenty leagues to the westward of Canceau,

[1] Hutchinson's *History of Massachusetts*. Hildreth, in his *History of the United States*, says that Cromwell alleged a sum of money promised by France, in consideration of the cession of Acadié, had never paid, and that the cession, in consequence, was not binding.

set up a claim to Chedabouctou, Denys's principal settlement. This man, whose establishment was situated at the head of the navigation (where Sherbrooke now stands), surrounded by a palisade, supported by four small bastions armed with two brass guns and some swivels, on his first arrival had cleared some land, and attempted to bring it into cultivation; but finding the soil unproductive, he had given up farming, and devoted all his time to the fishery and the fur trade, from which he derived considerable profit. These advantages, however, did not satisfy Giraudiere, who looked with envious eyes upon the smiling fields and luxuriant crops of his nearest neighbour, M. Denys, and determined, if possible, to get possession of them. By means of false representations, he induced the Company of New France to give him a grant[1] of the whole coast from Canceau to Cape Louis, a distance of twenty-five leagues, all lying within Denys's concession.

Having collected a force of 100 men at Canceau, Giraudiere proceeded to Chedabouctou, where he seized a vessel which had just arrived from France with a cargo of merchandise and provisions for M. Denys. He then summoned Denys to deliver up the place, notifying him at the same time, that he had obtained a grant of the coast, from Canceau to Cape Louis, from the Company. To this Denys replied, that the Company must have been deceived, or they never would have granted to another that which they had already granted to himself. Giraudiere rejoined, that he was furnished with a proper authority, and the means of compelling him to surrender the fort, if he would not give it up peaceably. At this juncture, to add to Denys's troubles, all his men, 120 in number, seeing that the ship had been seized, and that they would, in consequence, soon be in want of provisions, demanded their discharge. Promising the men that, if they would only remain to assist him in completing his defences, consisting of a rampart made of barrels filled with earth, and two bastions armed with eight pieces of cannon and some swivels, he would then

[1] I have not been able to ascertain when this took place, but it must have been before 1663, because Giraudiere's grant was from the old Company, which was dissolved in that year.

allow them willingly to retire to Cape Breton, and also furnish them with letters to the captains of the fishing vessels to give them free passages to France, they all agreed to remain for that purpose. When the defences were completed, all the men departed for Cape Breton, except twelve brave fellows, who would not abandon their master in his hour of need. Giraudiere, seeing the men depart, and supposing that the place would now be given up without resistance, again summoned Denys to surrender, telling him at the same time that it would be unwise on his part to risk his life in attempting to defend a place which he could not hope to hold against a superior force. To this Denys answered, that Giraudiere would run a greater risk in the attack than he (Denys) would in the defence, especially as the justice of his cause would combat in his favour. Giraudiere and his brother De Baye now spent some days in reconnoitreing the place, in the hope of finding a weak point in the defences which they might assault with a certainty of success; but failing in this, they embarked in their vessels and left the place, to the great joy of Denys, who naturally concluded they had abandoned their enterprise.

In this, however, Denys was disappointed, as De Baye returned a few days afterwards and asked to see the Governor, when he informed him that Giraudiere had taken possession of the settlement of St. Peter's in Cape Breton, which he was determined to hold until some satisfactory arrangement could be made respecting his right to Chedabouctou.

The conditions proposed by Giraudiere were, that Denys should give up Chedabouctou in exchange for St. Peter's, and that they both should go to France to submit their claims to the decision of the Company, each binding himself in writing to abide thereby. Denys, having agreed to these conditions, accompanied Giraudiere to France, when the Company declared that they had been imposed upon, annulled Giraudiere's grant, and re-established Denys in all his rights. The result was so far satisfactory; but Denys received no compensation for his losses in consequence of this affair, which he estimated at 15,000 crowns, partly on account of advances he had made for the maintenance and charge of 120 men, and partly for the cost of his buildings, clearings, and cattle, which were all lost and ruined so completely, that he was unable to establish himself again at Chedabouctou, and was obliged to retire to his settlement at St. Peter's.

I am grieved to say that this was not the last of M. Denys's misfortunes; for after his removal to St. Peter's, the whole of his buildings there were destroyed by fire, which compelled him to abandon Cape Breton, and to retire to his only remaining settlement at the Bay Chaleurs. The following is his own account of this calamity:—

'I was obliged to remove to Cape Breton, where I would doubtless have recovered from my losses, through meeting with some savages yet unknown, who came to seek me, bringing two long boats full of furs, worth about 25,000 francs, had not a fire unfortunately broken out (the cause of which could never be ascertained) in a loft where fire was not usually carried, and burnt down all my dwellings, all my wares, furniture, ammunition, victuals, flour, wine, arms; in short, all that I possessed in that place was consumed without being able to save anything; and all my people were obliged, as well as myself, to escape from the violence of the fire with no other covering but our shirts. The only things saved were half a cask of brandy, and as much wine, with about 500 sheaves of wheat, which were withdrawn with great difficulty from a barn which the fire had not yet reached; without which we should all have been compelled to have sought a subsistence in the woods with the savages until the coming spring.'

Unfortunately, Denys does not give us the date of this calamity, so that I am not able to say when he left Cape Breton. It is certain he was there in 1659, as it is stated in the Jesuits' 'Relations' of that year, that 'Monsieur Denys occupies the chief settlement belonging to the French in Cape Breton,' and that the 'Fathers André Richard, Martin Lione, and Jacques Fremin, were then in that island.'[1] It is also equally certain that he left before 1669, because, as Denys himself informs us, when a person named Huret, who was in charge of

[1] *Relation de Jésuites en Nouvelle-France, an.* 1659–1660. Paris: 1661.

Giraudiere's settlement at St. Mary's, was driven out by the English in that year, he went with all his people in boats to Denys's settlement at Nipisiguit, in Bay Chaleur, for refuge, where they were kindly received and supported all winter by Madame Denys, in the absence of her husband.

'For which,' he adds, 'I hold their note, which has never been paid; and behold! by my diligence and labour I have again had the opportunity of relieving in their misfortunes those who, not satisfied with their own possessions, coveted, seized, and destroyed mine, Providence having permitted me to toil for their subsistence and to give them bread in their troubles, all which I say without reproach.'

His settlement at Nipisiguit, the only one now left to him, seems to have been in a flourishing condition; he says his house was flanked by four bastions mounted with six pieces of cannon, and surrounded by a palisade eighteen feet in height; 'that he had a large garden in which vegetables flourished admirably; an orchard planted with apple and pear trees which withstood the cold; and that peas and corn grew passably well.'

The Company of New France, or, as it was sometimes styled, the 'Company of One Hundred Associates,' having been dissolved in 1663, a new one was established in the following year, which confirmed M. Denys in the possession of all his territory, upon condition of sending out fifty emigrants every ten years. From this time we find only some occasional notices of M. Denys's movements. It seems probable that he went to France some time before 1672—the year in which his book was published, and left his sons in charge of his settlement.

In the year 1677, Denys's right to exact a duty from all persons who took coal from Cape Breton was recognised by an ordinance of Jacques Duchesnau, Intendant of New France.[1]

[1] I make this statement on the authority of Mr. Murdoch, who says, in his *History of Nova Scotia*: 'The coal mines of Cape Breton began at this time to attract attention. Duchesnau, the Intendant of New France, issued an *ordonnance* dated August 21, 1677, which recognises and establishes the right of M. Denys to

In 1685, Richard Denys, acting for his father, granted a piece of land three leagues square, in Cape Breton, to the Seminary of Foreign Missions at Quebec, but its situation is not mentioned.

There is no record of the fact, but it is probable that M. Denys's patent was partially, if not wholly, cancelled about this time, because a new trading company, composed of the Sieur Bergier of Rochelle, Gabriel Gautier of Paris, and some others, who had for two or three years been in possession of Chedabouctou and other places on the coast, obtained in 1686 a grant of Cape Breton, St. John's, and the Magdalen Islands.

Finally, it is quite certain that his patent was entirely revoked before the year 1690, as he applied for and obtained at that time from Frontenac, the Governor of New France, a grant of fifteen leagues square at Miramichi, where his son Richard resided, lying within the limits of the concession which he had held for more than forty years.

Denys's book, entitled 'Description géographique et historique des Côtes de l'Amérique Septentrionale,' to which I am indebted for the substance of the greater part of this letter, was published in Paris in 1672. It contains much valuable information relating to Acadié and Cape Breton, minute and graphic accounts of the fisheries, and drawings of storehouses, fishing stages, and all the implements in use, down to a common fish barrel. The sixth chapter is devoted to a description of the harbours, rivers, &c. of Cape Breton. Beginning at St. Peter's, he takes us all round the island to the Gut of Canceau, then called the Strait of Fronsac. His description of St. Anne's, as might be expected from his connexion with that place, is very accurate, but he does not appear to have been personally acquainted with some of the other harbours. At

exact a duty from all persons who took coal from Cape Breton, or plaister from the Straits of Canceau, as grantee of the land by patent in 1654, governor, &c. This document fixes the duty at thirty sous for each ton of plaister (gypsum), and twenty sous for each ton of coal. Persons also who trade in furs within the limits of Denys's grants and government, which embraced the islands of St. John and Cape Breton, and the whole Gulf-shore from Canceau to Cape Rosiers, are declared liable to confiscation of their goods employed, and to a fine of 200 livres, unless they have license from Denys.'—Vol. i. p. 155.

to face p. 103.

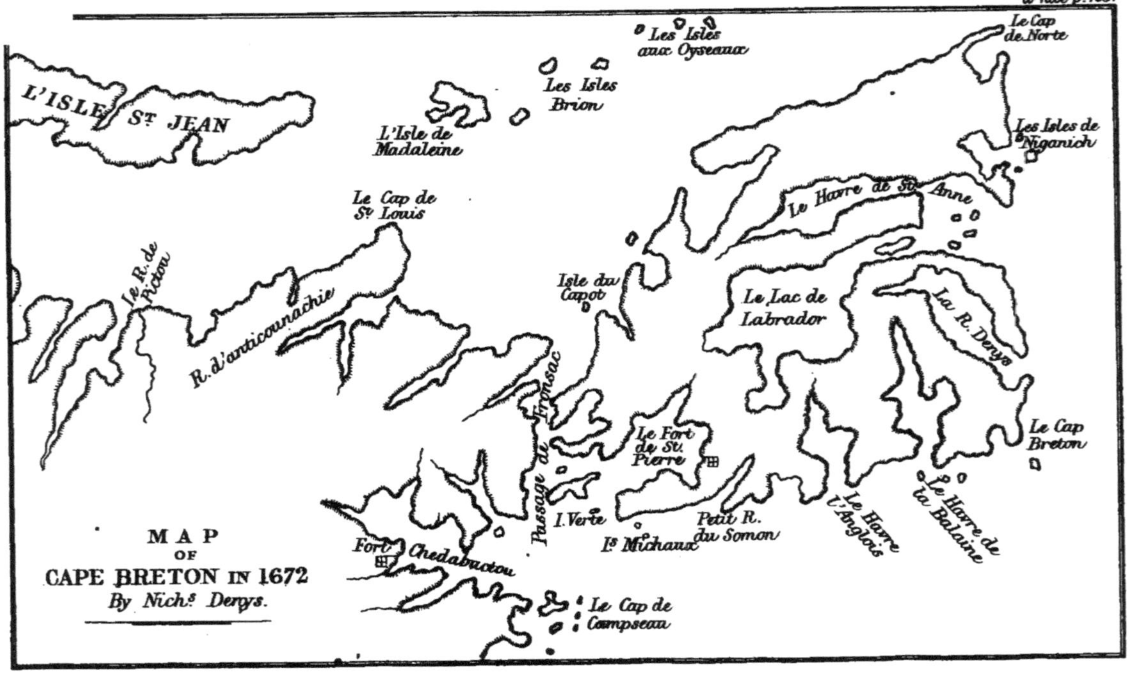
Les Isles
aux Oyseaux
Le Cap
de Norte
L'ISLE St JEAN
Les Isles
Brion
L'Isle de
Madaleine
Les Isles de
Niganich
Le Havre de St Anne
Le Cap de
St Louis
Le R. de
Picton
R. d'anticounachie
Isle du
Capot
Le Lac de
Labrador
La R. Denys
Passage de Fronsac
Le Fort
de St.
Pierre
Le Cap
Breton
I. Verte
Is Michaux
Petit R.
du Somon
Le Havre
l'Anglois
Le Havre de
la Balaine
Fort
Chedabucteu
Le Cap de
Campseau
MAP
OF
CAPE BRETON IN 1672
By Nichs Denys.

the Baie des Espagnols (Sydney) you will be surprised to learn 'there is a mountain of very good coal four leagues up the river.' This will be great news for the numerous parties now engaged in mining speculations! The most curious document in the book is the map of the island, of which you have an exact copy annexed. It is odd that two persons of such ability and intelligence as Champlain and Denys, who were both engaged in maritime occupations for so many years, should have compiled such wretched maps of Cape Breton. Considering that Denys's map was constructed so long after Champlain's, and that he himself had resided so long in the island, the latter is in reality the best of the two, save in the position of the entrance to the Bras d'Or Lakes, which Champlain supposed to be through Niganiche Bay. Denys gives us a tolerably accurate description of Sydney Harbour in his pages, but, you will observe, does not even give it a place in his map, whilst he makes the little harbour of Baleine, which will scarcely hold a dozen vessels, as large as St. Anne's, which he truly says has anchorage for a thousand.

In making these remarks I do not wish to throw any blame upon M. Denys, as he probably had not much time for making marine surveys, but to show the slow progress of geographical science during the two hundred years following the discovery of America. His whole time was, no doubt, occupied with the various mercantile and agricultural pursuits in which he had embarked, in places so far distant from one another, leaving him little leisure to bestow upon map making. Of all the Seigneurs of Acadié, he was the only one that succeeded in bringing any notable surface of land under cultivation. If he did not make so much progress as might have been expected with the number of men he employed, we must bear in mind that this was chiefly due, as he tells us, to the envy and rapacity of his neighbours, and not 'to his negligence or his want of knowledge of the country, with the advantages of which he was well acquainted.' He entertained a high opinion of the capabilities and resources of the country, for he adds: 'People might live in Acadié and Cape Breton with as much satisfaction as in France itself, provided the envy of one did not ruin the best intended designs of another, and that land cleared and cultivated by one should not be taken from him and given to another;' provisos which had been overlooked in more than one instance within his own experience.

The tact and courage which M. Denys displayed on so many occasions of difficulty and danger; the patience and perseverance with which he endeavoured to repair his severe losses; and the generosity and kindness which he exhibited towards the children and dependents of his bitterest enemies in their hour of need, justly demand our highest praise and admiration. To you, my friends, I feel that no apology is necessary for dwelling so long upon the fortunes of one so intimately connected with Cape Breton, and who, had he been permitted to pursue his liberal and enlightened views in peace and quietness during his long career, would have contributed in an eminent degree to the early settlement and advancement of your native land.

LETTER VII.

1654—1690.

Having in my last brought down the history of Cape Breton to the year 1690, we must now revert to Acadié, which, you will recollect, was taken possession of by Major Sedgwick (see p. 97) in the year 1654, although France and England were at that time at peace. In the following year a Treaty of Alliance was agreed upon at Westminster between the two nations, but Cromwell could not be persuaded to give up Acadié, alleging that it was, by right of discovery, the ancient inheritance of the Crown of England. To secure his hold of the country, letters patent were granted on August 10, 1656, by Cromwell to Sir Charles St. Stephen, Lord Delatour, Thomas Temple, and William Crowne, 'of all those lands in America called Acadia, and that part of the country called Nova Scotia.' The grantees had the exclusive right of trading with the savages, rendering yearly twenty moose skins and twenty beaver skins to the Lord Protector or his successors.[1] Colonel Thomas Temple was appointed Governor, and on April 14, 1657, by an Order of the Council, a ship was provided to carry him and his company to his plantation in Nova Scotia.[2]

In the year 1662, Charles II. confirmed this grant, and, it is supposed, at the urgent request of the people of New England, refused for a long time to listen to the solicitation of the French Government to give up the country. The fickle monarch, however, at length yielded to the entreaties of Louis XIV., and, wholly ignoring the rights of Temple and

[1] Documents in the Public Record Office.
[2] Ibid.

his associates, who had spent a large sum of money in repairing the Forts of St. John, Pentagoet, Port Royal, and Cape Sable, restored the whole of Acadié to France at the Treaty of Breda in 1667. Sir Thomas Temple, of course, made strong objections to this article of the Treaty, and contrived by various excuses to hold possession of the country, until 1670, when the King sent him out a positive order to deliver it up to M. de Andigny de Grandfontaine, who was appointed Governor of Acadié by the King of France.

England had, nominally, been in possession of Acadié from 1654 to 1670, but during all that time the French inhabitants had neither given up their houses nor lands except in the immediate vicinity of the forts of La Héve, Port Royal, St. John's, &c.

It was reasonably expected that the disorders which had so long prevailed would cease when a Royal Governor was appointed, with full powers over the whole colony, and that the country 'which had hitherto been little more than a resort for adventurers, whose occupations were concentrated in the fur trade, the fisheries, petty wars, and probably piracy,'[1] would now begin to make some progress. There was certainly ample room for improvement, for we learn that, according to a census taken in 1671, by order of M. de Grandfontaine, the whole number of inhabitants in Acadié did not exceed 400, not reckoning those who had intermarried with and been absorbed by the Abenaquis Indians.

In the year 1674, the Charter of the West India Company, which had been only ten years in existence, was cancelled, and the trade in the French Colonies in America was declared free to all French subjects. At the same time, the governments of Acadié and Cape Breton were made subordinate to that of Canada, Quebec being the residence of the Viceroy or Commander-in-chief of all New France.

In the short space of seventeen years Acadié had no less

[1] 'Nevertheless we are bound to remark that whilst others were chiefly engaged in war or the fur trade, M. Denys was making the most praiseworthy efforts to form agricultural establishments; he employed a great number of men in the cultivation of the soil.'—M. Rameau's *France aux Colonies*. Paris: 1859.

than five governors: La Grandfontaine, appointed in 1670, De Chambly in 1674, De Valliere in 1682, Perrot in 1684, and De Menneval in 1687.

Nevertheless the country did not prosper under the Royal Governors. The frequent changes were the cause of much mischief, as each governor on his appointment, aware that his reign would be a short one, made the best use of the time in enriching himself as speedily as possible. The Baron la Hontan, who resided in Canada and Newfoundland from 1683 to 1694, says, 'The French governors look upon their place as a gold mine given them in order to enrich themselves; so that the public good must always march behind private interest . . . M. Perrot was broke with disgrace for having made it his chief business to enrich himself . . . his chief business was to go in barks from river to river in order to traffic with the savages . . . M. de Menneval suffered the English to possess themselves of Port Royal because the place was covered only with single pallisados. But why was it not better fortified? I can tell you the reason: he thought he had time enough to fill his pockets before the English would attack it.[1]' La Hontan's testimony must, however, be received with caution; he had been dismissed from the French service, and probably wrote under feelings of irritation on that account. The Abbé Prevost says, 'La Hontan is a bad guide on important subjects.' Still there seems to have been much truth in his statements, as we have a corroboration thereof from another source: M. Bergier, who resided at Chedabouctou, 'having gone to the island of Cape Breton with three men, to collect furs from the savages, was attacked and robbed by Beaubassin, a son of De Valliere, who entered his cabin at three o'clock in the morning, accompanied by six men armed with fusils, drawn swords, and pistols; and an Indian chief also, who was coming to Chedabouctou, was met by De Valliere himself, and robbed of the skins of seventy moose, sixty martins, four beavers, and two otters.[2]'

[1] La Hontan's *Travels in Canada*. English Edition. 2 vols. London, 1735.
[2] Paris Manuscripts in archives at Quebec.

In consequence, probably, of the complaints of the honest and peaceable inhabitants of Acadié, the Viceroy sent M. de Meulles, the Intendant of New France, to inquire into the state of the country, who reported that he found all the French settlements in a state of ruin and desolation. In the year 1688, anticipating a war with England, Louis XIV. sent out the Sieur de Pasquine to examine and report upon the defences of the colony. Pasquine reported very favourably of the country, the fertility of the soil, the security of the ports, and the value of the mines and fisheries; but added that, owing to the dissensions of the proprietors, and the avarice of the governors, who traded with the English, the latter had obtained a monopoly of the fisheries and the commerce of the colony; and that the French inhabitants, who were under no restraint or discipline, neglected the culture of the soil and led a vagabond life in the woods. He recommended that the seat of government should be removed from Port Royal to La Héve or Canceau, either of which was in a more central position, and better situated for affording succour to Cape Breton and Newfoundland in case of need.

The population of Acadié, which, according to a census taken by De Meulles in 1686, was 912, including 30 soldiers, in less than three years, owing to the disorderly state of the country, dwindled down to 806.

In Cape Breton there was not a single family of European descent; the Indians, and perhaps one or two Jesuit missionaries, had sole possession of the island. The fishermen frequented the harbours as usual, but the only other visitors were the persons sent by Bergiers Company, whose headquarters were at Chedabouctou, to collect furs from the Indians.

So that when the war broke out in 1689, Acadié and Cape Breton were in a truly wretched condition, and alike incapable of making the slightest opposition to the attacks of the English. No assistance could be obtained from Newfoundland, as the French occupied only a single fortified post in that island.

The mention of Newfoundland reminds me that I ought

before this to have given you some account of the progress of an island destined, in later times, to become one of the principal markets for the produce of Cape Breton. English merchants and fishermen, chiefly from the West of England, had long occupied, as I have before told you, stations upon the eastern coasts of the island during the fishing season, but no attempts were made to establish regular settlements before the year 1610, when the 'Company of the Planters of Newfoundland,' composed of the Earl of Northampton, Lord Bacon, and many other influential persons, obtained a patent from James I., granting them the whole of Newfoundland, from the forty-sixth to the fifty-second degree of latitude, with all the seas and islands within ten leagues of the coast.[1] John Guy, who was appointed Governor, went out with a number of emigrants, who settled at Cooper's Cove, but the cold proved so severe, and the soil so unproductive, that the enterprise was abandoned in less than three years, although Lord Bacon—one of its chief promoters—declared that Newfoundland 'contained richer treasures than the mines of Mexico and Peru.'

In the year 1623, Sir George Calvert, soon after created Lord Baltimore, obtained a grant from James I. of 'all that entire portion of land situate within our country of Newfoundland,' and all islands within ten leagues of the eastern shore thereof, to be incorporated into a province called Avalon. Lord Baltimore sent out three vessels with settlers, but did not go out himself until April 1628, when he took up his abode at Ferryland, where a fort and a large house had been erected for him. On August 25 he wrote to the King that the fisheries had been disturbed by a Frenchman, one Mons. de la Rade, of Dieppe, who had three ships and 400 men, all well armed. He added, that he had driven off Mons. Rade, and captured seven French vessels which he had sent to England, and requested the King to send out two men-of-war to protect the English fisheries. On August 19, 1629, he again wrote to the king from Ferryland, 'giving thanks upon his knees

[1] I obtained this information, and all that follows relative to Newfoundland, up to the year 1700, from the original documents in the Public Record Office.

for the loan of a fair ship;' this was the 'St. Claude,' one of the prizes taken in the preceding year. A year's residence in Newfoundland seems to have been quite enough for Lord Baltimore, as he applied on August 19 to the king for a grant in Virginia, stating that he could not bear the climate of Newfoundland,[1] the land and sea being frozen from October to May, and that of 100 persons in his service, 50 had been sick at one time, whereof nine or ten died.

The fishermen of Newfoundland were about this time cruelly harassed by pirates. In eight years, viz. from 1612 to 1620, the damage done by the pirates was estimated at 40,800*l.*; besides the loss of 180 pieces of ordnance, and 1,080 fishermen and mechanics carried off by force. Captain Whitbourne, who was sent out in 1615 to hold a Court of Admiralty to enquire into certain abuses, says that one Peter Easton, a pirate, had ten sail of well-appointed ships, that he was master of the seas, and levied a regular tax on all the fishing vessels.[2] On August 8, 1625, the Mayor of Poole wrote to the Privy Council, saying that, unless protection were afforded to the Newfoundland Fleet of 250 sail, 'of the Western Ports,' they would be surprised by the Turkish pirates; and on the 12th of the same month the Mayor of Plymouth informed the Council that twenty-seven ships and 200 men had been taken by pirates in ten days. As there are no records of any further complaints, we may presume that the required protection was afforded by the Government.

Having obtained a favourable answer to his application for a grant in Virginia, Lord Baltimore seems to have taken little interest in his colony in Newfoundland. Adventurers of moderate means obtained grants of that part of the coast which had been before assigned to Lord Baltimore, and parcelled it out in lots to persons who paid a certain sum, and undertook to settle a certain number of fishermen or agriculturists.

[1] Sir David Kirke, writing on October 2, 1639, to Archbishop Laud, praises the climate of the country, and says the air agrees with all God's creatures except Jesuits and schismatics; 'a great mortality among the former tribe so affrighted my Lord of Baltimore that he utterly deserted the country.'

[2] Whitbourne's *Discourse and Discovery of Newfoundland.* London: 1623.

In the year 1637, the Marquis of Hamilton, the Earl of Pembroke, the Earl of Holland, and Sir David Kirke—(the same that took Quebec in 1629)—obtained a grant of the 'Province of Newfoundland, bordering upon the Continent of America,' from the forty-sixth to the fifty-third degree of latitude. The preamble to this grant states that it was given in consequence of Lord Baltimore and Cecil his son having deserted and left the plantation in no sort provided for, as also had several other persons who had grants of parcels of land, 'leaving divers of our own poor subjects in the said province living without government.' Cecil, Lord Baltimore, when he heard of this scheme, memorialised the King, and informed his Majesty that his father had sent out divers colonies of the King's subjects to plant, build houses, and erect forts; that he had sent out Captain Winne, Captain Mason, and Sir Arthur Aston, as governors; and that he had expended more than 20,000*l.* in the colony, but was compelled to leave on account of the severity of the weather; he therefore prays that his rights might not be trenched upon by 'some persons of quality,' who had a design of exacting a duty upon all the fish taken, &c.

Nevertheless, the 'persons of quality' above mentioned obtained their grant, and Sir David Kirke went out to manage the affairs of the new company, where his proceedings caused much dissatisfaction among both the English and the foreign fishermen. In 1639, the French Ambassador complained of Kirke's impositions upon strangers fishing on the coast of Newfoundland, and in 1640 the Justices of the Peace of Exeter forwarded several petitions to the Privy Council from merchants and others, complaining of injuries inflicted by Kirke and his associates, more especially of having set up taverns (which were expressly forbidden by the Privy Council), whereby the fishermen wasted their estates and grew disorderly. In consequence of these and subsequent complaints, commissioners were sent out in 1652 to examine into them, when Kirke's estates were sequestrated, but restored in the following year. The 'persons of quality,' who were so conspicuous in the organisation of the enterprise, seem to have withdrawn when Kirke got into trouble, as there is no mention of them in any of the documents relating to his alleged delinquencies. After Sir David Kirke's death, in 1654, his sons took possession of his estate in Newfoundland, as we learn from a petition presented to the King by his brother, Sir Lewis Kirke,[1] in 1660, praying that the ships sent out for the protection of the fisheries might give assistance to George, David, and Philip Kirke, then resident there, in recovering certain duties which had not been collected on account of the late wars.

To make his title to Newfoundland quite safe, Sir David Kirke had made over part of his grant to John Claypole, the son-in-law of Oliver Cromwell, hoping thereby to enlist the interest of the Protector in his favour. This answered very well for a time; but on the restoration of the Stuarts, in 1660, Cecil, Lord Baltimore, made the circumstance known to Charles II., with the object of raising a prejudice against the heirs of Sir David Kirke, and renewed his claims to Newfoundland. This ruse produced the desired effect; for by an Order in Council, dated May 9, 1663, Sir Lewis Kirke, John Kirke, and the heirs of Sir David Kirke, were required to 'quit their pretensions to the province of Avalon,' and all captains, officers, and others His Majesty's subjects, were commanded to aid and assist Captain Swanley, the agent of Lord Baltimore, in recovering possession of the country. Swanley acted as deputy-governor for Lord Baltimore for a short time, and was then succeeded by John Rayner, who was withdrawn before 1667, as appears by a Memorial presented by him to the king on January 2 of that year, in which he calls himself *late* Deputy-Governor of Newfoundland. There is no mention of Lord Baltimore or his deputies in the public records after this date, from which it may be inferred that he had abandoned the colony, finding it occupied by settlers or planters who carried on the boat-fishery at all the principal stations.

[1] Sir Lewis Kirke was appointed Governor of Quebec after its capture, in 1629, (see p. 73). In October 1660, he obtained the office of Receiver and Paymaster to the Band of Gentlemen Pensioners, Gentlemen-at-Arms, from the King. He died in 1663, and was succeeded in office by John Kirke, Gentleman Pensioner, with the same allowance and fees.

The French had always enjoyed the right of fishing on the northern and southern coasts; but they were not allowed to make use of the bays or harbours for any other purpose than curing their fish. This, particularly after the loss of Acadié, was the cause of so much inconvenience, that their Government resolved to remedy it by following the example of Cromwell, who had seized Acadié in a time of peace. In the year 1660, two ships of war were therefore sent out with 150 soldiers on board, besides ordnance and munitions for a fort, to take possession of the harbour of Placentia. In a very short space of time a fort and barracks were constructed, and houses for fifty families of fishermen and artisans. They held the place, which was called Plaisance,[1] until 1713, when it was yielded up by treaty, in spite of several attempts to dislodge them. It was to them an acquisition of great importance, both as a harbour of refuge for their ships, and as a convenient post for harassing the English fishermen in the time of war. The Baron le Hontan, who was some time on duty there, says the fort stood on a point of land so close to the narrow entrance of the harbour, 'that ships going in graze (so to speak) upon the angle of the bastion.'

About the year 1670, the mayors and merchants of the western ports complained to the king, in their petitions, that so many men were employed by the planters in the shore-fishery, that hands could not be found to man one-fourth of the ships formerly sent out, and that, in consequence, the fisheries of Newfoundland could no longer be considered the great nursery of seamen for his Majesty's Navy. These petitions do not seem to have produced much effect at that time; but the subject was again revived in 1675 with more success, when a committee of the Lords, to which it had been referred, recommended that the planters should be ordered to leave the country.

By an Order in Council of May 5 of that year, the commander of the frigate sent to Newfoundland to convoy the

[1] In some old maps Placentia Bay is called Plasancius, and is supposed to have been so named after Sancius, the youngest son of John Cabot.—Biddle's *Memoir of Cabot.*

ships engaged in the trade was required 'to warn and admonish our subjects dwelling in that country to remove from thence, and either to return into this kingdom, or to betake themselves to any other our plantations in America.' Sir John Berry, the commander of the frigate 'Bristol,' a humane and intelligent officer, to whom this disagreeable duty was committed, gave the warning required, but immediately afterwards reported by letter to the Secretary of State, that the people were too poor to move, that many false informations had been laid to their charge, and that the merchants were more to blame than the planters. On his examination before a Committee of the Lords, on April 13, 1676, Sir John Berry repeated what he had before stated, and 'assured their Lordships of the necessity of encouraging a Colony in Newfoundland, or else that the French would take advantage, by the intended removal, to make themselves masters of all the harbours and fishing stations about the island; or would otherwise entice the English Planters to come and settle among them, to the great prejudice of our fishery.' Captain Davis, who was present, 'and had conversed much in those parts,' declared himself of the same opinion. In consequence of these representations, the obnoxious Order of May 5, 1675, was rescinded, and on May 18, 1677, a new Order was issued, authorising the planters 'to be continued in possession of their houses and stages according to the usage of last years.' The captains of the convoy frigates were directed to make publication of this Order, and to see that nothing contrary thereto was attempted.

Nothing of importance occurred in Newfoundland until the war with France broke out in 1689, which I shall refer to in a future letter. The planters and western merchants seem to have lived together in harmony, as no complaints reached the ears of the home Government. The statistics relative to the fisheries, collected by the commanders of the convoy frigates, furnish us with some interesting information. From these we learn that 212 planters, of whom 99 were married, resided between Cape Race and Cape Bonavista, in 1680.[1]

[1] The family of Sir David Kirke, once the sole owner of the whole of Newfoundland, were residing at Ferryland in 1676, in the capacity of ordinary planters,

Belonging to them were 251 children, 1,695 men servants, 23 women servants, 454 head of cattle, 25 horses, 361 boats, and 196 stages: and that they made annually 67,340 quintals of dry fish, and 595 hogsheads of train oil.

At the same time, the western merchants had 97 ships, of the burthen of 9,305 tons, 793 boats, 133 stages, and 3,922 men, engaged in the fishing ports; and 99 ships of the burthen of 8,123 tons, mounting 415 guns, and navigated by 1,157 seamen, in carrying the produce of the fisheries to Europe, the West Indies, and South America. Their annual take was 133,910 quintals of dry fish, and 1,053 hogsheads of train oil.

It was, of course, impossible to obtain an accurate return of the produce of the French fisheries in Newfoundland by the English officers; but from an estimate made by Captain Twybourne, who was on the station in 1676, we learn that 102 ships, 1,836 boats, and 9,180 men were engaged in the fisheries on the northern and southern coasts. Captain Twybourne's estimate of the annual produce at 550,800 quintals of dry-fish, 9,180 quintals of cord fish, and 3,213 tuns of oil, based upon a catch of 300 quintals for each boat, is certainly too high, as we have seen above that the 793 boats belonging to the western merchants only took 183 quintals each.

The defenceless condition of all the fishing stations on the coast of Newfoundland, in the earlier years of the seventeenth century, invited the attacks of the numerous pirates which then covered the seas, as has been already mentioned. In later years, during the war with Holland, the Dutch cruisers, for the same reason, plundered the planters with impunity. In 1665 Admiral de Ruyter visited several of the principal ports, and victualled his fleet from the English ships before sailing for Europe. Again, in 1673, a Dutch squadron of four ships of forty guns each entered the harbour of Ferryland, where 'they plundered, ruined, fired, and destroyed the commodities, cattle, household goods, and other stores belong-

comprising his widow, Lady Kirke, his son George, with his wife and four children, his son David, with his wife and one child, and Philip, unmarried. Altogether they had sixty-six men servants, fourteen boats, three stages, and three oil-vats.

ing to the inhabitants.'[1] Notwithstanding these warnings, no steps were taken to protect even St. John's itself. In the year 1682, Capt. Talbot, of H.M.S. 'Tiger,' appointed to convoy the ships to Europe, memorialised the king, showing that there were no forts in the island, and that a single enemy's ship could at any time destroy all the boats and ruin the colony. He recommended that St. John's and some of the chief fishing ports should be fortified, and that the cost should be defrayed by charging the fishing ships or the colony with a tax, 'not more than they paid in the proprietor's time.' This wise counsel was not heeded; so it happened, of course, when war broke out a few years later, that almost every station, as will be related in due time, was devastated in mid-winter by a handful of Canadian militia.

The progress of Canada, which we have not noticed since the death of Champlain in 1635 (see p. 86) now demands our attention; the more especially because Quebec, the capital of the colony, was the seat of government of the Viceroy of all New France. Champlain, you will recollect, on his first arrival in Canada joined the Algonquins and Hurons in an expedition against the Iroquois, and gave such valuable aid to the former in their first rencontre with the enemy, by means of his arquebus, that the latter, who had never before witnessed the destructive effects of fire-arms, fled precipitately into the forest, abandoning their villages and leaving a great number of prisoners in the hands of the Algonquins. This affair seems never to have been forgiven nor forgotten by the Iroquois, who waged constant war against the French, and embraced every favourable opportunity of making secret and sudden irruptions into their settlements. The weak and defenceless condition of the colony, for more than thirty years after the death of Champlain, chiefly owing to the neglect of the 'Company of 100 Associates,' which had not brought out the number of emigrants agreed upon, was the chief cause of these hostile incursions. Like all their predecessors, they

[1] From a letter from Dudley Lovelace, who was a prisoner on board the Dutch fleet at the time. He says the Lady Kirke and her sons were the greatest sufferers on this occasion.—*Letter in Public Record Office.*

soon found that the fur trade was a much more profitable occupation than the slow and laborious process of clearing land and preparing it for cultivation. If they did encourage the Jesuit missionaries, as they were bound to do by their charter, to visit the savages in the depths of the forest, it was for the purpose of making use of them as pioneers to the fur traders who followed in their footsteps. Agriculture was almost entirely neglected, except under the walls of the forts, and even there, although the colonists planted the seed, the savages often reaped the harvest.

Urgent representations were made to Louis XIV. that the French authority in Canada was completely trampled upon and set at defiance by a tribe of savages, and that the colony, which under good management would soon rise into great importance, was fast going to ruin. A commissioner was therefore sent out to inquire into the administration of the affairs of the colony; at the same time, 400 soldiers were sent to protect it from the inroads of the savages. The Company, jealous of the interference of a royal commissioner in their affairs, which probably would not bear a close scrutiny, and weary of the contests in which they had been so long engaged with the fierce and implacable Iroquois, refused to incur any further outlay in the defence of the colony, gave up their charter with all its privileges, and in the year 1664 abandoned the country. The privileges which they had long enjoyed were then granted to the 'West India Company,' according to the system of the French Government at that period.

In the following year, the Marquis de Tracey went out to Canada as Viceroy, accompanied by M. Talon as intendant, or minister of justice, finance, and marine. A regiment of soldiers and a great number of settlers were sent out at the same time, with horses, cattle, and all kinds of tools and implements. The first object which engaged the attention of the new governor was the defence of the settlements. This he secured by erecting three forts on the river Richelieu, which so overawed the Iroquois, that some of the five cantons, into which the tribe was divided, sent deputies to sue for peace: others, however, kept aloof, and soon engaged in open hostilities with the

French; but De Tracey, although it was in the depth of winter, sent an expedition into the Mohawk country, which penetrated into their fastnesses, and created such alarm, that the Indians fled with precipitation into more distant retreats, where the French could not, for want of provisions, follow them. By these wise and energetic measures De Tracey secured the colony from the inroads of the savages, and the country for the first time began to show signs of improvement and real progress. Many of the officers and soldiers settled upon lands, granted upon the condition that they should render military service when called upon by the governor.

M. de Courcelles, who was appointed Viceroy in 1667, availed himself of the quiet state of the country to extend the power of France in the interior, by sending Jesuit missionaries to survey the remote regions bordering on Lakes Huron and Michigan. French settlements were advanced as far as the river Richelieu, and the construction of a fort was commenced at Cataraqui, on Lake Ontario, for the purpose of overawing the Iroquois. This fort was completed by the succeeding governor, after whom it was named, and long known as Fort Frontenac.

Canada enjoyed uninterrupted tranquillity during the vice-royalty of the Count de Frontenac, extending over a period of ten years; but a powerful English colony had been rapidly extending along the southern borders of the Iroquois country, which was destined at no far distant date to become a more dangerous neighbour than all the savages north and south of the Great Lakes.

When M. de la Barre arrived in Canada in 1682, as the successor of Frontenac, he found that the English colonists of the province of New York were rapidly advancing their settlements along the banks of the Hudson and its tributaries, and purchasing furs from the Iroquois at more liberal prices than were paid by the French traders. The Iroquois even bought furs from the Hurons, the allies of the French, and sold them to the English, which gave such offence to De la Barre that he determined to march into the Iroquois country to compel them to abandon their traffic with the English. Deputies from the

Iroquois met him on the shores of Lake Ontario, and in reply to his threat of devastating their country unless they gave up trading with the English, coolly informed him that he had not a sufficient force to carry his threat into execution, and insisted upon his immediately withdrawing his troops. Finding all the cantons leagued against him, De la Barre was obliged to submit to this humiliating condition, and to return to Montreal.

The Marquis de Denouville, who succeeded De la Barre in 1685, had an uneasy time of it during his short reign of four years. The French settlements were kept in a state of constant agitation and alarm by the inroads of the Iroquois, who wandered about in large bodies, wherever they pleased, with impunity, and at length became so emboldened by the manifest weakness of the French, that they made a sudden descent upon the island of Montreal in 1687, killed a number of the inhabitants, and carried off 200 prisoners.

In this emergency, the Count de Frontenac, who had during his former viceroyalty gained much influence over the Indians, was again sent out in the same capacity in the year 1689, with the hope of establishing friendly relations with the several cantons. Under ordinary circumstances, an able enterprising man like Frontenac might have succeeded in such an important mission; but unfortunately, the war, which broke out between England and France, on the accession of William and Mary, just at that time, brought such a powerful ally to the Iroquois, who now felt assured that they would be openly supported by the English settlers on the frontiers of New York, that they sternly rejected all the overtures of the French governor, and refused to enter upon any negotiations whatever. The cunning savages saw clearly enough that the weak and scattered settlements of the French[1] would soon be overpowered by the rapidly increasing population of the English colonies,[2] and wisely allied themselves with the strongest side in the approaching contest.

[1] Canada at this time contained only 9,818 inhabitants.—*Archives of Canada*, quoted by M. Rameau in *La France aux Colonies.*

[2] 'The population of the English colonies might at this time have reached 200,000, although half of this population, lying south of the Delaware and far removed from the scene of hostilities, took no part in the struggle.—Hildreth's *History of the United States.*

Seeing no prospect of coming to terms with the Iroquois, Frontenac decided upon making incursions into the English settlements at three different points, hoping thereby to intimidate the Indians, and to induce them to abandon their alliance with the English. Secret arrangements were made without loss of time. One party, consisting of 120 Frenchmen and a large body of friendly Indians, under the command of De Mantel, left Montreal in the depth of the winter of 1690, and forced their way through the forest, a distance of 200 miles, in twenty-two days, to Schenectady, a small town on the frontier of the province of New York. The unsuspecting inhabitants, aroused from their sleep by the war whoop, which gave the first signal of their danger, rushing half clad into the streets with the intention of flying to Albany, were massacred by the savages. Sixty-three persons, including women and children, were killed on the spot, and several were carried off prisoners to Montreal. The town was pillaged and burned; the fort was levelled with the ground. The inhuman victors did not altogether escape with impunity, having been reduced to such straits in their return through the forest, that they were obliged to subsist for several days upon horseflesh.

Another party, commanded by Portneuf, left Quebec for Casco Bay, where they destroyed the fort and ravaged the settlement; whilst a third, under Hertel, from Trois Rivières, attacked the village of Sementels, on the Piscataqua river, killed thirty of the inhabitants, burned the houses and barns, and carried off fifty prisoners, chiefly women and children, whom they compelled to bear the spoil of their own homes through the forests.

The barbarous conduct of the French and their savage allies, instead of intimidating and separating the Iroquois from the English, produced directly the contrary effect. The Iroquois solemnly promised to avenge the wrongs of their friends, and to stand by them in the coming struggle; this promise they faithfully kept for many long years afterwards, and thereby rendered valuable aid to the English on several important occasions.

These atrocities, committed at so many different points, and with such secrecy that no preparations could be made to meet them, caused such alarm through all the English provinces, that the people of New England and New York determined to drive the French out of Canada altogether, as the only means, in their opinion, of securing themselves against such dangerous neighbours.

Preparations were immediately commenced for equipping an expedition against Quebec by sea, and another against Montreal by land. As some time was required to raise volunteers and provide the means of transportation, Sir William Phipps was sent in the mean time with three armed ships and 700 troops, to reduce Acadié. This was an easy task, as the only forts in Acadié were Port Royal, with a garrison of eighty-six men, commanded by M. de Menneval, the Governor, and Chedabouctou, at the eastern extremity of the province, with a garrison of twenty men, commanded by Lieutenant de Montorgueil. Port Royal surrendered to Phipps's summons on May 21, 1690; but the little garrison at Chedabouctou made such a stout defence, that the English were compelled to set fire to the buildings before De Montorgueil would capitulate, in the beginning of June. The garrison of Port Royal was taken to Boston, but that of Chedabouctou (it is to be hoped in consideration of its gallant defence), was sent to the French post of Plaisance in Newfoundland.

The expedition against Quebec, comprising thirty-four ships and 2,000 volunteers, under the command of Sir William Phipps, sailed from Boston on August 19, but owing to contrary winds did not reach Quebec until October 16, just three days after the Governor, Frontenac, had received warning of the departure and destination of the expedition by an Abenaquis Indian from the Piscataqua. This short warning, however, gave Frontenac time to adopt such measures as were necessary for the defence of his post. The inhabitants gave all the help in their power to the few hundred irregulars which formed the garrison of Quebec, in repairing the walls and fortifications; and the militia flocked in so promptly from the out-settlements, that when Phipps, who had anchored his ships near Beauport, demanded the surrender of the place, Frontenac felt himself strong enough to peremptorily reject the summons. In fact, the force within the walls was quite equal in number to that of the enemy, with the advantage of a strong position protected by fortifications, and by a river not fordable except at low water. The chances were clearly in favour of the defence. Phipps landed 1,500 men on the 19th, upon the marshy ground at the mouth of the river St. Charles, but their advance against the town was completely checked by the fire of the French Irregulars, concealed and sheltered by the rocks and bushes covering the sloping ground in their front. A constant fire was kept up during the two following days by the fleet, but without effect, whilst the ships sustained so much damage from the enemy's guns that they were obliged to move higher up the river. On the 21st, six pieces of ordnance were landed at the mouth of the St. Charles, and a second attempt was made to assault the walls; but in their passage across the marsh, such a heavy fire of musketry was opened upon the troops by a large body of Indians and militia concealed in the bushes, that they were compelled to retreat in great haste, leaving all their cannon in the hands of the enemy. In consequence of this decisive repulse, Phipps prudently gave up all hopes of reducing Quebec, re-embarked his troops, and dropped down the river. Unhappily, the misfortunes of the expedition did not end before Quebec, as the fleet encountered a violent storm in the mouth of the St. Lawrence, in which one ship with sixty persons on board was wrecked on the desolate island of Anticosti; two others foundered with all hands, and some were driven as far to the southward as the West Indies. More than 1,000 men are said to have perished, in one way or the other, in this unfortunate expedition. The whole of the men wrecked upon Anticosti perished during the winter, except five brave hardy fellows, who left the island in a small boat as soon as the ice would permit, in which they made their way down the Gulf of St. Lawrence, and round the Atlantic coast of Acadié, to their home in Boston, a distance of more than 900 miles, in forty-four days.

The land force collected to attack Montreal never reached its destination. Owing to gross mismanagement on the part of the commissary, when it arrived at Lake George in the month of August it was obliged to return for want of provisions ere it had accomplished one-third of the distance between Albany and Montreal.

The signal failure of these expeditions relieved Frontenac from all anxiety for the safety of Canada. On the other side, the English colonists, exhausted by the cost of their equipment, and disappointed in their sanguine hope of striking the blow which was to have driven the French out of their strongholds on the banks of the St. Lawrence, had the mortification of finding that they could not even defend their own frontier towns against the midnight assaults of the savage allies of their enemy. Nearly one hundred persons were either killed or made prisoners, in 1694, in a village of New Hampshire; and the scalps of the English killed on the Piscataqua were presented as trophies of their exploits, by the chiefs of the Abenaquis to the Viceroy of New France. 'In the pages of Charlevoix,' says Bancroft, 'the unavailing cruelties of midnight incendiaries, the murdering and the scalping of the inhabitants of peaceful villages, and the captivity of helpless women and children, are diffusely narrated as actions that were brave and beautiful.'[1]

[1] My principal authorities for the above statements are Charlevoix's *History of New France*; Belknap's *History of New Hampshire*; Garneau's *History of Canada*; and Williamson's *History of Maine*.

LETTER VIII.

1690-1711.

When Port Royal was taken by Sir William Phipps, in 1690, the fortifications were demolished, but such of the inhabitants as agreed to take the oath of allegiance to the British sovereign were allowed to retain possession of their lands, according to the conditions of the capitulation. The French Government, ignorant of the fall of Port Royal, in the spring of the same year sent out the Chevalier de Villebon as Governor of Acadié. Villebon arrived at his destination a few days after the English fleet sailed for La Héve, but found no other sign of their conquest than the ruins of the fort with an English flag flying over them, without a single man to defend it. Learning from the inhabitants that Phipps's fleet was then at anchor in La Héve, Villebon wisely abandoned the vicinity of such dangerous neighbours, and proceeded to Nachouac, on the river St. John, which he made the seat of government. Here he resided for several years, and contrived, by intriguing with the Indians, to keep the English settlements on the coast of Maine in a constant state of agitation and alarm. Irritated at length beyond endurance by the frequent incursions of the savages, the Government of Massachusetts, in the spring of 1696, despatched two small sloops of war and an armed tender to intercept the vessel which annually brought out the stores for the fort of Nachouac, and supplies of arms and ammunition for the Indians. It so happened that in the very same spring the Marquis de Frontenac, Governor of Canada, had come to the determination of driving the English out of Newfoundland, destroying the port of Pemaquid on the east bank of the Kennebec, and then attacking either Boston or

New York. Two ships of war, 'L'Envieux,' commanded by M. d'Ibberville; and the 'Profond,' by M. de Bonaventure, with two companies of soldiers, were sent from Quebec with instructions to call at the Baie des Espagnols (Sydney) and collect fifty Micmac warriors to aid in carrying out the first part of the programme. On their arrival there D'Ibberville, who commanded the expedition, received despatches sent overland by Villebon from Nachouac, informing him that three English ships were cruising off the mouth of the St. John's river, and urging him to proceed thither without delay.

Nothing can more forcibly show the great influence which the French had obtained over the natives, than the readiness with which they responded to the call of the commander of the expedition. Although there was not a single Frenchman residing in Cape Breton, nor even a missionary[1] to administer the sacraments to the Indian neophytes, a band of fifty chosen warriors was soon mustered, prepared to submit to the discipline and confinement of a ship's crowded decks, and to embark upon a voyage of 300 or 400 miles, without a murmur, to aid their allies in an enterprise from which they could derive no benefit.

In consequence of the pressing demands of Villebon, D'Ibberville for the present relinquished his designs against the English settlements in Newfoundland, embarked his detachment of Micmacs, and sailed on July 4 for the Bay of Fundy. On his arrival at St. John's on the 14th, the English ships, although now in presence of a superior force, did not shrink from the combat. A smart action ensued; but the 'Newport,' of 24 guns, having been dismasted by the fire of the 'Profond,' became unmanageable and fell an easy prey to the enemy. The 'Sorel' and the tender fortunately escaped in the fog. Charlevoix says the Cape Breton Indians on board D'Ibberville's vessel 'contributed much towards the victory.' After this exploit, Villebon, with fifty Indians, started with D'Ibber-

[1] The French priest Baudoin, who accompanied the expedition, during his stay at Sydney baptised several Indians and married several others, proving that there was no other missionary in the island at that time.—Murdoch's *History of Nova Scotia*, quoted from Baudoin's *Journal*, which I have not seen.

ville's expedition for Pentagoet, where the Baron Castine[1] had collected a large body of Abenaquis Indians. From thence D'Ibberville sailed to Pemaquid, where he arrived on August 14, and immediately invested the fort, which fell on the following day. The whole of the garrison were made prisoners, and sent, according to the capitulation, to Boston. The fort was then demolished and the houses burnt down.

As soon as intelligence of this disaster reached Boston, several vessels were sent in pursuit of D'Ibberville's squadron. The English ships arrived on the coast just as D'Ibberville's were leaving Mount Desert's harbour at dusk on the evening of September 3. Villebon was captured next day on his way to St. John's, but D'Ibberville escaped in the dark, and sailed for Cape Breton without calling at La Héve to take on board a number of Indians who were waiting there to accompany him to Newfoundland. After landing the Micmacs in Cape Breton, with the exception of three, who had taken such a liking to their new vocation that they would not leave him, D'Ibberville sailed for Plaisance, where he arrived on September 12.

Before I give you an account of D'Ibberville's doings in Newfoundland, I must tell you that four years previously (1692) the port of Plaisance had obtained such notoriety as the resort of French privateers, that the British Government determined to destroy it, and sent out three 60-gun ships and two smaller vessels, under the command of Commodore Williams, for that purpose. The only defences of the place

[1] Lahoutan says, 'The Baron de Castine was a native of Oleron in Bearn, who had resided more than twenty years among the Abenaquis, by whom he was greatly respected. He had formerly been an officer in the Carignan Regiment in Canada. He married an Abenaquis squaw, by whom he had a numerous family. He made a large fortune by trading with the Indians, and was able to give handsome dowries to his daughters, who all married Frenchmen. The Abenaquis made him their great chief or leader, and always submitted to his authority. The Governor-Generals of Canada found his influence over the savages of great service on many occasions, and the Governors of New England had good reason to dread him.' He did not, however, succeed in converting the Indians, for, according to Lahoutan, 'It is in vain for the Jesuits to preach up the truths of Christianity to them; though, after all, these good Fathers are not discouraged; nay, they think that the administering of baptism to a dying child is worth ten times the pains and uneasiness of living amongst that people.'

were Fort St. Louis, with a garrison of fifty men, situated upon a rock 100 feet in height, on the eastern side of the narrow entrance of the harbour, and a battery hastily constructed by the governor, M. de Brouillan, manned by sailors from the privateers and merchant ships in the harbour; yet, strange to say, Williams, after six hours bombardment, gave up the enterprise and retired, having only partially destroyed a portion of the works.

At the very time that Williams was engaged in this disreputable affair, a powerful French squadron, under the command of the Chevalier du Palais, was lying at anchor in the Baie des Espagnols (Sydney), waiting the return of a fast-sailing vessel which had been sent out to gain some intelligence of Williams's movements. This vessel, after an unsuccessful cruise in the Gulf, was returning to rejoin Du Palais, when she encountered a heavy westerly gale of such long continuance that she was obliged to bear up for France. This mishap fortunately saved Williams's squadron and disconcerted Du Palais's plans; for, as Charlevoix observes, 'it is not likely that a commander, who had been repulsed by a paltry place like Plaisance, would have made much resistance to a powerful enemy.'

I have not time to enumerate the various attacks made by French ships of war and privateers upon the English settlements during the four years following Williams's unsuccessful attempt to destroy Plaisance.[1] Nothing, however, of much importance was accomplished by the enemy, beyond the capture and destruction of fishing and trading vessels, until the autumn of 1696, when D'Ibberville, as has already been men-

[1] I must, however, record the gallant exploit of Captain Holman of the English privateer 'William and Mary,' of sixteen guns. Holman, who learned from a prisoner that had escaped from Plaisance, that some French ships were going to attack Ferryland, by great exertions, with the aid of the inhabitants, erected four small batteries at the mouth of the harbour, and armed them with guns taken from his own vessel. On August 12, 1694, two French ships of forty and fifty guns arrived off the harbour and immediately began to bombard the place; but Holman gave them such a warm reception that, after a fight of five hours, the French ships were driven off, with a loss of eighty or ninety men. There were nine merchant-ships in the harbour at the time.—*Records in State Paper Office.*

tioned, arrived at Plaisance. Here he found a reinforcement of 400 Canadians waiting his arrival, which had been sent by the Governor-General of Canada to aid in the reduction of Newfoundland. Having equipped nine privateers belonging to St. Malo's, three corvettes and two fireships, and embarked the Canadians, D'Ibberville, accompanied by M. de Brouillan, the Governor of Plaisance, sailed for St. John's.[1] Owing to head winds, the expedition was not able to reach St. John's, and had to return to Plaisance, for a supply of provisions, having captured thirty-one vessels and destroyed some fishing establishments upon the coast. It was then arranged to make a simultaneous attack upon St. John's by sea and land, for which purpose Brouillan took command of the ships, whilst D'Ibberville and his Canadians marched across the Peninsula. The first intelligence of the impending danger was brought to St. John's by a messenger from Petty Harbour, which had been attacked by the French. As this place was only nine miles from St. John's, a force of eighty-four armed men were sent on the 18th November to its relief. The party had scarcely proceeded a mile from St. John's when it encountered D'Ibberville at the head of a body of French, Canadians, and Indians, in all about 400 men.

In the conflict which ensued, the English had thirty-four men killed and several wounded. The rest retreated to St. John's, closely pursued by the French, and took refuge in King William's Fort, where, with the other inhabitants, they held out for three days, when they were obliged to surrender, being short both of provisions and ammunition. This fort, which commanded the entrance of the harbour, had not long been erected; it was a place of some strength, and had enabled the inhabitants in the early part of the summer to successfully resist the attack of a strong squadron of French ships commanded by the Chevalier Nesmond. During the three days which the fort held out against D'Ibberville, all the houses, stores, stages, and provisions in the settlement were burned or destroyed.[2]

[1] Bacqueville de la Porterie's *Histoire de l'Amérique Septentrionale*. Paris: 1722.

[2] For these facts I am chiefly indebted to a deposition made by Messrs. Philips,

The season being far advanced, Brouillan returned with his ships to Plaisance; but D'Ibberville and his Canadians, accustomed to winter travelling, proceeded along the shore to the northward, and in the course of two months desolated all the remaining settlements in Newfoundland, except Carbonear and Bonavista, which could not be attacked without a naval force. More than 200 men were killed, and 600 sent prisoners to Plaisance.[1] In the spring of 1697, D'Ibberville was engaged at Plaisance in fitting out an expedition against Carbonear and Bonavista, when a squadron of ships arrived from France under charge of M. de Serigny, with instructions that he (D'Ibberville) should take the command, and destroy all the English trading posts in Hudson's Bay. Having accomplished this duty, he returned to Plaisance, where a council of war was held, at which it was decided that it was then too late in the season to make a descent upon the coast of New England, and the fleet sailed for France, to the great relief of the colonists, who had for nearly six months been kept in a state of alarm. The merchants and traders of the western ports of England, engaged in the Newfoundland trade, who had sustained such severe losses during the war, petitioned the king for reparation, and protection for the future. Twenty-nine vessels, of the value of 24,700*l.*, belonging to the little port of Bideford alone, had been captured, and several other ports had suffered in like proportion. Beyond all doubt the planters were the greatest sufferers; the inhabitants of Ferryland estimated their losses in goods, chattels, and fish, at 12,000*l.* In consequence of these remonstrances, a squadron, commanded by Sir John Norris, with two regiments of soldiers, was sent out in the spring of 1697, 'for the recovery of Newfoundland.' Norris arrived at St. John's on June 10, and found it abandoned by the French. The troops were

Roberts, and some others, now in the Record Office. The deponents further state 'that the French took one William Brew, an inhabitant, a prisoner, and cut all round his scalp, and then, by the strength of hands, stript his skin from the forehead to the crown, and so sent him into the fortifications, assuring the inhabitants that they would serve them all in like manner if they did not surrender.'

[1] Bacqueville de la Porterie.

landed, and a battery erected upon each side of the harbour's mouth; but nothing further was done worthy of notice. It was known that a French squadron of five ships, supposed to be part of M. Nesmond's fleet, was cruising on the coast; but it was decided at a council of war that the English squadron should remain in port.

The following abstract of the trade and population of Newfoundland in 1698 may be interesting:—

Number of Planters	284
" their children	462
" their servants	1,894
" boats owned by them	397
Quintals of fish made by them	101,152
Number of ships fishing and carrying fish	252
Their tonnage	24,318
Number of seamen employed	4,244
Quintals of fish caught by ships	114,770
" purchased by merchants	157,848
" carried to market	265,198

Happily, at this time, for the peace and comfort of the unprotected planters in Newfoundland, both England and France were so impoverished and exhausted by the enormous cost of the great military operations in which they had been engaged upon the Continent during the last six years, without any solid advantage to either side, that negotiations were opened at Ryswick, which terminated in a treaty of peace, signed on September 20. By this treaty it was agreed that each country should retain the territories which it occupied in America before the war, and that commissioners should be appointed to settle the disputed boundaries between the British provinces and the French colonies of Canada and Acadié. The commissioners on both sides, however, advanced such extravagant pretensions that no satisfactory arrangement could be made, and consequently the unsettled boundaries remained—a fruitful source of dispute in after years. The right of France to the Valley of the Mississippi was, however, recognised, founded on the discoveries of the Jesuit La Salle, who, with a party of traders, had in 1682 descended the river from its source to the sea, and planted the national flag on the shores of the Gulf of Mexico.

Although the first article of the Treaty of Ryswick stipulated that there should thenceforth be universal and perpetual peace between the two Sovereigns, the French had scarcely resumed possession of Acadié when Villebon, the Governor, caused a chapel to be built at Norridgewock, on the banks of the Kennebec, within the disputed territory, and attempted to drive the New England fishermen from the coasts of Acadié. These ill-advised measures, just after the establishment of peace, were not such as a man desirous of maintaining friendly relations with his neighbours ought to have adopted; but even these might not have led to any serious misunderstanding, as both England and France, at that period, were too apt to exhibit a very blameable indifference towards their colonies in America, had not a more serious cause of rupture arisen in Europe. This was the acknowledgment of the title of the son of James II. to the crown of England by Louis XIV., which gave such offence that, on the accession of Queen Anne, in 1702, war was immediately declared against France.

A state of peace and tranquillity was no doubt fully appreciated by the English colonists; but the attempts of Brouillan, who had succeeded Villebon in the government of Acadié in 1700, to drive them from the fishing-grounds, and the shelter which he afforded to the pirates, who committed great depredations upon the trade of Massachusetts during the peace, had raised such a feeling of indignation that the news of the declaration of war was hailed with joy by the colonists. Anxious as the English were to engage in hostilities, the French were the first to break the peace on the frontiers. In the winter of 1703, a party comprising 200 French and 140 Indians, commanded by the notorious Hertel de Rouville, who had headed the assault on Schenectady in 1690, attacked at midnight the village of Deerfield, in Massachusetts, killed 47 of the inhabitants and carried off 112 prisoners. On a preconcerted day in the same year, parties of Indians, led by French officers, burst into almost every farmhouse and hamlet, from Casco to the Piscataqua, sparing neither age nor sex in their savage fury. Heartrending narratives of similar atrocities may be found in the records of every settlement, from the

Kennebec to the Merrimac. Such deeds as these inspired the colonists with a deep hatred against the French missionaries, who, if they did not instigate, as was believed, certainly did not use the great influence they possessed over the savages, in endeavouring to stop such inhuman outrages.

In the summer of 1704, Colonel Church was sent from Boston in command of an expedition, comprised of three armed ships, fourteen transports, and 500 soldiers, to ravage the French settlements in Acadié, in revenge of these outrages. Almost every French village, between the Penobscot and Beau Bassin (Chignecto), at the head of the Bay of Fundy, was plundered and destroyed; houses and barns were burned; the dykes were cut, and the marshes inundated; many of the settlers were killed, and a great number made prisoners. In the following winter the Jesuit chapel of Norridgewock, with all the wigwams, which had been abandoned by Father Rasle and his converts, were burned by the English. This harassing warfare continued, with varying success, until 1707, when the Government of Massachusetts came to the determination of driving the French entirely out of Acadié, as the only means of relieving the colonies from the constant alarm inspired by such unquiet neighbours. Accordingly, in the spring of 1707, two regiments of militia were sent in transports, convoyed by the 'Deptford,' of fifty guns, under the command of Colonel Marsh, to reduce Port Royal, but they received such a warm reception from M. Subercase, who had been appointed Governor on the death of Brouillan, that Marsh was obliged to abandon the attempt and retire to Casco Bay, where he received a reinforcement of 100 men from Boston, with pressing orders to return immediately to Port Royal. In the meantime, Subercase also had been joined by fifty Canadians and a large body of Indians, commanded by the Baron Castine, which afforded such important aid during the siege which followed, that Marsh was again obliged to retire without effecting his object.

The French, justly elated by the successful defence of Port Royal against a superior force, lost no opportunity of harassing the English colonists, by land and water, making frequent incursions across the unprotected frontiers, and preying upon her commerce. The fishing-stations on the coast of Newfoundland, which had been reoccupied and repaired, were again desolated, and on January 1, 1708, M. de St. Ovide, the king's lieutenant at Placentia, having landed within five leagues of St. John's without being discovered, attacked and completely destroyed that town. The inhabitants of Carbonear, however, gallantly repulsed an attack made upon it by M. de Costabelle, the French commander-in-chief.

Small English squadrons had occasionally retaliated upon the French, by destroying their settlements on the southern coast; but the English planters were the greatest sufferers. The British Government had been urgently solicited to send out a naval force to protect the commerce of the colonists of New England; but her statesmen were too deeply engrossed with the campaigns in Flanders, in which Marlborough was then reaping such immortal renown, to pay much heed to their representations. Nevertheless, the colonists were neither discouraged nor dismayed. Seeing that there could be no peace for them so long as the French held Acadié, they set about preparations for another attempt upon Port Royal in the year 1710, and once more appealed to the mother country for assistance, offering to raise a body of troops to be paid by England, provided a squadron of ships was sent out to convoy them to their destination. This application, happily, was successful, and the colonists were assured that, if they could make themselves masters of Acadié, it should not again be given up by treaty. With this assurance, the New England provinces engaged heartily in the enterprise. Four regiments were soon raised and embarked in transports, convoyed by four ships of war, under the command of General Nicholson. The expedition arrived at Port Royal on September 24, when a summons was sent to Subercase to surrender the place. The Governor, who had heard vague rumours of a fresh invasion, had wisely exerted all his energy in repairing and extending his means of defence; but though convinced from the first that, with a garrison of only 260 soldiers, he could not defend his post with the remotest chance of success, he nevertheless refused to obey the summons. Part of the troops were therefore landed, ar several slight skirmishes occurred, but no serious attack was made. The engineers having reported on October 1 that the batteries were all armed and ready to open their fire, Nicholson, seeing the utter hopelessness of any attempt to defend the place against the force under his command, and desirous of saving the lives of the garrison, again sent an officer with a summons to the Governor to surrender. Subercase being now satisfied that there was no chance of defending his post against such an imposing force, prudently complied with the summons. Articles of capitulation were arranged and signed, and on the following day, October 5, an English force of 200 marines and 260 volunteers, under the command of Colonel Vetch, took possession of the fort. The French troops, and about 200 of the principal inhabitants, were sent in English transports to Rochelle. Those who wished to remain in possession of their lands were allowed to do so upon taking an oath of allegiance to the British Sovereign. Some complied with this condition, but a great number of the inhabitants fled into the interior. A few emigrated to Miramichi and Cape Breton.

With a change of masters came a change of names. Acadié was again called 'Nova Scotia'—the name bestowed upon it by James I. in 1621; and Port Royal, 'Annapolis,' in honour of the reigning Queen of England. We must now drop the old familiar names, and try to accustom ourselves to the pedantic titles conferred upon the country and its ancient capital by their new masters.

When it was too late, the French Government began to realise the value of the country, which had been lost by gross negligence. A recent writer (M. Rameau),[1] after noticing the rapid increase of the population of French descent during the thirty years following its conquest, observes that, if 100,000 livres a year had been spent by France in maintaining a regular garrison of 500 men at Port Royal, and if twenty-five or thirty families of emigrants had been sent out yearly since 1670, there would, in 1710, have been a population of 8,000 or 10,000 souls for the defence of the country. He adds, that France would also have been a great gainer in

[1] *La France aux Colonies.* Paris: 1859.

a financial point of view, as there would then have been no occasion for spending 30 millions upon the fortress of Louisbourg, which, after the loss of Acadié, became absolutely necessary for securing the command of the entrance of the St. Lawrence.

The English garrison at Annapolis suffered so much loss from sickness, and skirmishes with the hostile population which surrounded it, that in the course of seven months its strength was reduced to 150 men fit for duty. Bands of savages lurked in the woods in the vicinity, ready to pounce upon any unwary soldier that strayed beyond the limits of the fort; and upon one occasion seventy men and two officers, who had been sent up the river to reduce the inhabitants to subjection, were surprised by an ambush of savages, led by a noted chief called L'Aimable, when thirty of the men and the two officers were killed, and all the rest save one made prisoners. Elated by this success, 500 of the French inhabitants, whom we shall in future call Acadians, and a large body of Indians, at the instigation of the missionary Gaulin rushed to arms and invested the fort. The Marquis de Vaudreuil, Viceroy of Canada, who had despatched messengers in the winter with instructions to the missionaries to do all in their power to retain the Acadians and Indians in the interest of France, hearing of the state of affairs in Nova Scotia, was just on the point of sending 200 men from Quebec to assist in the reduction of Annapolis, when he received intelligence from Placentia that an English fleet was on its way to the St. Lawrence, and was therefore obliged to keep the men for the defence of his own capital. Disappointed in obtaining succour from Canada and Placentia,[1] the revolted Acadians laid down their arms and made their submission to the English Governor of Annapolis.

Encouraged by the success which had attended the expedition to Acadié, and alarmed at the rapid extension of the

[1] The Acadians had applied to M. de Costabelle, the Governor of Placentia, for an engineer to conduct the siege of Annapolis, and also for a supply of ammunition; but Costabelle, having learned that the garrison of Annapolis had been reinforced by 200 provincial troops, concluded that it was too late to comply with their requisition.

French posts in the valley of the Ohio, the Governors of the British provinces resolved to attempt the conquest of Canada. General Nicholson was therefore sent to England to urge upon the Ministry the importance of the enterprise, and to offer to raise a body of troops in the colonies, to march upon Montreal, if the Government would send out a naval force to attack Quebec. The British Government entered heartily into the project, and in the spring of 1711 sent out to Boston a fleet of fifteen ships of war, under Admiral Hovenden Walker, with forty transports carrying 5,000 troops, commanded by General Hill. If this powerful armament had sailed direct to Quebec, the object in view would in all probability have been effected; but so much time was lost at Boston in taking in provisions, collecting provincial reinforcements, and obtaining pilots, that it did not reach the mouth of the St. Lawrence before August 22, although it had sailed from Plymouth on May 4. Owing either to the incapacity of the admiral, or the ignorance of the pilots, the whole fleet during the same night got entangled amongst the rocks and shoals near the Egg Islands, on the north shore, in a thick fog. The ships of war fortunately put about just in time to clear the breakers, but eight transports, with 1,383 men on board, were wrecked upon the ledges, when 884 brave fellows, who had passed scatheless through the sanguinary battles of Blenheim, Ramillies, and Oudenarde, perished miserably on the desolate shores of the St. Lawrence. Two days afterwards, it was resolved at a council of war to give up the enterprise, on account of the ignorance of the pilots and the rapidity of the currents, and to proceed to Spanish Bay in Cape Breton, which had been selected as the most convenient rendezvous in case of the vessels being dispersed.

The Governors of the English provinces had meanwhile fulfilled their promise, by collecting several regiments of militia and volunteers at Albany, commanded by General Nicholson, ready to march upon Montreal. Nicholson, according to preconcerted arrangements, started from Albany on August 20, and had reached the shores of Lake George, when tidings arrived of the heavy disaster which had befallen the fleet. He was in consequence obliged to return to Albany. The loss of so many valuable lives at the Egg Islands was a great calamity, but if the expedition had reached Quebec in safety, it would, perhaps, have been still more serious, as neither Walker nor Hill were capable of conducting a siege of such importance. Besides, it would have received a warm reception from Vaudreuil the Viceroy, who had strengthened the fortifications, called in the militia, and collected a large body of Indians, including some even from a country so distant as Nova Scotia.

On September 4, the bulk of the fleet reached Spanish Bay, and anchored in the roadstead, 'in seven fathoms water, the East Point E.N.E. and the North Point of the Road N. by W., good ground,' or directly abreast of Lloyd's Cove. In the course of a few days the remaining ships, and some men of war which had been cruising in the Gulf and on the coast of Newfoundland, arrived at the rendezvous. Walker's fleet, consisting altogether of forty-two sail, was probably the largest naval armament ever assembled in Sydney Harbour.

Before the expedition left England, the two commanders had been instructed, after taking Quebec, 'to summon and attack Placentia, in Newfoundland.' This, one might suppose, would have been an easy task for a fleet of fifteen ships mounting nearly 900 guns, and a land force of 4,000 men, especially when we bear in mind that letters had been found on board of prizes brought by the cruisers into Spanish Bay, from M. de Costabelle, the Governor of Placentia, to M. Pontchartrain, 'Secretary of the Court of Paris,' stating that the little garrison was in want of supplies of all kinds, that a promised reinforcement of two companies of soldiers had not arrived, and that 'La Valeur'—the only armed ship on the station, had been lost. And yet, incredible to relate, although Placentia was only 150 miles from Spanish River, and almost in the direct homeward track of the fleet, a council of war, held on board the flagship, decided 'that it was not practicable to make any attempt against Placentia.' With such facts before us, we cannot be astonished that, as Admiral Walker tells us, 'loud and invidious clamours were raised against him on account of the late expedition to Canada,' and that the 'frivolous pamphleteers' were not so far wrong when they insinuated 'that the taking of Placentia on our way to Britain had been as easy as a citizen riding home in his chaise from Hampstead or Highgate, calling at a cakehouse by the way, to regale himself and his spouse with a glass of cyder and a cheesecake.' The doughty Admiral, however, performed one signal exploit before he sailed, which must be duly recorded. Remarking that 'it would be a pity such a squadron and such a body of land forces should leave America without doing something against the enemy in some part or other,' . . . and 'being informed by several officers who had been there, that a Cross was erected on the shore, with the names of the French Sea officers who had been here, which I looked upon as a claim of right they pretend to for the King their master, the island having always been in the times of peace used in common both by the English and the French, for lading coals, which are extraordinary good here, and taken out of the cliffs with iron crows only and no other labour, I thought it not amiss, therefore, to leave something of that kind to declare the Queen's right to the place; and having a board made by the carpenter and painted, I sent him ashore to fix it upon a tree, or in some convenient place where it might easily be seen, with the inscription following:—

In nomine
Patris, Filii et Spiritus Sancti
Amen
Omnibus in Christi Fidelibus Salutem.
Anna Dei Gratia
Mag. Britanniæ
Franciæ et Hiberniæ Regina
Totiusque Americæ Septentrionalis
Domina, Fidei Defensor, &c.
In
Cujus harum Insularum vulgo
Cape Breton
Proprietatis
Et Dominii
Testimonium
Hoc
Erexit Monumentum
Suæ Majestatis Servus
Et Subditus fidelissimus
D. Hovenden Walker Eques Auratus
Omnium in America Navium Regalium
Præfectus et Thalassiarcha
Monte Septembris
Anno Salutis
MDCCXI.'

This pompous and absurd 'monument' was most likely torn down by the first savage that passed that way, and the sole record of the Admiral's conquest of Cape Breton speedily obliterated. Few natives showed themselves whilst the fleet was in the harbour, but there were no doubt many lurking in the woods watching all that was going on. Several of the sailors, 'who went a good way up into the woods alone, met with no manner of insult from the Indians;' but a carpenter and two seamen belonging to the 'Eagle' transport were not so fortunate, having been killed and scalped whilst engaged in collecting wood from an old wreck in a remote part of the harbour. The Admiral supposes 'those men were killed for meddling with a wreck which the Indians believed themselves only to have a right to; for I was told by several of the New Englanders, who had often been upon the island and conversed with the natives, as also by the French, that they were a very inoffensive people.'

The troops raised in New England having been sent to Boston under convoy of the frigate 'Enterprise,' and a detachment of 400 men to Annapolis, the fleet left Spanish Bay on the morning of September 16, and arrived at Portsmouth in safety on October 10. The disasters attending this ill conducted expedition, however, were not yet ended, for the Admiral's flagship, the 'Edgar,' of seventy guns, with a crew of 470 men, was blown up at her anchorage in Portsmouth Harbour on the 16th of the same month, 'and not one man saved.'[1]

[1] For the materials used in compiling the preceding letter I am chiefly indebted to Charlevoix's *History of New France*; Lahoutan's *Voyages to Canada*; Documents in the State Paper Office; Admiral Walker's *Account of the Expedition to Canada*; Williamson's *History of Maine*; Douglas's *Summary*, &c. &c.

LETTER IX.

1711-1720.

THE FAILURE of Admiral Walker's expedition, as might be expected, caused great disappointment in England, and increased in no small degree the general desire for the establishment of peace with France. Although the armies of England and her allies, led by the celebrated Marlborough, had won victory after victory on the continent, the protracted contest at length became unpopular, and upon a change of Ministry an agent was sent to Paris, in 1711, with proposals for a peace, which proved very acceptable to the French Government. In the following year a suspension of hostilities was signed, and negotiations for a general peace were commenced.

At these negotiations the French Government, now fully aware of the value of Acadié, made great exertions to obtain its restoration, offering to give in exchange for it the post of Plaisance (Placentia), all the rest of Newfoundland with the fisheries, and the isles of St. Martin and Bartholomew; but Queen Anne rejected the offer, and insisted that it should be designated by the name of Nova Scotia, as well as Acadié, in the Treaty. The long discussions relative to Cape Breton clearly show the importance the French attached to its possession. Mr. St. John, in a memoir submitted to the Marquis de Torcy on May 24, 1712, proposed on the part of Queen Anne, 'That the subjects of His Majesty (Louis XIV.) should enjoy, in common with the Queen's, the island of Cape Breton,' and 'that the islands in the Gulf of St. Lawrence and in the mouth of the river of that name, which are at present possessed by the French, should remain to his most Christian Majesty, but expressly upon the condition that his said Majesty shall engage himself not to raise or suffer to be raised any fortifications in these islands or in that of Cape Breton—the Queen engaging herself likewise not to fortify or suffer any fortifications to be raised in the adjacent islands, and those next Newfoundland, nor in that of Cape Breton.' In his reply to this proposition, on June 5 the Marquis de Torcy stated: 'As the perfect good understanding that the King proposes to establish between his subjects and those of the Queen of Great Britain will, if it please God, be one of the principal advantages of the peace, we must remove all propositions capable of disturbing this happy union; experience has made it too visible, that it was impossible to preserve it in the places possessed in common by the French and English nations, so this reason alone will suffice to hinder His Majesty from consenting to the proposition of leaving the English to possess the isle of Cape Breton in common with the French; but there is still a stronger reason against this proposition: as it is but too often seen that the most amicable nations many times become enemies, it is prudence in the King to reserve to himself the possession of the only isle which will hereafter open an entrance into the river of St. Lawrence: it would be absolutely shut to the ships of His Majesty, if the English, masters of Acadié and Newfoundland, still possessed the isle of Cape Breton in common with the French, and Canada would be lost to France as soon as the war should be renewed between the two nations, which God forbid; but the most secure means to prevent it is often to think that it may come to pass.

'It will not be dissembled, but it is for the same reason, that the King is desirous of reserving to himself the natural and common liberty, as all sovereigns have, of erecting in the isles of the gulf and in the mouth of the St. Lawrence, as well as in the isle of Cape Breton, such fortifications as His Majesty shall judge necessary. These works, made only for the security of the country, can never be of any detriment to the neighbouring isles and provinces.

'It is just that the Queen of Great Britain should have the same liberty to erect what fortifications she shall think necessary, whether in Acadié or in the isle of Newfoundland; and upon this article the King does not pretend to exact anything contrary to the rights which the propriety and possession naturally give to that Princess.'

The demands of the French Government, supported by these just and candid arguments, were considered fair and reasonable, and it was accordingly agreed that France should have liberty to fortify any place or places in Cape Breton.

The cession of Acadié and Newfoundland to England, and the right of France to fortify Cape Breton, and prosecute the fisheries on certain parts of the coast of Newfoundland, were embodied in the 12th and 13th Articles of the memorable Treaty signed at Utrecht on April 11, 1713. In these articles it was stipulated that 'All Nova Scotia or Acadié, with its ancient boundaries, as also the city of Port Royal, now called Annapolis Royal, . . . the island of Newfoundland, with the adjacent islands, . . . the town and fortress of Placentia, and whatever other places in the island are in possession of the French, shall from this time forward belong of right wholly to Great Britain.' . . . 'That the subjects of France should be allowed to catch fish and dry them on that part of the island of Newfoundland which stretches from Cape Bonavista to the northern point of the island, and from thence down the western side as far as Point Riché; but that no fortifications or any buildings should be erected there, besides Stages made of Boards, and Huts necessary and usual for drying fish. . . . But the island of Cape Breton, as also all others, both in the mouth of the river of St. Lawrence and in the gulf of the same name, shall hereafter belong of Right to the King of France, who shall have liberty to fortify any place or places there.'

Charlevoix says 'that France was amply compensated for the loss of Newfoundland by the acquisition of Cape Breton, where the inhabitants of Plaisance found themselves more agreeably and more advantageously situated than they had ever been in Newfoundland; whilst the English were now absolute masters of the country where before they could not assure themselves of anything so long as they had us for their neighbours.' If you have read the accounts of the repeated raids upon the English settlements, you will not question the truth of the latter part of the paragraph; but I cannot understand how their position in Cape Breton was now so much improved, seeing that the French had held undisputed possession of the island for nearly a century, had erected forts and formed settlements therein, and carried on the fishery without interruption. The capabilities and resources of the island were well known, but nevertheless, it had been suffered to remain desolate and neglected ever since it was abandoned by Nicholas Denys. M. de la Potherie, who was 'Commissaire de Roi' in the squadron commanded by D'Ibberville in 1697, comparing Plaisance with Cape Breton, says, 'The land at the former place is all mossy, and will produce little or nothing; wheat never ripens; they have no fruits of France except strawberries; whilst in Cape Breton, which is a very beautiful island on the coast of Acadié, there are plains and prairies, vast forests filled with Oak, Maple, Cedar, Walnut, and the finest Fir trees in the world. If apples and stone fruits were planted, it would become a second Normandy. Hemp grows wild everywhere; Hops flourish well; the Wheat is better than in Quebec. For the chase there are Bustards, Partridges of France, Deer, Hens of the Wood, Turtledoves, Plover, Teal, and every sort of Water Fowl. The Fishery can be carried on with less risk than at Plaisance, the fishing grounds being close in shore.' This description, although rather too flattering, is upon the whole correct; the only wonder is, that the French did not profit by their knowledge of Cape Breton before they were obliged to cede Plaisance to England.

French writers of a later date do not seem to have regarded the loss of Acadié and Newfoundland with so much complacency as Charlevoix. The Abbé Raynal, for instance, says, 'One is afraid to express how much these sacrifices marked our humiliation, and how hard it was to give up three provinces which, with Canada, constituted the immense territory known by the glorious name of New France.' And Garneau remarks, 'that the treaty of Utrecht snatched from the feeble hands of Louis XIV. the portals of Canada, Acadié, and Newfoundland. From this treaty dates the decline of the monarchy and the coming of the Revolution.'

As England had now obtained undisputed possession of the whole Atlantic coast of North America, from Florida to Hudson's Bay, with the exception of Cape Breton, the construction of a fortified naval station in that island became an object of the first necessity to France, for the protection of her commerce and fisheries, and for maintaining the communication with Canada and the Gulf of St. Lawrence. The necessity and importance of such an establishment had been clearly demonstrated in 1708 by M. Raudot, Intendant of Justice, Police, Finances, and affairs in general, and his son, the Intendant of Marine, in Canada. These intelligent officers, who had introduced various important judicial and fiscal improvements into the colony, submitted an able and interesting memoir to the Court of Paris, containing a complete explication of the state of New France, and many valuable suggestions calculated to advance its prosperity. They proved by the statistics of the colony:—

1. That the fur trade, which had at first been the sole object of forming settlements in North America, must gradually decline, and could not, therefore, long sustain a great colony.

2. That the total income derived from the fur trade and fisheries, and the sums expended by the Government on the troops, seminaries, and pensions, amounting altogether to 650,000 livres, was quite insufficient for the support of a colony of twenty or twenty-five thousand souls.

3. They recommended that the commerce of the colony should be established on a broader and more healthy basis, by encouraging the trade in timber, planks, pitch, tar, salted meats, whale and seal oils, codfish, flax, hemp, &c.—commodities which could be produced in abundance. The opening up of these resources, it was argued, would reduce the price of European manufactures, which were now sold at exorbitant prices, because the colony would then pay for them in productions of its own; at the same time, many of the inhabitants, who now wasted their time in running about the woods in quest of game, would find useful and profitable employment upon their own farms.

4. To carry out this object, it would be necessary to have some convenient entrepôt on the seaboard, somewhere between Canada and France, open at all seasons of the year, where the productions of Europe and the West Indies could be stored ready for shipment to Canada; and where, in like manner, the productions of Canada might be collected for transhipment to all parts of the world. No fitter place for this purpose could be found than the island of Cape Breton, which, besides, could furnish codfish, oils, coal, plaister, and timber, of its own production.

5. The smaller class of Canadian vessels employed in the fisheries of the Gulf could then store their cargoes in Cape Breton ready for reshipment to Europe and the West Indies, thereby avoiding the risk of a voyage up and down the St. Lawrence, and saving at the same time a great and unnecessary expense.

6. Wine, brandy, linens, silks, and other French products, could be more easily supplied to English vessels at Cape Breton than at Quebec, for transmission to the British North American provinces and the West India islands, which would bring a great deal of hard money into the coffers of the French merchants.

7. The whale fishery, in the Gulf of St. Lawrence and on the coast of Labrador, could be prosecuted with more advantage from ports in Cape Breton than from Quebec, and ships even could be built there at a less cost than in France.

Lastly, that a fortified harbour in Cape Breton would afford a safe refuge for vessels chased by an enemy, driven in by storms, or in want of provisions. In time of war it would form a suitable rendezvous for cruisers and privateers; and France might monopolise the cod fishery on the coasts of Acadié by means of a few small frigates always ready to sally out and drive off foreign fishermen.

For these, and many other reasons which I have not space to recount, the French Government would undoubtedly have adopted the project of the Messieurs Raudot, when it was proposed, in 1708, if France had not then been engaged in a war with Great Britain which wholly engrossed her attention, and left her little leisure to think of her distant possessions in America. When, however, she was deprived of all her colonies on the Atlantic seaboard, except Cape Breton, by the Treaty of Utrecht, the realisation of their project became not only expedient, but absolutely indispensable, for the security of Canada and the islands in the Gulf of St. Lawrence.

As Plaisance, according to the treaty, was to be given up immediately, M. de Costabelle, the Governor, lost no time in sending off the garrison and inhabitants to Cape Breton, so that the latter might not lose their summer's fishing. Some of the people objected to leaving Plaisance, and would willingly have remained under English domination, but Costabelle urged all to go, except certain idlers and vagabonds, whom he discreetly left as a legacy to his successors. In the first instance, the garrison and inhabitants were sent to Havre à l'Anglois (Louisbourg), which was known to be favourably situated for carrying on the fishery. In the course of the summer, about 180 persons, chiefly fishermen and their families, arrived from Plaisance and the Isle of St. Pierre. Some of these settled at Baleine, Scatari, and the out harbours, but the majority took up their abode at Havre à l'Anglois. All were supplied with provisions by the French Government for some time after their arrival.

As Costabelle could not leave Plaisance until the English Governor arrived to take charge of the fort and munitions of war, which were to be delivered up according to the treaty, he despatched Major l'Hermité, an engineer officer, and M. de St. Ovide, a commander in the Royal Navy, to Cape Breton, to examine and report upon the capabilities of the harbours on the Atlantic coast, for the purpose of selecting the one best adapted for a great naval station. About the same time, an officer was sent to Nova Scotia to request the missionaries to use their influence in persuading the Acadians and Indians of that province to remove to Cape Breton.

It was well known that the Baie des Espagnols (Sydney) was the best harbour in the island, and most easy of access, being resorted to by navigators seeking shelter in stormy weather; but the entrance was so wide that it could not be fortified against an enemy with the artillery then in use. The other harbours on the eastern coast, having sufficient depth of water to admit large vessels, were St. Anne's and Havre à l'Anglois, both with narrow entrances capable of being effectually closed by suitable batteries against an enemy's ships.

In favour of the former it was said that a single fort would completely command the entrance, and that the spacious harbour inside, being surrounded with lofty rugged hills of great height, the position could not be turned by a land attack. Also that, independently of the fine fisheries in the bay, St. Anne's was situated at no great distance from Niganiche, the two entrances of the Labrador Lakes, and the Baie des Espagnols, all noted fishing stations. Within the harbour there was an extensive gravel beach for drying fish, whilst wood of the best description could be obtained close to the shore.

Very little seems to have been said at that time in favour of Havre à l'Anglois. It was admitted to be a good harbour, capable of being fortified at great expense; but Guyon, a pilot of some reputation, averred that there were only three fathoms of water in the entrance.[1]

L'Hermité and M. de St. Ovide having both reported in favour of St. Anne's, the Viceroy of Canada and M. de Costabelle, guided by their opinion, wrote to the Minister of Marine recommending the adoption of their report.

Several years elapsed before the Government came to a decision, which gave the French officers who had removed to Havre à l'Anglois an opportunity of making themselves better acquainted with its advantages. M. de Costabelle, who was the first Governor of Cape Breton, and resided some years at Havre à l'Anglois, must soon have seen how many advantages it possessed over St. Anne's, especially in its proximity to the open ocean, its facility of access, its great depth of water, and the fact of its being never entirely frozen up. Charlevoix,

[1] This was a great mistake. According to the late charts of the Naval Surveyors there are ten fathoms in the entrance of Louisbourg Harbour, but only three fathoms on the bar of St. Anne's.

writing in 1744, says the only objection to St. Anne's was the difficulty of entering the harbour, not being aware, apparently, that it was frozen up four or five months every winter, and for that reason could never have been of any use as an entrepôt of foreign trade at that season.

When the French Government decided in favour of Havre à l'Anglois, its name was changed to Louisbourg, in honour of the king; and, to mark the value set upon Cape Breton, it was called Isle Royale, which it retained until its final conquest in 1758, when its ancient name was resumed. To avoid confusion I shall adhere to its old name, a name so dear and familiar to you all. The names of some other places were changed about the same time; for instance, St. Peter's and St. Anne's were called Port Toulouse and Port Dauphin, both of which have been long forgotten.

Several of the officers who came from Plaisance to Louisbourg applied for grants of land in Cape Breton. One of these was M. de le Ronde Denys, grandson of that Nicholas Denys I have so often mentioned, who at one time had a grant of the whole island. Le Ronde Denys addressed a long letter to the minister, giving a description of the principal harbours in Cape Breton. He spoke very highly of St. Anne's, where, he says, his late grandfather had a fort of which the vestiges could then be seen (1713), and several fields under cultivation, which produced 'the finest grain in the world.' He then applies for a grant on the river Moulacady, which, he says, is the first river you meet on the right hand in going up Lake Choulacady, on which he proposes to settle a number of people from Canada and Acadié. He then informs the minister that he was well acquainted with New England, not nearly so valuable a country as Cape Breton, which is making great progress, and where more than 1,500 vessels are built yearly; and adds, that many things might be seen there which might be followed with great advantage in Cape Breton.[1] Le Ronde Denys was the officer sent to Boston in the spring of

[1] Quoted in Murdoch's *History of Nova Scotia*, from French manuscripts collected by the Commission appointed to examine the archives of Nova Scotia in 1844.

1711 by Costabelle, at the suggestion of the French minister Pontchartrain, to endeavour to persuade the people of Boston to refuse supplies to the expedition expected from England under Sir Hovenden Walker, for the conquest of Canada, when he probably became acquainted with the flourishing state of the English colonies.[1]

M. de Rouville, captain of infantry, a brother of Hertel de Rouville, who led the savages in the attack on Haverhill in 1708, applied to the minister for a grant of Niganiche, but without success. He probably obtained a grant at St. Anne's, as the northern arm of that harbour was long known by the name of Rouville's River. There is every reason to believe that M. de la Boulardrie, an officer of the navy, who greatly distinguished himself in the defence of Port Royal in 1708, and who came over from Plaisance to Havre à l'Anglois with part of the garrison, obtained at this time (1713) a grant of the rich and beautiful island lying between the two entrances of the Labrador, which still bears his name.

The principal officers of the Government at Plaisance had apparently enjoyed the privilege of employing a certain number of boats in the fishery; for we learn by a report addressed by Costabelle to the minister in the following year, that there was not sufficient room for the officers' boats on the beach at Louisbourg, and that they would have to look out for suitable places on the northern coast. If we may judge from the names of certain places marked on Charlevoix's map, Costabelle, Soubras, and Beaucourt had fishing stations on the shores of St. Anne's Bay.

When M. de St. Ovide de Brouillan was appointed Governor of Louisbourg in 1714, he sent M. de la Ronde Denys and M. de Pensens with letters to General Nicholson, asking him to allow such of the French inhabitants as desired, to remove to Cape Breton. This was readily granted; but very few of the Acadians accepted his invitation, as they had been allowed, ever since the fall of Port Royal, to exercise their religion and to enjoy their lands and tenements without

[1] Costabelle's letter, July 23, 1711, to Pontchartrain; intercepted by one of Admiral Walker's cruisers whilst the fleet was at Baie des Espagnols.

molestation. The Abbé Prévost allows 'that they had been well used by the English governors.' They saw no reason, therefore, why they should abandon the fertile farms, which for several generations had descended from father to son, according to the patriarchal custom of their forefathers, and remove to a new country still covered with dense forests, which would have to be cleared with great labour and expense. It is true they had been repeatedly called upon by Nicholson, the Governor of Annapolis, to take the oath of allegiance to the Queen of England, but they had always refused, and the matter had been allowed to drop, because it was supposed that if such a number of persons were driven out of the province, they would remove to Cape Breton, and strengthen the power of France in that quarter.

The fishermen, however, who had no fixed stake in the country, and could easily transfer their boats and fishing gear from one place to another, went in considerable numbers to Cape Breton, but did not meet the favourable reception they had been led to expect. No provision was made by the governor for supplying their wants, and, being in a destitute condition, they were completely at the mercy of the merchants and traders, who charged such exorbitant prices for supplies of all kinds that many were absolutely ruined. Most of the fishermen settled in the small harbours near Louisbourg, but small parties found their way to more distant places along the coast, wherever safe and sheltered inlets invited them to erect their huts and stages.

The Indians, accustomed to roam at their pleasure over an extensive country, refused to remove to a small island, where, they alleged, there were already as many of their tribe as could make a living upon the products of the chase. They acted wisely in coming to this decision, if it be true 'that in a population which lives by the produce of the chase, each hunter requires on an average seventy-eight square miles for his support.'[1] Nevertheless, both the Acadians and the Indians assured M. de St. Ovide that they would continue faithful and true to the King of France. The former added, that if any

[1] Schoolcraft's *History of the American Indians.*

attempts were made to interfere with the free exercise of their religion, or to compel them by harsh measures to take an oath of allegiance to the British Queen, rather than submit they would abandon all their possessions and fly to Cape Breton.

When Colonel Phillips was appointed Governor of Nova Scotia in 1720, he was greatly surprised to learn, on his arrival in the province, that the inhabitants lived as if they were still subjects of France, that they were furnished with priests from Louisbourg, and kept up a regular communication with their countrymen in Cape Breton. Phillips immediately issued a proclamation forbidding all commerce with Cape Breton, and calling upon all the inhabitants to come forward and take the oath of allegiance within four months from its date, promising to all that complied the free exercise of their religion, the security of their possessions, and the enjoyment of all their civil rights.

In this emergency, the Acadians sent Father Durand to Louisbourg to seek the advice of M. de St. Ovide, who strongly advised them to refuse to take the oath, hoping that, if the English governor persisted in forcing it upon them, many would take refuge in Cape Breton and St. John's Islands, where an industrious agricultural population was much needed. The settlement of New Orleans in 1717 had, from its superior attractions, drawn off a number of persons who had made preparations to go to Cape Breton from France, and even some of the people of that island had removed to St. John's (Prince Edward's) Island, where a French Company were about to establish a colony under the auspices of the Count de St. Pierre, first equerry of the Duchess of Orleans. It was expected that this fertile island, if brought into cultivation, would, from its proximity to Cape Breton, soon be able to supply Louisbourg with the provisions which had now to be brought from distant countries. Setting aside all political considerations, the acquisition of a large body of immigrants from Nova Scotia would be of great importance, both in Cape Breton and St. John's Islands. We need not therefore be surprised that M. de St. Ovide strongly urged the Acadians to refuse to take the oath of allegiance.

Without waiting for the return of their messenger from Louisbourg, the Acadians sent deputies to Governor Phillips to inform him that as soon as they could dispose of their lands they would remove either to Canada or Cape Breton; that they considered their residence in the province quite as beneficial to the English as to themselves; and that, without their control, when the missionaries were withdrawn the savages would not allow the English to live in peace, and most likely would raise an insurrection of all the tribes from Canceau to the Kennebec. In this dilemma Phillips went to England to lay the case before the Ministry, when it was decided to allow the matter to remain in abeyance until a more favourable opportunity. Thus the threatened storm was for a time averted, only to break out with redoubled fury at a future period.

Nothing worthy of record occurred at Louisbourg for some years after its foundation, until the year 1720, when the fortifications were commenced. From this time the population began to increase rapidly, by the arrival of a large body of officers, mechanics, and labourers engaged in the construction of the works, and by traders and others employed in the supply of provisions and other necessaries. The people of New England were not long in discovering the valuable market which Louisbourg offered for their surplus produce, although trade with the French colonies was strictly forbidden by the Treaty of Neutrality concluded at London on November 16, 1686. The French authorities at Louisbourg winked at, and probably encouraged, a business which administered to the wants of the people, and furnished a ready and profitable market for articles imported from France. But Shute, the Governor of Massachusetts, took a different view of the matter. In his speech at the opening of the Legislature, on March 5, 1721, he recommended, as you will observe by the following extract, that an Act should be passed prohibiting all Trade with Cape Breton: 'At the last Sessions there was a Bill drawn to prevent any trading with the French at Cape Breton, conformable to the Treaty of Neutrality stipulated between the two Crowns of England and France; but since it had not then the assent of the whole General Assembly, I must again recommend it, hoping it will have a better fate this Sessions, lest it should otherwise be thought by the Government at home, that we have more regard to some private persons' interests than to His Majesty's Treaties or the public good.'

It may be inferred, from the Governor's allusion to 'private interests,' that some of the legislators themselves had been concerned in the trade with Cape Breton, especially as in their curt reply they were so ready to deny all knowledge of any such traffic: 'The reason why the Bill to prevent any trading with the French at Cape Breton did not pass the House last Sessions, was not out of regard to any private persons' interests; for as we then did not, neither do we now know, or are we informed of any within this Government that do trade there; and we humbly presume, should an Act be now made for that purpose, it could add no strength or power to the Treaty of Neutrality mentioned by your Excellency, to which we would ever have a due deference; and if any do trade there, and it is contrary to any Act of Parliament, those gentlemen commissioned from home to inspect these matters, doubtless have and will discharge their duty in that affair.'

It is not likely the Governor would have brought this matter before the Assembly, unless he was in possession of sufficient information to justify his doing so, or that the House should have refused to comply with his request in such discourteous terms, if some of the members had not in some way or other been interested in the traffic.

Leaving the French busily occupied in the construction of the fortress of Louisbourg, I propose in my next letter to give you a slight sketch of the principal incidents of the Indian War, which broke out in 1720, and raged for more than five years on the coasts and frontiers of the British provinces.[1]

[1] I have already mentioned in the foot-notes some of the authorities consulted in preparing the preceding letter. In addition to those, I may refer you to Charlevoix's *History of New France*, Garneau's *History of Canada*, Douglas's *Summary*, Prévost's *Histoire générale des Voyages*, and *Memoirs of the French and English Boundary Commissioners of* 1755.

LETTER X.

1720–1727.

As I PROPOSE to give you in this letter a sketch of the leading incidents of the Indian War, from 1720 to 1725, it will be as well to preface it with a short account of the manners and customs of the aborigines of Nova Scotia and Cape Breton, compiled from the observations of writers who were well acquainted with them at that period. The natives of America, as you are aware, were called Indians, because it was supposed, when the continent was first discovered, that it was connected with the East Indies; this mistake was soon rectified, but nevertheless, the name then applied to them has been continued down to the present day. Bands of these people were found by the early voyagers in every harbour they visited. They all evidently had a common origin, their manners and customs were similar, their physical organisation identical. We are told by Bancroft that 'one primitive language, which the French called the Algonquin, greeted the colonists of Raleigh at Roanoke and the pilgrims at Plymouth. It was heard from the Bay of Gaspé to the valley of the Des Moins; from Cape Fear to the land of the Esquimaux.' Twelve distinct tribes occupied the coast between Virginia and Gaspé. That called the Micmacs, with which we are chiefly concerned, had sole possession of Nova Scotia, the islands of Cape Breton and St. John, and the eastern coast of New Brunswick. This tribe, according to Bancroft, did not exceed 3,000. But this must be a mistake, for you will recollect that when Poutrincourt was at Port Royal in 1606, 400 Micmac warriors rendezvoused there on their way to attack a distant hostile tribe called the Armouchiquois. Now if one half of the tribe were females, and every fifth male a warrior, there could not have been more than 300 at Port Royal, even supposing every man capable of bearing arms in the whole of Nova Scotia and Cape Breton was present, which was not very likely. Besides, if it be true, as generally believed, that the Indian race has been gradually decreasing, Cape Breton alone, which constitutes scarcely a seventh part of the country occupied by the Micmacs, must have contained a population of 1,500 Indians at the beginning of the last century; for according to the census taken by the Surveyor-General of Nova Scotia in 1859, there were then 600 Indians in the island.

The American Indians have been so often described by abler pens than mine, that it is not necessary to go into much detail. I shall therefore merely point out some of the most prominent characteristics of the Micmac tribe, derived chiefly from the observations of a French writer, M. Dieréville,[1] who visited Port Royal in the year 1700, as agent of a company of merchants of Rouen. Dieréville spent a year at Port Royal, and frequently accompanied the Indians in their hunting expeditions, for the purpose of making himself acquainted with their habits, and for collecting specimens of the natural productions of the country. One hundred years of intercourse with civilised men had no doubt in some degree modified their original habits, but apparently to a small extent; for on comparing Lescarbot's account, written in 1607, with Dieréville's in 1700, very slight variations are observable. I compile my sketch from the latter account, because it was founded upon observations almost contemporary with the events I shall soon have to relate.

The chase, in Dieréville's time, was still their chief occupation and means of subsistence. Game of all kinds peculiar to the country was abundant. Moose, cariboo, and wild fowl furnished them with food; beaver, martens, otters, lynxes, &c., with valuable furs for clothing as well as for trading with the French. When out upon an expedition they would sometimes live for several days without food; but when they succeeded

[1] *Relation du Voyage du 'Port-Royal.' De l'Acadie ou de la Nouvelle-France*, 1710.

in killing a deer, they ate it in a most ravenous manner, bolting the flesh without chewing, and washing it down with copious draughts of water. Beaver were found in every stream, and proved a source of great profit to the hunters. Much skill and cunning were required to capture the beaver; its senses of hearing and smelling were so acute that it was impossible almost to shoot it. The Indians themselves possessed a fine sense of smelling; they could scent a bear at a great distance. With the firearms furnished by the French they seldom failed to procure not only food enough for themselves, but also venison and game for the garrison of Port Royal. The man who excelled in the chase was raised to a position of high rank in his tribe, and was chosen captain or chief of a hundred warriors, by whom he was respected and obeyed, both in peace and war. A young man had little chance of obtaining a wife until he had proved himself to be a good hunter. If he fell in love with a girl, he applied to her father and mother, who at once gave their consent if he was known to be successful in the chase. If there was any doubt on this point, he was required to give practical proof of his skill, by feeding the whole family of his future father-in-law with game killed by himself, for some fixed period.

The marriage ceremony was very simple. The father and mother of the girl presented her to her lover, merely saying, 'This man is thy husband.' The young couple then went into the woods to spend the honey-moon and to hunt together. The game which they killed was brought to the wigwam of the bride's father, where a feast was prepared, to which all the Indians in the vicinity were invited. Here the exploits of the ancestors of the bride and bridegroom, their courage and cunning, and all they had done for the tribe, were related to the company by the bride's father; the guests then applauded his eloquence with shouts and yells, and the marriage was declared to be consummated.

An infant, immediately after its birth, was dipped in the coldest water that could be procured, even in mid-winter, to harden it, and fish-oil, or the melted fat of some animal, was poured down its throat before it was allowed to taste its natural aliment.

Feasts were given on the following occasions:—1. On the birth of a boy. 2. On cutting his first tooth. 3. When he began to walk; and lastly, when he killed his first game. At the last, the young hunter and his parents did not partake of the game. Feasting was quite an 'institution' amongst the Micmacs. The women prepared the food, but were not allowed to eat with their husbands. A stewed 'dog' was considered one of the dantiest dishes that could be placed before a chief. A feast was a scene of great merriment; there was much noise and laughter; but, to remind the party of more serious duties in the midst of their enjoyment, an old woman would suddenly rise and recite the story of her misfortunes, telling them how, some twenty or thirty years before, her children had been killed by the English, for the purpose of keeping alive and inciting their animosity against our countrymen. When the feasting was over, the young men retired to a distance to dance and sing, whilst those who felt disposed might rest undisturbed in their wigwams. Their dances were of the most absurd description, consisting chiefly of contortions of the body and extravagant grimaces, accompanied by no other music than beating a hollow tree with a short stick.

Whilst Dieréville was at Port Royal a celebrated chief, called Sagaino, who had been ennobled by Henry IV. for his services in the wars with the English, came thither with twenty or thirty of his followers, and was regaled by the governor with pipes, tobacco, and brandy. One man filled a pipe and handed it to the chief, who took a few puffs and then passed it round to all his men. Brandy was then handed round. This, he says, was merely a prelude, as they were afterwards supplied with peas, prunes, and flour, which they stewed together in a kettle of sea-water. They ate pork uncooked, tearing it to pieces with their fingers, the chief having first selected the best parts for himself. He adds, 'It is fortunate when they can get nothing but water to drink, for when they can get brandy they make beasts of themselves: they behave as in a frenzy.'[1]

[1] The Micmacs have never been charged with cannibalism, but beyond all doubt it was not uncommon among some of the Canadian tribes. When Admiral Walker's fleet was at anchor in Spanish River, a letter from Costabelle, the

The Indians were always distinguished for their hospitality. They relieved one another in cases of necessity, and shared their food with all who required it. When suffering from the keenest hunger, one that had the good fortune to kill an animal would not eat of it alone, but carry it to his cabin and divide it equally among his family and friends. When one Indian visited another, food was always given to the visitor before any questions were asked concerning his coming. An old Indian gave Dieréville the following reason for this custom: 'If I asked for what I wanted at first, I should have to go when I had got an answer, whereas, if I said nothing about it at first, I should at any rate get something to eat, if nothing else.' Notwithstanding their irregular mode of life they often lived to a great age. Old men were treated with the greatest veneration and respect. Their advice was always sought before starting upon warlike expeditions, and if an old and helpless man was left childless, some young man of the tribe was chosen to supply the place of a son.

When the French first settled at Port Royal the Indians worshipped the Sun as their God, which they called 'Nichakaminon,' meaning 'very great.' They acknowledged him as their maker. They also believed in a demon called 'Mendon,' whom they endeavoured to propitiate by praying to him to protect them from evil. The Jesuit missionaries succeeded 'in showing them the folly of these things,' but, more than one hundred years after their conversion to Christianity, many of their old superstitions had not been eradicated. Even now some of these remain. They will allow a dying person to breathe his last only upon a bed or mattress of spruce boughs, asserting that an Indian can only die upon the kind of bed he has been used to all his life.

Although fierce and implacable in war, and inspired with

Governor of Plaisance, to Pontchartrain, the Minister at Paris, dated July 24, 1711, was discovered on board a prize brought by a cruiser into Spanish River, in which Costabelle says, in reference to the expected attack on Quebec:—'Before the arrival of Rouville [at Quebec] they had despatched more officers and people that knew all the savages of this continent, to incite them to defend and take part of a feast which they would make of English Flesh at Quebec, in case they (the English) were so incensed as to make so fatal an enterprise as is reported.'

the most vindictive feelings against their enemies, they were endowed with many gentle and amiable qualities, which might have been turned to good purposes if the Jesuit missionaries had confined their instruction to religious matters only; but these had other objects in view. Pychon says in his 'Memoirs of Cape Breton,' 'It should be our business to appoint such missionaries for the savages subject to our dominion, as are incapable of separating the interest of religion from that of the Prince; by which means they would more surely deprive the enemy of all possibility of drawing them astray.'

The French soon discovered the best means of securing the Indians to their interests.[1] They indulged their humour and inclination; force was never used, but, on the contrary, mild and reasonable persuasion, which they had discovered would prevail where harsher measures had failed. Wherever a new post was established, they associated with the Indians on terms of the greatest intimacy; they accompanied them on their hunting expeditions; danced and sang with them at their feasts; and in frequent instances intermarried with them. By such means the Indian tribes, from the confines of New England to the eastern extremity of Cape Breton, had been completely won over by the French; whilst at the same time they had been inspired with such an inveterate hatred of the English, that whenever they were called upon, the Indians promptly obeyed the summons of their allies. I cannot give you a stronger instance of French influence than the reply of an Abenaquis Chief to Governor Dudley of Massachusetts, when the latter proposed to live at peace and amity with them. 'It is well that the kings should be at peace; I

[1] 'No other Europeans have ever displayed equal talents for conciliating savages, or, it must be added, for approximating to their usages and modes of life. The French traders and hunters intermarried and mixed with the Indians at the back of our settlements, and extended their scattered posts along the whole course of the two vast rivers of that continent. Even at this day, far away on the upper waters of these mighty streams, and beyond the utmost limits reached by the backwoodsmen, the traveller discovers villages in which the aspect and social usages of the people, their festivities and solemnities, in which the white and the red man mingle on equal terms, strangely contrast with the habits of the Anglo-Americans, and announce to him, on his first approach, their Gallic origin.'—Professor Merivale's *Lectures on Colonies and Colonization*. 1861.

am contented that it should be so, and have no longer any difficulty in making peace with you. I was not the one who struck you during the last twelve years: it was the Frenchman who used my arm to strike you. We were at peace, it is true. I had even thrown away my hatchet, I know not where, and as I was reposing on my mat, thinking of nothing, the young men brought a message which the Governor of Canada had sent, and by which he said to me, "My son, the Englishman has struck me; help me to avenge myself; take the hatchet and strike the Englishman." I, who have always listened to the words of the French Governor, search for my hatchet; I find it entirely rusted; I burnish it up; I place it in my belt to go and strike. Now, the Frenchman tells me to lay it down. I therefore throw it away from me, that no one may longer see the blood with which it is reddened. Thus let us live in peace. I consent to it.'

From this it is evident that the French Viceroy might, if so disposed, have prevented many of the atrocities perpetrated about this time upon the peaceful inhabitants of New England; but he seems to have pursued an entirely opposite course, though France and England were then at peace. He informed the Indians, who still continued hostile to the English after the Treaty of Utrecht, that they were not mentioned in the treaty, from which they naturally inferred that they were an independent people, and not subjects of Great Britain. Their hostility to the English was kept alive by the Jesuit missionaries in the pay of France, 'who were continually inciting them to act vigorously, and to drive all the English beyond the Kennebec.'[1] Arms, ammunition, and clothing were annually distributed amongst them for the same purpose. All through the winter of 1720 great agitation prevailed among the Indian tribes; mischief was evidently brewing, but no open acts of hostility were committed until the month of August, when the Micmacs of Nova Scotia and Cape Breton, who 'had the character of being more savage and cruel than the other nations,'[2] first broke the peace, although there is

[1] Hutchinson's *History of Massachusetts.*
[2] Ibid.

every reason to believe that it was done by a preconcerted arrangement with the other tribes.

The harbour of Canceau, at the eastern extremity of Nova Scotia, within sight of the shores of Cape Breton, had long been used as a fishing station by the French. After the conquest of Acadié, the New England fishermen and traders resorted thither in great numbers during the summer season, where they resided in temporary dwellings, which were mostly unoccupied during the winter. They had also large warehouses for the storage of their dry fish and merchandise; but, having neither naval nor military protection, the teeming warehouses offered a tempting prize to the Indians, as they could be plundered with little trouble or risk. On August 17, 1720, a large band of Indians, collected from various quarters, without the slightest warning burst at midnight into the little village of huts occupied by the traders and fishermen. Unarmed and incapable of making any resistance, the fishermen fled in boats to their vessels at anchor in the harbour, leaving the traders and their merchandise in the hands of the Indians. Four Englishmen were killed, and the warehouses were plundered of fish and merchandise valued at 20,000*l.* currency. The Indians kept possession of the place until a number of French fishing vessels arrived on the following night and carried off the spoil. The Indians had not forgotten the lesson taught them by the Canadian Viceroy; they considered themselves an independent people, telling the traders 'that they came to carry away what they could find upon their own land.'[1] The terrified traders and fishermen made no attempt to rescue their property; but 'a sloop happening to arrive next day, the master offered his services to go out and make reprisals; being furnished with a number of men, and joined by two or three smaller vessels, he took a commission from one Thomas Richards, a Canceau Justice, went after the French, and soon brought in six or seven small fishing vessels, all having more or less of the English property on board.'[2] Mr. Henshaw, a Boston merchant, who happened to be at

[1] Hutchinson's *History of Massachusetts.*
[2] Ibid.

Canceau at the time, went to Louisbourg at the request of the fishermen, to complain to the French governor; but the latter refused to interfere, on the ground that the Indians were not French subjects. Five Frenchmen, who were taken prisoners by the captain of the sloop, were sent to Annapolis, when, upon examination before the Governor and Council, it came out that they had been sent by their employers, who resided at Petit de Grat, to bring off the plunder. Whereupon Governor Phillips sent Major Armstrong to Louisbourg with a copy of the examination, and letters to M. de St. Ovide, demanding restitution of the stolen property, and satisfaction for the lives of the four Englishmen. St. Ovide informed Major Armstrong that he had sent M. de Pensens to Isle Madame to recover the property, and seize any Frenchmen who had been engaged in the affair; and also authorised Major Armstrong himself to visit Petit de Grat for the same purpose. M. de Pensens's mission proved unsuccessful, but Major Armstrong recovered fish and merchandise belonging to the Canceau traders, valued at 1,548*l.* 18*s.*

The Indians dispersed after effecting their object.[1] One party, which had come all the way from Minas, robbed a trader called Alden, on their return to that place, in the presence of many of the inhabitants.

Canceau, owing to its proximity to Cape Breton, was so much exposed to Indian attacks that Governor Phillips sent a small detachment of soldiers to protect it. Nevertheless, on July 14, 1721, 'Captain Watkins, who was engaged on a fishing voyage at Canceau, was surprised by a small body of Indians in the night while a-bed. His lodging was on an island (Durell's Island) a little distance from the fort; and although he was strongly importuned by several of his friends

[1] The Indians gave out that the attack on Canceau was made by way of reprisal for the seizure of two French ships at that place by Captain Smart, of H.M.S. 'Squirrel,' on September 18, 1718. Captain Smart, it appears, was sent by Governor Shute, of Boston, to complain of the illegal fishing of French subjects within the English limits, but obtaining no satisfaction from M. de St. Ovide, he seized two French vessels fishing at Canceau Island on his return. M. Dubois, the French Minister, remonstrated against this seizure, but Captain Smart's conduct was approved by the British Government.—*Record Office.*

to stay with them that night, as if they had secret impulse of some impending evil, yet all the arguments they could use could no ways prevail or influence him. He was a gentleman of singular good temper, respected and lamented by all that knew him. John Drew of Portsmouth (a pretty youth) was slain with him at the same time.'[1]

In the summer of 1722, the Indians captured sixteen vessels belonging to Massachusetts, on the southern coast of Nova Scotia. Nine of the fishermen were deliberately murdered in cold blood; all the rest were carried off prisoners to Malagash (Lunenburg). The news of this outrage caused great alarm at Canceau. Governor Phillips, who fortunately happened to be there at the time, immediately despatched two vessels manned with volunteers, under the command of John Elliot and John Robinson, in pursuit of the Indians. Proceeding along the coast, Elliot discovered seven of the captured vessels in a small harbour, and coming upon them by surprise, retook the whole and killed a great number of the Indians. Robinson also retook two of the captured vessels and killed several Indians. Those which escaped fled to Malagash, where a number of the fishermen were kept in close confinement. The Indians, exasperated at the loss of so many of their companions, were just on the point of putting the prisoners to death, when Captain Blinn, who had once been a prisoner in their hands, and for some cause or other had gained their friendship, arrived in a small vessel at Malagash, and ransomed the fishermen.[2]

In 1724, a band of sixty Indians had the audacity to attack Annapolis, when two soldiers were killed and four others dangerously wounded. In the same year an Acadian vessel, which had been seized by the Commandant of Canceau for illicitly carrying a cargo of cattle from Bay Verte to Louisbourg, was boarded by a party of Indians whilst lying at anchor in the night, in the Gut of Canceau, when the whole of the prize crew, consisting of a sergeant and eight soldiers, were either killed or made prisoners. The Governor of Nova Scotia, having reason to believe that the Indians were instigated to commit these out-

[1] Penhallow's *History of the Indian Wars.* 1859.
[2] Hutchinson's *History of Massachusetts.*

rages, and supplied with arms and ammunition by the French, sent Captain Bradstreet and Mr. Newton to Louisbourg in the month of August, 1725, to remonstrate with M. de St. Ovide on these and other outrages. The deputation, on its return, reported that St. Ovide denied all knowledge of the outrages complained of, and professed to be very friendly to the English; but the Council, notwithstanding, resolved 'that St. Ovide's reply was trifling, his promises of friendship not to be depended upon, and that no credit should be given to his pretended ignorance, there being too much proof to the contrary.'[1]

The Abenaquis Indians were not long in following the example set by the Micmacs. Having concerted measures with some neighbouring tribes for expelling the English settlers from their farms on the Kennebec, every village sent a quota of warriors to Norridgewock, the head-quarters of the Abenaquis, where a large force was soon collected. Spreading thence along the frontier of New England, they ravaged the settlements, burning houses and barns, and murdering the terror-struck inhabitants in cold blood. It would occupy too much of my space to enumerate even a tithe of the atrocities committed by these savages during the five years ending in 1726. I shall content myself with quoting Bancroft's eloquent and touching description of the sufferings of the people of New England in those troublous times. 'The Indians,' he says, 'were secret as beasts of prey, skilful marksmen, and in part provided with firearms, fleet of foot, patient of fatigue, and mad with a passion for rapine, vengeance, and destruction, retreating into swamps and fastnesses, or hiding in the greenwood thickets, where the leaves muffled the eyes of the pursuer. By the rapidity of their descent, they seemed omnipresent among the scattered villages, which they ravaged like a passing storm, and for a full year they kept all New England in a state of terror and excitement. The exploring party was waylaid and cut off, and the mangled carcases and disjointed limbs of the dead were hung upon the trees to terrify pursuers. The labourers in the field, the reapers as they went forth to the harvest, men as they went to the mill, the shepherd's boy among the sheep, were shot down

[1] Quoted by Murdoch, from *Archives of Nova Scotia.*

by skulking foes, whose approach was invisible. Who can tell the heavy hours of woman! The mother, if left in the house, feared the tomahawk for herself and children. On the sudden attack, the husband would fly with one child, the wife with another, and perhaps one only escape; the village cavalcade, making its way to meeting on Sunday in files on horseback, the farmer holding the bridle in one hand, and a child in the other, his wife seated on a pillion behind him, as was the fashion in those days, could not proceed safely, but, at the moment when least expected, bullets would whiz amongst them, discharged with fatel aim from an ambuscade by the wayside. The forest that protected the ambush of the Indians secured their retreat. They hung upon the skirts of the English villages "like the lightning on the edge of the clouds."'

Detachments of soldiers sent in pursuit rarely succeeded in overtaking the bands of Indians, who, after ravaging a village, instantly retreated into the depths of the forest. A reward of 15*l.*—afterwards increased to 100*l.*—was offered by the Governor of Massachusetts for every Indian scalp or captive brought in, but no really important effect was produced until the year 1724, when it was wisely decided to attack the Indians in their head quarters at Norridgewock, where the Jesuit Ralle resided. Ralle had been employed by the Viceroy of Canada to instigate the Indians to begin the war, as was clearly proved by his correspondence, which was seized by Captain Moulton in 1722. Hutchinson says 'he was ranked by the English amongst the most infamous villains, and his scalp would have been worth a hundred scalps of the Indians. His intrepid courage and fervent zeal to promote the religion he professed, and to secure his neophytes or converts to the interest of his sovereign, were the principal cause of these prejudices. The French, for the same reason, rank him with saints and heroes.'

An expedition, consisting of four companies of militia, commanded by Captain Harman, reached Taconic, on the Kennebec, on August 20, and came upon the village of Norridgewock by surprise two days afterwards. The village was defended by fifty warriors, who after a short conflict were defeated with great slaughter. The priest Ralle was unfortunately killed, although strict orders had been given to spare his life. Hutchinson says, Ralle had shut himself up in a wigwam, from which he fired and wounded a soldier, which so exasperated Lieutenant Jaques, that he burst open the door and shot the priest in the head. The Jesuit father, La Chasse, says he was shot at the foot of the Cross, which stood in the centre of the village, whither he had gone in the hope of allaying the tumult, by a volley from the English.[1]

The successful termination of this attack produced the best results. The loss of so many warriors, including six chiefs of great note, humbled the whole tribe. Utterly routed and dispersed, the Abenaquis gave little further trouble to the English settlers. 'From the day of the attack on Norridgewock, the tribe of that name was blotted out from the list of the Indian nations.'[2] They made, indeed, a feeble attempt to renew the war in the following spring, but finding that the English had adopted their own system of tactics with decided success, and that all hopes of driving the colonists across the Kennebec had vanished, they wisely proposed to make peace. The governors of the English provinces gladly accepted their advances; commissioners from the several colonies met the chiefs of the Indian tribes at Boston in November, when the terms of the peace were satisfactorily arranged. The most important condition of this treaty was the acknowledgment of the sovereignty of Great Britain. The French authorities, however, did not regard it with much favour. Beauharnois, the Viceroy of Canada, was so much displeased with the Indians for making peace, that he refused to send them the usual presents, and threatened to withdraw the missionaries. In the beginning of 1727, the missionaries, no doubt by instructions from head-quarters, endeavoured to persuade the Indians at Minas and Beaubassin to renew the war, but happily without effect. A long peace followed, interrupted only by some slight outrages not worth mentioning.

Sad and solemn must have been the reflections of the scattered remnants of the Abenaquis, as they ofttimes floated

[1] Kip's *Lives of the Jesuits.* [2] Ibid.

past the blackened ruins of the chapel of Norridgewock in their frail canoes. The scene has been described in touching language by an American poet. I give you an extract, hoping it may induce you to peruse the whole of Whittier's beautiful poem of 'Mogg Megone:'

> No wigwam smoke is curling there;
> The very earth is scorched and bare;
>
> . . . .
>
> And here and there on the blackening ground,
> White bones are glittering in the sun.
> And where the house of prayer arose,
> And the holy hymn at daylight's close,
> And the aged priest stood up to bless
> The children of the wilderness,
> There is naught save ashes sodden and dank,
> And the birchen boats of the Norridgewock,
> Tethered to tree, and stump, and rock,
> Rotting along the river bank!

LETTER XI.

1727–1744.

DURING the long peace following the Treaty of Utrecht, interrupted only by the Indian war (of which I gave you a short account in my last letter), both the French and English colonies in America made rapid progress. In Canada, the clearing and cultivation of the land were fostered and encouraged by the able and intelligent men who held the office of Viceroy during that happy state of tranquillity. Contiguous farms or clearings spread along both banks of the St. Lawrence, from Quebec to Montreal, and far up many of its tributaries; whilst even on the remote and secluded shores of Erie and Ontario, immigrants from Old France were rapidly forming agricultural settlements in the vicinity of the forts and trading stations. The savage Iroquois, who ever since the time of Champlain had been inveterate enemies of the French, were at length appeased and conciliated by the tact and ability of the Chevalier de Beauharnois, who administered the government for the unusual period of twenty years, ending in 1746. The fur trade, too, which had in a great measure been engrossed by the colonists of the province of New York, was by the introduction of a more liberal system of barter once more attracted to Montreal, which became the great mart of this lucrative branch of commerce.

By the permission of the Iroquois, the French erected several forts within their territory, destined to form part of a chain of posts connecting Canada with Louisiana. According to Rameau, the population of Canada, which in 1713 was only 18,169, had in 1739 reached 42,924.

Nova Scotia, although almost wholly occupied by a population of aliens, felt the beneficial effects of the peace. The fishery, carried on at Canceau by the people of New England, employed from 1,500 to 2,000 men during the summer season. In the year 1733, the exports of dry fish from that place amounted to 46,000 quintals; and the whale fishery, which had been recently established there, gave great promise of success. The Acadians, who were chiefly settled at Minas, Chignecto, and other places on the Bay of Fundy, disposed of their fish, oils, furs, &c. to the Boston traders in exchange for articles of British manufacture, and of their cattle and farm produce to the Louisbourg traders at Bay Verte, from whence an active but illicit traffic was carried on in defiance of the orders of the English governors. The coal mines at Chignecto were also leased at this time to a Boston Company.[1] Nothing seemed now to be wanting to ensure the prosperity of the province but a population of Englishmen, the only permanent residents being the Governor and Council, a few other officers and traders with their families, and a garrison of 150 men at Annapolis. Extensive grants of land were offered to induce settlers to come from New England, but without success, as it was generally believed that all the most fertile lands in the province were occupied by the Acadians. There was in reality a good reason for this belief, as we learn by a letter from Governor Armstrong, in 1730, to the Board of Trade, 'that the French are becoming a formidable body, and, like Noah's progeny, are spreading themselves over the face of the province.' He adds, 'All the Acadians, with the exception of five or six families on the eastern coast, have consented to take a simple and unconditional oath of allegiance,' but considers 'that the peace of the country was only thus settled so long as England and France were in alliance, and no longer.'

The Indians, who had for several years given no trouble to the English Governor, about this time (1732) began to exhibit great restlessness, and to commit daring outrages in various quarters. They plundered and destroyed the buildings and magazine erected by the Mining Company at Chignecto, and even compelled the Government to abandon the design of

[1] The Company obtained a grant of 4,000 acres, subject to a quit-rent of one penny per acre. The royalty on the coal raised was eighteen pence per chaldron.

building a blockhouse at Minas. Colonel Armstrong, who was at this time Lieutenant-Governor of the province, informed the Board of Trade that these outrages were committed at the instigation of M. de St. Ovide, the Governor of Louisbourg; but this, apparently, was mere surmise.

There is, however, no doubt but that the Viceroy of Canada had not given up all hopes of recovering Acadié, as he was regularly furnished by the missionaries with returns of the number of French inhabitants in every parish. The last census, which Rameau says was taken *secretly* in 1737, made the French population of Nova Scotia 7,598, having trebled in thirty years. The French were evidently preparing for hostilities; for in addition to the works at Louisbourg, which they were now pushing on with great vigour, military posts were established at St. Peter's and in St. John's Island, overlooking the coasts of Nova Scotia, and commanding the communication between Canceau and Bay Verte. To oppose these, England had only two miserable garrisons at Canceau and Annapolis, which together could not muster 300 men.[1] The weak and defenceless condition of the country had been repeatedly brought to the notice of the British ministry by the local governors, but without any effect. The position of the Governor of Nova Scotia at this period must have been an unenviable one. Surrounded by a disaffected population, and a tribe of savages ready to embark in any undertaking which promised plunder and profit, at the instigation of missionaries appointed and paid by a foreign government; with no subjects of his own nation to aid him in the hour of need; with two weak garrisons at situations so far apart that their forces could never be united in an emergency; and with the constant worry and irritation to which he was daily subjected in his capacity of chief magistrate of a community composed of petty officials and small traders, it is no wonder that Colonel Armstrong sank under the weight, and rashly terminated his life with his own hand on December 6, 1739.

[1] In 1739, there were at Louisbourg 800, at St. Peter's sixty, and at St. John's Island sixty regular troops; while, at the same time, England had barely 200 at Annapolis, and 100 at Canceau.

Major Mascarene, who assumed the administration of the Government on the death of Colonel Armstrong, soon found that the office was no sinecure. The Indians were daily growing more insolent, and rumours of approaching war with France were rife in the colonies, but no heed was paid by the British minister to Mascarene's remonstrances on the miserable condition of the defences of the important post of Canceau, only seven leagues distant from Cape Breton, and liable to be taken by surprise the moment war should be declared. Mascarene's opinion on this matter was soon verified by events which will be brought under your notice in a future letter. We must now turn to the affairs of Cape Breton, which will in future occupy the greatest share of our attention.

The history of Louisbourg at this period is emphatically the history of the whole island. For more than twenty years the French Government devoted all its energy and resources to one object—the completion of the fortifications. Even the English colonies contributed a great proportion of the materials used in their construction. When Messrs. Newton and Bradstreet, who were sent to confer with M. de St. Ovide, as already related (p. 164), returned to Annapolis, they reported that during their short stay at Louisbourg, in 1725, fourteen colonial vessels, belonging chiefly to New England, arrived there with cargoes of boards, timber, and bricks. It has often been stated that all the materials used in the fortifications and public buildings were brought from France; if you go into a fisherman's hut on the coast, he will tell you that his chimney is built of bricks brought from Louisbourg, which originally came from France. To some extent this may be correct; but you may rest assured the French engineers obtained them chiefly from New England at a much cheaper rate. The trade was a profitable one, and was prosecuted by the colonists, regardless of the consequences, namely, the construction of a fortress which soon became 'a national nuisance.'[1] The Acadians of Nova Scotia, certainly with more reasonable excuse, shared in the lucrative business of supplying the wants of the workmen, having in 1731 sent from 300 to 400 head of cattle, besides sheep and other pro-

[1] Douglas's *Summary*.

visions, chiefly from Minas and Bay Verte. To make themselves independent of supplies from foreign countries, the Governor of Louisbourg offered great inducements to the French inhabitants of Nova Scotia to remove to the island of St. John's, where the facility of clearing the land, and the fertility of the soil, it was hoped, would soon enable them to supply all that was needed. The first immigrants, who came to the island in 1719, were fishermen, who settled at Port le Joye (Charlotte Town) and Havre St. Pierre, but those who followed them in 1726 were farmers, who brought their cattle and effects. In 1735 the total number of inhabitants was 542.

It is rather extraordinary, considering the estimation in which it was held by the Government, that so little information can be found in the works of French authors concerning Louisbourg, from the date of its foundation in 1720 to the siege in 1745. The only event of any importance recorded in the pages of Charlevoix, is the disastrous wreck of 'Le Chameau,' of sixty guns, which occurred on the night of August 25, 1725. This unfortunate ship struck on a rock near Louisbourg, on her way from France to Quebec, and became a total wreck—not a single man was saved. Among the passengers were M. de Chazel, the new Intendant of Canada, M. de Louvigny, the newly appointed Governor of Trois Rivières, a son of M. de Ramezay, the late Governor of Montreal, a number of officials belonging to the colony, and several ecclesiastics. On the following morning the shore near Louisbourg was strewn with dead bodies. 'This misfortune,' we are told by Charlevoix, 'in the course of a single night brought more grief and loss upon the French colonies than they had suffered during twenty years of warfare.' The pilot on board the 'Chameau' was the same that had charge of the ship in which Charlevoix went to Canada in 1720, when he so narrowly escaped shipwreck on the coast of Newfoundland.

Although it was considered by the French engineers that they could hold the whole island by fortifying Louisbourg, as it was 'so very woody, that on whatever part the enemy should make a descent, there was no access to it by land,'[1]

[1] D'Ulloa's *Voyage to South America*. See note, p. 174.

it was, nevertheless, deemed advisable to erect small outlying forts at St. Peter's and St. Anne's. The former, situated on the isthmus separating St. Peter's Bay from the Labrador Lakes, was a post of great importance; 'being no more than eighteen leagues from Louisbourg and twenty-five from the island of St. John by the Lake of Labrador, it is of course the centre of communication to the whole island. From thence one may observe the least motion of the English, either at Canceau or in the Passage of Fronsac; and advice may be sent to the Commandant at Louisbourg in less than eighteen hours.'[1] The erection of a fort at St. Peter's did not escape the notice of the Lieutenant-Governor of Nova Scotia, who informed the President of the Board of Trade, in 1733, that, 'the French were very assiduous in carrying on their fortifications at the island of St. John's, at the Bay of Verte, and at St. Peter's, about six or seven leagues distant from Canceau.' At the same time he strongly urged the necessity of fortifying Canceau.

Great exertions were made to establish a fixed population in Louisbourg and its immediate vicinity, for the purpose of furnishing materials for a militia to support the garrison in time of need.[2] To prevent the fishermen who came out every spring from returning to France, an ordonnance was promulgated, which compelled the master of every ship going to America to take out a certain number of men, in proportion to the tonnage of his ship, bound to remain there for a term of three years. These men, who were called 'Engagés,' generally remained in the colony after their term of service had expired.[3] As it was sometimes impossible to hire the number required, the captains of vessels are said to have kidnapped

[1] Pychon's *Letters on Cape Breton and St. John's Islands.*

[2] With this object in view, distant settlements did not receive much encouragement, but nevertheless they were gradually rising up in favourable localities for fishing. In 1729, a large church, of which the foundations may still be seen, was erected at Niganiche (now called Ingonishe). In the year 1849, a church bell weighing more than 200 lbs. was found there, buried in the sand upon the beach. The following inscription was engraved upon it:—'Pour la paroisse de Niganiche j'ai été nominée par Jean Décarette et par François Urail, parrain et marraine. La Fosse Huet de St.-Malo m'a faite l'an 1729.'

[3] Pychon.

men on the coast of Normandy to complete their quotas. Pychon, who resided several years in Louisbourg, says the greater part of the inhabitants came out as 'Engagés,' and that many of them 'made the best figure in the colony.' The fixed population of Louisbourg, according to the Abbé Prevost, was about 4,000 when war broke out in 1744.

The rapid increase of the commerce of Louisbourg fully verified the predictions of the Messrs. Raudots (see p. 145). D'Ulloa gives us some interesting information concerning it in his 'Voyage to South America.'[1] He says, 'The principal, if not the only trade of Louisbourg, is the Cod Fishery, from which vast profits accrue to the inhabitants, not only on account of the abundance of this fish, but because the neighbouring seas afford the best of any about Newfoundland. Their wealth (and some persons among them were in very prosperous circumstances), consisted in their storehouses, some of which were within the fort, others scattered along the shore, and in their number of fishing barks; of these more than one inhabitant owned forty or fifty, which daily went on this fishery, carrying three or four men each, who received a settled salary, but were at the same time obliged to deliver a certain number of standard fish. So the cod storehouses never failed of being filled by the time the ships resorted thither from most of the ports of France, laden with provisions and other goods, with which the inhabitants provided themselves in exchange for their fish, or consigned it to be sold in

[1] Don Antonio D'Ulloa, a captain in the Spanish navy, accompanied the French Academicians to Peru, in the year 1735, to measure an arc of the meridian under the equator. He sailed from Callao in October, 1744, in a French ship called the 'Notre Dame de la Délivrance,' in company with the 'Louis Érasme' and the 'Marquis d'Antin.' All the ships had a large amount of treasure on board, stowed away under the cocoa with which they were laden. On July 21, 1745, when off the Azores, they fell in with the English privateers 'Prince Frederic' and 'Duke.' After a smart action of three hours, the 'Louis Érasme' and 'Marquis d'Antin' struck their colours. Whilst the privateers were engaged in securing their prizes, the 'Délivrance' crowded all sail, and steered for Louisbourg. On August 12 she made the island of Scatari, and on the following morning was captured by a ship of war off the mouth of the harbour. Ulloa resided two months at Louisbourg. He has given us some very interesting particulars concerning the place, its trade, the Indians, &c., of which I shall avail myself in the following pages. Ulloa's work was published in 1758.

France on their own account. Likewise, vessels from the French colonies of St. Domingo and Martinique brought sugar, tobacco, coffee, rum, &c. and returned loaded with cod. Any surplus, after Louisbourg was supplied, found a vent in Canada, where the return was made in beaver skins and other kinds of fine furs. Thus Louisbourg, with no other resources than the fishery, carried on a large and regular commerce both with Europe and America.'

A considerable traffic, as has been already mentioned, was maintained with the English colonies. The New England traders, who brought fruit, vegetables, oats, shingles, bricks, &c., in payment of their purchases of West India produce, at the same time introduced many contraband articles, such as flour, meal, biscuit, dry goods, and codfish. Whole cargoes of codfish were sometimes transferred from English to French vessels, under the cover of night, in Louisbourg harbour,[1] whilst in the outports, where there were no Custom-house officers, and on the coast of Newfoundland, this contraband trade was carried on without any attempt at concealment. The English fishermen, unhampered by harassing restrictions, and supplied with outfits at reasonable rates, were able to sell their fish to the French traders at prices much below the current value in Louisbourg. In the year 1740, according to a report sent to the Lords Commissioners of Trade by Captain Smith of H.M.S. 'Eltham'—the guardship at Canceau—48 schooners and 393 chaloups were employed in the cod fisheries of Cape Breton, at the following places:—

			Quintals.
At Louisbourg,	42 Schooners	which caught	25,200
"	200 Chalouts	"	40,000
Niganiche	64 "	"	13,500
Scatari	6 Schooners	"	3,600
"	18 Chaloups	"	4,500
Baleine	30 "	"	6,000
Lorambec	12 "	"	2,400
Fourchu	19 "	"	5,700
St. Esprit	23 "	"	6,900
Isle Michaux	5 "	"	1,250
Petit de Grat	18 "	"	4,500
L'Indienne	14 "	"	3,500
		Total	117,050

The number of fishermen was 2,445.

[1] Pychon's *Memoirs of Cape Breton.*

Yet, in spite of this apparent prosperity, we are told by Garneau[1] that the greater part of the inhabitants languished in misery. Trade and the fisheries enriched a few, but thousands lived in indigence, on account of the high prices charged for salt and provisions, and the exorbitant rate of interest (often as much as 25 per cent.) imposed upon the succours required by needy fishermen. These had no other resource to fly to, as the clearing and cultivation of the soil was discouraged by those who were making large profits from their ill-requited services.

The Government of Cape Breton (which embraced the Island of St. John's[2]) was constituted on the model of that of Canada. It consisted of a Governor or Commandant, a Commissary or Intendant, a Supreme Council, an Inferior Court or Bailiwick, and a Court of Admiralty.

The Governor had the direction of all the affairs relating to the security of the colony, and the command of the military establishment, consisting of the King's Lieutenant, a Major and Aid-major, a regiment of French regulars, and two companies of the Swiss regiment of Karrer.

The Intendant had charge of the military chest, ammunition, provisions, and stores of all kinds. He was entrusted with the administration of justice in civil matters, and could at any time call upon the Governor for the aid of the military to carry out the decisions of the courts if necessary.

In many important matters, such as the direction of the police, the granting of lands, the erection of fortifications, and the maintenance of religion and order, the Governor and Intendant possessed equal and joint authority. This arrangement, as Pychon justly observes, 'is suitable only to such countries as are within reach of the eye of the sovereign; for should there happen to be any clashing between these officers about their respective jurisdictions, it would lay a foundation for a perpetual quarrel and animosity if either of them should not

[1] Garneau's *Histoire du Canada.*

[2] The Lieutenant-Governor of St. John's Island, who received his orders from the Governor of Cape Breton, resided at Port la Joye (Charlotte Town), where he had a garrison of fifty or sixty men.

be thoroughly honest, and much more so, if neither of them was endued with a disposition to promote the general good.'

The Supreme Council was composed of the Governor, the Lieutenant-Governor (or King's Lieutenant), the Intendant, the Attorney-General, and four or five other persons chosen from among the merchants of Louisbourg. This Council, of which the Intendant was President, was entrusted with the administration of justice throughout the colony and its dependencies.

The Inferior Court, or Bailiwick, was composed of a judge, the Attorney-General, a secretary, and tipstaff. Its jurisdiction was chiefly confined to such matters as came under the cognisance of the police of the colony.[1]

The Admiralty Court consisted of a lieutenant, the Attorney-General, a clerk, and a tipstaff. Its principal duties were the prevention of illicit commerce, the entry and clearance of merchandise, and visiting and examining cargoes that arrived from foreign parts.

The spiritual affairs of the colony were administered by six missionaries, aided by six friars or religious brothers, who had charge of the hospital, and by some nuns from Quebec, who superintended the education of young females. One of these missionaries, the Abbé Mallard, had the exclusive charge of the Indians of Cape Breton and St. John's Islands. Ulloa says the Indians whom he saw at Louisbourg 'not only resemble those of Peru in complexion, but there is also a considerable affinity betwixt their manners and customs; the only visible difference is in stature, and in this the advantage lies on the side of the inhabitants of these northern climates. .... They were not absolutely subject to the King of France —they acknowledged him lord of the country, but did not alter their mode of living nor submit to his laws. So far from paying tribute, they received annually from France a quantity of apparel, gunpowder, muskets, brandy, and several kinds of tools, in order to keep them quiet and attached to French

[1] Pychon complains that this Court was destitute of the means of executing its decrees, as 'we have neither a common hangman, nor a tormentor (to rack criminals), nor so much as a jail.'

interests. For the same end priests were sent amongst them for instructing them in the Christian religion, and performing divine service and all the other offices of the church, as baptisms, burials, &c. And as the end to be answered was of the highest importance to French commerce, the persons chosen for these religious expeditions were men of parts, elocution, graceful carriage, and irreproachable lives; and accordingly they behaved with that prudence, condescension, and gentleness towards the Indians under their care, that besides the universal veneration paid to their persons, their converts looked upon them as their fathers, and with all the tenderness of filial affection shared with them what they caught in hunting, and the produce of their fields.' When the Indians came to Louisbourg to receive the King's presents, they sometimes hired themselves to the merchants; but soon growing weary of restraint, they returned to their hunting grounds, often accompanied by the Abbé in their immigrations from place to place. Upon going to a new place where they intended to make some stay, their first care was to build a wigwam and chapel for their priest. If all that Pychon tells us be true, the labours of the Indian missionaries at Louisbourg were devoted to less praiseworthy objects than the religious instruction of their converts. He says, 'their continual employment was to spirit up the minds of the people to fanaticism and revenge,' and to teach the poor savages 'that the English were enemies of God and companions of the devil, and since they did not choose to adopt the same way of thinking as the French, it was their duty to do them as much mischief as possible.' Pychon, as I will show you in the sequel, is not a very good authority on some subjects; but as his statements are corroborated by evidence from other quarters, there is good reason to admit their accuracy. We find even the Abbé Mallard himself, who after the fall of Louisbourg had retired to St. John's Island, endeavouring in 1747 to induce the Indians of that island to go to Louisbourg to attack six English houses which had been built outside the town.[1]

I must now direct your attention to a more important part

[1] Quoted from New York documents by Murdoch, in his *History of Nova Scotia*.

of my subject—the defences of Louisbourg, which the French Government considered impregnable. To give you a clear idea of their strength, and the position of the fortress, I must refer you to the map of the island at the end of this volume. You will observe that the first land made by a vessel coming from Europe, supposing a good reckoning has been kept, is the low rocky island of Scatari. If she is bound for Louisbourg, steering westerly with Scatari on the starboard, she will run close past a large rock covered with waving grass, elevated some fifty feet above the level of the sea, called Port Nova Island, which is connected by a reef of sunken rocks, easily distinguished by sheets of foaming breakers, with a low point, about a mile to the northward. This low point, perhaps, would hardly be noticed by a passing voyager; it is nevertheless a spot of some note. 'Heere diuers of our men went on land vpon the very Cape' (see p. 40), the very cape from which the island of Cape Breton derives its name. Two miles to the westward there is a small harbour, now called Baleine, the 'Port aux Baleines' of former days, where Lord Ochiltree established his settlement in 1629, from which he was so rudely expelled by Captain Daniel of Dieppe. Hence to the entrance of Louisbourg Harbour, a distance of barely two leagues, there are not less than three small ports well adapted for fishing and coasting craft. Just off the last of these—Big Loran or Lorambec—lies the sunken rock on which the ship of war 'Le Chameau' was wrecked in 1725. The aspect of the coast, from the Cape to the point on the east side of the entrance of Louisbourg Harbour, on which stood the lighthouse, is bleak, rugged, and desolate, presenting in front a range of rocky precipices, backed by a broken hilly country, rising in some places to a height of 250 feet, partially covered by woods of stunted spruce and birch. Approaching the harbour from the eastward, the most conspicuous object was of course the city, surrounded by massive walls bristling with cannon. Standing out like sentries in advance of the fortress, are three small rocky islands protecting the harbour from the swell of the Atlantic. Upon one of these, called Goat Island, there was a battery mounting thirty 28-pounder guns.

The harbour of Louisbourg, which is two miles in length and half a mile in width, with a depth of three to six fathoms, communicates with the open ocean by a channel only half a mile in length and one-third of a mile in width, having a depth of six to ten fathoms. A vessel arriving on the coast with a favourable wind, can reach safe anchorage in a few minutes after passing the lighthouse. This great facility of access, without any intervening bay or roadstead, was probably one of the principal reasons why Louisbourg harbour was chosen in preference to St. Anne's. Vessels can ride at anchor with safety in all parts of the harbour, although there is some agitation immediately in front of the town during easterly gales, when the rocky coast outside and the islands at the entrance, not more than half a mile distant, are exposed to the unbroken fury of the waves, and enveloped in immense sheets of surging foam. On the north-west shore, directly facing the entrance of the harbour, stood the Grand or Royal Battery, armed with twenty-eight 42-pounder and two 18-pounder guns. This battery, protected by a moat and bastions on the land side, was said, when garrisoned by 200 men, to be capable of successfully resisting a besieging force of ten times that number. It completely covered the entrance of the harbour, as its guns could rake the decks of any ship attempting to force the passage. On the shore just opposite the Grand Battery, there was a careening wharf, in a snug sheltered cove, for heaving down ships of the largest class, and near the mouths of the small streams, at the head of the north-east arm, a long range of wooden buildings for warehousing provisions and naval stores. From thence to the Barachois, at the other end of the harbour, the shore was dotted at close intervals by the huts and stages of the fishermen. Rugged hills covered with scrub, terminating in rocky precipices at the water's edge, bordered the eastern shore of the harbour, from the lighthouse to the head of the north-east arm. On the north-western shore, with the exception of small patches of cleared land near the huts of the fishermen and around the Grand Battery, the low range called the Green Hills, extending southerly as far as Gabarus Bay, was still covered by the primeval forest.

By referring to the 'Map of the Harbour and Environs of Louisbourg,' at a future page, you will observe that the town, situated upon the tongue or promontory lying between the south shore of the harbour and the sea, occupied, including the walls, an irregular quadrilateral area of about 100 acres. The site of the town was elevated some twenty or thirty feet above the sea, but the ground outside the walls was low and marshy, with here and there small ponds and rocky knolls. This broken swampy ground, which extended in one direction to the foot of the Green Hills, and in the other nearly as far as White Point, presented great obstacles to the advance of a besieging army. The walls or defences, which extended from the Western Gate on the harbour side nearly to Black Point on the sea-shore, a distance of 1,200 yards, were constructed according to the 'First System' of the celebrated French engineer, Vauban. As many of you may never have had an opportunity of seeing works of this description, I beg to submit the annexed section or profile for your information:—

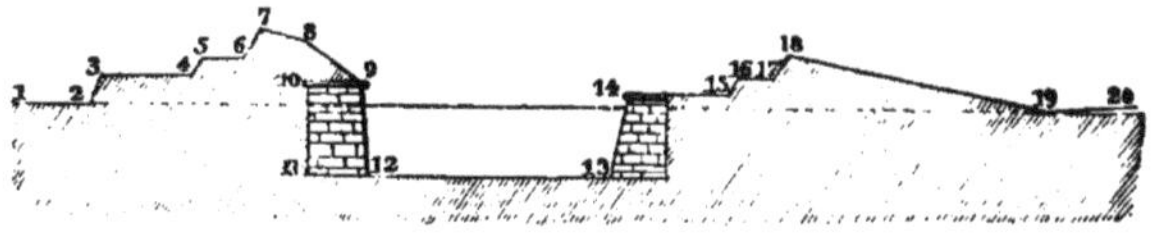

The line 1, 2, represents the level of the streets.

The outline of the Rampart is shown by the irregular figure 2, 3, 4, 5, 6, 7, 8, 9.

2, 3. Is the Inner Slope of the Rampart.

3, 4. The Terre Pleine or Platform upon which the cannon were mounted, 14 feet above the line 1, 2, and 25 feet in width.

5, 6. The Banquette, a level space five feet in width, three feet above the Terre Pleine. Musketeers standing on the Banquette can fire over the top of the Parapet.

6, 7. The Parapet, a breastwork five feet higher than the Banquette. The Parapet is pierced at certain intervals by openings called Embrasures, through which the cannon are discharged.

7, 8. The top of the Parapet sloping outwards, to enable the musketeers stationed on the Banquette to fire upon an enemy that may have gained a footing in the Covered Way, 14, 15, on the opposite side of the Ditch, 12, 13.

8, 9. The Outer Slope of the Rampart, resting upon the Wall or Escarp. The whole of the Rampart, from 2 to 9, is composed of earth covered with sods.

9, 10, 11, 12. The Escarp, or Wall, of strong masonry 10 or 12 feet in thickness, facing the Ditch. Its height at Louisbourg varied from 30 to 36 feet, according to the irregularity of the surface.

12, 13. The Ditch. At Louisbourg it was 80 feet in width.

13, 14. The Counterscarp, or sustaining Wall, of solid masonry, on the other side of the Ditch.

14, 15. A level space 20 feet in width, called the Covered Way, upon which a body of troops can be assembled ready to make a sortie upon an enemy's trenches.

15, 16. The Slope of the Banquette.

16, 17. The Banquette, four feet in width, and four feet above the Covered Way.

17. 18. A Parapet four feet in height, from which musketeers assembled in the Covered Way can fire over the crest of the Glacis upon the enemy.

18, 19. The Glacis, a bank of earth sloping gradually outwards until it meets the natural surface of the ground. It must be carried out far enough to enable the musketeers stationed behind the Parapet 6, 7, to sweep its sloping surface with their fire.

19, 20. The natural surface of the ground beyond the Glacis, generally on a level, as shown by the dotted line 1, 20, with the base of the Rampart.

If you refer to the 'Plan of the Town and Fortifications of Louisbourg,' at page 185, and the table of references annexed, you will observe that there were two bastions and two demi-bastions on the south-west or land front of the fortress, armed with heavy guns, and a circular battery of sixteen 24-pounders commanding the West Gate. Also two bastions on the eastern front, facing Point Rochefort, and another on the gravel beach, facing the harbour.

The north front of the town, facing the harbour, was defended by a strong wall of masonry, with parapet and banquette for musketeers, extending from the Batterie de la Grève to the West Gate, pierced by five gates leading from the town to the wharves.

The only portions of the circuit of the town unprotected by strong and permanent defensive works, were two intervals of about two hundred yards each between the Princess and Bourillon Bastions, and the Maurepas and De la Grève Bastions. The first of these intervals was enclosed by a pallisading and ditch, and protected from assault by the shallow water and rocky shoals lying between Point Rochefort and Black Point. The second was occupied by a deep pond, crossed by a temporary wooden bridge, which could easily be removed when required. Both of these spaces being covered by the collateral fire of the flanks of the adjoining bastions, no other defensive works were deemed necessary.

The principal entrance to the town was through the West Gate, over a drawbridge covered by the guns of the Circular and Dauphin Batteries. Access from the land side also was obtained by means of temporary bridges across the ditch, for the use of the garrison in making sorties during a siege; at other times they were open for the use of the inhabitants generally.

All the authorities I have consulted agree that in the circuit of the walls there were embrasures for 148 guns, but they differ widely respecting the number of guns actually mounted, some saying there were only sixty, others more than a hundred. As seventy-six fell into the hands of the victors, and some must have been burst or destroyed by the enemy's fire, we may reasonably conclude that the armament of the fortress at the commencement of the siege exceeded eighty guns, exclusive of those in the Grand and Island Batteries.[1]

The most conspicuous object within the walls was a stone building called the Citadel, standing in the gorge of the King's Bastion, with a moat next the town. It was provided with a glacis and covered way, and a parapet for musketeers, but had no artillery. The entrance from the town to the Citadel was over a drawbridge, with a guardhouse on one side and advanced sentinels on the other. Within the Citadel were apartments for the governor, barracks for the garrison, an arsenal, and a chapel which served as the parish church. There was also under the platform, or terre pleine, a magazine well furnished at all times with military stores. The other public buildings within the walls were a general storehouse, an ordnance storehouse, an arsenal, and powder magazine. The nunnery and hospital of St. Jean de Dieu were situated in the centre of the city. The latter, which had a church belonging to it, was an elegant and spacious structure, built entirely with stone.

The town was well laid out in wide regular streets, crossing each other at right angles, six running in an east and west,

[1] Captain Towry, of H.M.S. 'Shoreham'—the guardship at Canceau in 1735—reported to the Lords Commissioners of Trade, that he found at Louisbourg 48 guns at the Grand Battery, 26 on the Island, 24 at the Dauphin and 16 at the Queen's Bastions, and 6 on the Key—in all 118.—*From Documents in Record Office.*

and seven in a north and south direction. Some of the houses were wholly of brick or stone, but generally they were of wood upon stone foundations.

Louisbourg, as I have endeavoured to describe it, had between the years 1720 and 1745 cost the French nation the enormous sum of 30,000,000 livres, or 1,200,000*l.* sterling; nevertheless, as Dussieux [1] informs us, the fortifications were still unfinished, and likely to remain so, because the cost had far exceeded the estimates; and it was found such a large garrison would be required for their defence, that the Government had abandoned the idea of completing them according to the original design.

The Plan of the Town and Fortifications of Louisbourg, on the annexed page, reduced to a smaller scale from one prepared by Lieutenant-Colonel Gridley, who commanded the train of artillery at the siege in 1745, will, with the following references, I hope give you a correct idea of the position of the several works mentioned in the preceding pages:—

[1] *Le Canada sous la Domination française &c.* Paris: 1855.

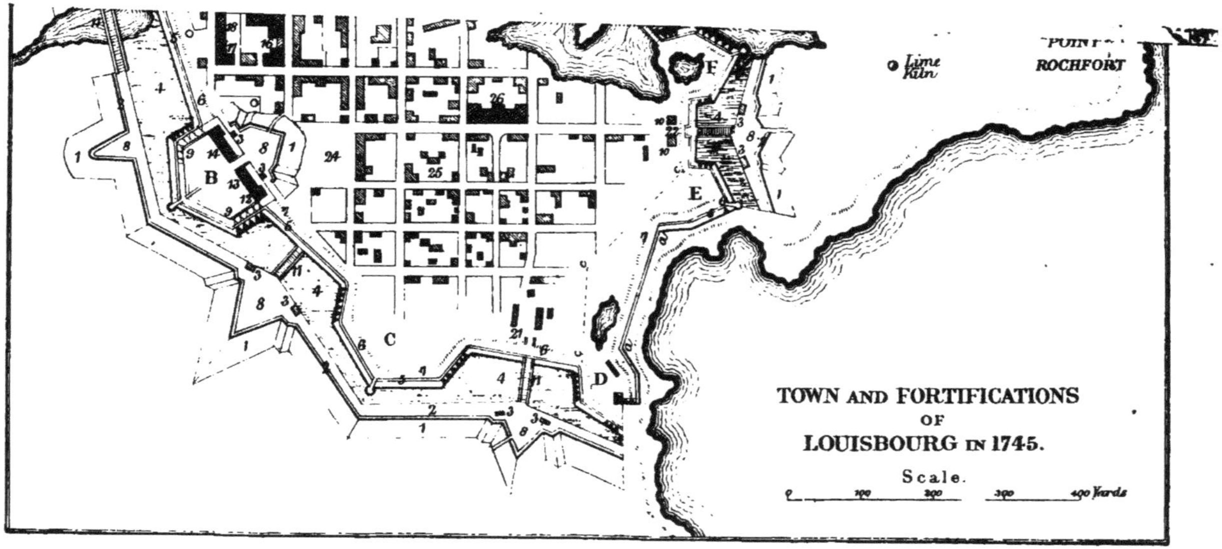
Lime Kiln
POINT ROCHFORT
B
C
D
E
F
TOWN AND FORTIFICATIONS
OF
LOUISBOURG IN 1745.
Scale.
0 100 200 300 400 Yards

an
we
wo

be
en
ne
sti
fa
ga
m
to

th
pe
tr
re
th

References to Plan.

A. Dauphin Bastion and Circular Battery.
B. King's Bastion and Citadel.
C. Queen's Bastion.
D. Princess's Bastion.
E. Bourillon Bastion.
F. Maurepas Bastion.
G. Batterie de la Grève.
1, 1, 1, 1, &c. The Glacis.
2, 2, 2, 2, &c. The Covered Way.
3, 3, &c. Traverses.
4, 4, &c. The Ditch.
5, 5, &c. The Parapet.
6, 6, &c. The Ramparts, and 7, 7, their Slopes.
8, 8, &c. Places of Arms.
9, 9, &c. Casemates.
10, 10, &c. Guard Houses.
11, 11, &c. Wooden Bridges.
12. The Governor's Apartments.
13. The Chapel or Parish Church.
14. Barracks for Garrison.
15. The Powder Magazine.
16. Fortification House.
17. Arsenal and Bakehouse.
18. Ordnance, and 19, General Storehouse.
20. West Gate; 21, Queen's; and 22, East Gate.
23, 23, &c. Gates in Quay Curtain, *b*, *b*, *b*.
24. The Parade.
25. The Nunnery.
26. The Hospital and Church.
a, *a*. Pallisading, with Rampart for Small Arms.
c, *c*, *c*. Picquet raised during the Siege of 1745.

LETTER XII.

1744–1745.

THE tranquillity which the colonies had enjoyed ever since the Treaty of Utrecht was unhappily terminated in 1774 by the war between England and France, brought on by the intermeddling of England in the affairs of the Continent. Irritated by this interference, the French Government espoused the cause of Charles Edward, the son of the Pretender, and projected an invasion of England for the purpose of placing him on the throne. Fifteen thousand men were collected at Dunkirk, and a fleet of twenty ships of the line was sent to conduct them to the shores of England.

Frustrated in this object by the appearance of a superior force under Admiral Sir John Norris, the project of invasion was for the present abandoned, and war declared against England on March 15, 1744. England declared war on April 10, but, though the intelligence of this event did not reach Boston until June 2, the colonies were not wholly unprepared for it, as they had been informed in the preceding October that there was every probability of a speedy rupture with France.

The French Government showed more alacrity in apprising their colonies of the declaration of war, having despatched a fast-sailing vessel to Louisbourg for that purpose, which arrived there about the middle of April. The Governor, M. Duquesnal, lost no time in turning this early information to account. Aware of the weakness of the garrisons of Canceau and Annapolis, which could barely muster eighty men each, he immediately decided upon fitting out an expedition to reduce both places before any aid could be sent from Boston.

Accordingly, several small vessels, carrying 70 soldiers and 300 militia, under the command of M. Duvivier, Aide-Major of Louisbourg, were despatched to Canceau, where they were joined by 300 Indians.

As the little garrison, which had no defences except a wretched blockhouse built by the fishermen, could offer no resistance to such a superior force with the slightest hopes of success, the commandant, Captain Heron, capitulated on May 13, upon condition that the ladies of the officers should have liberty to go where they chose, and that the troops and inhabitants should be conveyed either to England or Annapolis within the space of twelve months. The town of Canceau and the blockhouse were burnt, and the prisoners carried off in triumph to Louisbourg, where they remained until the autumn, when, at their own request, they were sent to Boston.

Having thus easily captured Canceau, Duvivier proceeded to execute the more difficult task of reducing Annapolis. The Indians of Cape Sable and the St. John's river, agreeably to instructions sent from Louisbourg to the missionary M. Loutré, were collected for the purpose of uniting with Duvivier's forces on their arrival at Annapolis; but owing to some unaccountable delay, for which Duvivier was much blamed by his Government, his forces did not reach Annapolis at the time agreed upon. Meanwhile Loutré, with his 300 savages, appeared before the town, to the surprise and dismay of the inhabitants, who had received no intelligence of the war. Loutré advised the Governor, Mascarene, to surrender the fort, informing him that a large force was on the way from Louisbourg to join him. Mascarene, however, had no idea of surrendering the post committed to his charge without a struggle. He immediately sent off a messenger to Boston to ask for aid, and began to repair the weakest points of his defences. The Indians made several attempts to gain possession of the fort, but being foiled by the gallant little garrison, retired to Minas to await the arrival of Duvivier. Loutré and his Indians had scarcely left when Duvivier arrived by another route at Annapolis, with sixty soldiers, several hundred militia, and a number of Indians. Fortunately, he was too late, for the Governor of Massachusetts, aware of the defenceless state of Annapolis, had sent a reinforcement from Boston, which arrived just in time to enable Mascarene to successfully repel the repeated attacks of Duvivier. This officer, who was a descendant of Etienne de la Tour, one of the first Seigneurs of Acadié, fully expected that when he appeared amongst them all the French inhabitants would rise in revolt and flock to his standard; but the Acadians had now lived so long in tranquillity under the mild and judicious sway of the English Governors, that they had no desire for change, and remained quiet on their farms. Finding that the Acadians would not join him, and that the ships of war expected from Louisbourg had not made their appearance, Duvivier retired by way of Minas to Bay Verte, from whence, having sent the troops to Louisbourg, he proceeded to Quebec.

If Duvivier had made a rapid march upon Annapolis and arrived there before Loutré and his Indians retired, nothing could have saved the place. Altogether the enterprise was badly conducted. The arrangements were defective, or else there was some gross neglect on the part of the officers employed to carry them out, for scarcely had Duvivier turned his back upon Annapolis, when the two ships expected from Louisbourg arrived off the harbour, with a number of soldiers on board. They captured two vessels from Boston, laden with stores for the garrison, but the commanders, learning that Duvivier had left, and that the garrison had been reinforced, wisely followed his example and returned to Louisbourg.

A naval force sent by Duquesnal to attack Placentia, under the command of M. de Brotz, met with no better success. Disappointed in his hopes, De Brotz, who commanded a privateer of sixteen guns, called the 'Labrador,'[1] directed his course towards the coast of New England, in the expectation of taking some valuable prizes. He was again doomed to disappoint-

[1] De Brotz's ship was built in and named after the Labrador Lake, which Douglas, in his *Summary*, calls 'a Gut in Cape Breton.' Several Irish soldiers who had deserted from Canceau were on board the 'Labrador' when she was captured.

ment, for he was himself taken by Captain Spry of the bomb ship 'Comet.'

Douglas says he was informed by the Marquis de la Maisonforte, that the French court, considering the weak and mutinous state of the garrison at Louisbourg, sent out express instructions to Duquesnal not to attempt any expedition which might alarm the populous neighbouring colonies; but Ulloa, who was there soon after the siege, as I have already told you (p. 174), says that 'one of the most considerable inhabitants[1] of Louisbourg, who claimed a large tract of land in Nova Scotia, desirous of recovering such a valuable property, availing himself of the present war, laid before the Ministry a scheme for the conquest of that country without any charge to the King, asking only to be allowed the services of a body of troops from the garrison. The Ministry entered into his views; and a commission was sent him for the expedition, accompanied by an order for furnishing him with the number of regulars required.'

The expeditions fitted out to take Canceau and Annapolis, whether with or without the sanction of the French Government, undoubtedly hastened, if they did not originate, the attempt of the colonists to reduce Louisbourg. Ulloa says that if they had not been undertaken, although England and France were at war, the hostilities in America might never have been carried beyond acts of privateering, without any thoughts of higher enterprises; but this act of violence (the destruction of Canceau) 'raised such a clamour not only

[1] This, of course, was M. Duvivier, the greatgrandson of La Tour, who laid a memorial before the French Government in 1735, on the same subject, in which he stated that he had several relatives in Nova Scotia who had never taken the oath of allegiance to the King of England; that the inhabitants were entirely devoted to him; that he had secretly arranged the means of taking the country from the English on the first instant of a rupture; and that he could reckon on the zeal of the inhabitants and of the greater part of the savages. He added, that with 100 men only from the garrison of Louisbourg, and a certain quantity of arms and ammunition to distribute to the inhabitants, he would pledge his head to make the conquest of that part of North America, comprising the fort of Canceau, where the English carried on a very great fishery, to the prejudice of the colony of Isle Royale.—See Translation of the Memoir in Murdoch's *History of Nova Scotia*, from which I have made this extract.

amongst the sufferers but through all Acadié, that the Governor and principal people of New England became alarmed, and began to consider their own welfare in danger. Accordingly, they held consultations on the means of preventing further mischief, and of taking satisfaction for the late insult; they with reason apprehended that the French must carry all before them in a country like theirs, every way open, without fortresses or troops; and they imagined that the French, from the facility of its execution, had really formed such a design; and that the first success, so easily obtained, would naturally animate that ambitious nation to greater enterprises.' The English colonists, as we are told by a later writer, 'had looked with awe upon the sombre walls of Louisbourg, whose towers rose like giants above the northern seas.'[1] They now began to feel the strength of the giants. Annapolis had indeed escaped, but Canceau, a place of great importance, had fallen into the hands of the enemy. Their fisheries on the coast of Nova Scotia had been ruined, their communication with Newfoundland cut off, and their ships captured by privateers at the very mouths of their own ports. The merchants of Louisbourg were not slow in availing themselves of their position for fitting out privateers; even M. Bigot, the Intendant, who never lost sight of his own interests, was the owner of several vessels of this description. It was at this time that Louisbourg, from its admirable situation for their purposes, was called by the privateers the 'Dunkirk of America.'

The British colonists were no doubt alarmed at this state of affairs; but they were neither discouraged nor intimidated. They proved themselves equal to the emergency. The French had indeed stolen a march upon them by the possession of earlier intelligence of the war; but the colonists, confident in their own strength and resources, were in no wise disheartened. Troops were raised for guarding the frontiers towards Canada, and for garrisoning the forts on the seaboard; reinforcements were sent to Nova Scotia, which, as we have seen, secured the capital of that province; and war was declared against the

[1] Garneau's *Histoire du Canada*.

Indians east of Passamaquoddy, who had taken an active part in the recent hostilities. Meanwhile, the colonists were not satisfied with merely putting their defences in order. As it was well known that France was making formidable preparations for war, and that Louisbourg would of course be the base of all operations directed against the colonies,[1] it was the general opinion of the leading men of Boston that the security of their trade and navigation could only be ensured by the reduction of that stronghold.

The feasibility of taking Louisbourg seems to have been first mooted by Mr. Robert Auchmuty, Judge of the Vice-Admiralty Court of Massachusetts, in 1744. There is an article, headed 'The Importance of Cape Breton to the British Nation' over his signature, in the 'Gentleman's Magazine' for July 1745, in which the best mode of effecting it is fully discussed.[2] As the accuracy of his statement does not appear to have been disputed at the time, I think we may fairly conclude that Auchmuty was the originator of the enterprise. Several

[1] 'M. Duvivier was sent to France in the winter of 1744–45 to solicit a force to conquer Nova Scotia. He was coming out in July, 1745, with seven ships of war for that purpose, when he captured a brig bound from Boston to London, from which he learned the conquest of Louisbourg, and consequently returned to France. —*Hutchinson*.

[2] Having described the situation of the island, the great value of its fisheries, and its importance to France as a nursery for her seamen, M. Auchmuty says that, if it were taken by England, the French would be obliged to abandon their fisheries; their communication with Canada would be cut off; Quebec must soon fall into the hands of the English; and the harbour of Louisbourg would become a safe retreat for British merchantmen and ships of war. He recommends that 3,000 men should be raised in the colonies, ready to co-operate with six ships of the line, and 2,000 regular troops to be despatched from Boston in time to anchor in Gabarus Bay by the middle of April, 1745, there to land and commence a regular siege, &c. He says in conclusion, 'that the city has a fosse and bastions regularly disposed; but both bastions and curtains are of masonry to the summit, which is thirty-six feet above the field; the quoins and embrasures are of hewn stones, cemented with mortar composed of their own lime, which is very bad, and salt-water sand, incapable of standing the frost, insomuch that every winter there is a repair almost equal to new. It is judged by the connoisseurs that the fire of their own cannon will shake down the works, and that they will not stand a battery. If the rampart is taken, the Citadel, and four other batteries that command the harbour, must yield; and, what facilitates the design, there are no outworks, glacis, and covert way.'

writers[1] say that Mr. Vaughan first suggested the practicability of taking Louisbourg; but General Pepperrell, who was probably well informed upon the subject, and a warm friend of Vaughan's, does not go that length; he says, 'Mr. Wm. Vaughan, a gentleman of Damariscouta, had the honour of *reviving*, at least, if not of having been the original mover or projector of this grand and successful enterprise.'[2]

At all events, whoever first proposed the enterprise, William Shirley, the Governor of Massachusetts, is alone entitled to the credit of submitting it to the British Ministry and the Legislature of his own province; and of having, when it was decided upon, devoted all his energy and influence to ensure its successful accomplishment. The intelligence brought by the Canceau prisoners, who were released in October, respecting the strength of the fortifications and the mutinous state of the garrison, induced him to believe that the place might be taken early in the following spring, before succour could arrive from France. Soon after the prisoners left Louisbourg, the soldiers, who had naturally been greatly discontented at the stoppage of the extra pay to which they were entitled for working on the fortifications, broke out into open revolt. Having com-

[1] Belknap says, 'Wm. Vaughan, a son of the Lieut.-Governor of New Hampshire, is said to have been the first who proposed the plan of this famous enterprise.' He adds, however, that several others claimed the merit.

[2] See a little work by him, on *The Importance and Advantage of Cape Breton.* London: 1746. Since the above was written, I find by the *New York Documents*, edited by Dr. Callaghan, that Lieutenant-Governor Clarke, of the Province of New York, was the first person that suggested the expediency of taking Cape Breton before any attempt was made to take Canada. In a letter addressed to the Duke of Newcastle sometime in 1743 (the exact time is not given), he says, 'Louisbourg is a place well fortified, and from whence the French can annoy our fisheries at Newfoundland, and guard their own navigation to and from Canada. That place is such a thorn in the sides of the New England people, that it is very probable that a large body of men may be raised there to assist in any such design. And if proper officers are sent from England in the summer to exercise them, they may by the ensuing spring be well disciplined, as all their youth are expert in the use of firearms, from the unrestrained liberty of fowling which obtains in all the Provinces; and I conceive the spring is the most proper season to attack the place, before the men-of-war and fishing vessels come from France, for in the winter they have few men except the garrison, and Boston being a proper port for our fleet to harbour in the winter, we may block up the harbour of Breton before the ships from France can come upon the coast.'

plained to their officers without obtaining any redress, they resolved to take the matter into their own hands. The Swiss Companies first gave the signal of revolt, and were soon joined by the rest of the garrison. They elected officers amongst themselves, seized the barracks, established guardhouses, and placed sentinels over the magazines and storehouses. Unfortunately, at this critical juncture the Governor Duquesnal died, and was succeeded by Duchambon, an officer of little experience, and of very inferior ability. M. Bigot, the Intendant, partially succeeded in satisfying the soldiers; but it is said they continued in this disaffected state all winter, and were again in open revolt when the English expedition arrived in Gabarus Bay.[1]

Convinced that there could not be a more favourable opportunity than the ensuing spring for effecting the object which he had taken up so warmly, Shirley sent a despatch to the British Ministry, dated November 10, 1744, in which he stated that Louisbourg had become the haunt of a number of privateers which preyed on the commerce of the colonies; and that unless it were taken without delay the fisheries would be ruined, and Nova Scotia, with a population of many thousand Acadians, would certainly once more fall into the hands of France. He then urged upon the Ministry the necessity of sending out a naval force to co-operate with a body of troops to be raised in the colonies. This despatch was sent by Captain Ryal, an officer who had been taken prisoner at Canceau, and had been detained several months at Louisbourg, for the purpose of giving any information that might be required by the Ministry respecting the fortifications. On the receipt of this proposal, orders were sent to Commodore Warren, then in the West Indies, to proceed with his squadron to Boston, to consult with Shirley and give all the aid in his power in the enterprise.

Without waiting for an answer to his proposal from the Home Government, Shirley early in January submitted his project to the General Court, with a request that it should be discussed under an oath of secrecy, lest its purport might get

[1] Garneau's *Histoire du Canada*.

abroad and reach the ears of the enemy. For some days the subject was kept secret; but a pious old deacon, one of the members of the Legislature, having been heard invoking the favour of Heaven upon the enterprise at his private devotions, it soon became public and excited the astonishment of all by its audacity. The question was fully discussed for several days in all its bearings. Hutchinson[1] has furnished us with a summary of the arguments on both sides, from which I make the following extracts:—

'On one side it was argued, that if Louisbourg were left in the hands of the French, it would prove the Dunkirk of America; that as their fishery was not profitable and their trade inconsiderable, they might lay aside both trade and fishery, and by privateering enrich themselves with the spoils of New England; to these dangers was added that of losing Nova Scotia, which would cause an increase of six or eight thousand enemies in an instant. The garrison of Louisbourg was disaffected—provisions were scant—the works mouldering and decayed—the Governor an old man unskilled in the art of war; this, therefore, was the only time for success; another year the place would be impregnable. We had nothing to fear from the forces at Louisbourg; before additional strength could arrive from France they would be forced to surrender. We had, it must be owned, no ships of sufficient strength to match the French men-of-war, unless, perhaps, a single ship should fall in by herself, and in that case five or six of ours might be a match for her; but there was no probability of men-of-war so early, and it was very probable English men-of-war from Europe or the West Indies would arrive before them. There was always uncertainty in war; a risk must be run; if we failed, we should be able to grapple with the disappointment, although we should have to bear the whole expense; but if we succeeded, not only the coasts of New England would be free from molestation, but so glorious an acquisition would be of the greatest importance to Great Britain and might give peace to Europe, and we might depend upon a reimbursement of the whole charge we had been at.'

[1] In his *History of Massachusetts.*

On the other side it was replied, 'That we had better suffer in our trade than by so expensive a measure deprive ourselves of the means of carrying on any future trade;—that we were capable of annoying them in their fishery as much as they could annoy us in ours, and in a short time both sides would be willing to leave the fishery unmolested;—that the accounts given of the works and garrison of Louisbourg could not be depended upon, and it was not credible that any part of the walls should be unguarded and exposed to surprise;—that instances of disaffection rising to mutiny were rare, and but few instances were to be met with in history where such expectation has not failed.—The garrison at Louisbourg consisted of regular experienced troops, who, though unequal in number, would be more than a match in open field for all the raw unexperienced militia which could be sent from New England; that twenty cruisers at that season of the year could not prevent supplies going into the harbour, it being impossible to keep any station for any length of time, and the weather being frequently so thick, that a vessel was not to be discovered at a quarter of a mile's distance;—that there was no room to expect any men-of-war for the cover of our troops;—that if only one sixty-gun ship should arrive from France or the French islands, she would be more than a match for all the armed vessels we could provide, our transports at Chapeau-rouge Bay (Gabarus) would be every one destroyed, and the army upon Cape Breton obliged to submit to the mercy of the French; that we should be condemned in England for engaging in such an affair without their direction or approbation, and we should be nowhere pitied, our misfortunes proceeding from our own rash and wild measures.—To these arguments were added the uncertainty of raising a sufficient number of men, or of being able to procure provisions, warlike stores and transports, and discouragement from the season of the year, when frequently for many days together no business could be done out of doors. Money, indeed, could be furnished, or bills of credit in lieu of it, but the infallible consequence would be the sinking the value of the whole currency to what degree no man could determine, but probably in proportion to the sum issued.—And, finally, if we should succeed, a general national benefit would be the consequence, in which we should be but small sharers and far short of the vast expense of treasure, and perhaps of lives, in obtaining it; and if we failed, such a shock would be given to the province that half a century would not recover to us our present state.'

As the opponents of the Governor's proposals had evidently the strongest arguments on their side, it is not surprising that, after several days' deliberation, the committee brought in an adverse report, which was accepted by the members of the Court. For a time all thoughts of the expedition were given up.

Notwithstanding this decision, Shirley did not give up the enterprise on which he had set his heart. He did not press the matter on the attention of the Court by further message, or by privately urging the members to change their views, but he encouraged his friends to carry about a petition signed by some of the leading merchants of Boston, Salem, and Marblehead, addressed to the members of the Legislature, praying, for various reasons set forth, among others the saving of the fishery from ruin, that they would reconsider their vote, and agree to the Governor's proposal of an expedition against Louisbourg. 'A second committee, appointed upon this petition, reported in favour of it, and on the 26th January their report came before the House, who spent the day in deliberating it, and at night a vote was carried in favour of it by a majority of one voice only. Never was any affair deliberated upon with greater calmness and moderation; the Governor, indeed, laid the affair before the Court, but left the members free to act according to their judgment, without any solicitation, and there appeared no other division than what was caused by a real difference in opinion on the true interest of the province.'[1]

No sooner, however, was this decision made, than all parties, including even those who had most strenuously opposed it, like true patriots united heartily to carry it into effect. Circulars were sent to the governors of all the provinces, requesting their

[1] Hutchinson.

co-operation with Massachusetts in raising a force of 4,000 men, which, it was estimated, would be sufficient to ensure success. Massachusetts, which then included the present State of Maine, agreed to raise 3,250 men; New Hampshire 300; Rhode Island 300; and Connecticut 500. Ten eighteen-pounder guns were furnished by New York, and a supply of provisions by Pennsylvania. As each of the provinces at that time had one or more armed vessels, a naval force of fourteen vessels, carrying altogether about 200 guns, was equipped as cruisers. Captain Edward Tyng, who commanded a small frigate of twenty guns, was made commodore of the little fleet. Instead of a commissary-general appointed by the Governor, a committee was chosen composed of members of the Legislature. This committee was authorised to enter the warehouses and cellars of the merchants, to take any provisions, clothing, or warlike stores they could find, at what they deemed a fair valuation. The next point was to select a commander of the expedition. As there were no officers in New England who had had any experience in actual warfare except with the Indians, this was a difficult task. Shirley was well aware that skirmishing with savages was a very different matter from besieging a strong fortress defended by disciplined troops; but as he had no alternative, he was obliged to select a commander from amongst the militia officers of the province. His choice fell, fortunately, as the result proved, upon William Pepperrell, a colonel of militia, residing at Kittery Point on the Piscataqua. Colonel Pepperrell was extensively engaged in the fisheries and other mercantile pursuits, in which he had acquired great wealth. He had held many important offices in his province, amongst others that of President of the Council—the highest office in the gift of the people—and was deservedly popular with all classes of his countrymen. Although Pepperrell had seen no service, he was from education and habits better fitted than any other militia officer for the responsible situation now conferred upon him. Born in 1696, when the Indian war was raging, which continued until 1713, with an interval of only four years' peace, young Pepperrell must from his childhood have become familiarised with the details of the atrocities perpetrated by the relentless savages in his own neighbourhood. In those unhappy times, when every man was from necessity a soldier; when sentinels stood at the church doors whilst those within prayed with their hands resting on their firelocks; when the militia were paraded for daily drill; when every one had to take his share in watch and ward; and when he himself, at the early age of sixteen, had been called upon to perform patrol duty, it is not surprising that he then became embued with that military spirit which so eminently fitted him for the arduous task imposed upon him by his countrymen. Although now in his 49th year, called away from his extensive business and domestic comforts, he shrank not from the duty, but cheerfully undertook the responsible office of chief of an expedition where success was doubtful, the danger certain.[1]

As soon as it became known that Colonel Pepperrell was appointed commander of the expedition, with the rank of lieutenant-general, volunteers, especially from his own province, offered their services with alacrity. In the short space of eight weeks the whole of the troops required were raised and equipped. The land force 'was composed of fishermen, who in time of war could no longer use the hook and line on the Grand Bank, but with prudent forethought took with them their codlines; of mechanics, skilled from childhood in the use of the gun; of lumberers, enured to fatigue and encampments in the woods; of husbandmen from the interior, who had grown up with arms in their hands, accustomed to danger, keenest marksmen, disciplined in the pursuit of larger and smaller game, all commanded by officers from among themselves, many of them church members, almost all having wives and children.'[2]

Eight regiments, comprising 3,250 men, commanded by Colonels Bradstreet,[3] Waldo, Dwight, Moulton,[4] Willard,

[1] *The Life of Sir William Pepperrell, Bart.* By Usher Parsons. Boston: 1856.

[2] Bancroft's *History of the United States.*

[3] After the siege of Louisbourg, Colonel Bradstreet was appointed Governor of Newfoundland.

[4] Colonel Moulton was second in command in the attack on Norridgwock, when Father Ralle was killed.

Hale, Richmond, and Gorham, were raised in Massachusetts; one regiment of 300 men in New Hampshire, commanded by Colonel Moore; and one of 500 men in Connecticut, by Colonel Burr. Colonel Wolcott of New Hampshire acted as Major-General, and Colonel Waldo of Massachusetts as Brigadier-General. The artillery was commanded by Colonel Gridley.[1] Mr. Vaughan of New Hampshire, who had taken a very active part in promoting the expedition, accompanied General Pepperrell as Lieutenant-Colonel unattached. The whole force, consisting of 4,300 troops, including officers, was embarked in ninety transports collected in Nantasket Roads, where they were joined by all the armed vessels except two or three which had been sent in the middle of March to cruise off Louisbourg. The Rhode Island force, of 300 men, did not reach Louisbourg until the siege was over.

Before the expedition sailed, a day of fast and prayer was held throughout the province to invoke the blessing of Heaven upon the enterprise. The well-known itinerant preacher, George Whitefield, who was then on his third tour through the colonies, 'gave his influence in favor of the expedition by suggesting, as a motto for the flag of the New Hampshire regiment, "*Nil desperandum, Christo duce.*" The enterprise, under such auspices, assumed something of the character of an anti-Catholic crusade. One of the chaplains, a disciple of Whitefield, carried a hatchet, specially provided to hew down the images in the French churches.'[2]

Governor Shirley's idea of the best plan of completing the great enterprise he had so successfully begun was so Quixotic, that I cannot resist the temptation of giving you at length Belknap's abstract of his (Shirley's) instructions to General Pepperrell.

'He was to proceed to Canceau, there to build a blockhouse and battery, and leave two companies in garrison, and to deposit the stores which might not be immediately wanted by the army. Thence he was to send a detachment to the village

[1] Colonel Gridley was afterwards engaged in the revolutionary army at the celebrated battle of Bunker's Hill.

[2] Hildreth's *History of the United States.*

of St. Peter's in the island of Cape Breton, and destroy it, to *prevent* any intelligence which might be carried to Louisbourg; for which purpose also the armed vessels were to cruise before the harbour. The whole fleet was to sail from Canceau, so as to arrive in Chapeau Rouge Bay about nine o'clock in the evening. The troops were to land in four divisions, and to proceed to the assault before morning. If the plan for the surprisal should fail, he had particular directions where and how to land, march, encamp, attack and defend, to hold councils and keep records, and to send intelligence to Boston by certain vessels retained for the purpose, which vessels were to stop at Castle William, and there receive the Governor's orders. Several other vessels were appointed to cruise between Canceau and the camp, to convey orders, transport stores, and *catch fish* for the army. To close these instructions, after the most minute detail of duty, the General was finally 'left to act upon unforeseen emergencies according to his discretion;' which, in the opinion of military gentlemen, is accounted the most rational part of the whole. Such was the plan for the reduction of a regularly constructed fortress, drawn by a lawyer, to be executed by a merchant, at the head of a body of husbandmen and mechanics — animated indeed by ardent patriotism, but destitute of professional skill and experience. After they had embarked, the hearts of many began to fail. Some repented that they had voted for the expedition or promoted it; and the most thoughtful were in the greatest perplexity.'[1]

If there had been any desire on the part of the leaders of the expedition to draw back, the intelligence received by Shirley, just on the eve of their sailing, would have afforded an ample excuse. It was fully expected by all that Commodore Warren, to whom Shirley had sent an express boat as soon as the enterprise was sanctioned by the Legislature, would have brought up his squadron from the West Indies to accompany them to Louisbourg; but Warren having called a council of his officers, it was agreed that it would not be advisable to comply with

[1] Belknap's *History of New Hampshire.*

Shirley's request without orders from the Admiralty. Warren's answer of course caused great disappointment; but it was determined to proceed at all hazards, and lest the men might be disheartened by such unwelcome news, it was kept secret from all except Generals Pepperrell and Wolcott.

The Massachusetts troops arrived at Canceau, the place of rendezvous, on April 1, and the Connecticut on the 10th. The New Hampshire arrived there about March 26. Here they were joined by the cruisers which had been despatched in the middle of March, which reported that the southern coast of Cape Breton was blocked up by drift-ice, and that it was impossible to effect a landing anywhere near Louisbourg. This delay afforded Pepperrell an opportunity of drilling his troops at Canceau, and of erecting a blockhouse armed with eight guns, for the defence of the place. The armed vessels were employed in cruising off Louisbourg, on the look-out for vessels from France, which generally arrived early in the spring. Early in April a large brig from Martinique, laden with rum and molasses, was captured off Louisbourg; and on the 18th of the same month the frigate 'Renommée' of thirty-six guns with despatches from France, kept up a running fight for some time with the Massachusetts cruisers; but being able to outsail them, she escaped, after two or three vain attempts to find a passage through the ice into the harbour. Some days previously, the same ship fell in with the Connecticut troops under convoy of their own and the Rhode Island sloops, all of which she might have captured if so disposed; but after some damage to one of the sloops she bore away. Her object was to get into Louisbourg as soon as possible; being prevented by the ice and the Massachusetts cruisers, she returned to France to report the alarming state of affairs on the coast of Cape Breton.

Whilst the expedition was detained at Canceau, Colonel Moulton was sent with a detachment to destroy the fort at St. Peter's and disperse the inhabitants. This was easily accomplished; the settlement was plundered, four schooners were burnt, and some prisoners taken. Another detachment, sent in an armed vessel commanded by Captain Donaheu up the Northumberland Straits, to intercept any vessels bringing supplies from Bay Verte to Louisbourg was not so fortunate, for in going through the Gut of Canceau, Captains Jacques and Hammond, having landed with a part of the troops to disperse a band of Indians on the shore, the first was killed and the latter wounded. No vessels were met with on their way to Bay Verte, where they burnt some houses and canoes.

On April 22, the troops at Canceau were gratified by the arrival of the 'Eltham,' of forty guns, which had been sent by Governor Shirley from Piscataqua, where she had gone to convoy the mastships to England; and still more so on the following day, by the appearance of three ships of war in the offing, which proved to be Commodore Warren's squadron from the West Indies. It seems that, upon receipt of Shirley's despatches by Captain Ryal, and the information furnished by that officer, the English Ministry, convinced of the importance of taking Louisbourg, at once sent out the sloop 'Hind,' with instructions to Warren to proceed to Boston, for the purpose of giving Shirley all the aid in his power in accomplishing that object. In compliance with these instructions, which did not reach Warren at Antigua until the day after he had written to Shirley, he immediately started with his squadron for Boston, in the hope of arriving there before the expedition sailed; but learning from a vessel which he met at sea that the fleet had left for Canceau, he bore up for that port, and arrived in the offing, as has been already related, on April 23, to the great joy of Pepperrell and the army. As soon as Warren reached Canceau, he sent a message on shore to announce his arrival, with a proposal to proceed to Louisbourg to blockade that port, to which Pepperrell sent the following answer by Colonel Bradstreet:—

'Canceau, 23d April 1745.

'Commodore Warren.

'Dear Sir,—I heartily congratulate you on your safe arrival with your squadron, the advice of which, by your favour of this day, gives me abundant pleasure. I am confident that nothing which the strictest vigilance and prudence can foresee, or bravery execute, will be wanting on your part, and doubt not you will succeed in preventing the introduction of provisions and supplies into Louisbourg, and that we shall soon have the pleasure of meeting there.

'WILLIAM PEPPERRELL.'

Warren had already requested Shirley, by letter written at sea, to send on any of His Majesty's ships that might arrive at Boston. He now despatched a small vessel to bring up any on the Newfoundland station, and then proceeded with the 'Superb,' of sixty, and the 'Launceston,' 'Mermaid,' and 'Eltham,' of forty guns each, to cruise before Louisbourg. The southern coast of Cape Breton was still (April 23) blocked up with drift-ice. This ice, as you are aware, comes down from the Gulf of St. Lawrence every spring, and is generally carried by the current to the eastward of Scatari, until it reaches the warm waters of the Gulf Stream, where it is soon dissolved; but occasionally, if the wind happens to change to the southward as it passes Scatari, large fields of ice are driven upon the coast, which block up Louisbourg harbour. This, however, seldom occurs—perhaps not once in ten years. In the present instance its occurrence proved of great service to the expedition in two ways; first, in affording Pepperrell and his officers time, during their detention at Canceau, to organise and drill their undisciplined troops; secondly, in preventing succours getting into Louisbourg.

Most of the troops had been nearly a month at Canceau, when intelligence was brought by one of the cruisers that a north-west wind had driven off all the ice, and the coast was now clear. Not a moment was lost. The troops, having embarked in the transports, set sail for Louisbourg on Sunday, April 29, with a light fair wind, fully expecting to reach Louisbourg before night. As they neared Gabarus Bay, where the disembarkation was proposed to be made, all eyes were eagerly on the look-out for the first sight of the redoubtable fortress, but the wind dying away, to the great disappointment of all it soon became evident that they could not reach their destination before the next morning. All hopes of effecting a landing in the dark, and taking the place by surprise, as proposed by Shirley, were now abandoned—that is, if any one in the expedition had ever seriously entertained such an absurd notion. Here we must for the present leave them, looking anxiously for a fair wind on the morrow.

LETTER XIII.

1745.

WHILST the fleet lies becalmed almost within sight of the ramparts, let us see what is going on within the doomed fortress, and what preparations are making for the coming storm. It does not appear that the Governor of Louisbourg had the slightest suspicion that the attacks on Canceau and Annapolis in the preceding year would have aroused the colonists to a sense of their danger, and induced them to undertake any serious attempt to avenge these insults. The Viceroy of Canada, however, seems to have been of a different opinion, and had offered to send a reinforcement to Louisbourg in the fall of 1744; but Duchambon, considering that there was no occasion for such succour, declined the offer. 'This,' says Ulloa, 'was the first, and not the least, error to which his disgrace for the loss of Louisbourg may be imputed, as with the succours offered he would have found himself at the head of a body of men more than sufficient not only to defend himself but to sally out and drive before them the raw and undisciplined multitude which was come against him.' The provincial cruisers had been seen passing and repassing Louisbourg; and some soldiers and axemen wintering in the woods near Menadou, had reported that several suspicious-looking vessels had been seen off that part; but no attempt to gain information concerning the character of these vessels was made until Commodore Warren's squadron appeared in the offing, when Duchambon, as he tells us in his Report addressed to the Minister of War, despatched a citizen and a soldier, with an Indian to guide them through the woods to the Strait of Canceau, 'to take prisoners,' but more likely to gain intelligence. He adds, this party took four prisoners, who rose upon them while asleep in the night. A few prisoners, both Frenchmen and Indians, were taken in the woods near Canceau whilst the expedition lay there, from whom Pepperrell obtained some information concerning Louisbourg; but it is not said whether they belonged to the neighbourhood or were spies sent by Duchambon. That no intelligence of the approaching danger should have reached Louisbourg is most unaccountable, when we consider that a fleet of 100 vessels had been at anchor for more than three weeks at Canceau, within sight of the French settlement of Nerica (Arichat) in Isle Madame. It was at first supposed that Warren's squadron were French ships waiting for the ice to clear off to get into Louisbourg; but all doubts respecting their real character were dispelled on April 27, when a large merchant ship got into that port, whose captain reported that he had been chased by a squadron and fired into. Even this information does not seem to have given rise to much apprehension, as it is said 'a grand ball was given at the Citadel on the night before the expedition arrived in Gabarus Bay, and that the company had scarce been asleep when they were called up by an alarm.'[1]

There was, indeed, ample cause for alarm. The English fleet, which we left becalmed on the evening of the 29th, favoured by a gentle breeze which sprang up in the night, was pressing on towards its destination. The leading ships were first descried from the ramparts of Louisbourg at early dawn on April 30. Before sunrise the western horizon was covered with a cloud of white canvas, every moment coming nearer and nearer, like an eagle with outspread wings, to pounce upon its prey. Before eight o'clock, the whole fleet was safely at anchor in the scarcely rippled waters of the capacious roadstead of Gabarus Bay, not more than a league distant from Louisbourg. At the same time, Commodore Warren's ships made their appearance in the offing. There was indeed, I repeat, ample cause for alarm. 'Surrounded by the enemy—all the ways for succour blocked up—besieged

[1] Hutchinson.

to face p. 206.

SIEGE OF LOUISBOURG IN 1745.
Scale.
0 500 1000 1500 2000 Yards
A Landing Place of Army.
B First Battery.
C Second Do
D Third Do
E Fourth or Advanced Battery.
F Fifth or Titcomb's Battery.
G Lighthouse Battery.
Warehouse
North East Arm
Careening Cove
Landing Cove
Grand Battery
Harbour
Rock
Lighthouse Point
Island Battery
Green Hills
Barachois
West Gate
CITY
Point Rochfort
Green Isd.
Black Pt.
Camp
Freshwater Cove
Flat Point
White Pt.
Cormorant Rocks
GABARUS BAY

in form with forces unequal to the defence of the place, and without any probability of receiving a reinforcement from Canada or from Europe,'[1] Duchambon saw what a sad mistake he had made in refusing the proffered succours of the Viceroy.

As you may easily imagine, Louisbourg presented a scene of confusion and dismay. Bells were rung, and cannon fired, to call in the people from the outskirts of the city and the neighbouring settlements. The troops, which had been in open rebellion all winter, were hastily assembled and addressed by the Governor. He appealed to their patriotic feelings, pointing out that the arrival of the enemy now afforded them a favourable opportunity of proving that they were good Frenchmen, and of winning forgiveness of their past misconduct. His harangue produced the desired effect. The injustice they had suffered at the hands of their superiors was forgotten. They acknowledged their fault and returned to their duty, sacrificing their own resentments for the good of their country. Their subsequent conduct proved the sincerity of their professions, but, unfortunately, their officers distrusted them, which, as will be seen, led to the most fatal results.[2] Meanwhile, the transports had scarcely come to anchor when preparations were made for an immediate landing. The first division of boats, filled with soldiers, proceeded towards White Point, apparently with the intention of landing there, but in reality for the purpose of drawing off in that direction a body of French troops which were coming to oppose them. This ruse had the desired effect. At a given signal the boats hastily returned towards Flat Point Cove, two miles further up the bay, and being joined by another division concealed behind the ships, pulled in for the shingle beach, where about a hundred men effected a landing under cover of two armed vessels, before the French detachment of 110 men, commanded by Captain Morpang, a celebrated rover, could reach the spot. The French troops gallantly attacked the invaders, but without the slightest chance of success, as the latter, reinforced by fresh arrivals, increased so fast in number that the

[1] Ulloa. [2] Garneau.

French were driven out of the woods, in which they were stationed, and compelled to retreat towards the city. In this affair the French lost six men killed and several prisoners, amongst the latter Captain Morpang himself. On their retreat, they set fire to all the houses on their way likely to afford cover to their pursuers. No further opposition was offered to the disembarkation of the army, of which about one half landed that day, and the remainder on the day following. Their first encampment was made between Flat Point and White Point, so near to the town that the enemy's shot sometimes fell into the camp, which compelled them to move further off to get out of range of such troublesome visitors. The camp was then pitched on the banks of a small stream of fresh water discharging into Flat Point cove, in the most favourable situation for landing stores and munitions of war, and for communicating with the fleet.

Although the English troops had now obtained a secure footing on the enemy's soil, within half a league of Louisbourg, without the loss of a single man, any impartial observer cognisant of the strength and respective positions of the rival hosts would have had no hesitation in pronouncing the odds entirely in favour of the besieged. On one side he would have seen a strong fortress constructed upon the most approved system of that day, with an armament of more than a hundred heavy guns and mortars, and two powerful outworks of thirty guns each, manned by 750 veterans and 1,500 militia; on the other, 4,000, undisciplined militia or volunteers, officered by men who had, with one or two exceptions, never seen a shot fired in anger all their lives, encamped in an open country, with no other shelter or protection than such slight earth-works as they could only construct during the night, and sadly deficient in suitable artillery. Under these circumstances the advantages were evidently on the side of the French; nevertheless, neither officers nor men ever despaired of success; and their general, without waiting to secure his camp by trenches or picquets, determined to avail himself of the advantages he had obtained by his unexpected arrival, to commence active operations before the enemy had recovered from his surprise, by despatching Lieutenant-Colonel Vaughan with a detachment of 400 men to reconnoitre the town and vicinity on the afternoon of May 1. The column marched through the woods until it arrived opposite the west gate of the town when it was first observed by the enemy; Vaughan and his men then gave three cheers in sight of the whole garrison and again struck into the woods. Passing through the defiles of the Green Hills in the rear of the Grand or Royal Battery, they reached the head of the north-east arm of the harbour after nightfall, and set fire to the warehouses, containing naval stores and a large quantity of wine and brandy (see Map, p. 206). It is stated in all the English accounts of the siege, that the smoke of the burning warehouses, driven by the wind towards the Grand Battery, so terrified the French, who supposed the whole English army was coming in that direction, that they spiked the guns, threw the ammunition into a well, and fled in their boats to the town. Next morning, whilst the English detachment, which had bivouacked in the woods, was proceeding by a circuitous route behind the Green Hills to the camp, Vaughan, with thirteen of his men, cautiously crept up to the top of the hill which overlooked the Grand Battery to observe its strength and position, when to his astonishment he found it apparently deserted. Having induced one of his party, a Cape Cod Indian, to climb up and enter the fort through one of the embrasures, to open the gate, Vaughan entered and took possession, and immediately wrote to General Pepperrell, 'that he had entered the Grand Battery at 9 A.M., and was waiting for reinforcements and a flag.'[1] Vaughan had not been long in possession, when, observing four boats full of armed men approaching from the town, he immediately marched down to the beach with his twelve men, and successfully opposed their landing in spite of a brisk fire of musketry from the boats and of cannon shot from the town, until a reinforcement arrived from the camp, when the French retired. English writers say that when Duchambon observed from the city that the Grand Battery was occupied by only a

[1] The French flag was hauled down, and a red coat, carried up by one of the soldiers in his teeth, was nailed to the flagstaff as a substitute.

handful of men, he sent the armed boats to recapture it. In his Report to the French Minister, Duchambon makes the following statement:—'In the evening, Captain Cheré, whose company held the Royal Battery, wrote me a letter stating the bad condition of his post, which might easily be taken, and that he believed it for the good of the service to spike the cannon and leave. The chief engineer was of the same opinion, and thought that the 400 or 500 Provincials in the rear could with cannon destroy the battery, defended by only 200 men. The Council of War was therefore in favour of spiking and dismounting the cannon, and removing the ammunition. The battery being not entirely destroyed, I next morning sent officers and men in boats to finish the work, who were repulsed.'

The Abbé Prevost[1] gives a somewhat different version:—'The Royal Battery being menaced by a numerous force, encamped at no great distance, and the Governor, aware of the importance of the post, but unable to spare men to reinforce it, sent orders to the captain commanding the battery to keep up a constant fire of artillery to deceive the enemy; adding, that if he should be attacked by a much superior force, to spike the cannon, and retire to the town in some boats which were under the walls of the battery. This officer, who was either deficient in courage or experience, had hardly received the Governor's order, when, upon some slight movement of the English, he embarked precipitately with all his people and threw himself into the city, exclaiming that the enemy was coming in great force; a mere imagination! proved by the fact that the flag of France floated over the fort twenty-four hours after the soldiers had left it. On the other hand, the English, seeing nobody moving on the ramparts, imagined that the garrison was occupied at some work in the interior, and passed two days in this doubt without taking courage to advance, until an Indian (their army being composed of all sorts of people) less timid than the rest, offered to go and reconnoitre the fort. He set out without arms, and pretending that he was mad, reached the gate, when he discovered the fort was abandoned, entered

[1] In his *Histoire générale des Voyages.* Amsterdam: 1774.

it, and pulled down the banner of France, which was all that remained to defend it. The English, who had observed all, ran in also, and easily repaired the cannon, which the deserters had not taken time enough to spike effectually. So that Louisbourg was battered with the same guns that were intended for its defence.'

You will observe there are several discrepancies in these accounts, which cannot be reconciled. This, however, is of little consequence. Whatever induced the French to abandon such a strong position so precipitately—the acquisition of the Grand Battery, with its heavy armament—proved an object of the greatest importance to the besiegers, as it gave them a secure footing within cannon-shot of the town, protected their communications between the camp and the north side of the harbour, and supplied them with much heavier siege artillery than they had brought with them.

Twenty-eight 42-pounders, and two 18-pounders, with 380 shells, a quantity of shot, and other munitions of war, were found in the Grand Battery. In the hurry of their departure, the French, after spiking the guns, had neglected to break off the trunnions and destroy the carriages, so that in the course of a few days the spikes were drilled out by the smiths, of whom there were several in the army, under the directions of Major Pomroy, himself a gunsmith, and the guns ready to return the fire of the city with good effect. Brigadier Waldo, who had command of the New Hampshire troops appointed to garrison the Grand Battery, fired the first shot into the city on May 3, which, being quite unexpected, killed fourteen men. The French maintained a constant fire of shot and shells from the Island Battery and the city, against the Grand Battery, but were not able to dislodge Waldo and his men, who kept possession of it during the siege. On Sunday, May 5, divine service was performed in the Grand Battery. The sermon, probably the first ever preached by a Protestant minister in Cape Breton, was upon the appropriate text, 'Enter into His gates with thanksgiving, and into His courts with praise.' Their devotions being concluded, the troops 'in the evening fired smartly at the city.'

Having landed all his troops in safety, and secured possession of the Grand Battery, Pepperrell commenced operations in due form against the town. As he had not a sufficient force to invest the place, he determined to confine his attack to the space extending from the West Gate to the King's Bastion. For this purpose, a site was chosen on the slope of one of the spurs of the Green Hills, for a battery, at the distance of 1,550 yards from the West Gate. The position of this battery is marked by the letter B. on the map, at page 206. As there was an abundance of brushwood close at hand, the parapet of the battery was formed of fascines or fagots of that material, covered with earth. Fascine batteries, as they are designated, can be constructed much more expeditiously than those of solid earth, which is of great importance, as the men can only work at them in the night, without lights, which draw upon them the fire of the enemy. The labour of bringing up guns and munitions from the camp to arm this battery, proved very severé, as they had to be transported across the marshes on sledges dragged by the men, often wading up to their knees in mud. Nevertheless, by May 5, this and a second fascine battery, 600 yards nearer to the city (marked C. on map), were constructed and armed with mortars and cohorns.

Aware of the character of the ground[1] between the town and the enemy's camp, Duchambon seems to have expected that the English would not have attempted to make an attack on that side, but rather would have made a dash at the south-eastern front, where, as has been already mentioned (page 182), there was an open space 200 yards in length between the Princess and Bourillon bastions, defended only by a dyke and piquets, as his first care before all the troops had landed was to enclose it with a solid plank-work, fifteen feet in height, on which were mounted a number of swivels.

[1] 'The land between Gabarus Point and the town is very uneven, marshy, and full of brambles. It is covered with turf twelve feet deep, which all the art of man can never dry up. Neither is there any possibility of drawing off the waters, the bogs being surrounded with high rocky ground. The bottom is a mixture of fat clay and round stones, that form a very hard cement. From this it is easy to judge of the difficulty of making a descent in this part of the bay, and of transporting artillery over such ground.'—*Pychon.*

The second fascine battery proved more successful than the first. Being only 950 yards from the West Gate, and subsequently armed with some of the 42-pounders brought from the Grand Battery, 'it proved,' as Duchambon reports, 'the most dangerous of any—sending its balls against the caserns and into the town, where they traversed the streets from end to end, and passed through houses. It never ceased firing during the siege.'

At a Council of War held on May 7, at which Commodore Warren was present, it was decided to send a flag of truce into the town with a summons to the Governor to surrender the place. The cannonading was suspended on both sides while the flag was in the city; but as soon as the messenger returned with the Governor's reply, 'that he would answer at the cannon's mouth,' it was resumed with great vigour on both sides. During the same night another fascine battery was commenced between the Barachois and the West Gate D, 440 yards from the city, for the purpose of covering the men working at the breaching battery, proposed to be established within 250 yards of the walls. Up to this time no attempts were made to interrupt the besiegers whilst raising their batteries, except by cannonading, which caused small damage; but when Duchambon found the besiegers were advancing their batteries so rapidly towards the West Gate, he came to the resolution of making a sortie to drive them from their last position. This was accordingly attempted on May 8, by a small body of troops, but was easily repulsed. If he had employed a sufficient force[1] he would most probably have succeeded, as it is not likely the raw Provincials could have held their ground, at close quarters, against 300 or 400 veterans,

[1] 'The most favourable time for defeating the English was when they began to open their trenches; but the French officers had no confidence in the garrison, on account of the mutiny, which had scarcely yet been appeased. In this situation they were afraid to make a sortie, which would have been certain of success against undisciplined troops. They thought it better to employ the soldiers guarding posts and serving the guns, than to expose them to the risk of passing over to the enemy, either for avoiding the punishment due for their disobedience, or to avenge themselves for the vexations which they had suffered from their chiefs.'—*L'Ulloa.*

which might easily have been spared for that purpose, seeing that no other part of his defences was menaced by the enemy. The soldiers, it is said, asked the Governor to allow them to make a sortie in force, but he persisted in believing that their object was merely to obtain a chance of deserting.[1] All the French, and most of the English writers, seem to have entertained the same opinion. It does not, however, seem to have been well founded; the simple fact, that only three men deserted during the siege, is a sufficient answer. If the soldiers had really been anxious to desert, they might easily have found opportunities of doing so without waiting for a sortie.

Although no breach had yet been made in the walls, it was unanimously advised, at a Council held on the morning of May 9, that Louisbourg should be attacked by storm on that night. This resolution, however, met with so little encouragement from the inferior officers and men, that it was prudently agreed to abandon the proposed attack until more cannon were mounted in the batteries, and a practicable breach made in the walls. Every exertion was now made to effect these important objects, by bringing up guns from the camp and the Grand Battery—a work of great labour and difficulty.

Whilst these preparations were in progress, rumours reached the camp that a large body of French and Indians was collecting in the woods to the northward. The settlement of St. Peter's, as I have already told you, had been ravaged and the inhabitants dispersed. At a later period similar outrages were perpetrated at St. Anne's and Niganiche by armed vessels sent by Commodore Warren. This wanton destruction of houses and fishing craft undoubtedly distressed the people of those settlements; but I must confess I cannot see how the reduction of Louisbourg could have been accelerated by such means. On the contrary, they must have produced a directly opposite effect, as the inhabitants, driven from their peaceful occupations at home, would naturally fly towards Louisbourg, to avenge their losses by joining the Indians hovering on the outskirts of the English camp.

[1] Garneau.

On May 10, a scouting party of twenty-five men was sent from the Grand Battery, under the command of James Gibson,[1] a subaltern of Brigadier Waldo's detachment, to obtain information respecting the strength and motions of the Indians. They reached a harbour on the north-east coast (the name is not given), where they were engaged in plundering some dwellinghouses, when they were unexpectedly attacked by 140 French and Indians. Twenty-two of the party were either killed or taken prisoners; but Gibson and two others concealed themselves in a house, and escaped during the night to the Grand Battery. While they were lying concealed, the Indians, after going through their war-dance, murdered all the prisoners in cold blood, including a sergeant named Cockran, whose fingers and tongue were barbarously cut off while alive. On the following day Gibson returned with a company to avenge this sad disaster. Having buried their murdered comrades, they burned every house in the settlement, including the masshouse and several stores. About 100 boats, and all the fishing stages, were also destroyed, and forty of the inhabitants made prisoners. This prompt action seems to have intimidated the Indians, as nothing more was heard of them for several days.

Up to this time, in consequence of the strict blockade maintained by Warren's squadron and the colonial cruisers, not a single vessel had been able to enter the harbour, until this night (May 13), when a brig from Bordeaux, laden with stores for the fishermen, ran in with an E.N.E. wind, and grounded opposite the King's Gate. An attempt was made to destroy the brig by sending a schooner fitted up as a fire-ship against her, but it did not succeed. One of the crew of the schooner

[1] After the fall of Louisbourg, Gibson, at the request of his brother officers, wrote an account of the siege, which was published in London in 1745. He says that he had had the honour of bearing H.M.'s commission in the Royal Regiment of Foot Guards at Barbadoes, and that he engaged in the expedition as a volunteer, without pay or allowance. As he left Louisbourg on July 4, with the ships that conveyed the French prisoners to Rochelle, and received the thanks of his brother officers for his Journal before he left, it must have been written on the spot, whilst every incident was fresh in his memory. He received a special grant of 550*l*. sterling from Parliament for his services.

was killed, and several wounded by musketry from the city walls.

Warren and Pepperrell, who held frequent consultations, were anxious to bring in the ships to attack the city from the harbour; but it was not considered prudent to make the attempt with so small a force, so long as the Island Battery, which protected the entrance, remained intact. It was quite evident that, owing to the shallowness of the water, this battery could only be feasibly attacked from the opposite shore near the Lighthouse; but there was no early prospect of being able to raise a battery there, on account of the difficulty of transporting artillery from Gabarus Bay. Fortunately, at this juncture, thirty cannon were discovered by a party stationed on the eastern side of the harbour, under water, near the Careening Wharf,[1] which were raised on the 16th, and taken to the Lighthouse, where Colonel Gorham was sent with a regiment to construct a battery. On the following day they were attacked by 100 Frenchmen, who had landed during the night at a cove about a mile to the eastward. A sharp fight occurred, in which the enemy lost five or six men killed, and several prisoners. The rest got off in their shallops. After this discomfiture, no further attempt was made to interrupt Colonel Gorham's men in the construction of the battery, which was traced out on a cliff, one flank facing the sea, the other the Island Battery, from which it was only 1,000 yards distant.

Meanwhile the troops had not been idle in making preparations for attacking the West Gate. On the 15th, the fifth fascine battery (marked F on map), commonly called 'Tidcomb's,' was constructed and armed with guns from the Grand Battery. The smart fire constantly maintained by this battery,

[1] Duchambon says in his Report: 'The Lieutenant of Artillery came to inform me that the enemy had discovered many cannon left as a reserve near the Lighthouse ten years ago; that he had reported to former governors many times, how an enemy might easily transport them to the Lighthouse and turn them against vessels passing in and out, and might also attack the Island Battery. Upon advice so important, and the enemy already having a breastwork there, I sent 100 men to surprise them and stop their works. They landed from three shallops, north of the harbour, and next day approached the Lighthouse, but they were repulsed by 200 of the enemy stationed there.'

and those previously raised, protected the troops engaged in digging the trenches for the advanced or breaching battery, which had been marked out at a distance of only 250 yards from the West Gate (E on map). This duty was so effectually performed, that on the evening of the 18th, having been armed with two 42 and two 18-pounders, dragged with incredible labour from the Grand Battery, it commenced firing upon the West Gate, and soon demolished the drawbridge and part of the adjoining wall. As this was specially intended for breaching the walls preparatory to an assault, and was within such a short distance of the ramparts of the town, it was indispensably necessary to provide for the safety of the gunners, by placing the cannon in trenches dug below the surface, faced by a parapet composed partly of fascines and partly of earth. The opposing hosts were now so near each other, that a sharp fire of musketry was constantly kept up, and several men were killed on both sides. One unfortunate man, who rashly exposed himself on the parapet, fell the moment he showed himself, pierced by five balls fired from the ramparts. Nevertheless, nothing daunted the gallant Provincials; fresh guns and mortars were brought forward daily, and the trenches extended to the southward in front of the King's Bastion.

On the same day that the advanced battery opened its fire with such decided success, an event occurred off the mouth of the harbour which, Pepperrell says, 'produced a burst of joy in the army, and animated the men with fresh courage to persevere.' Every spring the French Government sent a vessel from Brest to Louisbourg with a supply of military stores in time to reach Cape Breton as soon as possible after the ice left the navigation open. The vessel appointed for this service in the spring of 1745 was lying in Brest harbour ready to take in her cargo, when she was accidentally destroyed by fire; and as there was no other suitable ship in the port ready to take her place, the 'Vigilant,' of sixty-four guns, then on the stocks, was launched and fitted out for that purpose with all possible despatch. Owing to this unavoidable delay, the 'Vigilant,' which ought to have arrived at Louisbourg before Warren's squadron, did not reach the offing until May 18, and then unluckily in a thick fog. While standing off and on for the fog to clear away, she fell in with the frigate 'Mermaid,' of forty guns, commanded by Captain Douglas. As Douglas saw no chance of coping with such a powerful adversary, he made all sail towards Louisbourg, closely pursued by the 'Vigilant,' until he reached Warren's squadron just as the fog cleared off. The French Captain, the Marquis de Maisonforte, instead of making prize of the 'Mermaid,' as he expected, found himself, to his astonishment, in the midst of an enemy's fleet; but although his ship was overladen with arms and munitions of war, and so deep in the water as to be unable to use her lower tier of guns, De Maisonforte gallantly determined to defend himself to the last extremity. Of course, with such odds against him, there could be no doubt of the result. After a sharp contest, the 'Vigilant,' having lost a great number of men, struck her colours. A French author, the Abbé Prevost, whom I have often quoted, has the hardihood to assert that this single ship was nearly a match for the whole English fleet; he says:—

'The "Vigilant" was at first attacked by the frigate by which Maisonforte had been misled, then by two ships, one of fifty, the other of sixty guns, and in the end by the whole squadron. The fire, which began two hours after mid-day, was terrible on all sides. Maisonforte and his people performed prodigies of valour. The victory wavered until 9 P.M. nearly, when the French, having their rudder broken, all their rigging cut up, and their forecastle shattered to pieces, saw that their ship was near sinking. They yielded with more honour than their enemies could claim for their victory.'

The capture of the 'Vigilant' supplied the English with many articles much needed. The crew of 560 men was distributed through the fleet for safe keeping, and the ship was repaired by carpenters furnished by the army. Before the siege was over, she was manned by a crew collected from the army and the transports, and placed under the command of Captain Douglas.

Prevost says that this misfortune was the cause of the loss of Louisbourg, because the besiegers had become so discouraged with the resistance they had met with, and knew so little of the art of war, that the troops had already demanded of their officers permission to retire, when this unlooked-for success elevated their hopes and induced them to persevere! The capture of the 'Vigilant,' as I have already told you, undoubtedly inspired the army with fresh courage, but there is not the slightest foundation for Prevost's statement. The reduction of Louisbourg had certainly occupied a longer time than was expected, but the men neither murmured nor complained of the danger and fatigue to which they were daily exposed.[1] On the contrary, they cheerfully submitted to the orders of their superior officers, which they carried out with alacrity, after their own irregular fashion, it is true, and not with the strict discipline of regular troops; but they were always ready when called upon to take their places in a post of danger. When the engineer, Mr. Bastide, who arrived from Annapolis during the siege, proposed to make regular approaches under cover, they laughed at his zigzags and épaulements, and pursued their own random system, asking for no other cover than a dark night. Belknap,[2] who was personally acquainted with many, both officers and men, who were present at the siege says, 'Those who were on the spot, have frequently in my hearing laughed at the recital of their own irregularities, and expressed their admiration when they reflected on the almost miraculous preservation of the army from destruction. They indeed presented a formidable front to the enemy, but the rear was a scene of confusion and frolic. While some were on duty at the trenches, others were racing, wrestling, pitching quoits, firing at marks or birds, or running after shot from the enemy's guns, for which they received a bounty, and the shot were sent back to the city.'

[1] Major Pomroy, writing to his family at this time, said, 'Louisbourg is an exceedingly strong place, and seems impregnable. It looks as if our campaign would last long; but I am willing to stay till God's time comes to deliver the city into our hands.' To which his noble-hearted wife replied, 'Suffer no anxious thought to rest in your mind about me. The whole town is much engaged with concern for the expedition, how Providence will order the affair, for which religious meetings every week are maintained. I leave you in the hand of God.'—*Bancroft.*

[2] In his *History of New Hampshire.*

The General and Commodore, however, on whom rested all the responsibility, enjoyed no share of these happy feelings. On shore, the slight breaches made in the walls were repaired during the night with timber or such material as they had at hand; nearly 1,500 men were off duty, suffering from diarrhœa brought on by sleeping in the cold foggy nights upon damp ground, with no other covering than wretched tents or huts formed of spruce boughs; and about six hundred men were absent on scouting expeditions after the Indians,[1] who had again been seen in the neighbourhood and along the eastern coast. At sea also, Warren, who had not yet been joined by any of the ships expected from Newfoundland, had good cause for uneasiness, as he had learned from the master of a French ship captured off the harbour, laden with provisions and stores, that a squadron of four large ships and two frigates were at Brest ready to sail for the relief of Louisbourg. Warren, who had now been nearly three months at sea, had little hope of being able with four ships only to resist a superior force fresh from France, equipped with an abundance of munitions and stores; he had every reason, therefore, for wishing to get into the harbour for the purpose of attacking the town on that side, before the French squadron[2] arrived. If Warren's ships should be defeated outside the harbour, nothing could have saved the transports in Gabarus Bay, and the army on shore, being consequently cut off from its communications with Boston, from

[1] On May 20, 200 men were sent to the North-east Harbour (probably Menadou), where ten men, part of a boat's crew sent on shore by Captain Fletcher for water, had been murdered. They did not meet with the enemy, but brought in a French doctor and some other prisoners. On the following day another scout of 200 men was sent out to look after some hundreds of French and Indians who were said to be coming down on the camp. The party returned next day and brought in some cows, swine, and goats, but did not find the enemy.—Gibson's *Journal.*

[2] In consequence of the intelligence carried to France by the 'Renommée' (see page 201), a squadron of seven ships, under the command of M. Perrier, was despatched from Brest for the relief of Louisbourg. On July 19, M. Perrier fell in with and captured the English ship 'Prince of Orange,' Captain Smithurst, in 40½ west longitude, which had been blown off the coast of Cape Breton in a gale, from which he learned the surrender of Louisbourg. M. Perrier wisely returned to France. If he had not obtained this intelligence he would have fallen into the clutches of the English fleet at Louisbourg.—*Douglas.*

whence it received its supplies, must have been placed in a position of the greatest peril. In this emergency the Commodore held a Council of Naval Officers, at which he informed the General that it was decided, 'all H.M.'s ships and all the colony cruisers, except two, should go into the harbour and attack the town and batteries with the utmost rigour; that the "Vigilant" should be manned with 600 men selected from the army, to join in the attack; and that 1,000 men should also be distributed among the ships of war, ready to land and assault the town from the harbour.' If Pepperrell had had a sufficient number of troops at his disposal, this scheme might have been carried into effect with every prospect of success; but when it is borne in mind that about one-third of the army was at that time only just recovering from sickness and unfit for duty, and that a great number of men were absent on scouting expeditions, it must be admitted that the General was perfectly justified in declining the proposal of the Commodore.

Warren's scheme was therefore given up; but Pepperrell in the meantime did not relax in his endeavours to annoy the enemy. The batteries played incessantly upon the town with good effect. On the night of the 24th a fire-ship was towed by Lieutenant Gibson and five men from the Grand Battery, and grounded against the King's Gate. When the train was fired, the fire from the town became so hot that Gibson and his men were obliged to row close along the walls under the mouths of the cannon, until they reached the western side of the harbour. 'The fire-ship burnt three vessels, beat down a pinnacle of the King's Gate and great part of a stone house in the city. Being done in the dead of the night it caused great consternation.'[1]

As there were continual rumours afloat of French and Indians collecting and coming from remote parts of the island, who it was feared might attack the camp when so many men were absent at their duty in the trenches, it was deemed advisable to send out a detachment towards Mirá to intercept them on their way. Accordingly, on May 26, a party of 153 men were sent on that service from the Grand Battery. I will let

[1] Gibson's *Journal*.

Gibson, who was one of the party, tell his own story: 'A scout of 153 men marched to the W. N. W. part of the island, about twenty-five miles from the Grand Battery. Found two fine farms on a neck of land that extended nearly seven miles in length. First we came to a very handsome house with two large barns, two large gardens, and fine fields of corn. In this house took seven Frenchmen and one woman prisoners. Not more than five hours before our arrival, 140 French and Indians had been killing cattle here and baking bread for provisions on their march against our men, who held the Light-house Battery. This was the very same band that murdered nineteen of our men at the North-east harbour on the 10th. The other was a fine stone edifice, six rooms on a floor, and well finished. There was a fine walk before it, and two barns contiguous to it, with fine gardens and fields of wheat. In one of these barns were fifteen loads of hay, and room sufficient for sixty horses and cattle. At our departure from the first farm, set it all on fire. Turning back at a considerable distance, we saw some hundreds of the enemy hovering around the flames. Here we took three men, in a boat laden with provisions and sailing down to Louisbourg. The last house was situated on the mouth of a large salmon fishery, which was some few rods wide, and about half a mile above it was a large pond of fresh water which was nearly four miles over. On the 27th the scout returned to Grand Battery, all well and in high spirits.' [1]

As Warren's project could not be carried into effect for the reasons above stated, the two commanders came to the resolution of storming the Island Battery, which alone prevented the ships from getting into the harbour. At a Council of Army Officers it was agreed to make the attempt at all risks, although many of them were of opinion that it was a very hazardous undertaking. Inducements were offered to the men to volunteer for this dangerous enterprise, when 400 readily came forward, headed by Captain Brooks, a commander of their own

[1] The farms alluded to were probably situated near the confluence of the Mirà and Salmon rivers. Some of you, who are better acquainted with the Mirà River, may perhaps be able to fix their locality with more precision.

choosing. Having embarked in light whale-boats on the night of May 27, they rowed cautiously round Black Point, with the intention of landing on the eastern side of the island, close to the barracks, but having been discovered by the sentinels on duty at the guardhouse some time before they reached their destination, they were assailed by the whole garrison of 180 men before they could effect a landing. Many of their frail boats were sunk by musket shot before they touched the shore, on which a heavy surf was breaking at the time, which increased the confusion. In spite of all difficulties nearly half of the force succeeded in getting on shore, but their firelocks, being wetted by the surf, were useless; so that after sustaining a most unequal contest for more than an hour with the enemy, they were obliged to surrender. Sixty men were killed and 116 made prisoners. Among the first was their gallant leader, Captain Brooks, who was cut down by a Swiss soldier while in the act of hauling down the flag of the fort. This was the most serious reverse experienced by the Provincials during the siege. 'It saddened the hearts of the army, the more so when the exulting cheers of the enemy were next morning wafted to their ears, reverberating from hill to hill.'[1]

If there had, as Prevost asserts, been any discontent in the army, it would certainly have shown itself after a disaster like this, most probably in the shape of dissatisfaction with their General, who had, it was well known, been persuaded by Warren to undertake the enterprise contrary to the advice of many of his officers. No indications, however, of such discontent were exhibited by the troops, who neither lost confidence in their leader, nor ever despaired of ultimate success. They were as ready as ever to engage in any enterprise attended with danger or excitement. Nothing pleased them more than to be sent into the woods on scouting expeditions, to intercept the French and Indians, reported to be assembling in great numbers. Their taste for this kind of occupation was often gratified. Pepperrell states in a letter of May 28 to Warren, 'that 600 of his men had gone in pursuit of two large bodies of French and Indians, eastward and westward of us.' Perhaps

[1] Parsons's *Life of Pepperrell.*

some intelligence from Mascarene, the Governor of Annapolis, had reached the General, informing him that the French and Indians who had been besieging that place had been ordered by Duchambon to proceed with all haste to Louisbourg.[1] I will close this long letter with Gibson's account of an expedition to Scatari :—'On May 28, a scout of 400 men marched towards Scattaree, upon information that a great number of French and Indians were coming towards our camp, in order to cut them off. As our scout was marching down a hill at the North-East harbour, they came all on a sudden upon 160 French and Indians. A skirmish took place, in which the enemy had thirty-seven killed and forty-one wounded, as we were told by the French captain's wife, whom we took prisoner. They killed only ten of ours. Enemy made off without burying their dead. This was the same company that was on the W.N.W. neck of land on Sunday the 26th. We took their shalloways laden with provisions. On the 29th the scout marched to Scattaree,[2] where we burnt several houses and took six men and three women prisoners. Last night we (for I was amongst them) lodged in the woods. The French and Indians drew off. On the 30th, returned to the Grand Battery in great spirits.'

[1] A number of Canadians, commanded by M. Marin, who had wintered at Chignecto, having been joined by 300 Indians, appeared before Annapolis in the beginning of May. (Douglas says, 'there were 900 raggamuffins, Canadians, other French and Indians.') They captured two Boston schooners laden with provisions, but not being able to make an impression on the fort, they retired on the 24th to Minas, where they were met by an express from Duchambon, requesting them to go to the relief of Louisbourg. About 400 of them, who embarked in two sloops, two schooners, and sixty canoes, for that purpose, while lying in Amascouse harbour near Cape Sable, were attacked and dispersed by two Provincial cruisers.

[2] Gibson probably means Menadou, *in the direction of, or near to Scatari.*

LETTER XIV.

1745–1746.

THE ARMY had now (June 1) been a whole month in front of Louisbourg, but it was evident that, unless the ships could force an entrance into the harbour, the prospect of reducing the place was as remote as ever. The attempt to storm the Island Battery having failed, it was now determined to press on the construction of the battery at the Lighthouse with all possible despatch. More than 200 men had been employed on this service, but the labour of raising the guns at the Careening Wharf had proved so much greater than was anticipated, that they were not ready to open their fire upon the Island Battery before June 10. As these guns were only 18-pounders, it was deemed advisable to bring a mortar and some heavier cannon from Gabarus Bay—a work of great difficulty, as they had to be landed at a cove more than a mile to the eastward of the Lighthouse, and to be dragged over alternate intervals of rough rocky knolls and deep morasses by manual labour alone.

While these preparations were in progress during the first week of June, the bombardment of the West Gate and the King's Bastion was prosecuted with great vigour, notwithstanding the deficiency of suitable artillery, several of the 42-pounders and their largest mortar having been burst. There was, besides, a great scarcity of experienced gunners, though Warren had at different times supplied some from his ships. Still, in spite of these difficulties and disappointments, serious damage had been done to the defences near the West Gate, all the guns of the Circular Battery except two having been dismounted, and a breach twenty-four feet in depth made in the right flank of the King's Bastion, which it was expected would in the course of two or three days be sufficiently enlarged to admit of an assault. In this encouraging aspect of affairs, the long-expected ships began to arrive from Newfoundland, to the great relief of the Commodore, who could now muster (June 8) eight sail of forty to sixty guns, exclusive of the 'Vigilant.' On the same day that the English were gratified by the arrival of their long-looked for ships, the French, for the first time, heard of the loss of the 'Vigilant.' They had witnessed the capture of a large ship from the walls, but had no suspicion that it was the 'Vigilant' until this day, when her late commander, the Marquis de Maisonforte, at the request of Warren wrote to Duchambon informing him that it was reported through the English fleet that some prisoners had been treated with great cruelty and inhumanity in Louisbourg; that he had visited the ships in the English fleet, in which the crew of the 'Vigilant' were confined, and had ascertained that they were treated with great kindness and consideration. He hoped therefore that Duchambon would treat any English prisoners that fell into his hands in the same manner. Captain McDonald, the bearer of the flag of truce and the letter from the Marquis, reported that this intelligence caused great surprise and dismay in Louisbourg. This was just the effect intended. The Marquis had been asked to write the letter, not for the object stated to him, but for the purpose of discouraging the French by the intelligence of the loss of the 'Vigilant.'

As you must by this time be almost tired of my long story of the siege, I will now only mention a few circumstances which occurred about this time, and then hasten on to the crisis, which was evidently near at hand. On June 2 the French laid a boom from the West Gate to the Batterie de la Grève, to guard against fire-ships, and to prevent the English landing from boats on that side of the city. On the 5th a ship of 300 tons, armed with fourteen guns, laden with provisions for the fishery, was brought into Gabarus Bay; and on the same day, Gibson says, the trenches had now approached so near to the city 'that the French drank to us from the walls, we being so close that we could speak with each other.' On the 7th all the prisoners taken on shore and in the prizes, together with the crew of the 'Vigilant,' in all about 1,000 men, were sent in transports and prize ships to Boston, convoyed by two of the provincial armed vessels. On Sunday 9, two Swiss deserters came into the English lines, who reported that the garrison was kept constantly on the alert, expecting an assault every night,—that if succour did not arrive soon they would be obliged to surrender, being short both of provisions and ammunition,—and that great apprehensions were felt on account of the battery in the course of erection at the Lighthouse. On the same day (the 9th) two valuable prizes were taken and sent to Boston; and a sloop of 110 tons from Canada with provisions, chased by one of the cruisers, ran ashore behind the Lighthouse, when the crew escaped. The sloop was got off without damage. This made the twentieth prize taken up to this time.

The attention of all was now directed towards the Lighthouse Battery. Stores and ordnance were sent from Gabarus Bay in boats, close by the Island Battery, without interruption, and on the 11th, three of the eighteen-pounders being mounted, fire was opened upon it with such decided success, that the General and Commodore now felt assured of an early termination of their labours. This (June 11) being the anniversary of the accession of George II., it was determined to celebrate the day by a vigorous fire from all the batteries. The firing commenced at noon and was maintained until nightfall. With only three guns at the Lighthouse, the French gunners were driven off the platform of the Island Battery, and six cannon which the enemy had planted on the previous night near the West Gate were silenced. Bombs and red-hot balls were fired into the town from the trenches, which caused great consternation.

'The walls grew weak; and fast and hot
Against them pour'd the ceaseless shot,
With unabating fury sent
From battery to battlement;
And thunderlike the pealing din
Rose from each heated culverin;
And here and there some crackling dome
Was fired before the exploding bomb.'

BYRON.

Warren's squadron[1] having at this time been reinforced by the arrival of three large ships, he now felt himself strong enough to sail into the harbour. Having consulted with Pepperrell, arrangements were made by the two commanders for making a general assault upon the place by sea and land, as soon as the necessary preparations could be completed. As bands of French and Indians were, according to information obtained from prisoners, hovering in the woods,[2] it was deemed prudent to surround the camp and stores with a strong picket fence for their protection during the assault, when every available man would of course be engaged on that service. Ladders were put on board all the ships' boats, for the use of the sailors and marines in scaling the walls facing the harbour, and the transports were sent alongside the ships of war to clear them of their useless lumber. Scaling-ladders and fascines were also collected at the advanced battery, ready to be carried to the walls; and 600 men were selected from the army to strengthen the crews of the ships, which were to anchor in a line off the mouth of the harbour.

It was arranged that as soon as a fair wind sprang up, Warren should hoist a Dutch flag under a pennant at his main-top-gallant masthead, and that Pepperrell, if all were ready on his part, should answer it by lighting three fires of brushwood on Green Hill; Warren was then to sail into the harbour and anchor before the town, while Pepperrell, with all his available troops, was to march with drums beating and colours flying to the assault of the West Front.

While these preparations were in progress, the English batteries were not idle. The French also, seeing probably what was going on, replied with great vigour, especially against the Lighthouse Battery, which gave them great uneasiness. One of the Swiss deserters that came into the lines

[1] Warren's fleet now comprised the 'Superb,' 'Sunderland,' 'Canterbury,' and 'Princess Mary,' of sixty guns each; the 'Vigilant,' of sixty-four guns; and the 'Launceston,' 'Chester,' 'Mermaid,' 'Hector,' 'Lark,' and 'Eltham,' of forty guns each.

[2] On the 10th, a party of men were sent in boats to Mirá, to seize 400 stand of arms and some ammunition, which were said to be concealed there for the use of the Canadians and Indians expected from Annapolis. See note, p. 224.

on the 9th having said that a mortar at the Lighthouse would greatly annoy the Island Battery, Pepperrell, acting upon this hint, sent a large mortar from Gabarus Bay, which, together with four more guns, were ready for use on the morning of the 14th, when a smart fire was opened upon the Island Battery. In the course of the day, the barracks were in a great degree demolished, several guns dismounted, and the gunners, driven from the platforms, were obliged to run for shelter under the cliffs on the south side of the island. The shells were fired with such precision, under the direction of Colonel Gridley, who had superintended the construction of the battery, that out of nineteen fired in the course of the day, seventeen fell inside the fort, and one exploded on the top of the magazine.

On the 14th the whole of the ships anchored in a line off the town, which made an imposing appearance; and on the 15th, everything being ready for carrying out their plans, the moment the wind became favourable, Warren went on shore to confer with Pepperrell. 'The troops, being paraded, were exhorted in stirring speeches by both Warren and Pepperrell, to show their valour and heroism in the designed attack.'[1]

Duchambon, meanwhile, had not been a careless observer of the significant preparations in progress during the last few days. He saw that the storm which had long been gathering was about to burst upon his bealeagured fortress; and that the fleet of the enemy, which had been increasing in force daily, could now easily get into the harbour, as the Island Battery, his only safeguard, was no longer tenable. He had still sufficient strength to resist an assault on the West Front alone, but as it would require at least half of his troops to man the batteries on the harbour side, he clearly saw that any attempt to resist both the fleet and the army would be hopeless, and attended with a great loss of life; he therefore prudently resolved to surrender. On the afternoon of the 15th, while Warren was at the camp, Duchambon sent a messenger with a letter to Pepperrell, proposing a suspension of hostilities until the terms of capitulation could be agreed upon; to which the following answer was immediately returned:—

[1] Parsons's *Life of Pepperrell.*

'*To Governor Duchambon.*

'Camp, 15th, June 1745.

'We have yours of this date, proposing a suspension of hostilities for such a time as shall be necessary for you to determine upon the conditions of delivering up the garrison of Louisbourg, which arrived at a happy juncture to prevent the effusion of Christian blood, as we were together, and had just determined upon a general attack. We shall comply with your desire until 8 o'clock to-morrow morning; and if, in the meantime, you surrender yourselves prisoners of war, you may depend upon humane and generous treatment.

'We are your humble servants,

'PETER WARREN,

'WILLIAM PEPPERRELL.'

Next morning, Duchambon wrote to Warren and Pepperrell, stating the conditions upon which he proposed to surrender, which, being deemed inadmissible, they sent him their ultimatum as follows:—

'Camp before Louisbourg, 16th June, 1745.

'We have before us yours of this date, together with the several articles of capitulation on which you have proposed to surrender the town and fortifications of Louisbourg, with the territories adjacent under your government, to his Britannic Majesty's obedience, to be delivered up to his said Majesty's forces now besieging said place, under our command; which articles we can by no means accede to. But as we are desirous to treat you in a generous manner, we do again make you an offer of the terms of surrender proposed by us in our summons sent you May 7th last; and do further consent to allow and promise you the following articles, namely:—

'1st. That if your own vessels shall be found insufficient for the transportation of your persons and proposed effects to France, we will supply such a number of other vessels as may be sufficient for that purpose, also any provisions necessary for the voyage which you cannot furnish yourselves with.

'2nd. That all the commissioned officers belonging to the

garrison, and the inhabitants of the town, may remain in their houses with their families, and enjoy the free exercise of their religion, and no person shall be suffered to misuse or molest any of them till such time as they can conveniently be transported to France.

'3rd. That the non-commissioned officers and soldiers shall, immediately upon the surrender of the town and fortresses, be put on board his Britannic Majesty's ships, till they all be transported to France.

'4th. That all your sick and wounded shall be taken tender care of in the same manner as our own.

'5th. That the commander-in-chief, now in garrison, shall have liberty to send off covered wagons, to be inspected only by one officer of ours, that no warlike stores may be contained therein.

'6th. That if there be any persons in the town or garrison which may desire shall not be seen by us, they shall be permitted to go off masked.

'7th. The above we do consent to, and promise, upon your compliance with the following conditions:—

'1. That the said surrender, and due performance of every part of the aforesaid premises, be made and completed as soon as possible.

2. That, as a security for the punctual performance of the same, the Island Battery, or one of the batteries of the town, shall be delivered, together with the warlike stores thereunto belonging, into the possession of his Britannic Majesty's troops before 6 o'clock this evening.

'3. That his said Britannic Majesty's ships of war, now lying before the port, shall be permitted to enter the harbour of Louisbourg without any molestation, as soon after six of the clock this afternoon as the commander-in-chief of said ships shall think fit.

'4. That none of the officers, soldiers, nor inhabitants in Louisbourg, who are subjects of the French King, shall take up arms against his Britannic Majesty, nor any of his allies, until after the expiration of the full term of twelve months from this time.

'5. That all subjects of his Britannic Majesty, who are now prisoners with you, shall be immediately delivered up to us.

'In case of your non-compliance with these conditions, we decline any further treaty with you on the affair, and shall decide the matter by our arms, and are, &c.,

'Your humble servants,
'P. Warren,
'W. Pepperrell.'

In reply to this peremptory summons, the governor, Duchambon, who had no alternative, sent an hostage with a letter to Pepperrell on the same day, stating that he would surrender the town and fortresses, and the territories adjacent, upon the terms proposed, requesting only that his troops might be allowed to march out of the garrison with their arms, and colours flying, which should be then given up immediately afterwards. Pepperrell acceded to this request, and sent a hostage, as promised, as a guarantee for the faithful performance of the conditions agreed upon. That Duchambon had no alternative is quite evident from his Report to the Minister of War, in which he gives, amongst others, the following reasons for capitulating:—'On the 15th, the fleet drew up in a line off White Point, two leagues from the port, and piles of brushwood were made on Green Hill for signals. The fire of the enemy from cannon and mortars was without cessation from the beginning of the siege; the houses of the city were perfectly riddled with balls; the flank of the King's Bastion was demolished; the wooden and turf embrasures, that had been frequently repaired, were destroyed; a breach was made in the West Gate, through which an entrance was now practicable, by the help of fascines, which the enemy had been bringing forward for two days to their trenches; and all this had been done in the face of our cannon and musketry, which were served with an activity and vigour beyond expectation. This is proved, Monsieur, by the fact that of 67,000 kegs of powder we had at the commencement of the siege, there remained on the 17th June only 47 in the city, which quantity was absolutely necessary, on the eve of capitulation. We had also expended all our shells of 9 and 12 inches. I ought in justice to all the officers and soldiers of the garrison, and the inhabitants generally, to say, that they have all endured the fatigue and privation with intrepidity unequalled, passing all their nights without undressing, and sleeping on the bare ground; and those stationed on the ramparts found no repose, since the enemy's cannon balls reached every part of the city. Every one was worn out with fatigue and watching, and of the 1,300 men at the beginning of the siege, 50 were killed and 95 wounded, and many more were sick from the hardships they endured. On the 16th June, the inhabitants sent me a petition, stating that, as the forces of the enemy by sea and land were augmenting daily, without any prospect of the arrival of succours for us, nor any hope of our being able to hold out much longer, that it would be better to capitulate with the English commanders, in order to preserve the few lives that remain. This petition touched me with the deepest emotion. To think of surrendering Louisbourg, which had cost the King vast sums of money; that there were a number of inhabitants with families who were to perish immediately, or to lose the fruits of their labour since the commencement of the colony. But here was a practicable breach made in the wall by the enemy, and thirteen large ships all ready to join in an attack. In a conjuncture so critical, I directed the chief engineer, M. Verrier, to render an account of the fortifications and of the place, and the officer charged with the artillery, to give a report of the munitions of war; and upon their report I held a council of war, which decided unanimously, that, considering the forces of the enemy, and the state of the garrison and the place, it was necessary to capitulate.'

In a letter dated August 13, written by Duchambon to the Minister, after his arrival in France, he states that the English had 13,000 land and sea forces (about 5,000 more than the real number), while he had only 1,300. It is only charitable to suppose that he may have been deceived respecting the number of the English army, because, as Belknap observes, 'the ground was so uneven, and the people so scattered, that the French could form no estimate of their numbers:' but he surely could not so soon have forgotten that he delivered up 1,960 prisoners of war before he left Louisbourg. He must also have been wide of the mark in asserting that he used 67,000 kegs of powder during the siege; for, supposing that each keg contained only 25 lbs., he must in this case have expended 750 tons of powder in forty-eight days, or 15 tons per day! Pepperrell, on the other hand, says 9,000 balls and 600 bombs were fired against the city: allowing that 20 lbs. were used for each charge, the consumption did not exceed one-third of a ton per day. Duchambon, it may be presumed, made these exaggerated statements for the purpose of covering his own shortcomings. He committed many errors during the siege. The following, in my humble opinion, were the principal:—

1. He took no steps for ascertaining the character of the suspicious-looking vessels that passed and repassed the harbour so frequently during the month of April.

2. He did not send spies to Canceau to gain information.

3. When the English forces did arrive, he only sent 100 men instead of all the disposable force at his command, to oppose their landing.

4. He gave up the Grand Battery without destroying or removing the guns, which proved absolutely necessary to the besiegers.

5. He made no vigorous sorties upon the English when they first opened their trenches. His apologists say he could not trust his men outside the walls, but he does not give this excuse himself.

In addition to these, his gravest error was the refusal of the succours offered by the Viceroy in the autumn of 1744.

But Duchambon was not the only one to blame for the loss of Louisbourg. If you look at the map of the harbour, you will observe there is a hill (125 feet in height) between the Careening Cove and the Lighthouse Point, which overlooks the town, the harbour, and all the batteries. If the French had erected a strong fort upon this hill, it could, owing to the nature of the ground, have been made almost impregnable at a small cost; the English could not have taken up a position on the western side of the harbour, only half a mile distant; they could never have erected a battery at the Lighthouse, only one quarter of a mile distant, to silence the Island Battery; the ships could not have gone into the harbour, or, if they had forced a passage, could not have anchored in safety, exposed to the plunging fire of shot and shell of an elevated fort; and lastly, if the town itself, only one mile distant, had been taken, it could never have been held by an enemy. Supported by such a fort, there is every reason to believe that Louisbourg would have held out until the arrival of M. Perrier's squadron, which might have driven Warren's fleet off the coast, and have saved the place.

Having freely given my opinion of the conduct of the Governor of Louisbourg (worthless as it may be deemed by those better able to judge of such matters), let us now turn to the more agreeable task of paying a just tribute to the gallant Provincials for their great achievement. Hutchinson justly observes 'that if there had been no signal proof of bravery and courage in the time of action, there having been only one sally from the town, and a few skirmishes with French and Indians from the woods, in all of which our men behaved well, yet here was the strongest evidence of a generous, noble public spirit, which first induced to the undertaking, and of steadiness and firmness of mind in the prosecution of it, the labour, fatigue, and other hardships of the siege being without parallel in all preceding American affairs.' Many, no doubt, embarked in the enterprise under the impression that Louisbourg would fall at the first blow; yet, when they found out their mistake, they never murmured, but submitted patiently to sufferings and privations which they had never dreamed of, during a period of seven weeks. Every man was ready at a moment's notice to proceed to the post assigned to him, and to carry out, to the best of his ability, the orders of his superiors. Of this I can give no better proof than the fact, that not a single man was punished during the whole siege for a breach of discipline or neglect of duty. It is no disparagement of the provincial forces to say, that without the aid and protection of Warren's squadron they never could have succeeded; for one single

French ship like the 'Vigilant' could easily have captured or dispersed the whole fleet of armed cruisers and transports, and cut off their supplies. Even if the army could have held its position before Louisbourg, it would have been an act of reckless folly to have attempted to assault the town without the aid of the fleet, as the whole of the garrison and militia, still numbering nearly 2,000 men, concentrated upon the only threatened point, the West Gate, would have been more than sufficient to resist with success the whole provincial army; for, although 'the West Gate was defaced, and the adjoining curtain, with the flank of the King's Bastion, much damaged, there was no practicable breach.'[1] It is a singular fact, that the weather, which had been fine and dry for forty days, broke up immediately after the capitulation, and an incessant rain continued for ten days. If the rain had set in sooner, it must have proved fatal to hundreds of the men suffering from colds and dysentery, lying upon damp ground with no other covering than tents, chiefly made of common osnaburg, which would not have protected them from a single shower.

On the afternoon of June 17, according to the terms of capitulation, Warren sent a body of marines to take possession of the Island Battery, and then conducted his fleet and all the transports into the harbour. About the same time, the army, with Pepperrell at its head, marched through the South-west Gate into the city, and paraded between the casemates of the King's Bastion, in front of the French troops, drawn up in a parallel line to receive them. Salutations were exchanged, and the keys of the place were then delivered to Pepperrell. Finally, the English flag was hoisted on the ramparts, and a general salute fired from all the English batteries and the ships in the harbour. It was only now that the army saw the vast strength of the fortress which had fallen into their hands.[2]

[1] Hutchinson.

[2] 'When our forces entered the city, and came to view the inward state of its fortifications, they were amazed to see their extraordinary strength and device, and how we had like to have lost the limbs and lives of a multitude, if not have been all destroyed. And that the city should surrender when there was a great body of French and Indians got on the island, and within a day's march to molest us.'—*Prince's Sermon at the South Church in Boston, on the General Thanksgiving for the taking of Louisbourg.*

'As the troops, entering the fortress, beheld the strength of the place, their hearts for the first time sank within them. "God has gone out of his way," said they, "in a remarkable and almost miraculous manner, to incline the hearts of the French to give up and deliver this strong city into our hand."'[1] They had indeed ample cause for expressing their astonishment and thankfulness, when they reflected what inadequate means they had for reducing such a stronghold. Even Pepperrell himself, who was embued with deep religious feeling, attributed the event to the interposition of Divine Providence, in answer to the prayers daily offered up throughout all New England for the success of the enterprise.

On the same day that Pepperrell took possession of the city, the French troops, consisting of 650 regulars and 1,310 militia, were sent on board the English ships until transports could be got ready to take them to France. Seventy-six cannon and mortars, and a large amount of valuable property, together with six months' provisions, were found in the city. The loss of the English during the whole siege, including those who died in the camp from dysentery, did not exceed 130 men. The French are supposed to have had more than 300 killed, although Duchambon, who, we have seen, is not to be depended upon, says only 50, in his Report to the Minister of War.

On June 18, General Pepperrell sent Captain Bennet in a fast-sailing schooner with despatches to Governor Shirley, announcing the fall of Louisbourg. The news, which reached Boston at one A.M. on July 3, was everywhere received with most lively demonstrations of joy.

'The people of Boston,' says Dr. Chauncy, in a letter to Pepperrell of July 4, 'before sunrise, were as thick about the streets as on an election day, and a pleasing joy visibly sat on the countenance of every one met with. . . . We had, last night, the finest illumination I ever beheld with my eyes. I believe there was not a house in town, in no by-lane or alley, but joy might be seen through its windows. The night also was made joyful by bonfires, fireworks, and all other external

[1] Bancroft's *History of the United States.*

tokens of rejoicing.' The news soon spread through the adjoining provinces, and filled all hearts with joy. In New York, Philadelphia, and every town and village of New England, the event was celebrated by ringing of bells, fireworks, and illuminations.

'The news of this important victory,' Belknap says, 'filled New England with joy and Europe with astonishment.' News of this great achievement first reached England on July 20, by the frigate 'Mermaid,' Captain Montague, and on the 27th, duplicates forwarded by the 'Shirley Galley,' Captain Rouse, confirmed the happy intelligence. To show their sense of the importance of the conquest of Cape Breton, the Lords Commissioners of the Admiralty presented Captain Montague with a purse of 500 guineas, and appointed Captain Rouse soon after to the command of one of his Majesty's ships.[1] The Tower and Park guns were fired by order of the Regency, the King being at the time at Hanover. At night London was illuminated, and bonfires were made at many conspicuous places. In every city and large town throughout Great Britain, similar demonstrations of joy were exhibited, and when the King returned from Hanover, congratulatory addresses poured in from all quarters. General Pepperrell was made a Baronet of Great Britain, and Commodore Warren was promoted to the rank of Rear-Admiral of the Blue, in testimony of their great services. At the same time, General Pepperrell was directed to acquaint the officers and men of the New England army with his Majesty's gracious approbation of their services on this occasion. Shortly afterwards, commissions were sent out to Pepperrell and Governor Shirley, to raise and command two regiments of the line in the colonies, as a reward for their services in promoting, organising, and executing, the enterprise with such signal success.

[1] General Pepperrell recommended Captain Rouse to the Ministry for his valuable services during the siege. He commanded a privateer belonging to Boston in 1744, and took several prizes on the coast of Newfoundland. In 1748 he was promoted to the command of the 'Albany' sloop of war, and was subsequently employed several years on the Halifax Station. He commanded the 'Sutherland,' of fifty guns, at the second siege of Louisbourg, in 1758.

Nothing will give you a better idea of the views entertained by the British Ministry, of the importance of the conquest of Cape Breton, than a few extracts, which I now submit, from the Duke of Newcastle's reply of August 10 to General Pepperrell's despatches: 'I laid the despatches immediately before the Lords Justices, who had the greatest joy in an event which does so much honour to his Majesty's arms, and may be attended with such happy consequences to the trade and commerce of his Majesty's subjects; and their Excellencies recommended to me, in a particular manner, to assure you of the sense they have of your prudence, courage, and conduct, which contributed so greatly to the success of this enterprise. As I lost no time in transmitting copies of your despatches to my Lord Harrington at Hanover, to be laid before the King, I have now the pleasure to acquaint you that the news of the reduction of Louisbourg was received by his Majesty with the highest satisfaction, which the King has commanded should be signified to all the commanders and other officers, both of land and sea, who were instrumental therein. . . . . It is a great satisfaction to me to acquaint you that his Majesty has thought fit to distinguish the commanders-in-chief of this expedition, by conferring on you the dignity of a Baronet of Great Britain (upon which I beg leave most sincerely to congratulate you), and by giving a flag to Mr. Warren . . . . I am persuaded it is unnecessary for me to recommend it to you to continue to employ the same zeal, vigilance, and activity you have already exerted, in doing everything that shall be necessary for the security and preservation of Louisbourg, in which the Lords Justices are persuaded that you and Mr. Warren will have the hearty concurrence and assistance of Governor Shirley, who has had so great a share in the forming and carrying into execution this enterprise. As the perfect union and harmony which has happily subsisted between you and Mr. Warren has so eminently contrbuted to the success of that undertaking, the Lords Justices have the firmest confidence that the same good agreement will continue between you, and that you will employ yo joint endeavours for securing in the most effectual manner t valuable acquisition that has been made by his Majesty's forces under your command.'

Belknap says, 'The enterprising spirit of New England gave a serious alarm to those jealous fears which had long predicted the independence of the colonies; and that great pains were taken in England to ascribe all the glory to the navy, and lessen the merit of the army.' If any dependence can be placed upon various articles published in the periodicals of the time, which may be considered to represent the feelings of the people in general, it is evident that, so far from endeavouring to lessen the merit of the army, or to excite any unworthy jealousy of the colonists, their exploit was everywhere highly extolled, and held up as an example for the regular army, which had just before suffered some serious reverses on the Continent.[1] The extracts I have given above from the Duke of Newcastle's letter clearly show the high opinion entertained by the Ministry of the services of the provincial army.

Let us now return to Louisbourg. Both Warren and Pepperrell, who acted as joint Governors, naturally expected that the French Government would endeavour to recover the valuable fortress which had been so unexpectedly lost, by means of a naval force, as it was well known that the navy of France was at that time in a very efficient condition. Great exertions were therefore made to put the defences of the place in good order. The partial breaches in the walls and ramparts were repaired, and some of the least injured houses hastily fitted up for the reception of the troops, until barracks could be provided. 'All the houses in the city (one only excepted) had some shot through them more or less; some had their roofs beat down with bombs; as for the famous citadel and hospital, they were almost demolished by bombs and shot.'[2] The parapets and

[1] In the *Gentleman's Magazine* for July 1745, there is a Hymn to Victory, on the taking of Cape Breton, of which the following is the first stanza:—

> Beyond the wide Atlantic sea
> She rises *first* to crown our toils;
> Thither to wealth she points the way,
> And bids us thrive on Gallic spoils.

[2] Gibson's *Journal of the Siege.*

embrasures of all the English batteries, including that at the Lighthouse, were levelled, and their guns brought into the town, except the 42-pounders, which were sent back to the Grand Battery, from which they had been taken. As the 'Launceston' frigate had been appointed to accompany the transports to France, her guns were landed and taken into the town also. Consequently, in the course of a few weeks 266 good cannon were mounted on the ramparts of the town and batteries, and Louisbourg was in a better condition of defence than it ever had been in the hands of the French.

On the 18th, the day after the surrender, a storeship of 300 tons, armed with twenty guns, was taken off the harbour by one of the men-of-war.

Two schooners which the French had run on shore in the harbour were got off, but all endeavours to raise some vessels they had sunk at the beginning of the siege proved fruitless.

On the 27th, a number of inhabitants came in from Scatari in their boats, and gave themselves up according to the terms of the capitulation.

On July 4, the French prisoners and the inhabitants of Louisbourg, in all 4,130 persons, sailed for Rochelle in fourteen transports. M. Duchambon, and the officers of the garrison, with their families, left at the same time in the 'Launceston' frigate.

The French flag was kept flying on the ramparts of Louisbourg for some time after its surrender, for the purpose of decoying French ships into the harbour. This ruse proved very successful. On July 23, a large East Indiaman, the 'Charmante,' and a few days after another, the 'Heron,' ran into the trap set for them. These ships had received orders to touch at Louisbourg on their homeward voyage, where they would find a squadron of men-of-war, under whose convoy they might safely reach Europe.[1] The value of these two ships and cargoes was estimated at 175,000*l.* sterling. This was, however, a mere trifle in comparison with the value of the treasure on board the 'Notre Dame de la Délivrance,' which was captured on August 23. Don Antonio d'Ulloa, who was a pas-

[1] Ulloa's *Voyage to South America.*

senger on board this ship, as I have already told you (p. 174), has given us such an interesting account of her capture that I cannot resist the temptation of making a few extracts from his narrative. You will recollect that, after the capture of her consorts—the 'Louis Érasme' and the 'Marquis d'Antin'—by the English privateers off the Azores, the 'Délivrance' bore up for Louisbourg, because 'the captain, having consulted with his officers what course it was most advisable to steer, and having learned from one of them who had often been at Louisbourg in the island of Cape Breton, near Newfoundland, and had a perfect knowledge of the situation and nature of the place, that in the beginning of the summer two men-of-war were every year sent thither, to carry money and troops for that place and Canada, and likewise to protect the cod fishery,' concluded that the safest course would be to proceed thither, and continue his voyage to Europe under convoy of the men-of-war. They were at this time, according to reckoning, 96 leagues to the north-westward of the Island of Flores, one of the Azores.

On August 12 (Old Style), at 4 P.M., they first made land, which, on the following morning at 6 A.M., they found to be 'the island of Escatari, which lies about five leagues north of Louisbourg.' On the same morning 'we saw a brigantine[1] plying along the coast for Louisbourg. The "Délivrance" on this hoisted a French ensign, which was answered by the other firing two or three guns. This gave us no manner of uneasiness, concluding that the brigantine, suspecting some deceit in our colours, had fired those guns as a warning to the fishing barks without to get into harbour; and they put the same construction on this firing, immediately showing the greatest hurry in making for a place of safety. An hour afterwards, being near 8 o'clock, we saw coming out of Louisbourg two men-of-war, which we immediately took for ships belonging to a French squadron stationed there for the security of that important place, and that they had come out on the signal from the brigantine that a ship had appeared in sight, lest it might be some Boston

[1] This was the 'Boston Packet,' Captain Fletcher, the only colonial vessel that got a share of the naval prize-money.—*Hutchinson.*

privateer with a design on the fishery. Thus we were under no manner of anxiety, especially as they came out with French colours, and one of them had a pennant, and all the forts of Louisbourg, as well as all the ships in the harbour, which we could now plainly distinguish, wore the same disguise. Here I must refer to the reader's imagination the complacency and joy which swelled every heart, imagining that we now saw the end of all our fears and disasters—a place of safe repose after a voyage of such danger and fatigue. Then let the reader be pleased to think what an edge the melancholy disappointment gave to our astonishment and dejection when, amidst the indulgence of such pleasing ideas, we found our hopes destroyed, all our visionary schemes of delight ending in the real miseries of captivity.' Having unshotted his guns, the captain of the 'Délivrance' was preparing to salute the men-of-war, when they hoisted English colours and fired a shot which carried away his foretopsail halyards. The two ships proved to be the 'Sunderland,' Captain Brett, and the 'Chester,' Captain Durell.

Ulloa says he received very kind treatment from Captain Durell, who sent him to his own house, where he remained during his captivity; and also from Admiral Warren, who frequently invited him to his table. All his papers relative to the mensuration of the degrees of the meridian, together with his physical and astronomical observations, were of course handed to Admiral Warren, by whom they were transmitted to the Admiralty. Ulloa left Louisbourg in October, in the 'Sunderland,' Captain Brett, and arrived in England in December. During his residence in London he was elected a Fellow of the Royal Society. All his papers were handed to him when he left for Spain.

The cargo of the 'Délivrance' was ostensibly cocoa, under which there were stowed away 2,000,000 Peruvian dollars, and a large amount of gold and silver in ingots and bars, the value of the whole being 800,000*l.* sterling.[1] The fall of

[1] The specie taken in the consorts of the 'Délivrance,' 'Louis Érasme,' and the 'Marquis d'Antin,' captured off the Azores by the privateers 'Prince Frederic' and 'Duke,' amounted to 3,000,000 dollars. Forty-three waggons were employed

Louisbourg proved fatal to the French East India Company, as it was the port at which their ships often touched on their way to Canada to collect the furs, of which they enjoyed a monopoly.

The division of the prize-money, one-half of which was claimed by the Crown, the other by the officers and crews of the fleet, caused great dissatisfaction in the army. This division was made according to the usual practice in similar cases, but it was manifestly unfair that the provincial troops, who had left their comfortable homes and occupations to embark in an enterprise so foreign to their habits, and attended with such toil and danger, should have received comparatively a mere trifle arising from the sale of the provisions and clothing taken in the town. They were told that their share of the plunder was to be gathered on the land, which probably gave rise to an idea somewhat prevalent amongst them, 'that they had acquired a right to the whole island and its dependencies, which it was proposed to divide between the officers and men, until they were undeceived by Governor Shirley.' [1]

In the beginning of July, 700 of the New England troops, many of whom were sick and incapable of duty, were sent home, and their places filled by the Rhode Island contingent and a reinforcement from Boston. Having accomplished their great object, all the troops were anxious to get home. Besides, the pay of the Massachusetts men was so much less than that of the Connecticut and Rhode Island men, that it occasioned great discontent among the former. As Pepperrell had no authority to increase their pay, Governor Shirley was invited by the officers to visit Louisbourg. As the services of the Massachusetts men could not be dispensed with until two regiments of the line, which had been ordered to go from Gibraltar, arrived, Shirley, when he reached Louisbourg, in the middle of August, advanced their pay to forty shillings per month, which quieted their almost open rebellion. Owing to some delay in providing transports, and to a long and boisterous

to transport it from Bristol to London. 'When it was divided, each sailor received 850 guineas for his share.'—Mante's *History of the War*.

[1] Hutchinson.

passage, the Gibraltar regiments did not arrive upon the coast until the winter had set in, which obliged them to run south to Virginia, where they remained until spring. All the New England troops were consequently obliged to remain at Louisbourg during the winter. When Shirley left in September, there were 2,740 men in garrison, but putrid fever and dysenteries, which had broken out soon after the army got into the town, in the month of August became contagious, and carried off a great number of the men.[1] As winter approached the disease increased in virulence. In a letter dated December 10, to General Wolcott, Pepperrell says, 'It has been a sickly dying time amongst us. Upwards of 400 men have died since we came into the city.' On January 28 the deaths had reached 561, and there were at that date 1,100 men sick, and only 1,000 capable of duty. The burials, however, which at one time ranged from fourteen to twenty-seven, did not then exceed from three to five per day. It is painful, even at this distant day, to reflect upon the melancholy fate of the brave men who thus sank helplessly into their graves, after bearing unscathed the toils and dangers of the battlefield, so far away from their homes.

If you ever visit the ruins of Louisbourg, you will observe a patch of dark-green sward on Point Rochfort—the site of the old burying-ground. Beneath it lie the ashes of hundreds of brave New Englanders! No monument marks the sacred spot, but the waves of the restless ocean, in calm or storm, sing an everlasting requiem over the graves of the departed heroes.

All the inhabitants of Louisbourg, except a few families that went to join their friends in Nova Scotia, were sent to France in July, but those residing in the outports and fishing stations upon the coast were suffered to remain, upon taking the oath of allegiance. The missionary, Father Mallard, was also permitted to reside at St. Peter's, to attend to their

[1] 'After we got into the town, a sordid indolence or sloth, for want of discipline, induced putrid fevers and dysenteries, which at length in August became contagious, and the people died like rotten sheep; this destroyed or rendered incapable of duty half of our militia.'—*Douglas.*

spiritual wants. In the month of September a detachment of 300 men were sent to take possession of St. John's Island, but the French inhabitants were not disturbed.

In the month of October all the ships of war left Louisbourg for England except the 'Vigilant,' 'Chester,' and a fire-ship which remained to guard the port.

Warren and Pepperrell, who remained there all winter, as you may easily imagine had their hands full in maintaining order among the undisciplined troops and the crowds of traders that flocked to Louisbourg after its fall. For this purpose it was absolutely necessary to govern by martial law; both Pepperrell and Warren being compelled to sit in court three days a week to try delinquents.

On April 2, 1746, the Gibraltar troops, comprising Fuller's and Warburton's regiments, of 815 men each, and 245 men of Frampton's regiment, in all 1,875, arrived at Louisbourg, to the great joy of the New England forces, who were enabled in consequence to return to their homes. Warren, who received his commission of Governor on April 2, addressed the men before they left Louisbourg, and congratulated them on the speedy prospect of being united to their families and friends. He thanked them for their valuable services to their king and country, and promised his protection to any who might wish to settle in Louisbourg, or take up grants of land in the island.

About the middle of May, Warren and Pepperrell embarked in the 'Chester,' Captain Spry, for Boston, leaving Commodore Knowles[1] in charge of the Government, and Colonel Warburton acting Lieutenant-Governor. On their arrival in Boston, on June 1, they were received with salutes from the batteries and ships of war in the harbour. On June 24 they were welcomed, and thanked by the House of Representatives, then in Session, 'for the services rendered to His Majesty's subjects in general, and to the people of New England in particular.' Soon after this, Admiral Warren left Boston for England, to take the command of a squadron in the Channel; Sir William Pepperrell retired to his home at Kittery in Maine,

[1] Commodore Knowles had just arrived from the West Indies with two ships of the line—the 'Canterbury' and 'Norwich.'

where he was received with all the honour to which he was so justly entitled.

In concluding this long story, I venture to hope that you will not suppose I have dwelt too long upon the incidents of a siege which must ever be deeply interesting to the youth of Cape Breton. The historian Smollett designated it 'the most important achievement of the war of 1744;' and the authors of the 'Universal History' considered it 'an equivalent for all the successes of the French upon the Continent.'[1]

[1] In most cases, I have mentioned, either in the text or the footnotes, the authorities consulted in compiling my narrative of the Siege of Louisbourg; but I cannot dismiss the subject without acknowledging especially one valuable source to which I am largely indebted—viz., Dr. Usher Parsons's *Life of General Pepperrell*.

LETTER XV.

1746–1749.

INTELLIGENCE of the fall of Louisbourg had scarcely reached Quebec when the Viceroy, M. de Beauharnois, and the Intendant, M. Hocquard, drew up a long memorial addressed to the Count de Maurepas, Minister of Marine, urging the importance and facility of immediately recovering not only Cape Breton but Nova Scotia also. They stated they were well assured by the missionaries that nearly all the inhabitants of Nova Scotia were desirous of returning under the French dominion; that they would take up arms as soon as they received the support of a body of troops; and that the Micmacs, the irreconcilable enemies of the English, if supplied with powder and lead, and some provisions, would join the Acadians. They added that, as the English would not likely give up Louisbourg at a general peace, unless the King of France obtained important advantages over them in Europe, it would be advisable to send out an expedition at once. They estimated that ten ships of the line and 2,500 soldiers would reduce both Nova Scotia and Cape Breton; but even if they failed in retaking Louisbourg, a secure footing upon the island might be effected by establishing a military settlement at Baie des Espagnols. The French Government, exasperated at the loss of such an important fortress as Louisbourg, which had cost an immense sum of money and twenty-five years of incessant labour in rendering it, as it was supposed, impregnable, readily fell into these views, and at once directed an armament to be prepared of greater force than had ever yet been sent to America. Accordingly, during the winter and spring of 1746 an expedition was fully equipped, consisting of eleven ships of the line, thirty frigates, two fireships, and thirty transports carrying 3,150 soldiers. The fleet was commanded by M. de la Rochefoucauld, Duc d'Anville, and the troops by Adjutant-General M. de Pommerill.

The British Government, well informed of what was going on, sent Admiral Martin to blockade the port of Brest, and to watch the motions of the enemy. Notwithstanding, the French fleet managed to get out of port unobserved, on June 22, and being soon after joined by the transports from Rochelle, sailed for America. As soon as intelligence of the departure of the fleet reached England, Admiral Lestock sailed from Portsmouth with eighteen ships in pursuit, but after several attempts was obliged by contrary winds to return to England.

While the fleet was getting ready in France, the Viceroy of Canada was actively engaged in organising a land-force to act in concert with it on its arrival. All through the winter of 1745–46, a constant intercourse was kept up with the Acadians and Indians of Nova Scotia; and in the beginning of the following summer a force of 1,600 men, composed of regular troops, Canadian militia, Coureurs de Bois, and Indians, was collected at Bay Verte, under the command of M. de Ramsay.[1]

News of the impending danger reached Boston early in the summer, where it created the greatest consternation and alarm. 'England,' says Hutchinson, 'was not more alarmed with the Spanish Armada, in 1588, than Boston and the other North American seaports with the arrival of D'Anville's fleet in the neighbourhood.' Six thousand militia were called out to defend the town, and as many more were held in readiness in Connecticut, to march to Boston if necessary. Old forts were repaired and new ones erected, sentinels placed on commanding points to give notice of the approach of the enemy, and every preparation made for a stubborn defence. There was indeed ample cause for alarm, for D'Anville's instructions were to retake and dismantle Louisbourg; to reduce Nova

[1] While De Ramsay was waiting at Beaubassin for news of D'Anville's arrival, 200 Indians, led by M. de Montesson, crossed over in canoes to Port la Joie, in St. John's Island, and captured twenty-seven soldiers and seven sailors belonging to some English ships engaged in removing the French inhabitants.

Scotia; to destroy Boston, and ravage the coast of New England; and then to proceed to the West Indies to harass the English Sugar Islands. 'All this was for the purpose of avenging the capture of Louisbourg by the militia of New England, which had piqued the self-love of the French, who burned to measure their strength with the Americans.'[1] There is every reason to believe that the greater part, if not the whole, of these instructions would have been successfully carried out if the expedition had not met with a series of unparalleled disasters. The fleet had barely got clear of the land, after escaping Admiral Martin's vigilance, when it encountered westerly gales, which so greatly retarded its progress that it did not reach the longitude of Sable Island until September 2, where nearly all the ships were dispersed in a violent storm. The 'Mars' and 'Alcyde,' of sixty-four guns each, were obliged to bear up for the West Indies; the 'Ardent,' of sixty-four guns, to return to France; and several of the transports were driven on shore upon Sable Island. D'Anville, with only two ships of the line and a few transports, arrived on September 10 at Chebucto (Halifax), the port of rendezvous, where he expected to find M. de Conflans with three ships of the line and a frigate, which had been detached from the fleet soon after it left France, to convoy some merchantmen to Cuba, with orders to proceed from thence to rejoin the fleet on the coast of Nova Scotia. M. de Conflans having met more favourable winds, arrived on the coast in August, and cruised for some time between Cape Sable and Canceau, but hearing nothing of the fleet, returned to France, according to his orders.

In the course of the next five or six days, a few transports arrived at Chebucto, but D'Anville was so agitated and distressed by the misfortune which had befallen the fleet, that he fell suddenly ill, and died in a fit of apoplexy on September 16. On the same day, Vice-Admiral D'Estournelle, the second in rank, arrived at Chebucto with three ships of the line, and succeeded to the command of the expedition. M. de la Jonquière, a naval officer, who had been appointed Viceroy

[1] Garneau.

of Canada, and had come out in the flagship, was then made second in command.

Finding the expedition so greatly reduced in strength by the dispersion of the ships and the sickness of the men, D'Estournelle held a council of war on the 18th, on board the 'Trident,' and proposed to abandon the enterprise and return to France. Jonquière, and nearly all the land and sea officers, were of opinion that Annapolis, at all events, should be reduced before they returned to Europe. After a long debate the Council decided to attack Annapolis. Irritated at the opposition of the Council, the Vice-Admiral fell into a fever attended with delirium, in which he imagined himself among the English, and ran himself through the body with his sword.

During the long voyage across the Atlantic, a scorbutic fever had broken out and carried off more than 1,200 men, before the ships reached Chebucto. As the ships arrived, the sick were landed and encamped on the shore of Bedford Basin; but, in spite of every care and attention, as many more are said to have died there, as well as a great number of the Micmacs who had come to join the French. 'Nothing,' says Garneau, 'could be imagined more mournful than the situation of this fleet, enchained to the shore by the plague. The soldiers and their equipages encumbered the great barracks, erected in haste on the desert shores, the great ocean moaning in front, which separated them from their country, towards which they turned their last looks. A sombre despair seized upon all. The contagion was communicated to the faithful Indians who came to join the French. The scourge at the same time filled their enemies with horror, who kept aloof when the expedition might have been annihilated with little effort on their part. Admiral Townsend looked with terror from Cape Breton, where he was with his squadron, on the ravages which destroyed his unfortunate enemies.'

At length, however, the malady was stayed by the seasonable arrival of abundant supplies of fresh meat, brought in by the Acadians from Minas, Piziguit, Cobequid, and Chignecto; and several of the missing ships having dropped in from day to day, preparations were made by Jonquière, now the chief of the expedition, for re-embarking the troops and proceeding to the attack of Annapolis. M. de Ramsay, who had spent nearly all the summer doing nothing beyond keeping Annapolis in alarm by his presence, hearing no tidings of D'Anville, and winter approaching, had started on his journey to Canada, when he was recalled by an express sent by Jonquière, requesting him to return with all the forces he could muster, and proceed to Annapolis to await the arrival of the ships. When De Ramsay received this order the greater part of his forces were already far on their way towards Quebec; but he managed to collect a body of 400 Acadians and Indians, with which he marched to Annapolis, and encamped at some distance from the place to wait for Jonquière's arrival. The troops, which had begun to embark at Chebucto on October 10, were hastened in their movements by the capture of an English vessel off the mouth of the harbour, in which were found despatches from Governor Shirley to Commodore Knowles, informing the latter that Admiral Lestock was on his way from England with a fleet of eighteen ships. It is said these despatches were allowed to fall purposely into the hands of the French, to induce them to leave Chebucto, and that they were so alarmed that they struck their tents, sank one of their largest ships, which had been much damaged at sea, burned all the prizes they had taken, and set sail on the 13th with five ships of the line and twenty frigates and transports, for Annapolis. They were, however, again doomed to disappointment. Off Cape Sable the fleet encountered a severe storm, which dispersed the ships and compelled them to return to France. Only two of the French ships got so far as the mouth of Annapolis Basin, where, observing some English ships[1] in the harbour loosening their sails, they made off, after putting on shore a messenger with advices to De Ramsay that the fleet had gone to France. De Ramsay, in consequence, broke up his camp before Annapolis, and withdrew to Beaubassin, where he wintered. The ill luck which

[1] The ships at Annapolis were the 'Chester,' Captain Spry, the 'Massachusetts,' Captain Tyng, and the Ordnance schooner.

had attended this great expedition from the first did not end even here. The 'Mars,' of sixty-four guns, which had been obliged to run before the gale from Sable Island to the West Indies, was captured off Cape Clear on October 11, by the 'Nottingham,' Captain Saumerez; and the 'Mercury,' a hospital ship, was chased by the 'Namur' into a British squadron in the Channel, on November 24, and captured. Garneau tells us that when M. de Maurepas, the French Minister of Marine, was apprised of all these misfortunes, he made this simple and noble response: 'When the Elements command, they can easily diminish the *glory*, but not the *deeds* or *merits* of the Chiefs.'

The people of New England, and, in fact, of all the British colonies, who had been in a state of the greatest excitement and suspense for more than three months, waiting for intelligence from Louisbourg, the place first threatened, were at length relieved of the load of anxiety which had so long oppressed them, by advices from Annapolis of the departure of the last ship of D'Anville's great fleet. Storms and sickness had dispersed or weakened the mighty armament which was to have spread ruin and devastation through all the colonies, from Cape Breton to the Isles of the Caribbean Sea. Great was their joy, great their gratitude to God, for their preservation, which they attributed to the special interposition of Providence.

Although Louisbourg was the first place that was to have been attacked, less alarm was felt there than in New England, because, in addition to the garrison of 2,000 regulars and a corps of Provincials, commanded by Colonel Bradstreet, the squadron in the harbour, since the arrival of Admiral Townsend with three ships from England, comprised the 'Vigilant,' of sixty-four guns, the 'Kingston,' 'Canterbury,' and 'Pembroke,' of sixty; the 'Norwich' and 'Chester,' of fifty, and the 'Fowey,' 'Kinsale,' and 'Torrington,' of forty guns each: in all nine sail, which surely, with the forts and batteries fully manned, must have made a respectable defence against even the whole of D'Anville's fleet. Nevertheless, the garrison was kept all summer on the alert by rumours respecting the Brest fleet; and upon one occasion, about the middle of July, the

'Vigilant' was sent up to Gaspé to disperse some French ships, reported to be embarking men to join D'Anville before Louisbourg. Meanwhile, great exertions were made to put the fortifications in thorough repair, and to erect a new range of barracks near the Queen's Gate, before winter. The garrison, which consisted of the two Gibraltar regiments, three companies of Frampton's regiment, a provincial corps, and recruits for Pepperrell's and Shirley's regiments, was comfortably quartered in the hospital and the new barracks, well provided with supplies of all kinds, including an ample stock of excellent coal—the produce of Cape Breton—the want of which had been greatly felt during the preceding winter.

During the summer of 1746, Shirley's and Pepperrell's officers were busily engaged in recruiting for their respective regiments at Louisbourg, where some of the provincial troops enlisted, and also in Boston, St. John's, and Newfoundland. Nearly 1,000 men had been enlisted for each regiment, but they had not all joined the head-quarters at Louisbourg before winter set in. The Governor, Commodore Knowles, complained greatly, in the month of August, to Pepperrell, of the conduct of some of the officers and men of his regiment, and requested him to send his Lieutenant-Colonel to keep them in order. This request was immediately attended to, but Lieutenant-Colonel Ryan, instead of allaying the discontent and disorder which prevailed, added by his presence fresh fuel to the flames. He was soon after dismissed from the service for malpractices which are not worth recording. You may form a tolerable idea of his character from the following extract from a letter of Colonel Bradstreet's, of March 19, 1747, to Sir William Pepperrell:—'I am sorry to tell you that ever since the arrival of your Lieutenant-Colonel, your regiment has not been one hour at rest. Such disputes between him and the officers are surprising, and he is in the wrong in every one. They have worked him so now that he has taken to his bed, and is determined, since the Governor will not let him go to Old England or New, to settle about the regiment's bills, that he will die, which, if he keeps his word, he will do well, for then he will rid the world of a rogue and a fool.' There seems, from all accounts, to have been good reason for the Governor's complaints of the conduct of the newly-raised regiments, but it is equally clear that he himself was not altogether blameless in this matter. Knowles had imbibed a strong prejudice against the provincial troops, because they would not submit to the strict discipline which he had exercised on board a man-of-war. Douglas says 'he behaved in a most imperious disgustful manner.' On his first arrival at Louisbourg he took a dislike to the place, because the climate was not so agreeable as that of the West Indies, which he had just left. Before he had been three months in the island he stated in a letter to the Duke of Newcastle, that it was not worth keeping; that the whole island was nothing but rocks, swamps, and lakes, and that it could never be planted by settlers to advantage, because within a compass of several leagues there was not one acre of tolerable ground. And again, in January, 1747, that the cold was so severe that the sentries, although relieved every half hour, sometimes lost their toes and fingers; that the snow was in some places from twelve to sixteen feet deep; that nature never designed the place as a residence for man; and that, if Warren had done his country some service by taking Louisbourg, he (Knowles) hoped to do more by destroying it. Murdoch[1] supposes that Knowles's unfavourable account of the island was one reason why the British Government consented to restore it to France, and the 'fountain-head of all the dismal misrepresentations of Nova Scotia and Cape Breton so reiterated and believed in during the latter part of the eighteenth and beginning of the nineteenth century, when our year was said to consist of nine months winter and three months fog.'

Leaving the squabbles of Pepperrell's officers and the Governor to themselves for a while, I must now inform you of an important event that occurred in the beginning of this year (1747), on the other side of the Atlantic, which relieved Louisbourg and Nova Scotia from the threatened attack of another powerful French armament. The French Government, regardless of the disasters of the great expedition of the preceding year, and determined at all risks to recover Nova Scotia and

[1] In his *History of Nova Scotia.*

Cape Breton, fitted out another early in April, consisting of fourteen ships of war and twenty-two transports and store ships, under the command of M. de Jonquière, for that purpose. The fleet was ordered to proceed to Canada to land a large quantity of arms and ammunition for a body of Canadians and Indians collecting at Bay Verte to invade Nova Scotia, and then to endeavour to take Louisbourg. La Jonquière sailed from Rochelle about April 28, accompanied by two ships of war, commanded by M. de St. George, convoying six large ships to the East Indies, with the intention of keeping company, for mutual protection, until they got off the coast. The English Ministry, apprised of the fitting out and destination of La Jonquière's expedition, sent Vice-Admiral Anson and Rear-Admiral Warren with sixteen ships to intercept it. Gaining intelligence of the movements of the enemy, Anson and Warren sailed towards the coast of Spain, and fell in with Jonquière and St. George's combined squadrons off Cape Finisterre on May 3. After a severe and well-fought action, the French were totally defeated. Nine ships of war, including the 'Sérieux' and 'Invincible,' of sixty-six and seventy-four guns, the flag-ships of La Jonquière and St. George, all the East Indiamen, and several transports and store ships, with property on board valued at one million and a half sterling, were captured. More than 4,000 prisoners were taken, including Jonquière, who was severely wounded in the shoulder. For this gallant achievement Anson was created a peer and Warren a baronet. After this no further attempts were made by France during the year against the British colonies, as she had work enough on hand to guard her own coasts against the attacks of the English squadrons. Anson's and Warren's victory also relieved Nova Scotia from further apprehensions of De Ramsay and his Indian allies. He had remained all winter at Chignecto, and had scouts constantly on the look-out at Chebucto and other places, to gain the earliest intelligence of Jonquière's arrival, but hearing of the discomfiture of the expedition, he returned in the beginning of June to Canada.

Governor Knowles, as may easily be imagined, was greatly relieved by the news of Jonquières defeat; for, owing to troubles of his own, he was ill prepared to resist the attack of a powerful enemy. All the garrison was, in fact, in a state of mutiny, on account of his attempt to enforce an order sent from England to make certain trifling stoppages from the pay of the soldiers. To bring the men to their duty he was obliged to suspend the order until he received further instructions from England. In the month of August Sir William Pepperrell visited Louisbourg, as the Duke of Newcastle had sent orders to Governor Shirley to discharge all the troops levied during the preceding year for the proposed invasion of Canada, except so many as he and Governor Knowles might consider necessary for the protection of Nova Scotia and Cape Breton. Seven companies were retained for that service—all the rest were discharged. Shirley and Pepperrell were ordered, at the same time, to fill up all the vacancies in their regiments of the line.[1] As Sir William had found much greater difficulty than he expected in enlisting men for his regiment, which was still far from complete, many who had enlisted in New England having deserted, on the eve of his departure for Louisbourg he published a notice signifying that all deserters who should immediately return to their duty should be kindly received and forgiven, and have their passages paid to Louisbourg. He complains, in a letter written from Louisbourg on September 10, to the Secretary of War, that numbers of his men had been taken to man some of the small armed vessels employed to reconnoitre the enemy. Having settled the affairs of his regiment, cashiered his Lieutenant-Colonel (Ryan), and appointed Captain Blayney to command in the absence of the Major on leave, he embarked in Commodore Knowles's squadron on September 20, for Boston, where he arrived on October 2.[2] As Knowles had received orders to proceed from Boston to the West Indies, Lieutenant-Colonel Hopson, of Fuller's regiment, was left in charge of the government of Cape Breton. While Knowles's squadron was lying at anchor in Nantasket Roads, on November 17, he sent a press gang up to Boston, which seized

[1] From *Documents relating to the Colonial History of the State of New York.* Edited by E. B. O'Callaghan, LL.D.

[2] Parsons's *Life of Pepperrell.*

as many seamen as could be found on board the outward-bound ships, and a number of carpenters and labourers, to replace the men who had deserted whilst his ships were undergoing repairs. This outrageous proceeding was universally resented. A mob of several thousand persons attacked the Council Chamber and insisted upon seizing the commanders of the ships who were in town. In this emergency the militia refused to act, and Knowles was obliged to release all the men he had impressed. Knowles was a man of a harsh overbearing disposition, which often got him into trouble, but withal a brave and skilful officer, as was fully proved by his conduct in the West Indies a few months after he left Boston.

Nothing of importance occurred at Louisbourg during the winter of 1747–48, but as spring approached, Colonel Hopson, who had received the appointment of Governor of the island, in a letter to the Duke of Newcastle, of April 12, stated that he began to feel apprehensive of an attack upon the colliery at Burnt Head, which supplied Louisbourg with fuel. The French had obtained their coal chiefly from the cliffs at Cow Bay and Spanish River, but the English, during their occupation of the island, preferred that of Burnt Head and the Little Labrador. The principal colliery was at the former place, a well known promontory between Glacé Bay and L'Indienne Bay (Lingan). At that time, although the island was nominally in the possession of England, her power extended little beyond the walls of Louisbourg. Independent bands of Indians—inveterate enemies of the English—roamed at will over the other parts of the island. For this reason it was absolutely necessary to erect a fort at Burnt Head,[1] and garrison it with fifty soldiers under the command of a lieutenant, to protect the workmen engaged in digging coal and boating it off to the vessels. It does not appear that any regular fort was built at Little Labrador, but an officer and a few soldiers were stationed there also. The workmen employed in mining, or rather in digging the coal out of the

[1] The ruins of this fort may still be seen. Pichon says it was a place of respectable strength, and that, 'with fifty men, the English were able to defend themselves against the incursions of the savages, and to keep possession of the pit.

cliffs—for shafts were not necessary—were mostly Frenchmen who had remained at their old homes after the fall of Louisbourg, and taken the oath of allegiance. They resided at L'Indienne, Spanish River, the little entrance of the Labrador, and a few other places upon the coast—some occupied in mining, some in cutting wood, others in carrying these articles to Louisbourg. Those who dwelt at St. Peter's, St. Anne's, L'Ardois, and Isle Madame, were chiefly engaged in the fishery. The agitation prevailing at this time amongst the French of Nova Scotia, and their adherents in Cape Breton and St. John's islands, who were constantly passing and repassing from one country to the other, was well known to Governor Hopson, who evidently had good reason for apprehending an attack upon his colliery. In the beginning of July, forty Frenchmen, led by a rover named Jacques Costé, made a raid upon the little French settlements at L'Indienne and Labrador, burnt their houses and about 2,000 cords of firewood, and captured three small vessels. Costé carried off twenty-four men and women from L'Indienne, and an English officer and soldier from Labrador, to Canada, where he arrived on July 29. No attempt was made upon the fort and works at Burnt Head, which were defended by Lieutenant Rhodes and the usual garrison, but owing to the capture of the schooners and their crews, Louisbourg was deprived of its usual supply of coal for more than a month. Costé's daring outrages created such alarm among all the French remaining upon the island, that they fled to Louisbourg, where they were kindly received and supplied with food by Governor Hopson.

The Viceroy of Canada having learned from the missionary Germain that some French refugees from Cape Breton were at Tatmagonche, and about to proceed to the neighbourhood of Louisbourg to plunder and harass the English settlers, sent M. Marin with forty men to Beaubassin to join them, with as many Indians as he could muster. The Viceroy, it is said, hoped by these means to disgust the English with the island, and to induce the Ministry to restore it to France at the peace, which, he was aware, was near at hand. M. Marin, having collected a sufficient force, started for Cape Breton, and reached the environs of Louisbourg, where he fell in with a party of officers and ladies who were out probably upon a pleasure excursion. Four ladies, three officers and four soldiers of the garrison, and two navy officers, were captured by Marin. Upon hearing from the captives and the Governor of Louisbourg that hostilities between the two Crowns had been suspended, Marin released the ladies, but carried off the officers and soldiers to Nova Scotia. All of them were subsequently released, except a Swiss soldier who had deserted from the garrison at Louisbourg during the siege in 1745, whom he carried to Quebec.[1]

This harassing petty warfare, conducted by the French Canadians and their savage allies, created much uneasiness and anxiety, as it was never known when and where an attack would be made, and consequently no steps could be taken to meet it. The near approach of a general peace was therefore looked upon with great satisfaction in the colonies. The repeated disasters at sea, coupled with the exhaustion of his finances, having induced the King of France to express a desire for peace, which was favourably received by Great Britain and her Continental allies, plenipotentaries of all the Powers engaged in the war met in congress at Aix-la-Chapelle, in the month of March, to arrange the terms. The preliminary articles were settled and signed on April 30, but the definitive treaty was not executed until October 18. According to the fifth Article of this treaty—

'All conquests which have been made since the commencement of the war, or since the conclusion of the preliminary articles signed on April 30 last, either in Europe or the East and West Indies, or any other part of the world whatever, shall be restored, without exception.' This settled the fate of Cape Breton. Haliburton[2] says—

'A Memoir was sent by the French Court to the Count St. Severin, its Minister at Aix-la-Chapelle, upon the indispensable necessity of Cape Breton to France, and upon the

[1] *New York Colonial Documents.*

[2] In his *History of Nova Scotia.* He gives as his authority the *Histoire de la Diplomatique française.*

fatal consequences of leaving that island in the hands of the English, in relation to the free trade of Canada and Louisiana, and the general trade of the other Powers of Europe. He was desired to show merely a moderate wish to recover the island, as it was known that England had it not at heart to retain her conquest. He was also requested to give the Earl of Sandwich to understand that the loss of Cape Breton was less important in itself, than on account of the stress laid upon it by the public opinion in France, and that the King did not attach so much consequence to the matter itself, as not to prefer an equivalent in the Low Countries.' The French plenipotentiary, in accordance with his instructions, secured the island of Cape Breton for his master. But this was not all; for the ninth Article (after referring to the eighteenth Article of the preliminary treaty, which specified that six weeks should be the limit of the time allowed for restitution), stipulated that, 'while it is impossible, from the distance of the country, that what concerns America can be effected in the same time, or the term fixed for its perfect execution, His Britannic Majesty therefore engages, on his side, to send to the most Christian King, immediately after the exchange of the ratifications of the present treaty, two persons of rank and condition, to continue in France as hostages till such time as they have certain and authentic advice of the restoration of the royal isle called Cape Breton, and of all the conquests that the arms or subjects of His Britannic Majesty may have made, before or after the signature of the preliminaries, in the East and West Indies. Their Britannic and most Christian Majesties oblige themselves likewise to remit, on the exchange of the ratification of the present treaty, the duplicates of the orders given to the commissaries respectively appointed to restore and receive all which may have been conquered on each side, in the East and West Indies, conformable to the second Article of the preliminaries. . . . . Provided, nevertheless, that the royal isle of Cape Breton shall be restored, with all the artillery and ammunition found therein on the day of its surrender.'

Although the termination of the war was hailed with joy by

the nation, the Ministry was generally, and justly, blamed for restoring Cape Breton to France, and for submitting to the humiliation of sending hostages as a security for the faithful execution of that condition of the treaty. This dissatisfaction was greatly enhanced by the recollection that the Ministry had, only a year before, in answer to a recommendation of the Dutch Government to restore Cape Breton to France, for the sake of securing certain advantages on the Continent, declared 'that there might indeed be good reasons for giving up Cape Breton, if France had made any conquests upon Great Britain or any of the British dominions; but the case being quite otherwise, take this matter in what light soever, it must appear highly to the dishonour of the Crown of Great Britain to make a patched-up peace by the restitution of Cape Breton; and the Dutch Government may be assured that His Majesty will never listen to any accommodation of which that cession is to be the basis, it being well known to be contrary to the universal sense of all the people of Great Britain.' And further, by a knowledge of the fact that a certain noble Duke, supposed to be the Duke of Newcastle, in the ardour of his zeal had declared, 'that if France was master of Portsmouth, he would hang the man who should give up Cape Breton in exchange for it.'[1]

If the people of England had cause to be annoyed at the restitution of Cape Breton, the colonists had much more reason to be mortified that the conquest which they had achieved at the cost of so many valuable lives, and which they regarded with such just pride, not only as a proof of their own prowess, but also as a material guarantee for the security of their fisheries and commerce, should have been recklessly given up 'in exchange for a petty factory [Madras] in the East Indies, belonging to a private company whose existence had been deemed prejudicial to the commonwealth,'[2] The only recompense which the colonies received was a parliamentary grant of 235,200*l.* to indemnify them for the expenses incurred in taking Louisbourg.

[1] *Scots Magazine* for April, 1748.
[2] Smollett's *History of England*.

Little more remains to be told respecting Louisbourg at this period. Orders were sent out to remove the warlike stores to Annapolis, and several vessels were engaged during the autumn in that service, but the total evacuation could not be effected before the summer of 1749. As there was now, in consequence of the peace, no further occasion for keeping a large force in America, orders were received in Louisbourg, in March, to disband Shirley and Pepperrell's new regiments, and the six auxiliary companies which had been left for the protection of Nova Scotia. The evacuation of Louisbourg produced much disappointment and distress among the numerous officials, civil and military, who had abandoned their former occupations and obtained situations there. Notwithstanding the denunciations of Commodore Knowles, before referred to, many persons had found Cape Breton a desirable place of abode, and were very much chagrined at being obliged to leave it. In a letter, of September 21, from Boston, published in the 'Scots Magazine' for December 1748, the writer says, 'Captain Conolly is arrived at Louisbourg with orders for the garrison to evacuate that place; in consequence of which they have begun to ship off some of the stores for Annapolis Royal. Our letters from Louisbourg inform us that fresh provisions there are in such plenty, that the best beef is sold at two pence a pound, and a good fat ox costs but four pounds ten shillings, which here would yield seventy or eighty pounds. This plenty proves the value of the island of Cape Breton; and as its capital, Louisbourg, is a place of great strength, extremely proper for the centre of a fishery, and a victualling port, and as a large and commodious harbour, and in respect to its situation the most proper rendezvous between Europe and our colonies, it mightily aggravates our misfortune in being obliged to part with it.'

The new French Governor, M. Desherbiers, arrived at Louisbourg early in the summer of 1749, with two eighty-gun ships, twenty transports, and troops for the garrison, where he found Governor Hopson with the two Gibraltar regiments, waiting for transports to take them to Chebucto (Halifax). Being anxious, no doubt, to get rid of the English as soon as possible, he offered to transport the two regiments to Chebucto, which was accepted, and orders sent to Boston to discharge some vessels that had been taken up for that service. Hopson and the two regiments left in July for Chebucto, where Governor Cornwallis had just arrived to lay the foundations of Halifax, and on July 12 the French flag once more floated over the ramparts of Louisbourg.

The Frencl Government, being informed of the restitution of Louisbourg some time in August, notified the Earl of Sussex and Lord Cathcart, who had remained at Paris as hostages since the preceding October, that they were now no longer under the least restraint, but entirely at their own option to reside in France or return to their own country.[1] And so closed the last act of the Treaty of Aix-la-Chapelle—a treaty which proved to be, as many expected, a temporary truce, a mere cessation of hostilities, of very short duration.

'After four years of warfare in all parts of the world, after all the waste of blood and treasure, the war ended just where it began.'[2]

[1] 'At the news of the arrival of Lords Sussex and Cathcart in Paris, Prince Charles [the Pretender], it is said, displayed the highest indignation, and exclaimed, with more of patriotism than of prudence, 'If ever I mount the throne of my ancestors, Europe shall see me use my utmost endeavours to force France in her turn to send hostages to England.'—Lord Mahon's *History of England.*

[2] Campbell's *Lives of the Admirals.*

LETTER XVI.

1749–1755.

THE FIRST fruits of the peace of Aix-la-Chapelle were the settlement of Nova Scotia and the foundation of Halifax. England had now (in 1749) been in possession of the country ever since the Treaty of Utrecht, in 1713, but no settlements had been made except at Annapolis and Canceau. The Acadians, or French neutrals, as they styled themselves, were in possession of nearly all the best land in the province, and were rapidly increasing in number. According to Lafargue, the French population of Nova Scotia was 12,500 in 1748.[1] Nominally subjects of Great Britain, and disposed to live at peace under her protection, they were instigated by the French authorities in Canada and Cape Breton, through the missionaries, who exercised great influence over them, to harass and annoy the English settlements, and to aid and abet the savages in their inroads upon the province. They also kept up a regular communication with Louisbourg, which they supplied with cattle and other agricultural produce, and gave at the same time intelligence of all the movements of the English to the French authorities.

To neutralise this pernicious influence, the English Government, by the advice of Governor Shirley of Massachusetts, and of other persons well acquainted with the state of Nova Scotia, decided upon establishing a large settlement in some central and commanding situation. The harbour of Chebucto, one of the best in the province, lying half way between Canceau and Cape Sable, and within a short distance overland of the principal Acadian settlements on the Bay of Fundy, was

[1] See Rameau's *France aux Colonies*.

chosen for this important purpose. As a great number of soldiers and seamen had been discharged on the conclusion of the war, the Government encouraged them to go out as settlers, by offers of free grants of land, free passages out, subsistence for a certain period, arms and ammunition for their defence, and tools and implements for clearing and cultivating the soil. Attracted by these favourable conditions, about 1,200 persons with their families, in all 2,500, volunteered to go out, and embarked in transports, accompanied by Lieutenant-Colonel Cornwallis, in the sloop of war 'Sphinx,' who was appointed Governor of the province. The 'Sphinx' arrived at Chebucto on July 2, and all the transports also before the 12th. Some of the transports were then despatched to Louisbourg to bring in the English inhabitants of that place, and the two regiments which had remained there over winter.

I cannot attempt to give you a detailed account of the settlement, rise, and progress, of the new capital of Nova Scotia, which was called Halifax, after the Earl of that title, who was President of the Board of Trade at the time, as it would occupy a larger space than I have to spare. If you wish to make yourselves acquainted with these subjects, I must refer you for full information to Murdoch's 'History of Nova Scotia,' which has just been published. The preceding letters have spread out so far beyond the limits I anticipated, that I must devote the remainder of my pages to the affairs of Cape Breton only, except where it is absolutely necessary to refer to occurrences in the other provinces, bearing directly upon its history. With this object in view, I must now submit a short sketch of the principal transactions which within a few short years led to the second siege of Louisbourg.

On their first arrival at Chebucto, the Acadians had shown a very friendly disposition towards the English settlers. They sent deputies to Governor Cornwallis, acknowledging their subjection to the British Crown, but at the same time declined to take the oath of allegiance without any reservation. The Indians also sent in their chiefs to make their submission to the Governor. This promising state of affairs, however, did not last long. The peaceable disposition of the Acadians and Indians did not meet with the approval of the Viceroy of Canada, who, jealous of the establishment of a strong British post in the immediate vicinity of Louisbourg,[1] instigated the Indians to harass the settlers, with the hope, perhaps, of inducing them to abandon their new home in disgust. It was soon found unsafe to work in the woods or clearings, except in considerable numbers. Every straggler that wandered incautiously away from his party was either murdered or taken prisoner by the Indians, who lurked in ambush in the woods. On one occasion, even the town, which was surrounded with a picket fence for its protection, was attacked by a large body of Indians. Vessels also were seized and carried to Louisbourg; but it does not seem that this was done with the consent of M. Desherbiers, the Governor of that place, as the prisoners taken thither were promptly released and sent to Halifax. These atrocities at length became so frequent, and were executed with such audacity, that the Governor was obliged to raise a body of volunteers to scour the country, to drive the Indians from their hiding-places, and to offer a reward of ten guineas for their scalps. For a while these measures produced the desired effect, and would probably have ensured the pacification of the country, if the Viceroy of Canada had not at this time sent a force of 600 men, under the command of M. La Corne, to Bay Verte, to take possession of the isthmus which unites Nova Scotia to New Brunswick, for the purpose of securing the communication of Canada with Cape Breton by the overland route. As both England and France claimed this part of Nova Scotia, it was agreed at the Treaty of Aix-la-Chapelle to leave the settlement of the boundary[2] to Commis-

[1] The authorities at Louisbourg offered great inducements to some German settlers to go thither from Halifax. There are several letters, dated November 1752, in the Record Office, from some Germans who had left Halifax and gone to Louisbourg, to their friends at the former place, urging them to go to Louisbourg. The writers say that the Governor would give each family three years' provisions, fifty acres of land, cows, horses, oxen, and everything they needed. The writers advise their friends to go by way of Minas to Cobequid, and thence to Bay Verte, where they would get a passage to Louisbourg.

[2] The conferences of the Commissioners proved of no avail; the claims of each country were so widely at variance, that the Commissioners could not reconcile

sioners appointed by the two Crowns, who had gone to Europe in the month of September 1749 for that purpose; the action, therefore, of the Viceroy was clearly an infraction of the treaty, which Great Britain was not slow in resenting. In the spring of 1750, Major Lawrence was despatched with a body of troops to dislodge the French, but finding his force inadequate for that purpose, he was obliged to withdraw until he could obtain a reinforcement from Halifax. In the month of August he returned to Chignecto with a larger force, and effected a landing upon the eastern side of the Missaquash river, in spite of the opposition of the French, who during his absence had erected a strong post on the western side of that river, called Fort Beauséjour. Lawrence being still unable to dislodge the French, took possession of the old post of Beaubassin, where he built a fort which he named Fort Lawrence, and established himself there for the winter, while the French occupied Fort Beauséjour, on the opposite side of the river. Shortly afterwards the French built another fort on the shores of Bay Verte, near the mouth of the river Gasperaux, and a third on the St. John's river.

The Indians, encouraged and supported by the presence of the French garrisons on the isthmus, waged incessant war during the next three years upon the English settlers at Chebucto and its vicinity. While Desherbiers was Governor of Louisbourg, the barbarous atrocities of the savages were in some measure checked; but when the Count de Raymond succeeded him in 1751, the latter pursued a different policy, and instead of discountenancing their proceedings, strove by every means in his power to induce them to harass the English in their settlements and upon the coast. Pichon, who came out to Cape Breton in the capacity of secretary to Count Raymond, and ought to have been well informed upon the

them, and separated in 1753, without coming to any agreement. A long account of their proceedings was published by the French Government, in 1755, in two quarto volumes, entitled *Mémoires des Commissaires du Roi et de ceux de sa Majesté britannique sur les possessions et les droits respectifs des deux Couronnes en Amérique.* It contains much valuable information, and copies of many interesting documents relating to Nova Scotia and Cape Breton, from which I have drawn largely in compiling the preceding letters.

matter, says that when it was rumoured that the Abenaquis Indians had made peace with the English, the Count called a meeting of the Micmacs at Louisbourg, and urged them, in most violent and exciting language, to continue the war; also that he employed the missionaries to persuade the Abenaquis to violate the treaty they had made. The Count proved a troublesome neighbour to the English whilst he administered the government of Cape Breton, but he did not neglect the more important duties of his office. He opened a road from Louisbourg to St. Peter's, eighteen leagues in length, at an expense of 100,000 livres, of which traces still remain at various places along the coast, and in the spring of 1752 sent a party of officers to survey the coasts of the island, and to collect statistical information. Pichon, who accompanied the officers, gives in his 'Memoirs' some interesting information concerning the places they visited, from which I make the following extracts, as they will afford you some idea of the population and condition of the out-settlements at that time.

Leaving Louisbourg early in February, the party travelled along the coast to Gabarus and Fourché, where they found a few inhabitants engaged in the cod fishery. At the latter place there was a large settlement before the last war, when all the buildings were burned by the English, except a large storehouse, which was still standing. From Fourché they went to St.-Esprit, which they found was, 'notwithstanding all that it had suffered during the late war, recovering itself apace.' They next reached L'Ardoise, 'where there is a slate quarry, from which it takes its name.' Between Louisbourg and St. Peter's they found only 180 inhabitants, 'some of whom lived very comfortably, and others indifferently; but they fare best towards Gabarus, where there is plenty of game, and where the woodcocks [partridges] are so extremely tame that you may knock them down with stones.' Pichon justly speaks in terms of admiration of the natural features of Port Toulouse (St. Peter's). He found here 230 inhabitants, 'exclusive of the king's officers and troops, chiefly employed in summer in building boats and small vessels, and in winter cutting firewood and timber.' He says 'they were very industrious people; tilled the earth, and kept a sufficient quantity of cattle and poultry, which they sold at Louisbourg. . . . They were the first that brewed an excellent sort of antiscorbutic of the tops of the spruce fir;' and that they had a number of maple trees from which they extracted a sap in the spring, 'most agreeable to the taste, of the colour of Spanish wine, good for the breast, a preventive against the stone, and no way hurtful to the stomach. They boil it and make sugar from it.' St. Peter's was at that time a place of much importance, as it was thither 'the savages of Cape Breton and Acadié brought all the furs to exchange them for European commodities.' He considers St. Peter's a valuable military post, 'being so near to the "island of the Holy Family," in the Labrador, where almost all the savages live in a body with their missionary, and within easy distance of the settlements of Madame, Petit de Grat, Ardois, St.-Esprit, and the River Inhabitants. At the least appearance of danger, all these people, collected in a body, would make a small army, and with the assistance of a few fortifications render St. Peter's impregnable.' They found only 113 inhabitants at Descous, and upon the islands in the passage, 'who live as well as they can; that is, being greatly straitened by the barrenness of the soil, they subsist by means of a little commerce. Some maintain themselves by fishing and hunting; others by cruising winter and summer, and cutting wood for firing, which they sell for five livres the cord along the coast. The few horned cattle they are able to maintain are likewise a considerable relief to them; in short, their distress was so great as to excite our compassion. We quitted this country without any other regret than that of leaving such miserable people behind us.' At Petit de Grat and Grand Nerica (Arichat) they found thriving settlements of fishermen, the population of the two places being about 137. After visiting River Inhabitants, where about thirty persons were settled, mostly engaged in raising cattle, and in sawing boards at a mill which they had constructed, the party returned to Louisbourg. The same party then visited Baleine, Menadou, Scatari, the Bay of Morienne (Cow Bay), and L'Indienne, and found a few inhabitants at each of these places. Pichon says the coal pit which the English had opened at Burnt Head 'took fire in the summer of 1752, and entirely consumed the fort.' Traces of this fire may still be seen along the outcrop of the seam, as far as Little Glacé Bay. At Baie des Espagnols some Acadians had settled and begun to clear the land. He says there were beds of limestone and building stone on the banks of the river, and two coal pits. From thence the party visited the two entrances of the Labrador, 'which are separated by the island of Verderonne, which belongs to M. le Poupet de la Boulardrie.' There was a considerable number of settlers upon the Little Entrance of Labrador. Ruins of their old homesteads may still be seen at many places, in the woods on both sides of the strait, and a large burying-ground on the northern shore, where, a few years ago, the sites of the graves, designated by wooden crosses, were covered by a dense growth of spruce trees. Pichon says the Labrador was the most populous part of the island. An extensive cod fishery was carried on at Niganiche, but the vessels 'were obliged by the king's ordonnance to retire to Port Dauphin (St Anne's) towards the 15th August, because of the storms that rage in that season.' He says, 'Sometimes you see 150 boats employed in this business at Niganiche.' There were at this time very few inhabitants at Niganiche, and none whatever between that place and Just'au Corps (Port Hood). 'These places were hardly at all frequented.' The total population of Cape Breton, according to Rameau,[1] in 1752, was 4,125, of which 2,484 resided in Louisbourg and its environs; the remainder in other parts of the island.

From Just'au Corps the party crossed over to St. John's Island, and visited all the principal harbours and settlements. Pichon speaks very highly of the agricultural and fishing capabilities of the island, but says the Government discouraged, and even forbad the inhabitants from engaging in the latter business, because it was desirable that all their labour should be expended upon the soil, in order that Louisbourg might be supplied from thence with grain and cattle. The total number of inhabitants, who had mostly come from Nova Scotia, was at

[1] *La France aux Colonies.*

this period 2,663.[1] Owing to the unsettled state of affairs in Nova Scotia, new settlers were coming over from thence daily. I must not, however, say more about St. John's Island, as more important matters demand our attention elsewhere. I will merely give you one more extract from Pichon's Journal:— 'Though the island of St. John's is subject to a particular commandant, he receives his orders from the Governor of Cape Breton, and administers justice conjunctly with the subdelegate of the Intendant of New France. They reside at Port la Joye, and the Governor of Louisbourg furnishes them with a garrison of fifty or sixty men.'

The city and garrison of Louisbourg at this time obtained a considerable portion of agricultural produce from St. John's Island and Canada, but the great bulk of its supplies was furnished by the merchants of New England and New York. Cornwallis complained on several occasions to the Board of Trade, that there was often a great scarcity of provisions at Halifax, because the colonists preferred sending their produce to Louisbourg, where they received rum and molasses in exchange, which they frequently landed without paying any duty. He stated that in 1751 no less than 150 English vessels visited Louisbourg, and that the trade was rapidly increasing, insomuch that sometimes thirty Boston vessels might be seen in that port at the same time. This lucrative business was, however, fast drawing to a close, for it was evident that, owing to the encroachments of the French upon English territory, there would soon be an open rupture between the two nations. It was stipulated by the fifteenth Article of the Treaty of Utrecht, that 'the subjects of France, inhabitants of Canada and elsewhere, should not disturb or molest, in any manner whatever, the Five Indian Nations which were subject to great Britain;' yet, notwithstanding, they were extending a line of posts from Canada southwards, in order to cut off the communication between the English colonies and the Five Nations, and to connect the valleys of the St. Lawrence and the Mississippi. M. de Galissonière,

[1] *La France aux Colonies.*

the Viceroy of Canada, informed his Government[1] that the Alleghanies were the true frontiers, and the 'boulevards nécessaires' of Canada, which must be maintained at all risks; and that the isthmus of Acadié was the true boundary of that country, which he would endeavour to secure by enticing the Acadians to remove from Nova Scotia into the French territory, in order to obtain a population capable of defending it. This had been the policy of all the French Viceroys for many years, as we have already seen; and as they were of course aware that France was making great preparations for renewing the war, the Marquis du Quesne, who was Viceroy in 1754, took possession of several strong points on the Ohio, and strengthened and repaired the forts of Beauséjour and Gasperaux on the isthmus. For the present we must confine our attention to the transactions at Beauséjour, where M. du Chambon de Vergor[2] arrived as Commandant in 1754, having received the appointment at the suggestion of M. Bigot, the Intendant of Canada. At this time M. Pichon, whom I have so often mentioned, was 'Intendant Commissary' at Beauséjour, having been appointed to that office in 1753, when Count Raymond left Louisbourg.

When De Vergor arrived at Beauséjour, he found eighty families of Acadians residing there, whom the missionary De Loutré had induced to leave Nova Scotia. These poor people wished to return, but De Vergor would not allow them to do so. Having good reason to expect an attack from the English, he succeeded, with the aid of De Loutré's influence, in persuading about 400 more Acadians to come from Piziguit,

[1] Dussieux, in his *Histoire du Canada*.

[2] De Vergor was the son of Duchambon, who was Governor of Louisbourg in 1745. 'His father, Louis du Pont du Chambon, a lieutenant in the army, was married at Port Royal in 1709, to Jean Mius d'Entremont du Poubomcou, the daughter of Jacques Mius and Anne de la Tour. He was promoted to this post by favour of M. Bigot, who had been Intendant at Louisbourg under his father. Bigot, who procured him the appointment, is said to have written to him in these terms: "Profit, my dear Vergor, by your place; cut, clip—you have every power—in order that you may soon come and join me in France, and buy an estate in my neighbourhood."'—Murdoch's *Nova Scotia*. It is very likely that De Vergor was appointed because he had a great number of relations in the province, whom he might induce to take up arms and join their countrymen.

Minas, and other places, to help him in putting his post in good repair. Although the Bishop of Quebec had requested De Loutré to abstain from meddling in temporal affairs, which he assured him would lead to serious embarrassment, the latter received so much encouragement from the Marquis du Quesne to persevere in his policy of threatening the English with the Indians, who were entirely at his command, that he treated the Bishop's advice with contempt. Meanwhile, the Governor of Nova Scotia was not ignorant of the movements of the French, and their intention of attacking the English posts within the province; for our old friend Pichon—I say it with pain and sorrow—had turned traitor to his sovereign, and acquainted Captain Scott, the Commandant of Fort Lawrence, with all that was going on. Whatever could have induced an officer in his position to sacrifice his reputation for filthy lucre, is to me perfectly incomprehensible. Perhaps you may find some clue to this extraordinary conduct in the short memoir taken from the 'Biographie Universelle,' which you will find at the end of this letter. The information furnished by Pichon proved of great service to the English authorities, who resolved to anticipate the proposed incursions of the French and their savage allies, by reducing the forts of Beauséjour, Bay Verte, and St. John's, as speedily as practicable. Accordingly, in the spring of 1755, a force of 2,000 men was raised in Massachusetts, and sent to Chignecto under the command of Lieutenant-Colonel Monckton, where it arrived on June 2, and landed in front of Fort Lawrence, less than two miles distant from Beauséjour. The English force, including the garrison of regulars at Fort Lawrence, immediately began to make preparations for investing Fort Beauséjour, where De Vergor, informed on the previous day of the appearance of a fleet of English transports in the Bay of Fundy, had collected about 500 Acadians to aid in its defence. The fort was of a pentagonal form, with a bastion at each angle, and an armament of twenty guns and one large mortar. The garrison was composed of 150 regulars. De Vergor made a gallant defence, and held possession of his post for fourteen days, in spite of all the attempts of the English to dislodge him. I must refer you to Murdoch's

'History of Nova Scotia' for a detailed and interesting account of this siege, and must content myself with merely noticing the result. Finding himself closely pressed by the enemy, who was opening his trenches within a short distance of the fort, and disheartened by news received from Louisbourg, De Vergor called a meeting of his officers on June 14, when he laid before them a letter he had just received from M. Drucourt, the Governor of Louisbourg, informing him that it was impossible to send any help from thence, as an English fleet was cruising off the port. It was nevertheless determined to hold out by the Council, until the news became generally known in the garrison, when a number of the Acadians deserted, and the rest applied for leave to retire, seeing that the fort was incapable of defence against such a superior force. Under these circumstances De Vergor decided upon surrendering on the 16th, when the terms of capitulation were agreed upon, and the English took possession of the fort. The missionary, De Loutré, who was justly afraid of falling into the hands of the English, escaped from the fort in disguise before their troops marched in.[1] The garrison was sent to Louisbourg, upon condition that it should not bear arms in America for six months. The Indians, as a matter of course, fled to the forests and escaped, and the Acadians, 300 in number, were generously pardoned and dismissed, upon the assurance of M. de Vergor that they had been forced to bear arms upon pain of death.[2] Fort Gasperaux was surrendered on the following day to a detachment of 300 men sent by Monckton. A large quantity of stores and provisions were found in this fort, which had been brought from Canada for the use of the Indians and Acadians. The fort on the St. John river was then visited,

[1] De Loutré got safe to Canada, from whence he sailed for France in the month of August. He, however, did not escape the punishment justly due for his misdeeds in Nova Scotia, for the vessel in which he went was captured in the Channel, and De Loutré was kept 'in durance vile,' in Fort Elizabeth, Jersey, until the peace, in 1763.

[2] Pichon says that there were 600 Acadians who had been shut up in the fort against their will; and that he interceded for them after the fall of the place, 'imputing their conduct to the implicit obedience which these poor people paid to their missionaries.'

but the French had abandoned it after bursting the cannon and demolishing the buildings.

The conduct of the Acadians in the affair at Beauséjour caused much embarrassment to the Provincial Government, and proved beyond all doubt that no reliance could be placed upon their professed neutrality. Ever since the Treaty of Utrecht, in 1713, they had been allowed to remain in the country upon taking an oath of allegiance, with the understanding that they would not be called on to take up arms at any time against the French, in defence of the province. This condition was faithfully kept by the English Governors on their side, but it is too certain that the Acadians had frequently abused this indulgence, by conveying intelligence to their countrymen in Canada and Cape Breton, of all that was going on in the province, and by harbouring and aiding the Indians in their incursions against the English. How could the English Government, with due regard to the security of the country, overlook such open breaches of neutrality? Why, by requiring them to take an unqualified oath of allegiance without any reservation whatever. The Acadians positively refused to take such an oath, upon which the Governor and Council decided 'that effectual measures ought to be taken to remove all recusants out of the province.' Confining our view to Nova Scotia alone, the Government had no cause for apprehension just at that time, as the French had been driven out of the province, and it was protected by a considerable body of troops; but it was considered, and not without reason, that the intelligence of the defeat of General Braddock on his march against Fort Duquesne, and the fact that large reinforcements had been sent out from France to Canada and Cape Breton, might probably encourage the Acadians to rise in open rebellion. In this critical state of affairs, Governor Laurence and his Council sought the advice of Admirals Boscawen and Mostyn, who had just arrived at Halifax, when it was decided that the British settlements would never be secure until the Acadians were driven out of the province. It was also decided that, as they would merely remove to Canada and Cape Breton, if allowed to go where they pleased, and strengthen the enemy in these countries, they should be transported to and dispersed among the other British colonies, where they could not unite in sufficient numbers to cause any anxiety. Of the cruelty and injustice of this sentence there can be but one opinion. Many were no doubt guilty of the charges alleged against them, as for instance on the recent occasion at Fort Beauséjour, where 300 of them were taken with arms in their hands, but the great bulk of the Acadians were a peaceable, orderly, industrious people, as their descendants are at this day. But no distinction whatever was made between the innocent and the guilty; the iniquitous and tyrannical decision of the Council was carried out under circumstances of the harshest cruelty. More than 7,000 persons were transported from their happy homes, which had descended from father to son through three or four generations, and dispersed among the colonies bordering on the Atlantic, from Massachusetts to Georgia. Their lands and possessions were forfeited to the Crown; no recompense was made for their great losses; they were only allowed to carry with them their money and such quantity of their household goods 'as could be taken without discommoding the vessels.' Many escaped into the woods and sought a shelter from the Indians; others fled from the northern parts of the province to Canada, Ristigouche, the upper waters of the St. John, St. John's Island, and Cape Breton. I cannot dwell longer upon this painful subject. I must refer you to Haliburton's 'History of Nova Scotia' for a detailed account of the transaction, and to Longfellow's beautiful poem of 'Evangeline,' which is founded upon the facts I have briefly narrated. I will just transcribe the opening stanzas, convinced you will not rest until you have read the whole poem, which you will find well worthy of perusal:—

'This is the forest primeval. The murmuring pines and the hemlocks,
Bearded with moss, and in garments green, indistinct in the twilight,
Stand like Druids of old, with voices sad and prophetic,
Stand like Harpers hoar, with beards that rest on their bosoms.
Loud from its rocky caverns, the deep-voiced neighbouring ocean
Speaks, and in accents disconsolate answers the wail of the forest.
This is the forest primeval; but where are the hearts that beneath it

Leaped like the roe, when he hears in the woodland the voice of the huntsman?
Where is the thatch-roofed village, the home of Acadian farmers,—
Men whose lives glided on like rivers that water the woodlands,
Darkened by shadows of earth, but reflecting an image of heaven?
Waste are those pleasant farms, and the farmers for ever departed!
Scattered like dust and leaves when the mighty blasts of October
Seize them, and whirl them aloft, and sprinkle them far o'er the ocean.
Nought but tradition remains of the beautiful village of Grand Pré.'

The expulsion of the Acadians, cruel and unjust as it was, nevertheless established peace and tranquillity in Nova Scotia. No further attempts were made to disturb the English in their possession of the country, except by a party of 300 Acadians, who had escaped to the north side of the Bay of Fundy, and some Indians, led by M. de Boishébert, who arrived at Chignecto in the month of February 1756, and killed nine men belonging to a party of woodcutters in the vicinity of Fort Gasperaux. Lieutenant-Colonel Scott, who commanded at Fort Beauséjour, now called Fort Cumberland, immediately started in pursuit with 300 Provincials, and, coming up with the enemy, killed eight Indians and wounded many more. After this the Acadians gave no further trouble; but the Indians lurked about the country, murdering and scalping every straggler that fell into their hands, both on the isthmus and in other parts of the province, which compelled the Governor to issue a proclamation, on May 14, offering 'a reward of 30*l.* for every male Indian prisoner above the age of sixteen years, brought in alive; for a scalp of such male Indian 25*l.*, and 25*l.* for every Indian woman or child brought in alive.' This seems to have produced the desired effect, as we read of few Indian outrages within the province afterwards. The Acadians also abandoned the north shore of the Bay of Fundy and retired to Miramichi, where it is said there were about 1,500 of them settled under the charge of M. de Boishébert and the Jesuit Père Germain, in the beginning of 1757.

The prisoners taken at the fall of Fort Beauséjour, as I have already informed you (p. 275), were, according to the capitulation, sent to Louisbourg. I ought to have made an exception in favour of our old friend Pichon, who was allowed to go to Halifax. Pichon, as we have seen, had good reasons for not appearing at Louisbourg, although it was perhaps not known that he had been engaged in a traitorous correspondence with the enemies of his country. His biographer, M. Louis Dubois, seems to have been ignorant of this fact, as he does not mention it in his Memoir in the 'Biographie Universelle,' of which the following is a translation:—

'Pichon (Thomas) was born at Vire on the 30th April 1700. He was for a short time employed in the Bureau, where he might, if he had remained, have distinguished himself. In 1741 he was appointed by M. de Breteuiel, Minister of War, Administrator of Hospitals of the French Armies on the Danube and in Bohemia. Being made prisoner of war while on this service, Pichon was employed by the Empress Maria Theresa on a commission for settling the accounts of the French army. Having returned to France about the year 1743, he was appointed Inspector of the Administration "des fourrages" in Alsace, and in 1745 Director of the Hospitals of the Army of the Lower Rhine, until the beginning of 1749. Some injustice that he experienced, which was probably exaggerated by his suspicious character, induced him to leave France. He left for Canada in the capacity of Secretary to Adjutant-General Count Raymond, appointed Governor of Isle Royale or Cape Breton, with whom he remained a short time. He was then appointed by the Intendant of Louisbourg to the office of Intendant Commissary at Fort Beauséjour, which he filled for two years. This fort having been taken by the English in 1755, he went to England, where he remained until his death, in 1781. He resided in London under the name of Tyrrell, devoting himself to literary pursuits, until 1756, when he made the acquaintance of Madame le Prince de Beaumont, whom he married, and by whom he had six children. This lady left England about 1760, and having established herself in Savoy, in vain endeavoured to induce Pichon, who was a very obstinate man, to join her and their children. [Madame Pichon seems to have been ignorant of the reasons that compelled her husband to remain in England]. He was in correspondence with many learned men in London, where he composed several works, of which the greater part have remained in manuscript; such as a voluminous Treatise "de la Nature," &c. His best work was the "Memoirs of Cape Breton;" but we do not find in this curious and instructive book the memoirs promised by the title. Pichon bequeathed to his native town a good well-furnished library, which since 1783 has been opened to the public and is much frequented. It seems that he was of a suspicious character, which rendered him fanciful and capricious. His marriage with Madame le Prince de Beaumont, although apparently well assorted, was not a happy one: there was little sympathy in their characters; Pichon did not consult the happiness of a sensible and spiritual woman, who never ceased to love him with much disinterestedness notwithstanding the great difference of their religious opinions, even after they were separated.'

LETTER XVII.

1755–1758.

I INFORMED you in my last (p. 275) that near the close of the siege of Beauséjour, the commander of the fort, M. de Vergor, received a letter from the Governor of Louisbourg, telling him that no succours could be sent from thence, because an English fleet was blockading the port. I can imagine your asking how it happened that an English fleet was blockading a French port when the two nations were at peace? This I will endeavour to explain. The French, you are aware, ever since the last peace, had been pushing on their encroachments on the frontiers of New York and Pennsylvania, and, as it was well known to the British Government, were gradually strengthening their posts in Canada, with the purpose of recovering Acadié and of securing an uninterrupted communication between the St. Lawrence and the Gulf of Mexico. As France was not yet prepared for open war, the Ministry, all through the summer of 1754, tried to amuse, or rather deceive the English Court, by repeated assurances of friendship, in the hope of gaining time; but the English Ministry at length saw through this artifice, and wisely judging that, as a contest could not be avoided, it would be better to begin it at once, applied to Parliament for a large vote of money expressly for augmenting the army and navy. This brought matters to a crisis. The French Ministry, seeing that any further attempts at concealment were useless, immediately ordered a powerful armament to be fitted out for America. Twenty-five ships of the line were therefore got ready at Brest, Rochelle, and Rochfort, with all possible despatch, to convey 6,000 troops to augment the garrisons of Louisbourg and the forts on the Great Lakes and the Ohio, and the frigate 'Diane' was despatched early in March for Louisbourg, to announce their coming. The British Government, duly advised of these circumstances, despatched Admiral Boscawen with eleven ships of the line and one frigate, with two infantry regiments on board, on April 22; and Vice-Admiral Holborne, with six ships of the line and one frigate, on May 11, with instructions to attack the French fleet wherever they should meet with it. The French fleet, of twenty-five ships, sailed on May 3, but, having cleared the mouth of the Channel, nine of them returned to France. Of the sixteen that went on to America, it is said that ten carried only twenty-two guns each, being fitted out as transports for the conveyance of the land forces.

Boscawen's and Holborne's squadrons having joined company on the passage, were cruising on the banks of Newfoundland to intercept the French fleet, commanded by M. du Bois de la Mothe, when the 'Dunkirk' and 'Defiance,' of sixty guns each, being separated from the fleet in a thick fog on June 8, fell in with the French ships 'Alcide,' of sixty-four guns, and 'Lys,' pierced for sixty-four but carrying only twenty-two guns. After a severe action of five hours, in which the 'Dunkirk' lost ninety men, the two French ships were captured. The 'Lys' proved a valuable prize, having nearly 80,000*l.* on board, besides eight companies of infantry and several officers of distinction. Having sent the prizes to Halifax, Boscawen and Holborne sailed for Louisbourg, and cruised off the harbour for some time, to prevent the egress of the ships destined, as we have seen, to carry succour to M. de Vergor at Fort Beauséjour. Learning that four large ships and two frigates, with 1,000 soldiers on board, had got safely into Louisbourg, Boscawen sailed up the Gulf of St. Lawrence with the expectation of falling in with the rest of De la Mothe's fleet on their way to Canada. He was, however, too late; for the French Admiral, screened by the thick fogs which usually prevail at that season, had entered the gulf through the Straits of Belle Isle, reached Quebec in safety, and landed more than 3,000 troops under the command of Baron Dieskau.

When intelligence of the capture of the 'Alcide' and 'Lys'

reached England, the Ministry, considering that nothing could now prevent an open rupture with France, ordered all the French merchant ships in English ports to be seized and their crews imprisoned. The French minister, M. Rouille, remonstrated in strong terms against these transactions, stating 'that the king his master considered the capture of two of His Majesty's ships in the open sea, without a declaration of war, a public insult to His Majesty's flag; and the seizure of French merchantmen, in contempt of the law of nations, in his judgment an act of piracy; and demanded restitution of all the ships, guns, stores, and merchandise, and all the officers and men belonging to them.' To this Mr. Fox, Secretary of State, replied in substance that His Majesty had taken no steps but what the hostilities begun by France, in a time of profound peace (of which he had the most authentic proofs), rendered just and indispensable. It is quite evident that, entertaining sentiments so widely at variance, war could no longer be avoided; accordingly, we find that war was declared by England on May 18, and by France on June 9 following. Both countries, it was well known, had been actively preparing for the contest, though each endeavoured to throw the odium of breaking the peace upon the other. 'The French had evidently and flagrantly broken the bonds of peace by their audacious encroachments in America; but for the credit of England, a formal declaration of war should have preceded the first act of hostility on our part.'[1]

Nothing of importance occurred in America after the capture of the 'Alcide' and 'Lys,' except the defeat of the French under General Dieskau, near Lake George, by General Johnson, on September 8, when 600 of the enemy were killed and their general taken prisoner.[2]

[1] Campbell's *Lives of the Admirals.*

[2] Baron Dieskau was found alone, dangerously wounded, supporting himself on the stump of a tree, a little distance from the field of battle. The Indian who took General Dieskau went to England, where he was exhibited to the public, as appears from the following advertisement in the 'Public Advertiser':—

'Just arrived from America, and to be seen at the New York and Cape Breton Coffee House, in Sweeting's Alley, from 12 to 3, and from 4 to 6, to the latter end of next week, and then will embark for America, in the "General Webb," Captain

Admiral Boscawen returned with his fleet to England in the month of November, and the French ships left Louisbourg about the same time, the season for naval operations having come to a close.

The declaration of war, on May 18, 1756, was hailed with joy in England. 'Certainly the sound of war never echoed with more satisfaction than at the present conjuncture. It was the general request of the nation.'[1] It was hoped that, if it should prove successful, it would be followed by a treaty of peace, free from the ambiguities respecting boundaries which had kept the colonies in a constant state of war ever since the Treaty of Aix-la-Chapelle, and that everything would be so clearly defined that there could be no pretence for disputes in future.

The campaign in America, in 1756, for which such great preparations were made both at home and in the colonies, proved abortive, in consequence of the late arrival of the Earl of Loudon, the new Commander-in-Chief, at New York. Nothing of importance could at that late season be undertaken against the enemy; but at all events the British posts might have been reinforced, if so much time had not been wasted and frittered away in surveying and providing for the defence of Albany, the head-quarters of the army, which was in no danger. The important post of Oswego, on the shore of Lake Ontario, which had been victualled with great difficulty by Bradstreet, was left exposed to the attack of a vastly superior force collecting at Montreal, under the command of the Marquis de Montcalm. Oswego fell, basely deserted by General Webb, who had been sent to relieve it, and the garrison of 1,600 men were carried off prisoners of war to Montreal.

Boardman, a famous Mohawk Indian warrior!—the same person who took M. Dieskau, the French General, prisoner, at the battle of Lake George, where General Johnson beat the French, and was one of the said General's guards; he is dressed in the same manner with his native Indians when they go to war; his face and body painted, with his scalping-knife, tom-axe, and all other implements of war that are used by the Indians in battle. A sight worthy the curiosity of every true Briton.

'Price One Shilling each person.

'*** The only Indian that has been in England since the reign of Queen Anne.'

[1] Entick's *History of the Late War.* London: 1763.

Loudon, after this disaster, sent the provincial troops to their homes, and placed his own men in winter quarters.

The trifling successes achieved by the squadron of Commodore Holmes, consisting of seven ships of the line and two sloops, on the coast of Cape Breton during the summer of 1756, proved a poor offset to the disasters on the mainland; only one ship of war, the 'Arc en-Ciel,' of fifty guns, and a store-ship, the 'Amitié,' of 300 tons, having been captured off Louisbourg by the 'Centurion' and 'Success,' and carried into Halifax. On July 27, a smart action was fought also off Louisbourg, by Commodore Holmes, in the 'Grafton,' 70, accompanied by the 'Nottingham,' of 70 guns, and Jamaica sloop, with M. Beausier, in command of the 'Héros,' 74, the 'Illustre,' 64, and two frigates of 36 guns each. The engagement commenced in the afternoon and continued until dusk, when both parties withdrew without any decisive result. Next morning Holmes expected to renew the action, having kept his men all night lying at their quarters, but at daybreak discovered the French ships about five miles distant, bearing away with a fair wind for Louisbourg. The French commander says he found the enemy at such a distance next morning, that he gave up all hopes of getting at him, and therefore returned to Louisbourg with the loss of eighteen men killed and forty-eight wounded. The English loss was only six men killed and twenty-one wounded. Although the French had a squadron of six large ships in Louisbourg, the English Commodore kept such a sharp look-out, that no vessels could get in with supplies of provisions, nor could even boats go out to fish for the garrison, which was compelled in consequence to subsist for some time chiefly upon condemned codfish.

Although the failure of Loudon's operations and the loss of Oswego caused much disappointment in England, every exertion was made in the following spring (1757) to recover not only the places lost on the mainland, but also to reduce Louisbourg. In the month of January Lord Loudon held a Council at Boston, when it was determined to assemble a powerful land force at Halifax early in the spring, ready to co-operate with a fleet expected from England, in the attack on Louisbourg.

The fleet destined for this service, consisting of eleven ships of the line and some frigates, under the command of Admiral Holborne, together with fifty transports, conveying 6,000 troops under Viscount Howe, owing to delays caused by some changes in the Ministry, did not sail from Cork until May 8. It was supposed at the time that information of the destination of this expedition had been communicated to the French Government by some traitor or spy,[1] as the orders for its equipment had hardly been issued when active preparations were begun in Brest and Toulon for getting a fleet ready to go to the support of Louisbourg. Five ships, which sailed in April under M. du Rivest from Toulon, arrived at Louisbourg on June 4; and fourteen more, which sailed from Brest on May 3, under M. du Bois de la Mothe, arrived there on the 29th of the same month. On the very same day (the 29th), Lord Loudon arrived at Halifax with 6,000 regulars from New York, convoyed by only three small frigates; and on July 9, Holborne arrived at the same port with all his ships and transports in safety. The united forces of the two commanders, including the ships of war on the station, now amounted to fifteen ships of the line, eighteen frigates and sloops, and 12,000 effective soldiers. Nearly a month was wasted at Halifax in reviews and sham fights, accustoming the men to diverse sorts of attack and defence, &c., instead of proceeding against the enemy. At last, on August 1, the troops were embarked for Louisbourg, and were on the point of sailing, when one of the sloops which had been cruising off Louisbourg brought intelligence that De la Mothe had arrived there with a large fleet. Much discussion then arose whether it would, under these circumstances, be advisible to proceed with the

[1] This information, it afterwards appeared, was furnished to the French Government by a spy, one Dr. Henacy, who had established himself in London as a physician, and thus gained admission into society, where he picked up such intelligence as he thought would be useful to his employers. When he was arrested, in March 1758, copies of important papers were found at his lodgings in Arundel Street, proving that he had sent to France the first tidings of Admiral Holborne's intended expedition to America, an exact account of the number of ships and of the troops on board, the day of their departure, &c.—Entick's *History of the Late War*.

enterprise; but it was speedily brought to a close by the arrival of an English ship from the coast of Newfoundland, with despatches found on board a French packet she had captured, bound from Louisbourg to Brest, from which it appeared that, in addition to a garrison of 6,000 regulars, there were in the town 3,000 militia and 1,300 Indians, and in the harbour, seventeen sail of the line and three frigates. In consequence of this intelligence, a Council of War was held, when it was unanimously decided to give up all idea of attacking Louisbourg. Having left three battalions at Halifax, and sent two to the Bay of Fundy, Loudon returned with the remainder of the troops to New York, where he arrived on August 30.

Admiral Holborne being now relieved of the charge of the transports, sailed with fifteen ships of the line, four frigates and a fireship to Louisbourg, but it is hard to say with what object; for, having stood in within a couple of miles of the batteries, and observed the French fleet preparing to unmoor, he made sail with all possible haste to Halifax. Holborne reported that the French fleet consisted of nineteen ships and five frigates, which he considered more than a match for his own, and therefore retired. Many instances might be named of English Admirals having engaged, and beaten too, an enemy of vastly superior force;[1] Holborne would have done well had he followed their example; he would not then have been exposed to the taunts of a French writer,[2] who says, 'M. du Bois made ready to put to sea as soon as the enemy appeared. Our people had all but one heart and one voice to engage the enemy; but this famous and long-expected M. Holborne took it into his head that our number was nearly equal to his, and therefore he made the best of his way back to Halifax.' Being reinforced by the arrival of four ships from England, Holborne again proceeded to Louisbourg about the middle of September,

[1] 'Admiral Holborne, one of the sternest condemners of Byng, wrote that, having but seventeen ships and the French nineteen, he dared not attack them. Pitt expressed himself with great vehemence against the Earl (Loudon), and we naturally have too lofty ideas of our naval strength to suppose that seventeen of our ships are not a match for any nineteen others.'—Walpole's *Memoirs of the Reign of George II.*

[2] Pichon.

and cruised off the harbour, but could not draw the French out to an equal engagement. He continued to cruise off the port until September 24, when towards evening the wind began to blow very hard from the east, but veering round suddenly to the southward, a heavy gale set in, which continued with great violence until eleven o'clock next morning. Most of the ships were within two miles of the breakers, and must have been driven on shore if the wind had not as suddenly changed to the westward. Several of the ships, which were dismasted in the gale, and obliged to throw many of their guns overboard, sailed direct for England, where they arrived in November. All the rest got safe to Halifax except the 'Tilbury,' of sixty-four guns, which was wrecked on the coast to the westward of Louisbourg,[1] when Captain Barnsley, eight of his officers, and about one half of the crew were drowned. The French inhabitants on shore, by great exertions humanely saved about two hundred of the crew, including fifteen officers. The French fleet left Louisbourg for France in October, carrying with them the 'Tilbury's' crew. One of their ships, the frigate 'Hermione' of twenty-eight guns, was captured in the Channel on November 22nd, by the 'Unicorn,' of twenty-four guns, Captain Moore, after a smart action of five hours. She had fifty of the 'Tilbury's' crew on board, who were loud in their praises of the kindness and humanity of the people of the small fishing village near which they were wrecked, who concealed them from the savages and supplied them with all the necessaries required in their destitute condition. Leaving eight of his ships under Lord Colville at Halifax, to protect the trade and watch Louisbourg, Admiral Holborne sailed with the few remaining ships of his fleet to England. During the gale which proved so fatal to the English, several of the French ships were driven from their anchorage in Louisbourg harbour, but only one, the 'Tonnant,' was driven on shore; she was got off again with little difficulty when the wind shifted.

The failure of the projected attack on Louisbourg, for which such a large and costly armament had been equipped, caused great disappointment and discontent in England and the

[1] On a reef near St.-Esprit, now called Tilbury Rock.

colonies; but even this failure was of small moment compared with the disasters and losses on the frontiers of Canada, where the French General, Montcalm, taking advantage of the absence of Lord Loudon and the great bulk of his army, had ascended Lake George with a force of 8,000 French and Indians, and laid siege, on August 2nd, to Fort William Henry, which was held by Colonel Monroe with a garrison of 2,000 men. The pusillanimous General Webb, who was encamped at Fort Edward, only fourteen miles distant, with 4,000 men, instead of marching to Monroe's relief, sent him a letter advising him to capitulate. This letter fell into Montcalm's hand, who immediately forwarded it to Colonel Monroe, but that gallant officer refused to surrender until August 9, when he had burst many of his guns and exhausted all his ammunition. Nor was this the only disaster: Colonel Palmer, who embarked with 400 men upon Lake George, to make a night attack on Ticonderoga, fell into an Indian ambuscade on July 24, when the whole of his force, except two officers and seventy men, was either killed or taken prisoners. Although the English had a decided superiority in numbers, the French were everywhere successful; a large and valuable territory was relinquished, and the frontiers of New York and Pennsylvania were exposed to the irruptions of hordes of ruthless savages. In the words of Bancroft, 'The English had been driven from every cabin in the basin of the Ohio; Montcalm had destroyed every vestige of their power within that of the St. Lawrence. France had posts on each side of the lakes, and at Detroit, at Mackinaw, at Kaskaskia, and at New Orleans. . . . As the men composing the garrison of Fort Loudon in Tennessee were but so many hostages in the hands of the Cherokees, the claim of France to the valleys of the Mississippi and the St. Lawrence seemed established by possession. . . . America and England were humiliated.' Pitt, in the House of Commons, when censuring the conduct of Loudon, indignantly exclaimed, 'Nothing was done, nothing was attempted. . . . We have lost all the waters, we have not a boat on the lakes. Every door is open to France.' Dark and gloomy were the prospects of England.

Incompetent ministers at home, weak and incapable generals[1] abroad, had brought the nation to the very brink of ruin. In this sad state of affairs, Pitt, who had been compelled to resign on account of the aversion of the King and the intrigues of his enemies, was by the universal voice of the nation reinstated in his office of Secretary of State, though at too late a period to avert the disasters I have recorded. With full confidence in his genius and patriotism, the people looked with hope to the future. Nor were they disappointed. The war begun in 1756 with such serious reverses, eventually proved, as Macaulay[2] has well said, 'the most glorious war in which England had ever been engaged.'

When Parliament met, on December 1, 1757, the King declared that 'it was his firm resolution to apply his utmost efforts for the security of the kingdom, and for the recovery and protection of the possessions and right of his crown and subjects in America and elsewhere, as well by the strongest exertions of our naval force, as by all other methods.' Both Houses having expressed an earnest desire to afford all the assistance in their power for attaining these objects, Pitt set about the work with diligence and vigour, and took most active measures without a moment's delay, not only for recovering the forts that had been lost in America by the incompetence of Loudon, but also for effecting the conquest of Canada. To accomplish this great object he saw at once that it would be necessary to reduce Louisbourg—the key of the St. Lawrence—and to obtain possession of the French posts of Ticonderoga and Crown Point, in order to open the way for the invasion of Canada. For the first enterprise, a combined naval and military force would be required, ready to commence operations as soon as the season would permit. For the second, a large army of regulars would be indispensable, supported by as many troops as could be raised in the colonies. The command of the first was entrusted to Admiral Boscawen, an officer of great experience, and to General Amherst, who had greatly distinguished himself in

[1] Speaking of Loudon, Franklin says in his autobiography, 'He is like St. George on the sign-boards, always on horseback, but never rides on.'

[2] His *Essay on William Pitt*.

Germany. General Abercrombie, who was appointed Commander-in-Chief in place of the Earl of Loudon, was instructed to reduce Ticonderoga and Crown Point. The colonies were at the same time encouraged to raise men, with the assurance that they should be reimbursed, and that provincial officers under the rank of colonel should possess the same privileges as officers of equal grade in the regular army. As you, of course, feel more interested in matters that relate to the past history of your own island, I will endeavour in the first place to give you an account of the second siege of Louisbourg, and afterwards briefly notice the campaign on the Continent.

As it was well known that new batteries had been erected and the fortifications much improved since Louisbourg was taken in 1745 by 4,000 Provincials and ten ships of the line, and that the garrison was fully four times as strong as at that period, and could now receive succours by means of the roads constructed by Count Raymond from the outports and interior, where the population had been considerably augmented by the arrival of a number of the Acadians expelled from Nova Scotia, it was considered that a land force of 12,000 men and a fleet of at least twenty ships of the line would now be required to reduce it. The disappointment caused by the failure of the expedition of the previous year, chiefly due to delay in reaching the scene of action, warned the Ministry on the present occasion. The whole month of December was employed in naval preparations, with such diligence that the fleet and transports were ready to sail from Spithead, where they were anchored, on February 8. The great preparations going on in the English ports did not escape the notice of the French Government. In fact, the spy Henacy, before mentioned (p. 286), had kept up a regular correspondence all winter with a friend employed in the Secretary of State's office at Paris, until he was arrested on March 9 in London.[1] Learn-

[1] 'For this illicit correspondence with the enemy of our country, in time of open war, Dr. Henacy was tried, convicted, and condemned to be hanged and quartered, as in cases of high treason; but after several reprieves he obtained His Majesty's pardon, not for any discovery, as the world were made to believe, but by an extraordinary foreign interposition, which would not have had the same weight at a court that properly resented the disappointment the nation met with in the expeditions against Louisbourg and Rochfort.'—*Entick.*

ing from this source that the expedition was intended to attack Louisbourg, the French Government saw the immediate necessity of sending out reinforcements, and accordingly made great exertions to equip ships for that purpose. Two squadrons were accordingly fitted out—one of six ships of the line and one frigate, at Toulon, under the command of M. du Quesne, and another of six ships of the line and two frigates, at Rochfort, under M. de la Cloué. On the arrival of the first at Rochfort, M. du Quesne was to take command of the united squadrons, to convoy forty transports with 3,000 troops to America. This purpose was, however, successfully frustrated by the foresight and vigilance of Pitt, who stationed a squadron, under the command of Admiral Osborne, in the Straits of Gibraltar, to intercept the French fleet from Toulon, and another, under Admiral Hawke, in the Basque Roads, to watch the Rochfort fleet. Admiral Osborne carried out his instructions with great success. Not a single enemy's ship was allowed to pass through the Straits, and two of the finest vessels belonging to M. du Quesne's squadron—the 'Fourdroyant'[1] of eighty-four, and the 'Orpheus' of sixty-four guns—were captured while attempting to join M. de la Cloué's squadron in the Spanish port of Carthagena. Admiral Hawke fell in with the Rochfort expedition on April 3, a few leagues from the shore, just as it was starting for Louisbourg and Quebec; but, owing to a change of wind, the whole of the French ships got safely into St. Martin's, under the guns of the forts on the Isle of Aix, before he could come up with them, except one brig,

[1] The capture of the 'Fourdroyant,' of eighty-four guns, with a crew of 700 men, by the 'Monmouth,' of sixty-four guns, and 470 men, was the most gallant naval exploit of the 'Seven Years' War.' When Admiral Osborne fell in with the French fleet off Carthagena on February 27, he made signals to the 'Monmouth,' 'Swiftsure,' and 'Hampton Court,' to chase the 'Fourdroyant,' but the 'Monmouth' was the only one that could overreach her. Having come within gun-shot at 5 A.M., Captain Gardiner began the action, but finding that he could make no impression upon her at that distance, he laid his ship on the quarter of the enemy at 7 A.M., within pistol-shot, when a terrible contest ensued, in which both ships lost their mizen-masts and sustained great damage in their hulls. At 9 o'clock the gallant Gardiner fell mortally wounded by a musket-ball in the head, but his lieutenant, with equal bravery, fought out the action until 1 o'clock, when the 'Fourdroyant' struck.

which was driven on shore by the 'Hussar' and burnt. The greater part of the men-of-war and transports, in their haste to escape ran ashore behind the Isle of Aix in shoal water, where the English ships could not follow them. Boats were then sent to destroy them, but they contrived, by throwing overboard their guns, ammunition, and stores, to get afloat and warp up to the mouth of the Charente. Although none of the vessels were captured, the main object of the French expedition was completely frustrated, as neither the guns and stores thrown overboard could be recovered, nor the ships repaired in time to reach Louisbourg before it was blockaded by Admiral Boscawen. Still, notwithstanding the vigilance of the English Admirals on the coast, M. Beaussier, with four ships of the line, two frigates,[1] and sixteen transports, carrying 550 men of the regiment of 'Volontaires Étrangers' and 600 of the regiment of 'Cambise,' together with a large supply of provisions and munitions of war, contrived to get out of Brest unperceived on March 12, and reached Louisbourg in safety not long before the English fleet arrived in Gabarus Bay.

The English expedition, after waiting at Spithead about ten days for a favourable wind, set off on February 19, not, however, without suffering a serious mishap in the loss of the 'Invincible,' seventy-four guns, one of the finest ships in the navy, which ran ashore on the Dean Sand, near St. Helen's, and became a total wreck. Sir Charles Hardy,[2] the second in

[1] These ships were the 'Prudent' and 'Entreprenant,' seventy-fours; the 'Bienfaisant,' 'Capricieux,' and 'Célèbre,' sixties; and the frigates 'Apollo' and 'Comet,' of thirty guns each; all of which were taken or destroyed during the siege, except the 'Comet,' which got out a few days after the troops landed.

[2] Sir Charles Hardy arrived at Halifax on May 20, and reported that three or four ships of war had got into Louisbourg. When this news reached England it caused some alarm, as we learn from the following extract from a letter of Earl Temple to Pitt, of July 3:—'What alarms me most is the account Lady Hester brought of some men-of-war, a few, very few, being got into Louisbourg; because upon the issue of that attempt I think the whole salvation of this country and Europe does essentially depend.'—*Chatham Correspondence.*

How differently the gallant Wolfe thought of the matter! Having told his uncle, in a letter from Halifax, that a few ships had got into Louisbourg notwithstanding Hardy's vigilance, he added: 'If they had thrown in twice as much, we should not hesitate to attack them; and for my part, I have no doubt of our success. If the command, arrived off Louisbourg on April 2, with a few of the ships, but the whole of the men-of-war and transports did not reach Halifax until May 9. While the fleet lay at anchor in Halifax Harbour, taking in supplies of fresh provisions and water, it was joined by all the ships of war on the station; and the army was reinforced by the arrival of Bragg's regiment from the Bay of Fundy, and 200 carpenters under Colonel Meserve, and 538 Rangers, or Provincial troops, from Boston. On May 28, when the expedition sailed for Louisbourg, it was composed of the following sea and land forces:—

The Namur of	90 guns	Admiral the Hon. E. Boscawen Captain Buckle
Royal William	80 ,,	Rear-Admiral Sir Charles Hardy Captain Evans
Princess Amelia	80 ,,	Commodore Philip Durell Captain Bray
Terrible	74 ,,	Captain Collins
Northumberland	70 ,,	,, Lord Colville
Vanguard	70 ,,	,, Swanton
Oxford	70 ,,	,, Spry
Burford	70 ,,	,, Gambier
Somerset	70 ,,	,, Hughes
Lancaster	70 ,,	,, Edgcumbe
Devonshire	66 ,,	,, Gordon
Bedford	64 ,,	,, Fowke
Captain	64 ,,	,, Amherst
Prince Frederic	64 ,,	,, Mann
Pembroke	60 ,,	,, Simcoe
Kingston	60 ,,	,, Parry
York	60 ,,	,, Pigot
Prince of Orange	60 ,,	,, Fergusson
Defiance	60 ,,	,, Baird
Nottingham	60 ,,	,, Marshall
Centurion	50 ,,	,, Mantell
Sutherland	50 ,,	,, Rous;

the frigates 'Juno,' 'Gramont, 'Nightingale,' 'Hunter,' 'Boreas,' 'Hind, 'Trent,' 'Port Mahon,' 'Diana, 'Shannon,' 'Kennington,' 'Scarborough,' 'Squirrel,' 'Hawk,' 'Beaver,' 'Tyloe,' and 'Halifax;' the 'Etna' and 'Lightning' fire-ships, and one hundred and eighteen transports, carrying the following land forces:—

French fleet comes upon this coast, the campaign will, I hope, be decisive.'—Wright's *Life of Major-General Wolfe*. London: 1864.

1st Regt. Royals . .	854	45th Regt. Warburton's .	852
15th " Amherst's .	763	47th " Lascelles' . .	856
17th " Forbes' .	660	48th " Webb's . .	932
22nd " Whitmore's .	910	58th " Anstruther's .	615
28th " Bragg's . .	627	60th,[1] 2nd Bat., Monckton's	925
40th " Hopkins' . .	655	60th, 3rd " Lawrence's .	814
35th " Otway's . .	565	78th . . . Frazer's .	1,084

Also five companies of Rangers, a brigade of artillery and engineers, and 200 carpenters; altogether exceeding 12,000 men, exclusive of officers, and troops left for the defence of Halifax, consisting of the 43rd Regiment, under Colonel Kennedy, of 659 men, and detachments from the 1st, 29th, 35th, 45th, 47th, second battalion of 60th and 78th Regiments, and artillery, in all 1,600 men.

As General Amherst had not arrived from Germany when the expedition sailed from Spithead, the army, as well as the fleet, was placed under the command of Admiral Boscawen, so that no time should be lost waiting at Halifax in case the General should not arrive there so soon as was expected. Having, therefore, completed all his arrangements, the Admiral, agreeably to his instructions, sailed from thence, as before mentioned, on May 28, for Louisbourg, with his fleet and transports, numbering in all 157 sail. Fortunately, on the very same day General Amherst arrived in the 'Dublin,' seventy-four, Captain Rodney, and met the expedition at the mouth of the harbour, when he immediately went on board the 'Namur,' the flagship, and sent the 'Dublin,' whose crew was very sickly, after a voyage of seventy-three days, into Halifax.

Having now taken command of the land forces, General Amherst immediately began to organise the troops preparatory to their landing at Louisbourg, by dividing them into three brigades: the first, consisting of the 1st, 22nd, 40th, and 48th Regiments, and the second battalion of the 60th Rifles, under Brigadier-General Whitmore; the second, of the 15th, 28th, 45th, 58th, and 78th Regiments, under Brigadier-General Lawrence;[2]

[1] The 60th Rifles were originally raised in America, in 1756, under the designation of 'The Royal Americans;' they were composed chiefly of German and Swiss immigrants, who had arrived in the colonies in great numbers some years previously.

[2] Colonel Lawrence was at this time Governor of Nova Scotia. During his absence Lieutenant-Colonel Monckton acted as Governor.

and the third, of the 17th, 35th, and 47th Regiments, and the third battalion of the 60th Rifles, under Brigadier-General Wolfe. Pitt himself had, before the expedition left England, selected these three officers to command brigades. Wolfe, at at that time one of the youngest colonels in the army, had, 'by his zealous endeavours, on the 23rd September previous, to instil some life and vigour into the expedition against Rochfort, fruitless though they were rendered by the pusillanimity of the chiefs, caused him to be singled out as one likely to redeem the military reputation of England.'[1] As Wolfe was the youngest of the brigadiers in rank, the most active part of the service fell to his lot, and afforded him an opportunity, as you will shortly see, of proving that Pitt had made a judicious choice in selecting him for a post of such importance.

Meanwhile the fleet and transports proceeded on their voyage. On the 30th, the wind blowing hard and directly ahead, many of the transports were greatly dispersed; but the men-of-war kept well together and arrived in sight of Gabarus Bay on the morning of June 1, where the Admiral learned from Captain Rous, of the 'Sutherland,' who had been reconnoitreing the Harbour of Louisbourg, that there were thirteen ships of war in the port, two of which only arrived on May 30. On the morning of June 2 the fleet and about one-third of the transports came to anchor in Gabarus Bay, where they were joined on the following day by the remainder. On the same evening, General Amherst, together with Brigadier-Generals Lawrence and Wolfe, got into a boat and rowed along the shore as near as the surf would permit, in order to ascertain the most suitable place for effecting a landing. Preparations for landing were made on the 3rd, but the weather was so boisterous, and the surf so heavy, that the design was given up. For the same reason nothing could be done for several days; the south-east wind, driving in a heavy swell which broke in foaming surf upon the rocky shore, rendered landing from boats quite impossible.

While the troops are waiting for a favourable opportunity to land, let us glance at the dispositions made by the enemy

[1] Wright's *Life of Wolfe.*

to face p. 297

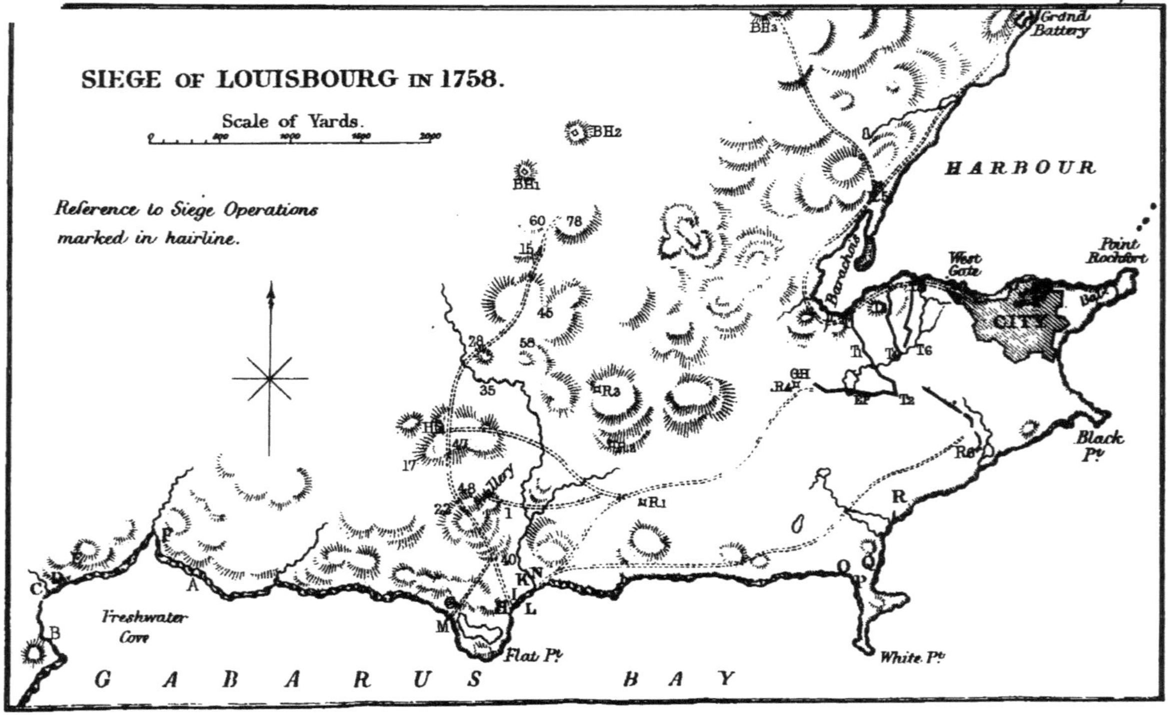
SIEGE OF LOUISBOURG IN 1758.
Scale of Yards.
0
500
1000
1500
2000
Reference to Siege Operations marked in hairline.
HARBOUR
Grand Battery
Point Rochfort
West Gate
CITY
Barachois
Black Pt
White Pt
Flat Pt
Freshwater Cove
G A B A R U S B A Y
BH1
BH2
BH3
R1
R3
GH
T6
T2
R6
60
78
15
45
58
28
35
17
47
48
22
40
A
B
C
D
F
K
N
L
M
O
R

to oppose them. The French Government, as already mentioned, correctly informed by the traitor Henacy of the destination and sailing of the large armament from England, had, notwithstanding the vigilance of the English Admirals, succeeded in sending reinforcements to the garrison of Louisbourg, which enabled the Governor, the Chevalier de Drucour, to make what he considered effective measures to prevent a landing. All along the shore, from Black Point to the Head of Fresh Water Cove—a distance of nearly five miles—strong breastworks were thrown up wherever a descent was considered practicable. At the head of Fresh Water Cove, where a gravel beach a quarter of a mile in length offered the most favourable place for landing, batteries were erected mounting eight guns, so effectually concealed by felled trees closely packed together, with their tops towards the shore, that, viewed from the sea, they presented the appearance of a smooth green field with here and there a tuft of spruce. This position was defended by a large body of troops commanded by M. de St. Julien, and a band of savages under a celebrated chief.[1]

There were eight guns and two mortars in position near Flat Point Cove, and eight more near White Point, the only places where the rough shingle beaches afforded some facility for landing. The rocky and rugged cliffs, occupying the intervals between these armed posts, were deemed inaccessible, and in a great measure left unguarded. The English accounts say that these works were defended by 3,000 men. French writers admit that there were 2,000 regulars, besides large bands of irregulars and Indians engaged in the duty of opposing the landing of the English, and that only 300 men were left in Louisbourg.[2]

[1] This chief was killed in the contest which ensued; he was a stout, well made man, and exhibited great daring and intrepidity. He had been rewarded for former services by a medal, which he wore round his neck. It was handed to Admiral Boscawen.—*Entick.*

[2] By referring to the Plan annexed you will observe the positions of the guns and mortars employed to oppose the landing of the troops.

At the head of Fresh Water Cove.

C. One Swivel.
D. Two Swivels.
E. Two Six-pounders.
F. One Twenty-pounder and Two Six-pounders.

Owing to a continuance of boisterous weather and a heavy surf, no attempt was made to land until the morning of the 7th, when the swell having somewhat abated, the signal was made to prepare to land, and the troops were embarked in boats for that purpose; but a thick fog coming on, the order was countermanded. The weather having again moderated towards evening, it was determined to renew the attempt next morning, with the three following brigades, which had already been told off for that object:—

The first, or right brigade, composed of detachments of the 1st, 17th, 47th, 48th, 58th, and 60th Regiments, led by Brigadier-General Whitmore, Colonels Burton and Foster, and Majors Prevost and Darby.

The second, or centre brigade, composed of detachments of the 15th, 22nd, 35th, 40th, 45th, and 60th Regiments, under Brigadier-General Lawrence, Colonel Wilmot, Lieutenant-Colonel Handfield, Majors Hamilton and Hussey.

The third, or left brigade, composed of the 78th Highlanders, five companies of Rangers, twelve companies of Grenadiers, and a corps of Light Infantry[1] consisting of 550 of the best marksmen to be found in the different regiments, led by Brigadier-General Wolfe, Colonels Frazer, Fletcher, and Murray, and Majors Scott, Murray, and Farquharson.

The right division was ordered to proceed towards White

Near Flat Point and Flat Point Cove.

G. One Seven-inch Mortar.	I. Two Six-pounders.
One Eight „ „	K. Two „ „
H. Two Swivels.	N. Two Twelve „

Near White Point.

O, Two Six-pounders.	Q. Two Six-pounders.
P. Two Twenty-four do.	R. Two Twelve do.

[1] "Our Light Infantry, Highlanders, and Rangers, the French termed the *English Savages*, perhaps in contradistinction to their own native Indians, Canadians, &c., the true French Savages. . . . Some were dressed in blue, some in green jackets and drawers, for the easier brushing through the woods, with ruffs of black bear-skins round their necks; the beard of their upper lips, some grown into whiskers, others not so, but all well smutted on that part, with little round hats like several of our seamen. . . . The Rangers are a body of irregulars, who have a more cut-throat savage appearance, which carries in it something of natural savages: the appearance of the Light Infantry has in it more of artificial savages.'—*Entick.*

Point, and the centre towards Flat Point, as if with the intention of landing at those places, but in reality to draw off the French forces from the neighbourhood of Freshwater Cove, where the descent was to be made by Wolfe's brigade.

The 'Kennington' frigate and 'Halifax' corvette were anchored off Freshwater Cove, to cover the troops in landing; the 'Gramont,' 'Diana,' and 'Shannon' frigates off Flat Point; and the 'Sutherland' ship of the line and 'Squirrel' frigate off White Point, to mislead the enemy and annoy the troops stationed at those places.

To further distract the attention of the enemy, the 28th Regiment was embarked in a small fleet of sloops, and sent past the harbour's mouth under convoy towards Lorambec, a small harbour three miles to the eastward of Louisbourg, with instructions to make a show of landing, but not to attempt to do so without further instructions.

LETTER XVIII.

1758.

On the morning of June 8—a day which will ever be memorable in the annals of the British Army—the swell having in some measure subsided, Commodore Durell was sent before daybreak to examine the coast, and on his return reported that although there still was a heavy surf upon the shore, the troops might land without danger from that cause. The order was therefore immediately issued for the men to embark in the boats before daybreak, ready to take up their respective positions in the order already designated. As soon as the boats were ready to start, the ships stationed at the places already mentioned opened a brisk cannonade upon the enemy's works, and kept it up until the boats nearly reached their destinations. The left division, commanded by Brigadier General Wolfe, pulled in with great vigour towards Freshwater Cove, the real point of attack; while the right and centre divisions advanced more slowly towards White Point and Flat Cove, to draw the attention of the enemy from the left. This feint, however, did not deceive the enemy, who soon divined its object, and waited quietly behind his cover at Fresh Water Cove until the leading boats of Wolfe's division arrived within musket-shot of the shore, where they were met all at once by a terrific fire of red-hot balls, grape and round shot, and a continuous discharge of musketry from the lines. Wolfe, seeing the impossibility of landing upon the beach, waved his hat to the leading boats to withdraw; but the signal being mistaken by Lieutenants Hopkins and Browne, and Ensign Grant, who with 100 infantry led the attack, for what their brave hearts most ardently desired—the order to advance

—they pushed on with great vigour and gained some shelter under a rocky point on the right of the beach (A, on Plan, p. 297), which being supposed inaccessible, had been left unguarded by the enemy. Many of the soldiers, as they sprang on shore from the boats, were dragged into the water by the recoiling surf and drowned; but the rest, led by the gallant subalterns, landed in safety, climbed up the rocks, and formed in a compact body on the summit, exposed to a flanking fire from the Cove batteries. Observing the success of this daring attempt, Wolfe immediately gave orders to the troops to advance in support of their comrades on shore,[1] and was himself one of the first to jump out of his boat into the raging surf, to escape the galling fire to which all were exposed from the flanking batteries and the incessant roll of musketry, scarcely twenty yards distant. All the troops followed the example of their leader with alacrity; Grenadiers, Rangers, Light Infantry, Highlanders—all strove which should get first on shore to share in the contest. 'Cannon and musketry were not their worst antagonists. The sea, which had grown more and more boisterous since they had set out, now lashing the coast, dashed them against the rocks, shattering several of the boats, upsetting others; and many a brave fellow, who hoped ere night to win renown in the field, found an instant watery grave.'[2] Wolfe's example was speedily followed by all the

[1] The gallant conduct of Major Scott, as related by Pichon, is deserving of special notice. 'Being ordered to go with his men to the support of those who had landed, and his own boat, which arrived first, being stove the instant he landed, the Major climbed up the rock by himself, in hopes of joining the hundred men, but finding no more than ten, he with this small band gained the summit of the precipice, where he found himself in front of seventy Frenchmen and ten Indians, from whom he was separated only by a small copse of fir trees. Nevertheless, he would not abandon a post on which the success of the whole enterprise depended. Two of his men were killed and three wounded; three balls were lodged in his own clothes; still he held his ground until seconded by the arrival of a support. The English troops, perceiving that this was the only chance of succeeding, followed his example, and notwithstanding the surf, which drove back the boats and drowned great numbers, landed here in defiance of the French batteries, which played upon them most vigorously.'—*Memoirs of Cape Breton.*

[2] Wright's *Life of General Wolfe.*

A traveller who recently visited Freshwater Cove, or, as it is sometimes called, Kennington Cove, says that two hundred paces from the shore, towards the wood men of his brigade, as well as by the troops of Lawrence's and Whitmore's divisions, which landed at a more convenient place a little further to the left (marked B on Plan, at p. 297), in the face of a continual discharge of shot and shells from the enemy's lines. The rear was brought up by General Amherst himself, who, from personal observation, was able to bear willing testimony to the bravery and resolution of all the troops engaged in this arduous undertaking.

The enemy—paralysed and thrown into confusion by the boldness and success of the British troops—made but a feeble resistance to the progress of Wolfe, who lost no time in following up the advantage he had gained. Attacking the defenders of the battery F (see Plan) with the bayonet, it was speedily carried; all the others, E, D, C, fell in rapid succession. The enemy, having made no preparations for a hand-to-hand fight, and alarmed by a report that General Whitmore had landed at White Point and cut off their retreat to Louisbourg, fled precipitately, one body along the coast, the other into the woods, leaving all their guns, stores, ammunition, and implements in the hands of the invaders. The whole of the guns enumerated at p. 297, fell into the hands of a party sent in pursuit of the fugitives along the shore. The main body was chased through the woods by Wolfe and Lawrence, almost up to the gates of Louisbourg. As the pursuers approached the town they were fired upon by the guns on the ramparts, which showed the Brigadiers at what distance from the fortress their camp might be pitched with safety. Thus, in six short hours of a summer's morning the first great step of the expedition was successfully accomplished—a footing was established upon the soil of Cape Breton, from which the troops never retreated a single inch during the siege; proving that there were neither difficulties nor dangers which could not be overcome by British troops led by a skilful commander.

The French seem to have placed their whole reliance upon

that skirts the rising ground in the rear, may still be seen the lone graves of the British soldiers whose lives were lost on that memorable occasion, marked by a few grey moss-clad stones standing erect amidst tufts of heath and crowberry.—*Cape Breton News*, January, 19, 1867.

their batteries, impressed with the belief that they could not be carried. Their men had been trained to fight behind cover, and were therefore thrown into confusion the moment they found themselves attacked with the bayonet by a body of British troops goaded and exasperated by the losses they had suffered in landing under such unparalleled difficulties. Besides, as they did not anticipate a defeat, no place of rendezvous had been fixed upon where they might have rallied and made a stand against their enemies, many of whom were only half-armed, having lost or damaged their muskets in landing through the surf.

The loss of the British troops in executing this great achievement was:—

	Killed.	Wounded.
Captain[1]	1	0
Lieutenants	2	5
Ensigns	1	0
Sergeants	4	2
Corporals	1	1
Privates	41	51
Totals	50	59

The enemy's loss in killed and wounded is not known, but two captains, two lieutenants, and seventy privates were taken prisoners. Pichon's statement that 200 were killed and taken prisoners cannot be correct. It is not likely that the French lost 130 men killed, protected as they were by breastworks, while the English lost only fifty killed, exposed to the enemy's cannon and musketry, without any shelter whatever.

As the French had now abandoned all their outworks and retired within the walls of Louisbourg, it will be well, before proceeding with the narrative of the siege, to notice the condition of the fortifications and the strength of the forces prepared to defend them. Some writers, in order to find an excuse for the second fall of Louisbourg, have stated that the works had never been repaired since the siege of 1745; that they were in a most ruinous condition, and quite incapable of stand-

[1] The officers killed were Captain Baillie and Lieutenant Cuthbert, of the Highland Regiment; Lieutenant Nicholson, of the 15th Regiment; and one ensign (name not given) of the Rangers.

ing a bombardment. This is not correct. While the English had possession of Louisbourg, from 1745 to 1749, much labour and expense were incurred in repairing the walls, which had sustained but slight damage during the siege; bombproof casemates were constructed, and large barracks erected near the Queen's Gate. After it reverted into the hands of the French, during the seven years preceding the second siege, a half-moon battery, mounting twenty guns, was constructed upon Point Rochfort, a curtain of masonry was built between the right flank of the Maurepas and the left flank of the Princess Bastions, which formerly was occupied merely by a pallisading, and a bastioned curtain erected between the Queen's and Princess's Bastions to give additional strength to the ditch.

The garrison of Louisbourg, when the English landed, consisted of,

			Men.
Twenty-four Companies of Infantry and two Companies of Artillery; the usual force in all			1,200
The Second Battalion of the regiment of Volontaires Étrangers			600
"	"	Artois	500
"	"	Burgoyne	450
"	"	Cambise	650
		Total	3,400

There were also in the town a body of 700 burgher militia and a band of Indians, and in the harbour the following ships of war:—

Le Prudent	74 guns.	La Chèvre	16 guns.
L'Entreprenant	74 "	La Biche	16 "
Le Capricieux	64 "	Le Fidèle	36 "
Le Célèbre	64 "	L'Echo	32 "
Le Bienfaisant	64 "	La Diane	36 "
L'Apollon	50 "	L'Aréthuse	36 "

The 'Bizarre,' sixty-four, escaped out of the harbour on June 8, and the 'Comète,' thirty, a few days afterwards, in spite of the vigilance of Sir Charles Hardy. The French Commodore wished to leave Louisbourg with the rest of his squadron, but could not obtain the consent of the Governor, M. de Drucour, who employed many of the officers and crews in the town.

Very little progress was made for several days in landing artillery and stores, on account of the weather; in fact, although tents and provisions were landed daily, the siege artillery and ammunition could not be got on shore before the 20th. Meanwhile, an encampment for the whole army was formed upon a low range of undulating hills on both sides of the rivulet which runs into the sea in Flat Point Cove. The position occupied by each regiment will be best understood by referring to the Plan (p. 297), indicated by figures corresponding with the number of the regiment. It will also be seen that the space covered by the encampment constituted a segment of a circle two miles in length, the head-quarters (H. Q.) being about midway between the northern and southern extremities. As Flat Cove was found to be the most convenient place for landing artillery and stores, a road was formed from thence through the encampment to the extreme left occupied by the Light Infantry. Three redoubts, marked R. 1, R. 2, and R. 3, were also commenced about half a mile in advance of the camp, to protect it from any attacks in front; and two blockhouses, B. H. 1 and B. H. 2, were erected in rear of the Light Infantry's quarters, upon commanding sites, from which a watchful look-out was maintained to guard against the Indians or Canadians expected from the interior. For the further security of the camp, a detachment was stationed at the head of Freshwater Cove, to meet any attack from that quarter.

Having now provided for the security of the camp, and received intelligence from some deserters that the French had dismantled and abandoned the Grand Battery, and burned every house within two miles of the town, General Amherst sent Wolfe with 1,200 men selected from the Highlanders, Grenadiers, Light Infantry, and Rangers, round the head of the North-east harbour, to take possession of the Lighthouse Battery, which commanded the Island Battery and the shipping; at the same time, artillery, tools, and provisions were sent by sea to Lorambec for their use. This important service was successfully accomplished the same day, the enemy having abandoned all their posts upon the route, and also two camps at Lorambec, in which were found a quantity of provisions, dry fish, and wine.[1] Finding the Lighthouse Battery deserted

[1] Pichon says the loss of the wine caused no regret, as the 'soldiers were so used to profusion, that they would neither work nor go upon a sally unless they were half drunk.'

and the guns spiked, Wolfe established a camp for the main body of his troops on the Lighthouse Point, and then posted 300 men at Lorambec to protect his communication with the fleet, and 300 more at the head of the North-east harbour, under the command of Major Ross. As there was still a wide interval between Major Ross's post and the quarters of the Light Infantry, a blockhouse (B. H. 3) was shortly afterwards erected upon the Miray road, about a mile to the eastward of the latter, which possessed the double advantage of securing the communication between the North-east harbour and the camp, and of intercepting succours coming from Miray. A detachment of Light Infantry and Rangers was also posted about half-way between the camp and the North-east harbour, which completed the communications of the main body of the army with the troops stationed at Lorambec and the Lighthouse. As one of Wolfe's objects was to destroy the shipping in the harbour, batteries were erected on the hill near the Careening Cove, and on the low ground between that Cove and the Lighthouse, armed with 24 and 12-pounder guns and mortars. All these arrangements being completed, fire was opened upon the ships on the night of the 18th, which obliged them to haul over nearer to the town. Leaving Wolfe now busily employed in making a road from Lorambec, for transporting heavy guns to the Lighthouse Battery, let us return to the main army.

From the 13th to the 16th, the weather was so boisterous that heavy guns could not be landed at Flat Cove; the operations on that side were confined to the completion of the redoubts in front, and the blockhouses in rear of the camp. These operations, however, were not carried on without some interruption, as the enemy kept up a vigorous fire from the town upon the workmen, and upon one occasion sent out 300 men in open day to attack Redoubt, R. 3, who were repulsed by the Light Infantry sent by Brigadier Lawrence, the commanding officer on the left of the camp.

On the 17th, the General, accompanied by the commanding officers of the Artillery and Engineers, reconnoitred the ground in front of the town, to select the most suitable place for opening the trenches. They decided that the ground between the head of the Barachois and a small eminence about a quarter of a mile to the south-westward, which they named Green Hill,[1] was the best adapted for their purpose, the ground further to the right being swampy and incapable of drainage. A road was also marked out from the landing-place at Flat Cove, with branches to the artillery camp and head-quarters, for the transportation of siege guns, ammunition, and stores. These roads, owing to the broken, rocky, and swampy nature of the ground, were made with great difficulty, the men being exposed to a heavy fire from the ramparts. The shot often fell thickly among the men, and occasionally even into the left of the camp. The formation of the roads, and the construction of a redoubt upon Green Hill, gave ample occupation to the army for the next ten days, and caused so much uneasiness to M. de Drucour, that he ordered the frigate 'Echo' to run out of the harbour at all risks, and proceed to Quebec for succours from the Viceroy. The 'Echo' got safely out of the harbour in a thick fog, not, however, without observation from the Lighthouse, from whence information thereof was forwarded to the Admiral, who sent the 'Sutherland' and 'Juno' in pursuit. The 'Echo' was soon overtaken, and brought into Gabarus Bay on the 19th.

Brigadier Wolfe, meanwhile, was not idle on his side of the harbour. His guns, it is true, had made little impression on the shipping, but having obtained some 24-pounders from Gabarus Bay, and mounted them at the Lighthouse, he began to fire with great vigour upon the Island Battery on the night of the 19th. The enemy replied on the following day with equal vigour from the island, the new battery on Point Rochfort, and the ships in the harbour. The contest was maintained with great spirit on both sides, until the evening of the 25th, when the Island Battery was silenced, all the embrasures destroyed, and the parapets reduced to a heap of ruins. Having made everything secure at the Lighthouse, and mounted

[1] This was not the Green Hill so often mentioned in the account of the first siege. *That* was nearly a mile distant from the King's Bastion; *this*, a small detached knoll, marked G. H., barely half a mile from the same work.—See Plan, p. 297.

some additional guns, Brigadier Wolfe left the north side in charge of a sufficient number of troops, and withdrew, together with the remainder of his forces and light artillery, to head-quarters. All the posts were left well guarded, to keep up the communications with the camp, and to prevent the arrival of succours from the interior. As the destruction of the Island Battery had now removed the only obstacle to the entry of the English ships into the harbour, M. de Drucour blocked up the entrance by sinking four ships of war in the narrowest part of the channel between Battery Island and the Nag's Head Rock—viz., the 'Apollon,' of 50 guns, the 'Fidèle,' of 36, and the 'Chèvre' and 'Biche,' of 16 guns each. The sunken ships were fastened together by strong chains directly across the entrance, and their masts were cut off below the surface of the water. On July 1, two more ships were sunk, the frigate 'Diane,' and another, of which the name is not given. There were now only five ships of the line and one frigate in the harbour.

Let us now return to the front of the town. The investment being completed by means of the redoubts, blockhouses,[1] and military posts, on one side, and by the fleet on the other, the engineers marked out a line of entrenchment at a distance of 600 yards from the most advanced salient of the fortress, with the design of attacking the Dauphin and King's Bastions. The length of this entrenchment, or first parallel, from its northern extremity at the water's edge, near the Barachois, to the southern extremity midway between Green Hill and the King's Bastion (T, T. 1, T. 2, on Plan), was about 500 yards. As the only access to the proposed parallel was across the bog from Green Hill, it was necessary in the first instance to construct an épaulement or rampart (E. P.) composed of fascines and gabions mixed with earth and sods, for the protection of the men employed in making a road across the bog, and of the troops in passing between Greenhill and

[1] On the night of the 26th, a party crept out of the town carrying with them a tar-barrel, and got close to the Blockhouse B. H. 3, with the intention of setting fire to it, before they were discovered. They were driven off by a detachment from the Light Infantry camp. On the same day a party of Indians carried off three sailors belonging to the transports, who had incautiously landed at the head of Gabarus Bay, contrary to orders.

the trenches. This was necessarily a work requiring time and labour, the width of the épaulement being sixty feet, its height nine feet, and its length nearly one quarter of a mile. As the road from Flat Cove was now finished, large quantities of fascines and gabions were brought forward to Green Hill, where Redoubt, R. 4, was completed on June 25. All available hands were now employed in the construction of the épaulement; next to the Pioneers, the body of Carpenters, under Colonel Maserve, were found the most useful in this service; but unfortunately, the smallpox breaking out, not less than ninety-six men, including the colonel and his son, fell victims to the malady in the course of a few days. The loss of these valuable men was much felt at this juncture; their place was poorly supplied by 200 men brought from Freshwater Cove, who had been relieved by 200 marines. Most of the work had to be done in the night time, which exposed the men to great hardship and suffering, not only from sickness, but also from the fire of the town and shipping. One frigate, the 'Aréthuse,' moored close to the mouth of the Barachois, not more than half a mile from Green Hill, kept up a constant fire upon the épaulement, and annoyed the men exceedingly.

On the morning of July 1, a large party, which left the town and approached the Barachois, were attacked by Wolfe with a corps of Light Infantry, and driven back into the town. Taking advantage of the confusion, Wolfe seized an eminence on the north side of the harbour, and began to erect a battery and redoubt, R. 5, which, when completed in the course of a few days, opened a destructive fire on the town and shipping.

Hitherto the attention of the besiegers had been wholly absorbed by the progress of the works preparing for the attack on the Dauphin and King's Bastions; but as nothing further could now be done than to push on the construction of the épaulement and the road across the bog in that quarter, it was determined to make a diversion on the right, by throwing up some batteries between Greenhill and the shore, to the eastward of White Point, for the purpose of drawing off a part of the garrison to the defence of the south front of the city.

Accordingly, on July 1, a body of troops were pushed forward to the right, which forced back the enemy towards Black Point; and on the 3rd, Brigadier Wolfe threw up a redoubt near the shore, R. 6, within 650 yards of the ravelin of the Queen's and Princess's Bastions. From this time until the 9th nothing worthy of note occurred, all the disposable force being occupied on the left in forming the road across the bog and in making fascines for the épaulement, which employed 500 men daily; and on the right, in mounting guns and mortars on the batteries thrown up by Brigadier Wolfe. On the night of the 9th, however, this monotonous and weary work was interrupted by an incident attended with serious loss of life on both sides. A company of Forbes's Grenadiers, stationed at the redoubt, R. 6, it is feared, for want of proper watchfulness, was surprised by five pickets of the enemy, supported by 600 men, which came from Black Point, when a desperate encounter took place. The contest was sustained with great obstinacy by the single company of Grenadiers, against a vastly superior force, until Major Murray arrived with a corps of Whitmore and Bragg's Grenadiers, who soon drove the enemy back into the town in great confusion. In this affair Lord Dundonald, who commanded the post, one corporal, and three men, were killed; seventeen men were wounded; Captain Bontein of the Engineers and Lieutenant Tew were taken prisoners; and one sergeant and eleven men were missing. The loss of the enemy was, Captain Chauvelin and another officer of the same rank, and seventeen men killed and one lieutenant and four men made prisoners. The wounded were carried off by their comrades.

Several small bands of Indians had been hovering round the outskirts of the camp for some time, and intelligence had come from Halifax, that a considerable number of Canadians and Indians had left St. John's Island for Louisbourg early in June, under the command of M. de Boishebert,[1] an officer, according to Pichon, who 'piqued himself more for his bravery than his humanity;' but no indication of their arrival in the

[1] Captain Knox, who was at Fort Cumberland (formerly Beauséjour), says some French deserters came there on June 17, who reported that M. de Boishebert had gone to Louisbourg with 300 or 400 Canadians.—*Journal of the War.*

vicinity of the camp was observed until the night of July 11, when a large fire was seen in the woods to the northward of the Blockhouse, B. H. 3, on the Miray road, supposed to have been made by the Canadians, to notify M. de Drucour of their presence. This supposition was verified on the following day by a waggoner who had been taken prisoner on the 11th, by some Indians on the north side of the harbour, and who had fortunately made his escape during the night. The waggoner, who had been taken to their camp in the woods, reported that there were 250 Canadians. If Boishebert had conducted his men, during the night, between the British posts to the harbour, he would probably have found boats in answer to his signal, to carry them into the town; but instead of doing this, he made an unsuccessful attack upon Major Sutherland's detachment, then stationed on the Miray road. Wolfe's Grenadiers and the Light Infantry, aroused by the smart firing on their left, were soon at the scene of action. The latter, under Major Scott, went in pursuit, but the Canadians, favoured by the darkness of the night, effected their escape. A deserter from the enemy stated that there were only 100 men in the party that attacked Major Sutherland's post on the 15th, and that M. de Boishebert with 300 men was still at Miray with boats ready to cross the river.

On the same night, the 'Aréthuse' frigate, which had been long watching for an opportunity to escape, and which some three days before had been driven from her anchorage near the Barachois by the fire from Wolfe's battery, R. 5, got safely out of the harbour in a thick fog. Signals were made of 'ships going out,' from the Lighthouse, but the 'Aréthuse,' concealed by the fog, escaped the ships sent by Sir Charles Hardy in pursuit. The fire from this ship, which was kept up night and day upon the works near Greenhill, had been a source of great annoyance to the troops, and I dare say, as Pichon observes, 'her departure gave more pleasure to the English than to us.'[1]

The laborious and exhausting duty of making the road across the bog, and the épaulement to protect it, being finished on the

[1] The 'Aréthuse' was captured by the English frigates 'Thames' and 'Venus,' on her way from Brest to Rochfort, on May 18, 1759.

14th, heavy siege guns and mortars were brought up to Green-hill, and the first parallel was commenced on the right. The troops, elated by the prospect of work so much more congenial to their taste than road-making, set to work with great vigour, and soon had one face ready to receive part of the armament of twenty 24-pounders, seven mortars, and some 12-pounders, with which it was proposed to arm the first parallel. While these works were in progress, the enemy poured into the trenches a constant shower of shot and shell, especially directing their fire towards the Magazine, of which the position had been pointed out by a deserter.[1] As the enemy's pickets still kept up an incessant fire of musketry from the glacis and ground in front of the West Gate upon the trenches, Brigadier Wolfe on the evening of the 16th, at the head of a strong corps, drove them into the town, and took possession of the hills in front of the Barachois, where he effected a lodgement in the midst of a brisk fire of shot and shell from the town and shipping, which enabled the besiegers in the course of a few days to push on their trenches on the left towards the Dauphin Bastion. The batteries now being armed from right to left with heavy siege guns and mortars, and manned by three brigades, a telling and destructive fire was opened upon the city, causing much damage to the works near the West Gate. Everything was thus progressing favourably, when an accident happened which caused great joy in the English camp and proportionably distressed the enemy. On the evening of the 21st, an explosion of powder occurred on board the 'Entreprenant' 64, at anchor in the middle of the harbour, which blew up, and set fire to the sails of two ships near her, the 'Capricieux' and 'Célèbre.' The fire raged with great fury; both ships were destroyed, as no assistance could be sent from the town, owing to the constant fire of the English batteries. The only two remaining ships, the 'Prudent' and 'Bienfaisant,' were saved with great difficulty, the seamen employed in towing them out of danger being exposed to the fire of the batteries and the explosions of the guns of

[1] This man was killed on board the 'Prudent,' on the night of the 25th, when she was attacked by the English sailors, and thus escaped the ignominious fate he so well deserved.

the burning ships. Several small craft were burned at the same time; as Pichon observes, 'in short it was a night of horror and desolation.'

During the next few days the trenches were pushed on with great rapidity. The second parallel, T. 3, T. 4, commencing at Wolfe's post near the Barachois, was pushed on to the right, a distance of nearly 600 yards, from the extremity of which another oblique trench, T. 5, T. 6, was opened towards the left. On the extreme right two batteries of thirteen 24-pounders and seven mortars were raised between Green Hill and the seashore, although the enemy's skirmishers still held their ground outside the walls near Black Point.[1] On the 22nd the Citadel was set on fire by the shells of the besiegers, and on the following night the barracks, which burned with great violence. On the 25th the enemy, apprehensive of an assault, kept up a vigorous fire of shot, shell, scraps of old iron, or anything they could pick up, upon the trenches, especially upon a boyeau or branch trench, opened on the left, which on that day had reached within sixty yards of the glacis of the Dauphin Bastion. The crisis was evidently not far distant. The long lines of British Infantry were closing in from day to day, like the coils of a serpent around his prey. The General, now determined, as he said in his despatches, 'to make quick work of it,' obtained 400 seamen from the fleet, to assist in working the guns, and sent an additional force of 300 miners to push on the approaches towards the West Gate, already so near that the skirmishers frequently drove the artillerymen from the ramparts.

At this juncture, Admiral Boscawen informed the General that he intended to send in his boats on the night of the 25th, to capture or destroy the 'Prudent' and 'Bienfaisant,' the only two ships remaining in the harbour. To distract the attention of the enemy, the General gave orders that a vigorous cannonade should be kept up from all the batteries, and that scaling-ladders should be sent to the front, to induce the

[1] During the night of the 22nd they made prisoner a lieutenant of the 60th Regiment, who had lost his way going his rounds at an advanced post in the vicinity.

enemy to believe that the besiegers intended to make an escalade. About noon, by the Admiral's orders each ship equipped a barge and pinnace manned by full crews armed with muskets, cutlasses, poleaxes and pistols, under the charge of a lieutenant and mate, which were sent in the course of the day in twos and threes, to disarm suspicion, alongside Sir Charles Hardy's squadron, lying off the harbour. The boats, which carried 600 men, divided into two squadrons, one commanded by Laforey, the other by Balfour—the two senior masters of the fleet—started at midnight, and, favoured by a thick fog, entered the harbour in perfect silence, going close past the Island Battery, and within hail of the town, without being perceived. Having discovered the position of the 'Prudent' and 'Bienfaisant,' Laforey's division immediately rowed close alongside the former, and Balfour's alongside the latter, giving three hearty British cheers in reply to the fire of the sentinels. On the order being given, the crews, seizing their arms with the most intrepid activity, followed their brave leaders and boarded the ships on each bow, quarter, and gangway. Surprised and confused by such a sudden and unexpected attack, the enemy made little resistance; both ships were taken, with the loss of only one officer and three or four seamen.

The report of firearms, and the well-known cheers of the British seamen, soon let the garrison know that their ships were in danger. Regardless of the lives of friends as well as foes, every gun that could be brought to bear from the town and Point Rochfort was discharged against the ships and the English boats. But nothing daunted the brave sailors.[1]

[1] The celebrated navigator, Captain Cook, won his first laurels at Louisbourg, having been engaged as a petty officer on board of one of the British ships of war, when he had a share in this exploit. He was soon after promoted to the rank of mate, and served in that capacity on board the 'Mercury,' at the siege of Quebec, in the following year. He was employed by Admiral Saunders to make a survey of the St. Lawrence below Quebec, and afterwards made Master of the 'Northumberland,' in which he spent the winter of 1759–60 at Halifax. In 1762 he was at the recapture of St. John's, Newfoundland. In 1764 he was appointed Marine-Surveyor of Newfoundland and Labrador. He also explored the interior of Newfoundland, and discovered several large lakes in the heart of the country.—*Cook's Voyages.*

Having secured the French crews below, under guard, the next point was to tow off their prizes—a work not easily accomplished in the face of the fire of the French batteries. Notwithstanding, the 'Bienfaisant' was carried off in triumph to the head of the North-east harbour, out of the reach of the enemy's guns; but the 'Prudent,' being fast aground, was set on fire, a large schooner and her own boats being left alongside to give the crew the means of escaping to the town. For their gallant services on this occasion, Mr. Balfour was made Commander of the 'Bienfaisant,' and Mr. Laforey of the 'Echo,' of thirty-six guns, captured on June 19.

All obstacles now being removed, the Admiral next day went on shore and informed the General that he intended to send in six of his heaviest ships to bombard the town from the harbour; but this proved unnecessary, for while the two commanders were conferring together, a messenger arrived with a letter from the Governor, offering to capitulate upon the same conditions that had been granted to the English at Port Mahon. In answer to this request the General sent the following reply:—

'In answer to the proposal I have had the honour just now to receive from your Excellency by the Sieur Loppinot, I have only to tell your Excellency that it hath been determined by Admiral Boscawen and myself, that his ships shall go in to-morrow to make a general attack upon the town. Your Excellency knows very well the situation of the army and the fleet, as well as of the town; and, as the Admiral as well as myself is very anxious to prevent the effusion of blood, we give your Excellency one hour after receiving this, to determine either to capitulate as prisoners of war or to take upon you all the bad consequences of a defence against this fleet and army.' M. de Drucour, who, considering the gallant defence he had made, thought himself and the brave men under his command entitled to the honours of war, immediately held a council of war, when it was decided to defend the town to the last extremity. This decision was communicated to the General and Admiral in the following terms:—'To answer your Excellencies in as few words as possible, I have the honour to repeat to you, that my resolution is still the same, and that I will suffer the consequences and sustain the attack you speak of.' As soon as M. Drucour's determination became known in the town, the principal inhabitants and traders sent a petition by M. Prevot, the Intendant of the colony, earnestly imploring him to accept the terms proposed, and spare them and their families the horrors of a general assault. M. Prevot, convinced that, in the present state of affairs, any attempt to prolong the defence would be quite useless, and attended with the loss of many valuable lives, strongly supported the prayer of the petitioners. The Governor, satisfied that he had done all in his power to defend the post entrusted to him by his Sovereign, at length yielded to the arguments of the Intendant, and sent M. Loppinot to inform General Amherst that, submitting to the law of force, he was ready to accept and sign the terms of capitulation demanded.

LETTER XIX.

1758.

In my last two letters I gave you a narrative of the siege of Louisbourg, compiled chiefly from English documents. Before I submit a copy of the Articles of Capitulation, I think it is but fair that you should hear M. Drucour's own account of the siege, and his reasons for complying with the hard terms of his conquerors. Soon after his arrival in England, a prisoner of war, M. Drucour wrote the following letter to a friend in Paris, in justification of his conduct at Louisbourg:—[1]

'*Infandum, regina, jubes.* I wish, Sir, I could erase from my memory the four years I passed in Louisbourg. The bad state of the place, the impossibility of making it better, the subsistence of a garrison and inhabitants supported there at the King's expense, and threatened with famine once a month, gave no little uneasiness and anxiety to all who were charged therewith. This situation—*manet alta mente repostum.* Many old officers, from all the provinces of the kingdom, have been witnesses of my conduct; and I dare assert it was never impeached. But he who views objects at a distance only may judge differently. I hope, Sir, this was not your case; but that you said, "It must have been impossible for Drucour to act otherwise." Of this I cannot so easily convince you till I have the pleasure of seeing you. Meanwhile, know that twenty-three ships of war, eighteen frigates, sixteen[2] thousand land forces, with a proportionate train of cannon and mortars, came in on the 1st June, and landed on the 8th. To oppose

[1] From a translation in the *Annual Register* for 1758. The letter is dated October 1, from Andover.

[2] Only 12,000. See p. 295.

them, we had at most but two thousand five hundred men of the garrison, and three hundred militia of the burghers of the town and St. John's Island, a fortification (if it could deserve the name) crumbling down in every flank, face, and courtine, except the right flank of the King's Bastion, which was remounted the first year after my arrival.[1] The covered-way was covered as much as it could be, and yet was commanded and enfiladed throughout, as well as the Dauphin's and King's Bastions. In the harbour were five men of war.[2] This was our force. The succours I expected from Canada did not arrive till the end of the siege,[3] and consisted of about three hundred and fifty Canadians only, including sixty Indians.

'The enemy was at first very slow in making his approaches; for on the 15th July he was three hundred toises from the place. He was employed in securing his camp by redoubts and épaulements, thinking we had many Canadians and Indians behind him.[4] We, on our part, used every method to retard and destroy his work, both by the fire of the place and that of the ships in the harbour. The commodore of these ships[5] warmly solicited leave to quit the place; but, knowing the importance of their stay to its safety, I refused it. It was our business to defer the determination of our fate as long as possible. My accounts from Canada assured me that M. de

[1] The bad condition of the works is here greatly exaggerated. It does not agree with English accounts.

[2] There were seven ships of the line and six frigates in the harbour on June 1.

[3] The Canadians and Indians arrived at Miray before July 10.

[4] Wolfe gives the Cape Breton Indians a very bad character in his letter, July 27, to his uncle:—'The Indians of the island gave us very little trouble. They attacked one of my posts and were repulsed; and since that time they have been very quiet. I take them to be the most contemptible *canaille* upon earth. Those to the southward are much braver and better men; these are a dastardly set of bloody rascals. We cut them to pieces wherever we found them, in return for a thousand acts of cruelty and barbarity.'—Wright's *Life of Wolfe.*

[5] In the *Gentleman's Magazine* for April 1760, it is stated, 'We are advised by private letters that the Marquis de Gouttes, who commanded the French squadron at Louisbourg when taken by the English, has been degraded from his rank, his patent being burnt by the common hangman, and condemned to twenty-one years' imprisonment.'

Montcalm was marching to the enemy, and would come up with him between the 15th and 20th July. I said, then, "If the ships leave the harbour on the 10th June (as they desire), the English Admiral will enter it immediately after;" and we should have been lost before the end of the month, which would have put it in the power of the generals of the besiegers to have employed the months of July and August in sending succours to the troops marching against Canada, and to have entered the river St. Lawrence at the proper season. This object alone seemed to me of sufficient importance to require a council of war, whose opinion was the same with mine, and conformable to the King's intentions. The situation of the ships was not less critical than ours. Four of them were burnt, with two corps of caserns, by the enemy's bombs. At last, on the 26th July, no ships being left, and the place being open in different parts of the King, the Dauphin, and the Queen's Bastions, a council of war determined to ask to capitulate.

'I proposed much the same articles as were granted at Port Mahon;[1] but the generals would listen to no proposals, but our being prisoners of war. I annex their letter and my answer [see page 315], by which you will see that I was resolved to wait the general assault, when M. Prevot, commissary-General and Intendant of the colony, brought me a petition from the traders and inhabitants, which determined me to send back the officer who carried my former letter, to make our submissions to the law of force; a submission

[1] The condition upon which M. de Drucour laid the greatest stress was, 'That all the honours of war shall be granted the garrison on their surrender, such as, to march out with their firelocks on their shoulders, drums beating, colours flying, 24 charges for each man, &c., &c.,' which had been granted by Marshal Richelieu to Governor Blakeney and his garrison at Port Mahon in 1756, with the observation, 'The noble and vigorous defence which the English have made, having deserved all the marks of esteem and veneration, that every military person ought to show to such actions; and Marshal Richelieu being desirous also to show General Blakeney the regard due to the brave defence he has made, grants the garrison all the honours of the war that they can enjoy, &c.' Drucour and his garrison were certainly, in my humble opinion, entitled to the same generous terms; an acknowledgment of the bravery of the conquered foe would not have lessened the merits of the conquerors.

which in our condition was inevitable. This condition was such, that for eight days the officers had not, any more than the private men, one moment's rest. In all besieged towns there are entrenchments where those who are not on duty may retire, and be covered from the enemy's fire; but at Louisbourg we had not a safe place even for the wounded; so that they were almost as much exposed every minute of the four-and-twenty hours, as if they had been on the covered-way. Nevertheless, the men did not murmur in the least, nor discover the smallest discontent; which was owing to the good example and exact discipline of their officers. None deserted but foreigners, Germans, one of whom prevented an intended sally. As he had gone over to the enemy two hours before, it was not thought prudent to make it. The burning of the ships and of the caserns [barracks] of the King's and Queen's Bastions hindered our making another. A third had not better success; we proceeded no farther than the glacis of the covered-way, having missed the quay of a small passage which it behoved us to turn in order to take the enemy in flank: so that, of four sallies which were intended, one only succeeded,[1] in which we made thirty grenadiers and two officers prisoners, besides those that were killed, among whom was a captain. We had about three hundred and thirty killed and wounded during the course of the siege, including officers. The crews of the king's ships are not comprehended in that number.[2]

'As to the landing, it must have been effected by sacrificing lives in one part or another, it being impossible to guard such an extent of coast with a garrison of 3,000 men, and leave men in the place for daily duty. We occupied above two leagues and a half of ground in the most accessible parts; but there were some intermediate places we could not guard; and it was precisely in one of these that the enemy took post.[3]

[1] This was on the extreme right, on the night of July 9, when the young Earl of Dundonald and four others were killed.

[2] In the English accounts, the total loss of the French in killed and wounded during the siege is stated to have been 1,000.

[3] This is not strictly true. An inspection of the Plan at p. 297 will show that Fresh Water Cove, where the troops landed, was more strongly guarded than any other part of the coast.

'The captain of a ship strikes when his vessel is dismasted, his rigging cut to pieces, and several shot received between wind and water. A governor of a town surrenders the place when the breaches are practicable, and when he has no resource, by entrenching himself in the gorges of bastions, or within the place. Such was the case of Louisbourg. Add to this, that it wanted every necessary for such operations. General Wolfe himself was obliged to place sentinels on the ramparts; for the private men and the sutlers entered through the breaches and gaps with as much ease as if there had been only an old ditch. Of fifty-two pieces of cannon, which were opposed to the batteries of the besiegers, forty were dismounted, broke, or rendered unserviceable. It is easy to judge what condition those of the place were in. Was it possible, in such circumstances, to avoid being made prisoners of war?

'I have the honour to be, &c.

'LE CHEVALIER DE DRUCOUR.'

Admitting the general accuracy of the Governor's statement, it is evident that he had no alternative, being compelled to accept the conditions imposed by the conquerors, as specified in the following Articles of Capitulation:—

'*Articles of Capitulation between their Excellencies Admiral Boscawen and Major-General Amherst, and his Excellency the Chevalier Drucour, Governor of the Island of Cape Breton, of Louisbourg, the Island of St. John and their appurtenances.*

'I. The garrison of Louisbourg shall be prisoners of war, and shall be carried to England in the ships of His Britannic Majesty.

'II. All the artillery, ammunition, provisions, as well as the arms of any kind whatsoever, which are at present in the town of Louisbourg, the islands of Cape Breton and St. John's, and their appurtenances, shall be delivered, without the least damage, to such commissioners as shall be appointed to receive them, for the use of His Britannic Majesty.

'III. The Governor shall give his orders that the

which are in the island of St. John's and its appurtenances, shall go on board such ships of war as the Admiral shall send to receive them.

'IV. The gate called Port Dauphin shall be given to the troops of His Britannic Majesty, to-morrow at eight o'clock in the morning, and the garrison, including all that carried arms, drawn up at noon on the Esplanade, where they shall lay down their arms, colours, implements, and ornaments of war. And the garrison shall go on board to be carried to England, in a convenient time.

'V. The same care shall be taken of the sick and wounded that are in the hospitals, as of those belonging to His Britannic Majesty.

'VI. The merchants and their clerks, that have not carried arms, shall be sent to France, in such manner as the Admiral shall think proper.

'(Signed) LE CHEVALIER DE DRUCOUR.
EDWARD BOSCAWEN.
JEFFERY AMHERST.

'Louisbourg, 26th July, 1758.'

According to the 4th Article of the Capitulation, Major Farquhar, with three companies of Grenadiers, took possession of the West Gate on the following morning, and the garrison delivered up their arms and colours to Brigadier Whitmore on the Esplanade. To provide against any risk of breaking the capitulation, the arms were sent out of the town, and strong guards were placed over the stores and magazines, and upon the ramparts. The following account of the guns and munitions of war found in Louisbourg, after sustaining a siege of forty-eight days, will give you some idea of the vast amount of such articles required for the defence of a fortified place of such importance:—

218 Pieces of Iron Ordnance.
11 Iron Mortars.
7 Brass do.
7,500 Muskets and Accoutrements.
13 Tons Musket Balls.
80,000 Musket Cartridges.
600 Barrels Powder.

9,600 Round Shot.
1,190 Grape, Case, and Canister Shot.
1,053 Shells.
12 Tons Lead.
6 Tons Iron.

Besides many hundreds of wheelbarrows, shovels, pickaxes, and other implements.

The loss in killed and wounded, according to the Governor's letter (p. 320) was 330.

The number of prisoners of war was—

Military officers	214	
Soldiers fit for duty	3,374	
Do. sick and wounded	443	
		3,031
Naval officers	135	
Sailors and Marines fit for duty	1,124	
Ditto sick and wounded	1,347	
		2,606
Total		5,637

On August 15,[1] all the prisoners of war sailed for England in ships specially provided for that purpose, convoyed by the 'Burford' and 'Kingston.' The merchants, traders, and other inhabitants, were sent to France. On July 30, the 'Shannon' frigate, commanded by Captain Edgecumb, charged with the Admiral's despatches, and carrying Captain Amherst, with those of the General, sailed for England.

Immediately after the surrender, General Amherst proposed to proceed to Quebec with the entire army; but upon consultation with the Admiral, who considered the season too far advanced to go up the St. Lawrence, that idea was given up.

On August 7, a detachment under Major Dalling was sent to take possession of St. Ann's and Espagnol (Sydney), and Lord Rollo was sent with the 35th and two battalions of the

[1] Every kindness and attention were shown to the officers and their families, as well as to the inhabitants in general, by the English commanders, after the surrender of Louisbourg. Pichon says:—'The Admiral has shown all the respects to Madame de Drucour as were due to her merit; every favour she asked was granted. True it is, that such behaviour does honour to the discernment of the gentlemen that showed it. This lady has performed such exploits during the siege, as must entitle her to a rank among the most illustrious of her sex; for she fired three cannon every day, in order to animate the gunners.'

60th Regiment, to take possession of St. John's Island. In a letter of September 13, from Louisbourg, Admiral Boscawen informs Mr. Pitt that Lord Rollo learned there were 4,100 inhabitants in the island, and that most of them had delivered up their arms. He says there were 10,000 head of horned cattle in the island; that Quebec had been in a great measure supplied from thence with beef and cattle; and that many of the inhabitants raised as much as 1,200 bushels of corn yearly. It is stated in the 'Annual Register,' that Lord Rollo found the Governor's house decorated with the scalps of Englishmen, murdered by the savage allies of France. Be this true or not, it is quite certain that the Indians here found shelter after their frequent irruptions into Nova Scotia, where they committed most cruel outrages upon the defenceless inhabitants.

On August 28, Sir Charles Hardy sailed for the Gulf of St. Lawrence with seven ships of the line and three frigates, carrying three regiments and some artillery, under the command of Brigadier Wolfe, with instructions to destroy all the French settlements, especially those of Miramichi, Bay Chaleur and Gaspé, and to disperse or carry off the inhabitants. None of these places were of any great strength, but they were thickly settled, and gave shelter to a set of Canadian renegadoes and savages who infested the confines of Nova Scotia, making raids into that province whenever opportunity offered. This disagreeable duty was soon accomplished. Vast magazines of fish, provisions, and merchandise, were destroyed, and the inhabitants dispersed in all directions. It was a most distasteful occupation to Wolfe, who had not been accustomed to wage war upon poor fishermen. Writing from Louisbourg on September 30 to General Amherst (who had left for Boston), Wolfe says, 'Your orders were carried into execution as far as troops could carry them. Our equipment was very improper for the business, and the numbers, unless the squadron had gone up the river [St. Lawrence], quite unnecessary. We have done a great deal of mischief—spread the terror of His Majesty's arms through the whole Gulf, but have added nothing to the reputation of them.' It was hoped by these harsh measures to alarm the French at Quebec, and prevent their sending succours to Montcalm in his operations on the Lakes.

On August 30, Colonel Monckton was sent with two regiments, a detachment of Artillery and a body of Rangers, up the Bay of Fundy. Having landed 400 Regulars and Rangers at Cape Sable, under the command of the Major of the 35th Regiment, Monckton proceeded to the St. John river, where he found all the French had retired into the interior. He repaired the fort and began to build barracks for 300 men. In attempting to cross the falls of that river, the armed sloop 'Ulysses' was lost, which prevented the troops going up. The detachment landed at Cape Sable was more successful; the French settlement was destroyed, and 100 men, women, and children, including their missionary, M. des Enclave, were made prisoners and sent to Halifax. Two armed sloops cruised off the Cape to intercept any Indians who might endeavour to escape, or, as Captain Knox says in his Journal, 'to prevent the *vermin* from getting off in their canoes.' It does not appear, however, that any of the *vermin* were captured.

While General Amherst was thus engaged in securing the fruits of his conquest, news of the defeat of Abercrombie before the Fort of Ticonderoga arrived from New York, which determined him to proceed with all the troops that could be spared to the assistance of Abercrombie. Amherst embarked at Louisbourg on August 30, with six regiments for Boston, and marched direct to the seat of war, but was too late to be of any service, as he did not reach the British camp before October 5. Before he left Louisbourg he gave orders that the 15th, 58th, and 3rd battalion of the 60th Regiment should be sent to Halifax, under the command of Brigadier Lawrence, the Governor of Nova Scotia, and that the 22nd, 28th, 40th, and 45th Regiments should be established as a garrison at Louisbourg, under Brigadier Whitmore, the newly-appointed Governor.

The following ships were sent to winter at Halifax, under the command of Commodore Durell, to be in readiness to proceed upon the expedition against Quebec in the following spring:—

	Guns.		Guns.
Princess Amelia	80	Captain	64
Prince of Orange	70	Nottingham	60
Vanguard	70	Pembroke	60
Devonshire	66	Centurion	54
Prince Frederick	64	Sutherland	50

All the rest of the fleet sailed from Louisbourg early in October (the exact date is not given) for England, under the command of Admiral Boscawen. The Admiral in the 'Namur,' and Sir Charles Hardy in the 'Royal William,' with the 'Bienfaisant,' arrived at Spithead on November 1. The other ships which came out with them parted company soon after they left Louisbourg. On October 27, off the Land's End, they fell in with six or seven French ships of the line and two frigates from Quebec, and though he had but three ships, Boscawen offered them battle. Wolfe, who was on board the 'Namur,' says, 'Boscawen did his utmost to engage them.'[1] A few shots were exchanged in the close of the evening, but the enemy slipped away in the night, and next morning were nearly out of sight. This was supposed to be the squadron of M. de Chauffreuil, which failed in its attempt to get into Louisbourg in the spring, 'where,' Wolfe says, 'they would inevitably have shared the fate of those that did, which must have given an irretrievable blow to the marine of France, and delivered Quebec into our hands, if we chose to go up and demand it.'[2]

I must now tell you how the news was received in England. Captains Amherst and Edgecumb, who arrived on August 18 with the first intelligence of the fall of Louisbourg, immediately proceeded to London and laid their despatches before the King, who presented each of them with a gratuity of 500*l.* The news soon spread through the kingdom, and was received with most lively demonstrations of joy. The reduction of a strong place like Louisbourg, defended by a powerful garrison; the destruction of eleven ships of war; the capture of 5,600 prisoners, with 248 pieces of ordnance, 7,500 stand of arms, and a great quantity of ammunition and stores, was considered a mighty triumph for the British arms, especially when it was borne in

[1] Wolfe's letter to his uncle, November 17, 1758.

[2] Wolfe to Colonel Rickson, December 1, 1758, in Wright's *Life of General Wolfe*.

mind that this great triumph had been effected at a comparatively small loss of life.[1] On Sunday, the 20th, a form of prayer and thanksgiving was read in all the churches in London and within the bills of mortality, and in all other churches and chapels throughout England, on the Sunday following. On September 7, eleven sets of colours taken at Louisbourg were presented to the King at his Palace of Kensington, from whence they were conveyed with great pomp to St. Paul's Cathedral by His Majesty's orders, and deposited there amidst the roar of cannon and other noisy demonstrations of joy and triumph. Addresses of congratulation were presented to the King by all the large towns and corporations in the kingdom. I cannot give you a better idea of the sentiments of the people of England at that time on the importance of the possession of Cape Breton, than by submitting a copy of the Address presented by the Lord Mayor and Corporation of London :—

'Most Gracious Sovereign,

'Amidst the joyful acclamations of your faithful people, permit us, your Majesty's most dutiful and loyal subjects, the Lord Mayor, Aldermen, and Commons of the City of London, in common council assembled, humbly to congratulate your Majesty on the success of your arms in the conquest of the important fortress of Louisbourg, the reduction of the islands of Cape Breton and St. John, and the blow there given to a considerable part of the French Navy.

'An event so truly glorious to your Majesty, so important to the colonies, trade, and navigation of Great Britain, and so fatal to the commercial views and naval power of France, affords a reasonable prospect of the recovery of all our rights and possessions in America, so unjustly invaded, and in a great measure answers the hopes we formed when we beheld the French power weakened on the coast of Africa, their ships destroyed in their ports at home, and the terror thereby spread over all their coasts.

[1] The English loss was 21 commissioned and non-commissioned officers, and 150 privates, killed; and 30 commissioned and non-commissioned officers, and 320 privates, wounded.

'May these valuable acquisitions, so gloriously obtained, ever continue a part of the British Empire, as an effectual check to the perfidy and ambition of a nation whose repeated insults and usurpations obliged your Majesty to enter into this just and necessary war; and may these instances of the wisdom of your Majesty's councils, of the conduct and resolution of your commanders, and of the intrepidity of your fleets and armies, convince the world of the innate strength and resources of your kingdoms, and dispose your Majesty's enemies to yield to a safe and honourable peace.

'In all events, we shall most cheerfully contribute, to the utmost of our power, towards supporting your Majesty in the vigorous prosecution of measures so nobly designed and so wisely directed.'

When Admiral Boscawen, who was a Member of Parliament, took his seat in the House on December 12, he received the thanks of the Commons for the service rendered to his king and country. The thanks of Parliament were also conveyed to General Amherst, then in America; but as Wolfe, who had contributed so largely to the success of the enterprise, held a subordinate position, he could not be noticed by Parliament. Pitt, however, who duly appreciated his services, soon afterwards promoted him to the rank of Major-General.

No better proof can be given of the opinion entertained of the importance of the fall of Louisbourg by the mercantile community, than the fact that the insurance on vessels bound to America, which had during the last few years ranged at from twenty-five to thirty, immediately fell to twelve per cent.[1] 'The taking of Louisbourg,' according to the 'Annual Register' for 1758, 'was an event the most desired by all our colonies; that harbour had always been a receptacle convenient to the enemy's privateers, which infested the English trade in North America. It was the most effectual blow that France had received since the beginning of the war; for with Louisbourg she lost the only spot from whence she could carry on her codfishery, her main depôt for the reinforcements to

[1] *Scots Magazine*, September 1758.

support her armies in North America, and the bulwark of Canada.'

In concluding this letter, allow me to say a few words respecting Wolfe, whose name will ever be associated with that of Louisbourg in the heart of every British soldier. Nothing, it is true, contributed more to the successful termination of the siege than the harmony which subsisted between the commanders of the land and sea forces; but it is no disparagement to either of these officers to say, that no small portion of the merit of the achievement was due to the prompt, daring, and untiring energy of Wolfe, in carrying into execution the boldest plans of his general. Chosen by Amherst to head the troops at Freshwater Cove, he was one of the first, after his flagstaff had been shattered by a bar-shot, to leap on shore and scale the cliffs, exposed to the galling fire of masked batteries and crowds of musketeers; he then led a detachment through the woods, a distance of six miles, amidst ambuscades of lurking savages, to the Lighthouse Point, where he erected a battery which commanded one of the most important outposts of the enemy—the Island Battery; this duty accomplished, and recalled to the front, he traced out the batteries on the right, near the sea-shore, within half a mile of the Queen's Bastion; and shortly afterwards, at the head of the Light Infantry and Highlanders, repulsed a sortie from the West Gate, and seized an important post, where he effected a lodgement in front of the Barachois; in short, wherever there was difficulty or danger, or hard blows to be encountered, Wolfe was always in the foremost rank; 'obstacles were but the stepping-stones to his success;' wherever he led, all were ready to follow, happy to serve one who had justly gained the affection of the whole army, from the general down to the rudest soldier. No monument nor sculptured stone recalls his memory near the scene of his gallant exploits; even the mouldering ruins of Louisbourg—'once mistress of the seas'—have been almost obliterated; but there are still a few families, descendants of men that were present, who hand down from generation to generation many a stirring story of the siege; and the hardy fishermen of Gabarus, returning at nightfall from their daily toil on the deep, oft point out the spot where he landed—still known by the name of 'Wolfe's Rock.'[1]

[1] Authorities consulted in compiling the preceding narrative of the siege of Louisbourg:—General Amherst's *Official Report of the Siege*; Captain Knox's *Journal of the War in America, from* 1755 *to* 1759; Manté's *History of the War*; Entick's *History of the War*; Wright's *Life of Major-General Wolfe*, &c., &c.

LETTER XX.

1758–1763.

You will probably recollect that I told you (page 290), when Pitt resolved to make America the field of his operations against France, in the beginning of 1758, he decided in the first instance, in order to open the way to the invasion of Canada, to reduce the fortress of Louisbourg—the key of the St. Lawrence—and the forts of Crown Point and Ticonderoga, for the purpose of cutting off the communications of Canada with the French encroachments on the Ohio. The first and most important of these objects was, as I told you in my last two letters, successfully accomplished; but General Abercrombie, at the head of an army of 16,000 men, was, I grieve to say, ignominiously repulsed by the French General, M. de Montcalm, with a force of 4,000 men only. When this disastrous news reached Amherst at Louisbourg, he started for Boston with six battalions, and marched overland to the British camp on Lake George, but arrived too late to be of any service. The troops, on going into winter quarters, learned with great satisfaction that Abercrombie had been recalled, and that Amherst had been appointed Commander-in-Chief in America. The failure of the attack upon Ticonderoga was, however, in some measure compensated by the dashing exploit of Colonel Bradstreet, who crossed Lake Ontario with a large force, in sloops and open boats, and laid siege to Fort Frontenac, on the north side of the St. Lawrence. Part of the garrison fled on Bradstreet's first appearance; the rest surrendered on the following day (August 25). A large supply of provisions and ammunition, intended for the French troops in the valley of the Ohio, was captured; also several vessels employed on Lake Ontario, including nine armed ships of eight to eighteen guns each. In the South, after much needless delay, Brigadier Forbes arrived with a large force in sight of Fort du Quesne[1] on November 24, which he found abandoned by the garrison of 500 men, which, after setting fire to the fort, had descended the river in boats.

Thus ended the first campaign in America. With the exception of the defeat of Abercrombie before Ticonderoga, the British arms had been everywhere successful. The indefatigable Montcalm, who had so nobly sustained the honour of his country, was even in consequence disheartened. In the February preceding, he had addressed the Minister in these desponding terms: 'For all our success, New France needs peace, or sooner or later must it fall; such are the numbers of the English, such the difficulties of receiving supplies.'

At the opening of Parliament, on November 23, the Commons, in reply to the King's speech asking for further supplies to carry on the war, congratulated His Majesty on the success of his arms, acknowledged their real satisfaction with the measures that had been taken, and with implicit confidence in the integrity and zeal of the Premier, cheerfully and unanimously voted nearly thirteen millions sterling for the service of the next year. Pitt, now satisfied that he had generals capable of executing his designs, devoted all his energies to the accomplishment of one great object—the conquest of Canada. For this purpose he proposed to send an armament of ships and land forces up the St. Lawrence, to co-operate with the army under General Amherst in the reduction of Montreal and Quebec. As it was of the utmost importance that the expedition destined for the St. Lawrence should arrive in the river before the French could send out reinforcements to the garrison of Quebec, a fleet of twenty-one ships of the line and a proportional number of frigates, commanded by Admirals

[1] Fort du Quesne was named 'Pittsburg,' in compliment to England's great Minister. It still retains the name; but the little fort, then surrounded on all sides with interminable forests, at the confluence of the Alleghany and Monongahela rivers, has been replaced by a large and populous city, with its hundreds of foundries, forges, and manufactories, which have acquired for it the title of 'the Birmingham of America.'

Saunders, Holmes and Durell, together with sixty transports carrying 7,000 troops under the command of Major-General Wolfe, were despatched from Portsmouth on February 17, with orders to proceed to Louisbourg, where the expedition was to be reinforced by contingents from the British provinces. Admiral Saunders, in the 'Neptune,' of ninety guns, with whom Wolfe had embarked, arrived with great part of the fleet off Louisbourg on April 21, but finding the harbour blocked up with ice, bore up for Halifax. As information had been received before the expedition left England, that the French Government was sending out troops and stores to Canada, a squadron of ten ships, under Admiral Durell, was sent from Halifax on May 4, to the Isle aux Coudres, about sixty miles below Quebec, to intercept the French transports and store-ships. Durell, however, was too late; seventeen ships, convoyed by three frigates, got up the river safely to Quebec before he arrived at Isle aux Coudres; he only succeeded in capturing three of the enemy's ships, with 120 recruits, 1,800 barrels of powder, and other stores, which he sent into Louisbourg.

Having been joined by all the missing ships, and taken on board six companies of Rangers, the expedition left Halifax for Louisbourg, where it arrived on May 18. Here the fleet had to remain more than a fortnight waiting for the arrival of the Provincial troops from New England and the Bay of Fundy. In the meantime, the troops were occasionally paraded and exercised on shore, and a brigade was selected from the garrison of Louisbourg, composed of the Grenadier companies of the 22nd, 40th, and 45th Regiments, which had greatly distinguished themselves during the siege. Major Murray, with the local rank of Lieutenant-Colonel, was appointed Commander of the Louisbourg Grenadiers. The movements of the English expedition seem to have been watched by scouts employed by the French, while it lay at Louisbourg, as Captain Knox says in his Journal, that on May 30, 'some carpenters who were in the woods heard French and Indians,' and that in consequence, on June 1, a party of Rangers was sent out to scour the woods.

On June 1, all the reinforcements expected having arrived, the land force, consisting of ten battalions of Infantry, six companies of Rangers, three companies of Louisbourg Grenadiers, and a detachment of Artillery and Engineers, in all 9,000 men, being embarked, the fleet began to move out of the harbour. There was still some loose ice floating about, which caused delay among the transports, but on the 6th all the vessels had got clear of the land. 'As each transport sailed out of the bay, the soldiers, who crowded the decks, rent the air with shouts of joy, while the prevailing toast of the officers was, 'British colours on every French fort, port, and garrison in America.'[1] Captain Knox says in his Journal, 'I had the inexpressible pleasure to observe at Louisbourg, that our whole armament, naval and military, were in high spirits; and though by all accounts we shall have a numerous army and a variety of difficulties to cope with, yet under such admirals and generals, among whom we have the happiness to behold the most cordial unanimity, together with so respectable a fleet, and a body of well-appointed regular troops, we have reason to hope for the greatest success.'

On June 7, the fleet made the coast of Newfoundland, on the 9th it passed the Bird Islands, and on the 26th came to anchor off the Isle of Orleans, a few miles below Quebec. It would occupy far more space than I can afford, to attempt to give you the very briefest outline of the operations of the British army before that city; but I cannot resist the temptation of submitting an account of the death of Wolfe, in the battle on the Plains of Abraham, which decided the future destiny of Canada, from the pen of the accomplished historian Bancroft: 'Wolfe, as he led the charge, was wounded in the wrist, but still pressing forward, he received a second ball, and having decided the day, was struck a third time, and mortally, in the breast. "Support me," he cried to an officer near him, "let not my brave fellows see me fall." He was carried to the rear, and they brought him water to quench his thirst. "They run, they run!" spoke the officer on whom he leaned. "Who run?" asked Wolfe, as his life was fast ebbing.

[1] Wright's *Life of Wolfe*.

"The French," replied the officer, "give way everywhere." "What!" cried the expiring hero, "do they run already? Go, one of you, to Colonel Burton, bid him march Webb's regiment with all speed to Charles River to cut off the fugitives." Four days before, he had looked forward to early death with dismay. "Now, God be praised, I die happy." These were his words as his spirit escaped in the blaze of his glory. Night, silence, the rushing tide, veteran discipline, the sure inspiration of genius, had been his allies; his battle-field, high over the ocean river, was the grandest theatre on earth for illustrious deeds; his victory, one of the most momentous in the annals of mankind, gave to the English tongue, and the institutions of the Germanic race, the unexplored and seemingly infinite West and North. He crowded into a few hours actions that would have given lustre to length of life, and, filling his day with greatness, completed it before its noon.' Such was the death of Wolfe, after a short and glorious life. He entered the army at the early age of fourteen, and had served seven years in Flanders, when he was thanked, in the presence of the army, by the Duke of Cumberland, for his conduct at the battle of Laffeldt. Subsequently, whilst employed in Scotland in keeping the clans in subjection after the rebellion of 1745, he was one of the first that proposed to enlist the hardy, intrepid Highlanders in the Royal Army; and he was one of the first to lead them to victory at the landing at Louisbourg, and in scaling the Heights of Abraham. Bitterly did the gallant 78th avenge his death, chasing the flying Frenchmen to the banks of the St. Charles, and cutting down with their broadswords everything that came in their way. Wolfe had not quite completed his thirty-third year when he fell. Glorious was the victory which he won, and important its consequences, but all must admit that it was dearly bought. I will conclude this short tribute to his memory with an extract from a letter written by his successor in command, Brigadier-General Townshend, to a friend in England: 'I am not ashamed to own to you, that my heart does not exult in the midst of this success. I have lost but a friend in General Wolfe, our country has lost a sure support and a perpetual honour. If the world were sensible at how dear a price we have purchased Quebec in his death, it would damp the public joy. Our best consolation is, that Providence seemed not to promise that he should remain long among us. He was himself sensible of the weakness of his constitution, and determined to crowd into a few years actions that would have adorned length of life.'

Just as the first ships left Louisbourg for the St. Lawrence, General Amherst set out from Albany with the intention of driving the French out of Ticonderoga and Crown Point, and of then marching overland to join General Wolfe before Quebec. At the same time, General Prideaux and Sir William Johnson, with a large force of Provincials and Indians, marched against Fort Niagara. Prideaux having been accidentally shot by one of his own gunners, Sir William Johnson took the command, defeated 2,000 French troops sent to succour Niagara, and on July 24 took the whole garrison prisoners. If Amherst had acted with equal vigour, perhaps Montreal might have been taken also; but owing to delays and obstructions, he did not reach Ticonderoga until July 21, when he found it abandoned by the enemy. On August 1, learning that the French had also abandoned Crown Point and gone down the Lake to Isle aux Noix, where M. Burlemaque had collected a force of 3,500 men, determined to make a stand, Amherst began to fit out vessels and rafts to attack him, but could not get ready to start until October 11, when he encountered such stormy weather that he was obliged to return to Crown Point and dispose his troops in their winter quarters.

Although Quebec, the capital, had fallen, Canada was not yet conquered. The Chevalier de Levis collected an army of 10,000 men at Montreal during the winter, and made his appearance on the Heights of Abraham on April 27, 1760, with the intention of laying siege to Quebec. On the same day General Murray, the Governor of Quebec, who had barely 3,000 effectives under his command, rashly marched out and attacked the French at Sillery, but being overpowered by numbers, he was defeated with great loss and compelled to retire into the fortress, where he held out with great gallantry until May 15, when he was relieved from his critical position by the arrival of an English squadron under Commodore Swanton, from the banks of Newfoundland. Next day, Swanton having attacked and captured all the French ships lying above the town, the Chevalier de Levis immediately raised the siege, abandoned all his artillery and field equipage, and retreated towards Montreal.

As soon as the season would permit, General Amherst left his winter quarters at Crown Point and marched to Oswego, upon Lake Ontario, where he was obliged to wait until August 14, for the arrival of the Provincial reinforcements, when the whole army embarked and proceeded across the Lake and down the St. Lawrence to Montreal. Owing to the great delay incurred in reducing the posts of the enemy upon the river, and the dangers and difficulties of the navigation[1] without good pilots, Amherst did not reach Montreal until September 6, when his army landed at La Chine and encamped upon a plain before the town. Next day, General Murray arrived from Quebec with his troops, and anchored in the front of the town; and just at the same time, Colonel Haviland, in command of a corps from Lake Champlain, made his appearance on the south side of the river. Thus, enclosed on all sides, the Marquis de Vaudreuil, who had by his unjustifiable conduct in instigating his countrymen to make encroachments on British territory, brought on the war between England and France, was obliged to submit to the humiliation of signing a capitulation, which transferred not only the city of Montreal, but the whole of Canada, to the British Crown.

While Generals Amherst and Murray were completing the conquest of Canada in the summer of 1760, operations of a very different character were going on in Cape Breton. Fearing that the French Government would make great efforts to recover her lost possessions in America, and as a first step would endeavour to retake Louisbourg—the key of the Gulf

[1] On the night of September 4, eighty-four men were drowned, and a great number of batteaux of artillery and stores were sunk in passing the rapids near Isle Perrot.

of St. Lawrence—the British Ministry determined to raze the fortifications to the ground, to prevent the possibility of its again falling into the hands of France. Bitterly as you, who have seen Louisbourg in its present state of desolation, may regret the destruction of the ancient capital of Cape Breton, it was at the time, no doubt, the best policy the British Government could have adopted, especially since a first-rate naval station had already been provided at Halifax, not far distant. It was therefore obviously quite unnecessary to maintain a large garrison, such as Louisbourg required, at a great and useless expense, with Halifax, possessing so many superior advantages, close at hand. The order to demolish Louisbourg was issued by Pitt early in February 1760, but it did not reach Governor Whitmore at Louisbourg until May 31. As the three regiments of Infantry in garrison at Louisbourg were not accustomed to operations of that kind, a party of Engineers, with a company of Sappers and Miners, were sent out from England to aid and direct their labours, in the 'Fame,' of seventy-four guns, Commodore Byron,[1] who was appointed to command the ships lying in Louisbourg during the demolition of the works. Soon after his arrival at Louisbourg, Governor Whitmore having received intelligence that some French ships had arrived in Bay Chaleur, and that they had taken a number of English prizes in the Gulf, Commodore Byron immediately sailed with the 'Fame,'[2] 'Dorsetshire,' 'Scarborough,' 'Achilles,' and 'Repulse,' for Ristigouche, where he found a French frigate of thirty-two guns, two large armed store-ships, and nineteen smaller vessels which had been mostly taken from English traders. These three French ships formed part of a squadron of six vessels which had left France early in May with troops and stores for Montreal, hoping to

[1] The Hon. John Byron, grandfather of the celebrated poet, accompanied Commodore Anson in his voyage to the Pacific in 1740. He was midshipman in the 'Wager' when she was wrecked on a desert island to the south of Chiloe. Byron has left a well-written narrative of his sufferings. Lord Byron has used the incidents of the 'Wager's' shipwreck in his *Don Juan*. He rose to the rank of Admiral, and died in 1798.'—Lord Mahon's *History of England*.

[2] The 'Fame,' 74, accompanied by the 'Achilles,' 60, sailed from Plymouth on March 27. Four days after, Commodore Byron fell in with and captured the privateer 'Pallas,' of Bayonne, of 16 guns, with a crew of 130 men.

get up the river and past Quebec before the English ships came thither from Halifax. Three of these unlucky ships were taken in the English Channel, and the remainder, upon reaching the Gulf of St. Lawrence, learning that Lord Colville's squadron had gone up to Quebec, put into Bay Chaleur, where the troops were landed and a battery erected for their defence.

When Byron got his vessels up to the battery on July 8, after some delay, in consequence of the shallowness of the water, he found it manned by 250 soldiers, 700 Acadians, and an equal number of Indians. The three ships, which proved to be the 'Marchault,' of thirty-two, 'Bienfaisant,' twenty-two, and the 'Marquis Marloye,' eighteen guns, and the nineteen English prizes, were captured; two batteries and 200 houses were destroyed, and the settlement totally ruined. After this exploit Byron returned to Louisbourg, where he found the destruction of the fortifications had not proceeded so rapidly as he expected, two of the regiments in garrison there having been taken by Lord Colville to Quebec, from whence they were sent to join General Amherst before Montreal. Nevertheless, the work of destruction went on with great vigour, for in the short space of six months all the fortifications and public buildings, which had cost France twenty-five years of labour and a vast amount of money, were utterly demolished—the walls and glacis levelled into the ditch—leaving in fact nothing to mark their former situation but heaps of stones and rubbish. Nothing was left standing but the private houses which had been rent and shattered during the siege, the hospital, and a barrack capable of lodging 300 men. 'On October 17, the day before His Majesty's ship 'Fame' left Louisbourg, the last blast was given to the complete demolition of the fortifications of that important fortress, the whole being by that time reduced to the houses of a few fishermen.'[1] All the artillery, ammunition, stores, implements—in short, everything of the slightest value—even the hewn stones which had decorated the public buildings, were transported to Halifax.

[1] *Scots Magazine*, November, 1760.

The loss of Cape Breton was a severe blow to the navy of France, as the fishery on the coast was one of the chief nurseries of her seamen. According to a document placed in my hands by the late Chief Justice Dodd of Sydney, about forty years ago, no less than 15,000 men were employed in the fisheries of Cape Breton, when Louisbourg was taken in 1758. I cannot do better than give you the following copy of this document:—

'*State of the Fisheries carried on by the French in the Island of Cape Breton, previous to the British taking possession in* 1758:—

	Decked Vessels.	Shallops.
Egmont Bay, near Cape North	—	30
Niganish Bay and Cove	—	245
Niganish Island	—	30
Port Dauphin, or St. Anne's	100	—
Entrance of Great Bras d'Or	20	40
Petit Bras d'Or	—	60
Spanish River, or Sydney	6	—
Indian Bay, or Lingan	—	50
Scattarie Island	—	200
Main à Dieu	—	190
Lorambec	—	80
Louisbourg	300	300
Gabarus Bay	—	50
Fourché	—	50
St. Esprit Island	—	60
Grande Rivière	—	60
L'Ardoise	—	14
St. Peter's	100	—
Petit de Grat, Isle Madame	—	100
River and Bay of Inhabitants	100	—
Different Places in the Gut of Canso	100	—
Totals	726	1,555

726 Decked Vessels, at 8 men each	5,808	
1,555 Shallops, at 6 men each	9,330	
Total	15,138	men.
726 Decked Vessels, at 700 quintals	508,200	
1,555 Shallops, at 300 quintals	466,500	
Total	974,700	quintals.

This was the amount in fish annually exported from Cape Breton.'[1]

[1] If this account is accurate, the fishermen must have increased six, and the catch eight fold, since 1740!—See Captain Smith's *Report on the French Fisheries*, p. 175.

There can be no stronger proof of the value of Cape Breton, in the estimation of the French, than the fact that, when negotiations for a peace were mooted in the year 1761, the French Minister, the Duc de Choiseul, offered to cede the whole of Canada to England upon certain conditions, of which the most important was the restitution of Cape Breton. As Mr. Pitt would not consent to this condition, the French Government broke off the negotiations and recalled their agent from London. France and England were both desirous of suspending hostilities, but the former had lost so much territory in America, that she saw no hopes of acquiring a fair share of the fisheries, which were of so much importance to her navy, unless she could obtain possession of some British post that she might offer in exchange. With this object in view, the French Government, in the spring of 1762, sent out four ships of war and 1,500 troops under the command of the Count d'Haussonville, to seize St. John's, Newfoundland, and to hold it until negotiations for peace should again be opened. This was no difficult matter, as the forts in St. John's harbour had been suffered to go to decay and were garrisoned by only sixty men. St. John's was taken by D'Haussonville on June 27, as well as all the ships in the harbour, including the English sloop of war 'Grammont,' of twenty-two guns. The French General then set about repairing the fortifications, with the intention of keeping possession thereof, for the reasons above stated. When intelligence of the capture of St. John's reached Halifax early in July, the Governor and Council were thrown into a state of consternation and alarm, though there was little cause for apprehension, as the place was defended by 1,500 regular troops, a body of militia, a line-of-battle ship, and a frigate. Louisbourg was in much greater danger, as it was occupied by only one weak regiment, and totally destitute of any kind of defences. When General Amherst, the Commander-in-Chief in America, heard of what had occurred, he sent Colonel Amherst with a body of troops, with orders to call at Halifax and Louisbourg for reinforcements, to retake St. John's. Amherst left Louisbourg on September 7, and having been joined by Admiral Lord Colville's squadron, of one ship of the line and four frigates on the way, effected a landing at Torbay, a few miles to the northward of St. John's. After some sharp skirmishing, he recaptured the forts on September 18, and made prisoners of the whole garrison, of 700 men. The French ships, however, eluded the vigilance of Lord Colville, having escaped in the night and got out to sea without being discovered.

By a singular coincidence, the capture of the 'Alcide' and 'Lys,' on the Banks, in 1755, and the retaking of St. John's—the first and last acts of hostility of the 'Seven Years' War'—both occurred within a few leagues of Cape Race; for while Colonel Amherst was occupied in driving the French out of Newfoundland, the Ministries of England and France were engaged in arranging preliminaries of a peace, which were subsequently signed at Fontainebleau on November 2. Although England obtained a great acquisition of territory and many other advantages by the terms agreed upon, the mercantile men of the chief towns were very averse to peace, having made great profits by the exclusive trade they enjoyed with other countries, owing to England's supremacy at sea. Nevertheless, the English Ministers, satisfied that a continuation of the war would soon exhaust the resources of the empire, and that all the chief objects of the war had been successfully accomplished, concluded and executed a definitive treaty at Paris on February 10, 1763. By the 4th Article of this treaty, Canada, Cape Breton, and the countries adjacent, were ceded to England in the following terms:—'His most Christian Majesty renounces all pretensions which he has heretofore formed or might form, to Nova Scotia or Acadia, in all its parts, and guarantees the whole of it, and with all its dependencies, to the King of Great Britain. Moreover, His most Christian Majesty cedes and guarantees to his said Britannic Majesty, in full right, Canada, with all its dependencies, as well as the island of Cape Breton, and all the other islands and coasts in the gulf and river St. Lawrence, and, in general, everything that depends on the said countries, lands, islands, and coasts, with the sovereignty, property, possession, and all rights acquired by treaty or otherwise, which the most Christian King and the Crown of France have had till now over the said countries, islands, lands, places, coasts, and their inhabitants, so that the most Christian King cedes and makes over the whole to the said King, and to the Crown of Great Britain, and that in the most ample manner and form, without restriction and without any liberty to part from the said cession and guarantee, under any pretence, or to disturb Great Britain in the possessions above mentioned.'

Concerning the Fisheries it was stipulated by the 5th Article, that 'The subjects of France shall have the liberty of fishing and drying on a part of the coasts of the island of Newfoundland, such as is specified in the 13th Article of the Treaty of Utrecht; which Article is renewed and confirmed by the present treaty (except what relates to the island of Cape Breton,[1] as well as to the other islands and coasts in the mouth and in the Gulf of St. Lawrence); and His Britannic Majesty consents to leave to the subjects of the most Christian King the liberty of fishing in the Gulf of St. Lawrence, on condition that the subjects of France do not exercise the said fishery, but at the distance of three leagues from all the coasts belonging to Great Britain, as well those of the continent as those of the islands situated in the said Gulf of St. Lawrence: and as to what relates to the fishery out of the said Gulf, his most Christian Majesty's subjects shall not exercise the fishery but at the distance of fifteen leagues from the coasts of the island of Cape Breton; and the fishery on the coast of Nova Scotia or Acadia, and everywhere else out of the said Gulf, shall remain on the footing of former treaties.'

By the Treaty of Utrecht, the French were allowed to catch fish and dry them on the land, on that part of the coast of Newfoundland 'which stretches from Cape Bonavista to the northern point of the island, and from thence, running down by the western side, reaches as far as the place called Point Riché;' but since France had by the present treaty (1763)

[1] Cape Breton was in this case excepted, because, by the 13th Article of the Treaty of Utrecht, France was secured in the possession of the island, with the liberty of fortifying any place or places therein.

been deprived of all her territory bordering on the Gulf, and left without a single port where she could erect a building of any description except a fishing hut, the two small islands of St. Pierre and Miquelon, on the southern coast, were ceded to her by Great Britain, by the 6th Article, as follows:—

'The King of Great Britain cedes the islands of St. Pierre and Miquelon, in full right, to His most Christian Majesty, to serve as a shelter to the French fishermen; and His said most Christian Majesty engages not to fortify the said islands; to erect no buildings upon them, but merely for the convenience of the fishery; and to keep upon them a guard of fifty men only, for the police.'

These short extracts from the 'Treaty of Paris' will clearly show, without any comments of mine, the glorious results of the 'Seven Years' War' on your side of the Atlantic—namely, the acquisition of the whole of Canada and the vast regions beyond the Great Lakes, the present province of New Brunswick, and the islands of St. John's and Cape Breton. France, on the other hand, which first brought on the war by encroaching upon the territory of her neighbour in a time of profound peace, lost all her possessions in North America except the colony of Louisiana, and obtained in return only the miserable islands of St. Pierre and Miquelon.

As soon as the preliminaries of the peace became known in Paris, a great outcry was raised against them, as you may naturally suppose, but without any effect. A document denouncing every stipulation in the proposed treaty in the strongest language was freely circulated in Paris, and became the chief subject of conversation at the time.[1] I will give you a few extracts, for the sake of showing the importance of the possession of Cape Breton and the fisheries in the eyes of the French merchants. 'When we consider the vile concessions made of our own territories, rights, and possessions, which shall we most wonder at—the ambition and arrogance of the British Ministry, or the pusillanimity or perhaps treachery of

[1] From the *Scots Magazine* for December, 1762. The editor says that some persons of distinction—the supposed authors of this document—were committed to the Bastile.

our own? Let us begin with what relates to the very valuable fishery in the North American seas. In the first place, then, we have given up Isle Royale, or Cape Breton, to regain which at the last peace we relinquished all Flanders and every conquest in Europe. In the next place, we have abandoned all the most valuable coasts from whence the dry cod was usually got. By the 2nd Article of the Preliminaries, France cedes to Great Britain, besides Cape Breton, all the other islands in the Gulf and River of St. Lawrence, without restriction; and by the 3rd Article we are excluded from fishing within three leagues of any of their coasts. The consequences of these cessions are obvious. We have nothing left us but a precarious right, subject to cavil and insult, to the *morue verte*, or mud-fish, a commodity not marketable in Portugal, Spain, or Italy, but only fit for our own home consumption. Ever since the happy Treaty of Utrecht, France has enjoyed great advantages in the dry cod fishery. At the breaking out of this war, we had in the Bay of Fundy, in Acadié, in Cape Breton, in St. John's, at Gaspé, and other places in the Gulf, above 16,000 fishermen, who carried on most successfully, in shoal water, the *pèche sédentaire* [shore fishery]. Now all this is in the hands of the British. All our settlements are unpeopled. From the single island of St. John's, Admiral Boscawen removed 5,000 inhabitants. What, then, is left to France? Nothing but the north coast from Cape Riche to Cape Bonavista, with liberty to land, and erect stages for a short season; so that we must carry and recarry both our fish and fishermen, while the British settled on the spot, and carrying on the *pèche sédentaire*, will forestall us, and undersell us at every market in the Mediterranean. Miquelon and St. Peter's—two barren rocks—indeed, are to be ours; yet even for them we have shamefully pledged the royal word, engaging not to erect in them any fortifications; so that even they, with their guard of fifty men for the police, will always lie at the mercy of the British.'

As the history of Cape Breton must exclusively occupy my remaining letters, I will close this with a glance at the state of Canada, Nova Scotia, and Newfoundland in 1763, at the termination of the 'Seven Years' War.' During the twenty years preceding the peace, although great numbers of the inhabitants had been withdrawn from their regular pursuits to serve in the army, Canada made great and substantial progress. The frugal and industrious Canadians, under the judicious direction of the Viceroys, devoted themselves to the cultivation of the soil, and rapidly spread along the shores of the Great Lakes and up the tributaries of the St. Lawrence, following close upon the heels of the coureurs des bois,[1] towards the north-west, and forming settlements in the vicinity of the military posts towards the south, which Montcalm and his generals were pushing on in the rear of the British provinces. The population of Canada, which in 1739 (see page 168) amounted to 42,924 souls, had risen in 1763, when the Governor-General Murray ordered a census to be taken, to 69,275, all of French descent, except 775 immigrants, brought out from Scotland by two officers of the 78th Highlanders, settled in the county of Saguenay. General Murray's census did not include the coureurs des bois, voyageurs, and traders, dispersed through the western country and among the Indians.[2] The French inhabitants of Canada had no reason to complain

[1] I cannot refrain from giving you a short account of these 'coureurs des bois' from the pen of a recent writer. In the pursuit of the fur-bearing animals, 'these men pushed up unknown rivers, or arrived at lakes not yet explored, and gained an influence with the Indian tribes not yet baptised, purchasing from them their beaver skins on their own account. Frequently they accompanied the Indians, as welcome allies, on their hunting or war excursions. Not only did they follow the example of Champlain, but of the Jesuit missionaries too. Like them, they prayed over the sick, or made the sign of the cross over the dying, performed wonders, and told the wild Indians Bible histories, which pleased those children of nature so exceedingly, that they often repaid them with whole packs of beaver skins. . . . They ventured wherever a beaver or a bear could live; and from the Canadian lakes they have spread themselves over the whole of the wide north-west of America. They have given the names now in use to almost all the localities. . . . The British and the United States beaver hunters were their pupils, and it was only by the aid of the French Canadians that they found their way in the western Labyrinth.'—Kohl's *Discovery of America*. London: 1862.

[2] Mr. Kohl is not therefore very correct when he says, 'The French, however, who for the most part only filled Canada with monks and adventurers, got scarcely beyond this fur-hunting—which is but the rudest way of turning a country to account—and beyond that hunting for souls, which, with all the zeal bestowed upon it, has produced but few lasting results.'—*Discovery of America*.

of the treatment they received from their new masters; the terms of the capitulation, which guaranteed to them their possessions, the free exercise of the Roman Catholic worship, and the preservation of the property belonging to the religious communities, being faithfully fulfilled. This just and liberal conduct of the British authorities gained the confidence of the Canadians, who never swerved from their allegiance during the revolutionary war, which broke out not long afterwards, although pressingly urged to join the united colonies. The greatest loss which the Canadians suffered at this time was due to the peculations of the late Intendant, M. Bigot, in consequence of which the French Government refused to pay the bills drawn by him in favour of the parties who had furnished supplies during the war.

Let us now turn to Nova Scotia, where it was confidently expected that the English settlers would enjoy some tranquillity after the expulsion of the Acadians in 1755. This hope, owing to the breaking out of the war in the following year, was not realised, for the Indians, now believing that the French would again obtain possession of the country, began their old practices of disturbing the English settlers, and committed several murders at Lunenburg, Chignecto, and even on McNab's Island, in the harbour of Halifax. The Acadians also, who had concealed themselves in the woods when their countrymen were expelled, and many who had secretly returned to the province, hung about the settlements at Minas, Chignecto, and other places, keeping the inhabitants in constant alarm. But this unhappy state of affairs did not last long, for as soon as it became known that Louisbourg, Quebec, and Montreal had fallen, and that the British arms were everywhere triumphant, the Indians sent their Chiefs from all parts of the province to make their submission to the Governor at Halifax, and to sign a treaty of peace. As every disposition to conciliate the Indians was manifested by the Government, and effective measures adopted to protect them from the impositions of the traders, by establishing truck-houses where provisions and clothing were supplied in exchange for furs at a regular scale of prices, they soon became friendly and peaceable. The Acadians also, who were lurking about the country, and many hundreds who had sought refuge at Miramichi, Ristigouche, St. John's River, and other places, finding the authority of the British Government firmly established, and that all hopes of aid from France had passed away, sent deputies to Halifax to make their submissions. All fears of danger from the presence of the Acadians having now vanished, those who had been transported to Massachusetts were allowed to return in 1763 and form a settlement at Clare, in the county of Digby.

Several new settlements were established during the war; for instance, Liverpool, Chester, and Lunenburg, on the Atlantic coast; and Amherst, Onslow, Truro, Cornwallis, Horton, Falmouth, Granville, &c., on the Bay of Fundy. Some of the new settlers came from England, Ireland, and Germany, but by far the greatest number came from Connecticut, Massachusetts, and Rhode Islands. Notwithstanding these arrivals, the population of the province, which, before the expulsion of the Acadians in 1755, was 14,000, amounted in 1763 to only 13,000. There is this, however, to be said, that 6,000 disaffected Acadians had been replaced by 5,000 loyal subjects chiefly of British descent. The trade of the province does not seem to have been very flourishing, as the whole amount of exports in 1763 was only 16,300*l.* In taking leave of Nova Scotia, I must not forget to inform you that a Constitutional government was established in 1758, consisting of a governor and twelve legislative councillors appointed by the Crown, and twenty-two representatives chosen by the freeholders of the counties and townships. The first General Assembly, as it was styled, met at Halifax on October 2 of the same year.

I have not much to tell you about your neighbour, Newfoundland. Happily, the planters, who had suffered so much during the early years of the eighteenth century from the French, were not molested for nearly fifty years after the Treaty of Utrecht. In 1762, as I have already told you, (p. 341), St. John's was taken by the Count d'Haussonville, but it was almost immediately after retaken by Colonel Amherst. With the exception of this misfortune, and the occasional visit of a French privateer, the country had enjoyed uninterrupted tranquillity and made great progress. The population, which in 1698 was only 3,224, in 1763 had risen to 13,112; and the produce of the fisheries had increased from 215,922 to 386,274 quintals. During the same time, the fish taken by the planters alone had increased from 101,152 to 235,944 quintals. In the year 1763, the planters also exported 694 tierces of salmon, 1,598 tuns of train oil, and furs valued at 2,000*l.*[1] When the fishery in 1731 only averaged 200,000 quintals, its importance was duly recognised: 'As the fishery is of great use in breeding able seamen, the natural strength of this kingdom; as, moreover, we have from Newfoundland great quantities of peltry, i.e. the furs and skins of deer, fox, otter, minx, and bear, with some beaver, we ought therefore greatly to prize Newfoundland.'[2] The cod fishery was not at that time the only source of profit in the vicinity of Newfoundland, for I learn by a notice in the 'Scots Magazine' for March 1764, that a valuable whale fishery had been discovered and prosecuted with success during the preceding three years:—'Since our people have been in possession of the Gulf and River of St. Lawrence, they have discovered a very valuable whale fishery there, which was unknown to the French. Upon this discovery, the people of New England fitted out ten vessels of near 100 tons burden each for that fishery in 1761, and had such success, that in 1762 they sent out fifty vessels for the same purpose. Last year were employed upwards of eighty: and we are assured a still larger number will be employed the ensuing season. The quantity of whalebone imported from New England within these two years has already reduced that commodity from 500*l.* to 350*l.* the ton.' In 1729, Newfoundland, which had been nominally appended to Nova Scotia, was made a separate Government, and courts of justice were established, whereby the property of the planters was protected from the ravages of many lawless vagabonds who came out in the spring as fishermen, and supported themselves during the

[1] Anspach's *History of Newfoundland.* London: 1819.
[2] M'Pherson's *Annals of Commerce.* London: 1805.

winter by plundering the inhabitants. I must here close my brief notice of Newfoundland with the observation, that during the twenty-five years preceding the peace of 1763, Newfoundland was governed by several naval officers, who afterwards distinguished themselves in the service of their country, such as Byng, Hardy, Rodney, and lastly, Graves—whose gallantry in Lord Howe's action of June 1, 1794, is known to all.[1]

In conclusion, I may observe that St. John's Island (Prince Edward's) which in 1758 had a population of more than 6,000, had in 1763 become almost a wilderness; the old clearings, which during the French occupation supplied Quebec with large quantities of wheat, had almost returned to a state of nature, being everywhere covered with wild strawberries and a young growth of spruce and birch.[2]

[1] Whilst Captain Graves was Governor of Newfoundland, Captain Cook was employed in making a survey of the coasts. According to Dr. Forster, Cook discovered some wonderful coal mines; he says, 'There are in Newfoundland, as well as in Cape Breton, such rich coal mines, that if the Crown would but grant leave to work them, their produce would be sufficient to supply all Europe and America abundantly with this commodity; and some are even so commodiously situated, that the coals might be thrown directly from the coal-works themselves into the ships, as they lie close to the shore. This piece of intelligence [which will be quite new to you] I had from my late friend the great circumnavigator, Captain Cook, who for several years successively had explored the shores of this island, taken their bearings and respective distances, and laid them down on charts.'—*History of Voyages and Discoveries in the North.* By John Reinhold Forster. Translated from the German. London: 1786.

[2] McPherson's *Annals of Commerce.*

LETTER XXI.

1763–1768.

PEACE being once more restored, and the conquest of Canada and Cape Breton, the chief object of the war, accomplished, a proclamation was issued on October 7, 1763, providing for the security of these valuable acquisitions. Canada, as a matter of course, had a separate Government, but the islands of Cape Breton and St. John's were annexed to the Government of Nova Scotia. To induce the officers and soldiers who had been engaged in the late war to settle in the colonies, free grants of land were offered as a reward for their services. Every person having held the rank of a field-officer was entitled to a grant of 5,000 acres; captains, 3,000; subalterns or staff-officers, 2,000; non-commissioned officers, 200; and privates, 50 acres each. To mark the sense entertained by the Government of the services of the navy in the conquest of Cape Breton, similar grants were offered 'to such reduced officers of the navy of like rank as served on board ships of war in North America at the time of the reduction of Louisbourg.' A number of officers eagerly embraced the opportunity of securing grants in Canada and Nova Scotia, but none were allowed to take up grants in Cape Breton, for the reasons mentioned in the following extract from a letter addressed by the Lords Commissioners of Trade and Plantations to Governor Wilmot,[1] on November 26, 1763:[2]—'We

[1] Colonel Wilmot was appointed Governor of Nova Scotia on October 8, 1763.

[2] You will have observed that I have occasionally referred to 'Documents in the Record Office' in the preceding letters; I am almost wholly indebted to these Documents for the information I have obtained relative to Cape Breton, in this and the subsequent letters.

cannot close this letter without mentioning the islands of St. John and Cape Breton, which, being annexed to the Government of Nova Scotia, are now becoming pressing objects of your particular care and attention; their advantageous situation in respect to the fishery renders them of the greatest importance to this country, and no measures should be left untried that may tend to promote and encourage the carrying on this fishery to the utmost extent it is capable of.' Wilmot was instructed at the same time to have an accurate survey made of St. John's and Cape Breton; to report, in the meantime, all information he could collect respecting their resources, extent, soil, &c.; and what establishments might be necessary for effectually uniting them to Nova Scotia. He was required also to state what plan of settlement would be most advantageous; but until the survey was completed, he was ordered to make no grants whatever in either of the islands to any particular persons; and 'to discourage every attempt that might in its nature and consequence operate as a monopoly.' In the month of March following, he was again cautioned 'against making any grants of land, upon any pretence whatever, in St. John's and Cape Breton Islands.' In conformity with these instructions, Captain Samuel Holland was directed to make a survey of Cape Breton, which, as you may well imagine, occupied several years, and retarded the settlement of the island. Frequent applications were made to Lieutenant-Colonel Tulleskein,[1] the commanding officer at Louisbourg, by persons desirous of carrying on the fishery, for grants of land for that purpose, but he could merely give them licences to occupy fishing lots, without any other legal title.

Before Governor Wilmot's instructions became generally known, several applications were made for large grants of land in Cape Breton. In 1763, John Greg, a merchant, and three others, applied for 40,000 acres between Mirá River and

[1] When the fortifications of Louisbourg were dismantled, and the Governor, with two of the regiments, withdrawn in 1760, Colonel Tulleskein, in command of the 45th Regiment, was left in charge of the place. He accompanied Colonel Amherst, in 1762, with part of the 45th Regiment, to retake St. John's, N. F. where, Amherst says, 'He seconded me in everything I could wish.'

Indian Bay. They proposed to carry on the fishery upon a large scale, and to found a town at the head of Cow Bay.

On April 3 in the following year, the Duke of Richmond petitioned the King for a grant of 'the whole island of Cape Breton and its appurtenances in fee to himself and several others of the nobility and gentry who were desirous of settling the said island.' This petition was referred to the Lords of Trade, who reported on May 23, 'that, as it was their duty to consider the public interest only, and to lay before His Majesty such plans as would in their judgment most effectually conduce to the promoting and extending of the commerce of the kingdom, by encouraging the speedy settlement of those valuable territories and islands ceded and confirmed to His Majesty by the late Treaty of Peace,' they could not advise His Majesty to comply with the prayer of the petitioner. They then refer to the reasons they had given against the Earl of Egmont's application for a grant of St. John's Island,[1] and add, 'The same argument operates more strongly upon our judgment in the present instance, as the island of Cape Breton is considerably larger than that of St. John's;' whereupon the King in Council adopted their Report and refused to grant the island. There is no mention made in the Records of the fate of Mr. Greg's petition, but it was probably refused for similar reasons.

On May 17 of the same year, the Sieur Gratian d'Arrigrand, who had obtained a concession of a large tract of land in 1751 from the French Government, petitioned the British Government for a confirmation of his title, offering at the same time to take the oath of allegiance to His Majesty. On July 10, the Lords of Trade, to whom the petition was referred, advised that a grant of 20,000 acres should be given to D'Arrigrand, to include the improvements he had made in the vicinity of Louisbourg, but it does not appear that their recommendation was acted upon, as there is no further mention of the matter.

[1] I found a copy of Lord Egmont's petition for a grant of St. John's Island, but could not find in the State Paper Office the opinion given by the Board of Trade thereon, and their reasons for reporting against the petition.

On March 22 of the same year, Captain Bradstreet, who states in his memorial that he had been many years employed in the provincial naval and military service, applied for a grant of 6,000 acres near St. Peter's Island, but there is nothing more said about it in the Records.

The valuable coal-fields of Cape Breton at this time seem to have attracted the notice of speculators; for we find that, on March 19, 1764, Brigadier-General Howe and several other officers of distinction who had served in the late war in America, petitioned the King for a grant of land in Cape Breton, being 'desirous of becoming adventurers in opening coal-mines and of endeavouring to establish a colliery for the better supplying the several colonies and garrisons on the Continent with fuel. That, to enable them to carry this their design into execution, they humbly pray to have granted to them as their allotment a tract of land on the east shore of that island, extending from the Point on the north side of Mirá Bay to the south-east side of the entrance into the Labrador and seven miles inland, and supposed to contain about 55,000 acres.' They offered to pay 2*s*. sterling per chaldron (London measure) on every chaldron exported. The area of the tract designated, you will find on reference to a map of the island, contains at least 100,000 acres, including the most valuable portion of the Sydney coal-field.

Other competitors soon appeared. In the month of May, Sir Samuel Fludyers and three others applied to the Lords of Trade for 'a lease of all the coals in the island of Cape Breton,' offering, 'upon having the mines for ten years free of tax, to pay 2*s*. 6*d*. sterling for every chaldron they ship, for the further term of ten years, 3*s*. 9*d*. for the next ten years, and 5*s*. per chaldron for the last ten years of their lease.' Finding, perhaps, that Brigadier-General Howe's offer was likely to be accepted, Sir Samuel Fludyers and his friends made a second application to the Lords of Trade [date is not given] upon terms much more advantageous to the Government. In this application they ask for a grant of 100,000 acres 'between the rivers Mirá and the great branch of the Labrador, taking the seacoast and harbours between the said rivers within the grant,' and a lease of all the coals in the said grant for thirty years. They undertook also to settle thereon not less than one hundred people every five years; to build a town on one of the harbours; to pay a quit-rent after the first ten years, of 2*s.* 1*d.* sterling, upon every 100 acres of land; and a royalty of 2*s.* 6*d.* sterling per chaldron during the first ten years, and 5*s.* per chaldron during the next twenty years, on all coal exported.

Neither of these applications seem to have been favourably entertained by the Ministry, although the Lords of Trade recommended on July 10 that a lease should be given to Brigadier-General Howe and his associates, and that it would be desirable to grant leases of the coal mines, because it would be the means of lowering the price of coal in England, from whence large quantities were now exported to America; would be a boon to the colonies, where fuel was becoming daily scarcer; and that a large revenue might be derived from it.

I have not been able to find any exact account of the population of Cape Breton at this time (1765). M. Rameau[1] says, according to the best information he could obtain, there were, immediately after the fall of Louisbourg, not more than 700 Acadians and 300 Frenchmen in all Cape Breton. Mr. Charles Morris, who was employed by Governor Wilmot in 1765 to visit and report on the state of the island, says there were at that time twenty-eight families of Acadians residing in Isle Madame, chiefly engaged in the fishery, and a Guernsey firm that had commenced business at Arichat in the preceding year. He adds, that the Acadians had built small vessels during the winter of 1764–65 at Just au Corps,[2] seven leagues to the northward of the Gut of Canceau, for the French merchants at St. Pierre and Miquelon. If Rameau's estimate be correct, there must have been several other small French and Acadian settlements along the coast to the northward and eastward. As the English population, including the garrison of 300 men at

[1] *La France aux Colonies.*

[2] Mr. Morris states that during the French occupation of the island, fifty men were constantly employed at Just au Corps quarrying freestone for Louisbourg and the French forts in the West Indies.

Louisbourg, did not probably exceed 500, there could not have been much more than 1,500 persons in the whole island in 1765, exclusive of the Micmac Indians.

Governor Wilmot, writing to the Board of Trade on December 10, 1763, warmly recommended that the Government should propitiate the Indians by giving them presents annually, as had been the custom of the French when they had possession of the island. He says, 'I have been told that a chief of the island of Breton having made an unsuccessful application at Louisbourg for some small supplies, has declared his necessity and resolution of going immediately to the French at St. Peter's or Miquelon for that purpose; and I am fearful that they very readily, and perhaps bountifully, supplied this man's wants, and would gladly seize the opportunity of re-establishing once more that interest with these people, by means of whom they so long and effectually obstructed the settlement of this country, and well knowing of what consequence it would be to gain the hearts of the natives of it against any future enterprises. And I apprehend, my Lords, that any favourable reception this man may have met with, will undoubtedly be communicated to the Indians of this province, particularly to those bordering on the Gulf of St. Lawrence [where, as he states in another letter, they can muster 400 fighting men], by which such an intercourse may be established between them and the French as may prove very prejudicial to His Majesty's interest in these parts of his dominions.' Governor Wilmot seems to have obtained his information from an authentic source, for Captain Thompson wrote to the Secretary of the Admiralty on April 16 following that, while cruising on the coast of Newfoundlandland in His Majesty's sloop 'Lark,' in the month of September previous, he met a party of Cape Breton Micmacs off the island of Codroy, headed by two chiefs named Oulat and Bernard, who asked him for a supply of various useful articles, such as cloth, shirts, muskets, powder, shot, hatchets, and codlines. The chiefs also requested that he would furnish them with three gold-laced hats and ten ruffled shirts for their own special use, and some red, green, and white ribbons for their squaws. All these articles were sent out by the Government, in His Majesty's ship 'Tweed,' soon after, and Governor Wilmot was about the same time instructed to make similar presents to the Indians in Nova Scotia. This policy, however, does not seem to have produced the desired effect, for great numbers emigrated in the course of the two following years to the French islands of St. Peter's and Miquelon. In the autumn of 1765, about 200 Indians landed in the Bay of Despair, on their way, it was supposed, to the island of Miquelon, where some of their tribe and about 150 Acadians from Nova Scotia had formed a settlement and built a straggling town, with the intention of remaining there until the return of the French fishing-fleet in the spring.[1] The arrival of so many disaffected Acadians and Indians in the vicinity of the English fishing-stations created so much alarm, that Sir Hugh Palliser, the Governor of Newfoundland, wrote to the Commandant at Louisbourg, urging him to recall the passports he had granted, and not to issue any more to the Indians. At the same time he gave peremptory orders to the intruders to withdraw from the country. Sir Hugh viewed the introduction of a foreign element with great repugnance, and, in his opinion, of dangerous consequence.[2] Governor Wilmot held the same view; he wrote to the Governor of Newfoundland soon afterwards, informing him that a considerable number of Micmacs was preparing to go thither with the intention of furthering the designs imputed to the French of recovering the country.

It does not, however, appear that the French entertained any such design. It is more probable that the wandering Indians were attracted by the hunting-grounds in the interior of the island, where, it is said, 'they proved the most destructive enemies of the few remaining aborigines of Newfoundland.'[3]

The restless state of the Indians in Nova Scotia about this

[1] See a letter from St. John's, N. F., dated October 28, 1765, in *Scots Magazine* for December, and another from Halifax, dated February 19, 1766, in the same periodical for July.

[2] Pedley's *History of Newfoundland*. London: 1863.

[3] Ibid.

time caused much uneasiness to the authorities. Michael Francklyn, who had been appointed acting-governor of that province on the death of Governor Wilmot in 1766, wrote to the Lords of Trade on September 3 of the same year, stating that the Indians were much dissatisfied because a Jesuit priest had not been sent to them as promised, declaring that the Government meant to deceive them. 'Last year,' he adds, 'they showed how capable the French are of drawing them together whenever they think proper, which they actually did by some means unknown to the Government, in the summer; for the whole body of Indians were collected from every part of the province, and assembled at Isle Madame, not far from the head of the Labrador; and as they passed through the different townships to the rendezvous, they declared they were to meet French forces, and threatened to destroy the out-settlements when they should return. This alarmed the inhabitants to so great a degree that for several weeks together they were kept in continual apprehensions, and some part of the time even in arms; and with difficulty this body of Indians were dispersed, partly by the influence of some gentlemen sent by the Government, and partly upon finding themselves deceived in their expected support from the French.' He then continues, that they did the same thing this year, but not in such great numbers, and declared they would allow no settlements to be made at Pictou, nor on the eastern coast of the Continent towards Cape Breton. On this occasion they were persuaded to disperse by a Canadian priest, specially sent from Bay Chaleur for that purpose. Francklyn says they are completely under the guidance of the French at San Pierre, and recommends that two Canadian priests whose fidelity and attachment to the English can be relied upon, should be sent among them 'as the most eligible plan of warding off the apparent danger.' He further states that he had written to Governor Palliser to instruct his cruisers to stop as much as possible all communication between the Indians and Acadians with the French at St. Peter's and Miquelon. Whatever may have been the object of these hostile demonstrations on the part of the Indians, there is no evidence to show that they received the slightest encouragement from the French Government. This is satisfactorily proved by their abstaining from any acts of violence, or from using threatening language to the English settlers after this period, with whom they lived upon friendly terms in the most remote and secluded places, where, if they had been so disposed, they might have kept the scattered inhabitants in a continual state of agitation and alarm. Those who had gone to Newfoundland, probably for the sake of hunting and fishing, as they still do in small parties, gradually returned to Cape Breton, where they had ample room for following their usual avocations, and were at liberty to roam over the whole island without interruption from the few English inhabitants of Louisbourg. 'After the English had established their power in the province,' Murdoch says, 'the Micmacs became tractable, peaceable, and friendly, with great readiness not only adhering strictly to their treaty engagements, but being most scrupulous and attentive to abstain from doing the slightest injury to the white people, or to abstract the value of one penny of their cattle or goods, showing that they deeply respected and well understood the rights of property.'[1]

The administration of the civil government of Cape Breton now demands our attention. The island having been annexed to Nova Scotia by Royal Proclamation on October 7, 1763, the Governor, in opening the Legislative Session on March 24 following stated, 'that he should consider what profits and advantages might thence be derived to the province in general, as soon as he should receive His Majesty's instructions and know his further pleasure relating to this acquisition.' No steps, however, were taken for giving the island a voice in the Legislature until December 10, 1765, when it was ordered by the Governor and Council: 'That the island of Cape Breton should be erected into a distinct county, to be known by the name of the "County of Breton," comprehending the islands of Madame and Scatari, and all islands within three leagues, and that a writ should be issued for choosing two representatives;' and further, that 'the freeholders should be at liberty to

[1] *History of Nova Scotia.* Halifax: 1867.

choose non-residents;' a very necessary proviso, no doubt, when we bear in mind that in the month of July previous, the Attorney-General had been ordered by Governor Wilmot 'to make inquiry whether there was a sufficiency of people for making a jury to be summoned at Louisbourg to try a man who had been charged with having committed a murder there.' A writ having accordingly been issued to the Provost-Marshal, directing him to summons the *Freeholders* of the County of Breton to make choice of two representatives, John Grant, Esquire, and Mr. Gregory Townsend were elected, who proceeded to Halifax to take their seats in the Assembly on June 3, 1766. The validity of their election having been called in question, on the ground that 'the return varied from the tenor of the writ, which directed that the choice should be made by *Freeholders*, and the return specified that the same had been made by the *Inhabitants*,' it was on June 5 'Resolved and ordered that Messrs. Butler, Morris, Smith, Brenton, and Burbridge be a committee to examine into the validity of the said election and report thereon.' On June 7, the committee reported as follows:—

'1st. That the usage of choosing representatives in this province has always been by a majority of Freeholders in the County or Town for which such Representatives are chosen, in pursuance of a resolution of the Governor and Council passed August 22, 1759.

'2nd. That the Writ by which the above members are returned directs the Provost-Marshal in direct words to summon the *Freeholders* of the County of Breton qualified by the said resolution to make choice of two Representatives for that County.

'3rd. By the return of the said Writ, that the above Election has been made by the *Inhabitants* of the said County, and it does not appear to us that there is one Freeholder qualified as above directed in that County.

'Lastly. The Committee therefore are of opinion that the said Election is contrary to the Resolution aforesaid, not conformable to the precept of the Writ, and ought not to be admitted.'

The House agreed to the Report of the Committee on June 14, and the Government, foreseeing that some question might be raised of the legality of taxing people who were not represented, immediately submitted a Bill entitled, 'An Act for the more effectual recovery of His Majesty's Dues in the islands of Cape Breton and St. John and islands adjacent,' which was debated and passed on June 17. It certainly was rather hard upon the people of Cape Breton, to refuse to give them such rights to property as would qualify them to return members to the Assembly, and then to tax them without their consent. It could not be expected that they would submit quietly to this injustice; and accordingly we find that they immediately sent a petition to the Lords Commissioners of Trade and Plantations, in which they stated: That they had been settlers in the island ever since its reduction, and that many of them had aided in that conquest: that their great distance from the capital of Nova Scotia was the cause of innumerable difficulties, from which the Governors of that colony had taken no measures to relieve them: that they were neither consulted at home nor represented in the Assembly: that they were oppressed by the most grievous impositions on almost every necessary commodity, and charged exorbitant rents for the liberty of dwelling in the wretched ruins of the town of Louisbourg: that they had no courts of justice to which they could apply for the redress of wrongs: that they had in vain applied to the Governors of Nova Scotia for absolute grants of land: and that spirituous liquors, so essential in carrying on the fisheries 'in this *intemperate* climate' were highly taxed by the Legislature of Nova Scotia, while they were excluded from every benefit common to the settlers of the said province. In support of these allegations, they referred their Lordships to Colonel Tulleskein, Colonel Pringle, and Captain Holland, who, they said, 'were well acquainted with the just grounds of their application' . . . 'and prayed their Lordships to take their case into consideration and apply such remedies as they might deem necessary for their relief.'

No notice whatever was taken of this petition until May 28

in the following year, when the Lords of Trade reported to His Majesty that no grants could be given in Cape Breton until the survey then in progress should be completed, as was well known to the people of Louisbourg; that the island had been erected into a distinct county and a writ issued for choosing two representatives, [you have already seen how this had been settled twelve months previously], and that a commission had been issued for holding a Court of Quarter Sessions and for erecting a Court of Common Pleas. 'This,' they add 'being the state of affairs in Cape Breton, and the inhabitants of Louisbourg having been made participant in every advantage and privilege enjoyed by your Majesty's other subjects in the continental part of Nova Scotia, they have no foundation either in reason or justice to complain. On the contrary, we think that every attention has been paid to their interests, under their unauthorised state of settlement, they had any just right to expect.'

The people of Louisbourg had certainly just reason to complain that they were not represented in the Assembly, but in other respects they do not appear to have had good grounds for the allegations contained in their petition. They were well aware that grants could not be issued until the survey was finished; and as to the want of Courts of Justice, their statement was not correct, for we find in the Records that, in January 1764, George Cottnam, Esq., was appointed a Justice of the Peace; and in June following, Gregory Townsend, William Russell, and George Cottnam were appointed Justices of the Court of Common Pleas, to hold pleas at the town of Louisbourg four times in the year. In 1766, a Collector of Duties, with a salary of 75*l.*, and a waiter, with 40*l.* a year, were appointed. On September 2 of the same year, Lieutenant-Governor Francklyn tells the Lords of Trade that the people of Louisbourg had been taught by some ill advisers to dispute the payment of duties because they were not represented in the Assembly. He adds, the matter will soon be decided, 'for a suit is already commenced, which, after the opposition they have made to laws, was found indispensably necessary.' He concludes in the hope 'that when the island shall be divided into property, the people will be better disposed, and that the settlement will become considerable.'

Before we proceed further, I must again return to the subject of the mines of Cape Breton, in which you are all so much interested. The failure of General Howe's and Sir Samuel Fludyer's applications in 1764, did not deter others from attempting to secure leases; for we find that in 1765 'a design was on foot for establishing a company to work to advantage the coal mines, which have this great superiority over all others, that the coals are within three feet of the surface, and the most excellent ever seen. There will be no occasion for digging underground, or making drains to carry off the water, as in England, for the mines consist of entire mountains of coal, and are sufficient to supply all the British plantations in North America for ten centuries.'[1] This will remind you of Nicholas Denys's assertion, made more than one hundred years previously, 'that there was a mountain of very good coal four leagues up Spanish River.' (See p. 103.)

It is also stated in a letter from Halifax, 'that some New England people, digging for a coal mine in the island of Cape Breton, had discovered a vein of lead ore, samples of which they carried to Boston, where measures were taking for turning it to account.'[2]

In the following year a letter was received in London from Halifax, Nova Scotia, saying that a valuable copper mine had just been discovered near Port Toulouse (St. Peter's), eighteen leagues distant from Louisbourg, in the isle of Cape Breton.'[3]

From the Records it appears that a licence was granted, on September 10, 1766, to William Hutton, to occupy a place [situation not named] in the Isle of Breton, for making salt, and leave was given to dig coals for that purpose, 'except where the troops were at work.' Most of these discoveries were mere myths and never heard of afterwards; but serious intentions existed, no doubt, of working the coal mines. Anticipating that applications would be made to the Lords of Trade, Lieutenant-Governor Francklyn wrote to their Lordships on

[1] Extract from a letter from Halifax, in the *Scots Magazine* for April, 1765.
[2] *Scots Magazine*, July, 1765. [3] Ibid. March, 1766.

September 30, 1766, upon the subject, and sent such statistics as he considered would be useful. He says the troops at Louisbourg had dug at Cow Bay between November 1, 1761, and June 30, 1764, 4,167 chaldrons of coal for the use of the King's troops at Louisbourg and Halifax, which had cost the Crown nearly 800*l.*, exclusive of utensils and stores, making the whole cost 5*s.* per chaldron. He says, 'There is at Cow Bay a picketed fort 100 feet square, with a blockhouse, barracks and stores for lodging the workmen, tools and provisions. Also, a wharf convenient for loading close to the mines. That the mine is in good order and well propped. The vein appears to be good and large (he is told twelve feet thick and half a mile wide). That twenty men may be employed daily. That vessels of 100 tons can load at the wharf between June 1 and October 15, when the wharf must be taken down and rebuilt in the spring, the bay being so open and the drift of ice so violent as to carry it away in the winter season.' He estimates that the coal can be sold at the mines for exportation at 12*s.* 6*d.* per chaldron, and proposes that, if the mines are leased, the lessees should be bound to take all the coal to Halifax for reshipment in vessels that would otherwise go from thence in ballast. He calculates that the shipping of the province will be increased, and 'the revenues arising on spirituous liquors also much increased, as great part of the expenses attending the digging and shipping the coals will be expended amongst the labourers, tradesmen, and inhabitants of Halifax.' He proposes also to appropriate the money arising from the mines to making roads from Halifax to Cape Sable and thence round to Annapolis; from Halifax to the Gut of Canceau 'to a ferry not far from St. Peter's, whence, he is told, there is a good road to Louisbourg; and from Halifax to Cobequid (Truro), and thence to the river St. John and New England.' In conclusion, he estimates that from 500*l.* to 1,000*l.* a year may be raised from the mines, which would make thirty or forty miles of road. Francklyn's proposals did not, however, meet with the approval of the Home Government, for instructions were sent out on December 2 following, stating 'that His Majesty would not at present authorise or permit any coal mines to be opened or worked in the island of Cape Breton, and ordering that all petitions and proposals for that purpose should be dismissed.'

Nevertheless, Lord William Campbell, who was sworn in Governor of Nova Scotia on November 27 of the same year, granted an exclusive right for eight months, on April 13 following (1767), to Benjamin Gerrish and two other merchants of Halifax, to dig 3,000 chaldrons in the island, 'anywhere except from such places where His Majesty's troops were at work digging for the use of the troops.' Gerrish and his partners agreed to pay 500*l.* for this privilege, and to ship at least 1,500 chaldrons to Halifax, and sell it there at no higher rate than 32*s.* 6*d.* per chaldron. They opened a mine at Spanish River, from whence they shipped during their term to Halifax, 1,783; to New England, 143; to Great Britain, 217; and to Louisbourg, 76—in all, 2,280 chaldrons, when they applied for an extension of time, alleging that they could not raise and dispose of the quantity agreed upon, because, 1. Their works had fallen in; 2. Larger quantities than usual had been brought from Europe; and 3. 'A large quantity of coal had been smuggled from Cape Breton to New England by one Alexander Lee of Louisbourg, which reduced the price so low that it would not pay them.' Being called upon to give an explanation of his reasons for granting permission to Gerrish and his partners by the Secretary of State for the Colonies, Lord William Campbell replied, that having been 'told the coal composed the surface of the island, and could be easily taken away by any adventurer,' he considered it was better to use them and apply the proceeds to the making of roads in the province. If the English Government had adopted the same policy, the valuable mines of Cape Breton would not have been so long suffered to remain unproductive, and the settlement of the island would have made more rapid progress. Before he had been six months in Nova Scotia, Sir William strongly advised Lord Hillsborough, the Secretary of State, to grant land to the people of Louisbourg, who were, 'since the island was annexed to Nova Scotia, obliged to pay the duties of impost and excise established in that province, which they considered a great hardship, as they had not any lots of land or houses granted them there.' He added, if they were allowed to purchase houses and lots, the place would soon become considerable again, 'being much in the way of trade, and a good harbour for the fishery. . . . It will revive a large town now going to ruin, and it will be of benefit to the Revenue, as the people will cheerfully pay the taxes when they have got property there.'

Although Captain Holland's survey of the island was completed in the early part of 1767,[1] and several applications were made for grants of land, it does not appear that any were passed until some years afterwards, or that the people of Louisbourg obtained any absolute titles to their holdings. I could not find a copy of Holland's Plans in the Record Office, but ascertained that the island was laid out in townships or lots of 20,000 acres each. The first applications for grants in 1767 were from—

	Acres.
Lieutenant Richard Shea of the Marines, for	10,000
" Thomas Carroll "	10,000
" John Thompson, late of 93rd Regiment .	10,000
William Mitchell, late surgeon 60th Regiment . .	20,000
Lieutenant Alexander Fowler, late of 74th Regiment .	10,000

And from Sir Edward Hawke, Philip Stevens, Esq., Martin Blade Hawke, Chaloner Hawke, Esq., and George Papps, Esq., for lots Nos. 15, 19, 22, 33, and 60 respectively. At a Council held at St. James's on August 26, 1767, the memorials of these applicants were referred to the Lords Commissioners of Trade and Plantations, to report thereon, but there is no record of the result of their deliberations.

Up to this time, the once celebrated capital of Cape Breton had retained some slight resemblance of its former importance, by the maintenance of a garrison of 300 men; but even this weak prop of its fallen fortunes was rudely upset by the withdrawal of the whole of the troops in 1768, in consequence

[1] On April 16, 1767, Mr. Howard, midshipman of His Majesty's armed ship 'Canceau,' applied to the Lords of Trade for compensation for taking Captain Holland's Survey to England, 'having been at great expense in bringing the Plans,' &c.

of an order of General Gage, the Commander-in-Chief in America, to call in the troops from all the outposts, and to concentrate them in Halifax, to be ready to embark for Boston, where some of those disturbances had occurred which preceded the breaking out of the revolutionary war. The troops composing the garrison of Louisbourg, belonging to the 59th Regiment, under the command of Major Milward, arrived at Halifax on August 14; with them departed a host of small traders who had been living upon their disbursements, and the population of the place was considerably reduced in consequence. Amidst these changes the Government exhibited some consideration for the interests of the remaining inhabitants, as Mr. Francklyn, who acted as Lieutenant-Governor during the temporary absence of Lord William Campbell, was instructed by Lord Hillsborough to 'signify to the inhabitants of the island of Cape Breton the tenderness with which his Majesty considered, and the attention that would be paid, to the improvements they had made under the temporary licences which had been granted to them by the Government of Nova Scotia.'

Subsequently (on September 26) Mr. Francklyn, at the request of Lord Hillsborough, forwarded to England a list of licences of occupation granted in Cape Breton by the Government of Nova Scotia, of which the following is an exact copy:—

To George Cottman, Esq., for 600 acres at Lorambec.

„ William Russell, Esq., for 60 acres at Louisbourg, fishing lots at Baleine and Mainadieu, and 50 acres of land at Little Bras d'Or, with garden, houses, stages and flakes belonging thereto.

„ James Gething and Lawrence Kavanagh, for 500 acres at Little St. Peter's, where they have built a house, storehouses, stages and flakes, and have a large quantity of cattle.

„ John Reilly, for a lot 50 by 100 rods at Mainadieu, where he has built a house, fishing flakes and stages.

„ Captain Antrobus, of the Navy, for a lot of land at the head of the North-east Harbour, where he has built a house, fenced in 8 or 10 acres of land, and was desirous of having 500 acres there.

To Elias Gerrot, late pilot in the Navy, for a lot in a cove beyond the Grand Battery, where he has fenced in 10 acres and built a flake and stage. Gerrot was recommended by the late Admiral Boscawen.

„ Major Robert Milward, of the 59th Regiment, for a lot on the north side of the road leading to Mainadieu, where he had fenced in 15 or 20 acres, built a house and outhouses, and was desirous of having 500 acres.

Mr. Francklyn sent at the same time the following list of parties who had made improvements without any title whatever:—

At Louisbourg.—Lawrence Kavanagh, Thomas Wheeler, Richard Wheeler, Thomas Mortho, William Brimigion, Mathew Roe, Gregory Townsend and William Russell, who had each fenced in small lots of 3 to 5 acres.

At Manadou.—John Gould, Cornelius Bollong, Richard Wheeler, Alexander Ley, John Neale, and Thomas Huxford, who had built dwelling houses, stages, and flakes.

At Baleine.—Thomas Meadoz, Benjamin Cann, and William Gerrot, who had built houses, stages, and flakes.

At Gabarus Bay.—Richard Collins, Edward and Thomas Macdonald, John Clewly, Francis Joice, Peter Jervois, John Perry, and —— Curdo, who had built dwelling-houses and stages.

At Le Brasdor.—James Townsend, John Bagnal, Peter Jermaine, and Boniface Benoit, who had built fishing stages and houses.

At Miré River.—Francis Nairing, a discharged soldier, and Richard Mascall, who had built houses, and made some small improvements.

At Petit de Grat.—Charles Fougier, Charles Duga, Lewis Budro, Joseph Budro, John Peters, Peter Fougier, and Joseph Gaudein, in all 47 Acadian men, women and children, who were recommended by the late Governor

Lawrence, and obtained licences to carry on the fishery in 1763, from Lieutenant-Colonel Tulleskein.

This meagre list embraces all the heads of families in Cape Breton in 1768, according to the best information Mr. Francklyn could obtain; but there is every reason to believe that it was very incorrect, as many families undoubtedly occupied lands and fishing lots in remote and secluded places, who escaped observation. In the course of this year also a number of Acadians who had emigrated to St. Pierre and Miquelon in 1765, came back and settled in the island of Madame, and on the eastern coast of Nova Scotia, where they were allowed to remain upon taking the oath of allegiance to His Majesty. The return of these people produced a very good effect upon the Acadians who had not left the province, as it convinced them that they were much better off in Nova Scotia and Cape Breton, under British rule, than in the French islands, and many of those who had hitherto kept aloof, sent deputations to the Governor requesting permission to take the oath of allegiance.

At the same time (September 26), Francklyn forwarded to Lord Hillsborough a plan of the town of Louisbourg, and on August 10, a minute report on the condition of the houses. According to this report, there were at that date only 142 houses standing in Louisbourg, of which thirteen were in good repair; sixty in tolerable repair· sixty-six in bad repair, the windows, floors, and partitions having been taken away; three in ruins.

Of these, nineteen, which had been used for public purposes, such as the hospital, Governor's, Intendant's, and Judges' residences, victualling office, bakehouses, stables, barracks, and gaol, were constructed of stone and were all standing; all the rest were of wood. Only twenty-six houses were occupied on August 10, viz. :—

1 by Mr. Cottnam, Chief Magistrate.
1 „ William Russell, late Barrack Master.
1 „ F. W. Strasbourger, late Town Adjutant.
2 „ Lawrence Kavanagh, Merchant.
1 „ Mr. Cottnam, for public uses.

1 by Mr. Townsend, late Deputy Paster?
1 „ Mr. Keho, a Fisherman.
1 „ Mr. Wheeler, a Trader.
1 „ Mr. Truman. a Trader.
1 „ William Phipps, Esquire, a Trader.
1 „ Mathew Ro e, a [illegible]
1 „ Monsieur Dion, a Pilot.
1 „ Silvanus Howell, Mariner.
1 „ Roger English, discharged Sergeant-Major, 45th Regiment.
1 „ Mr. Mortho, a discharged Sergeant.
1 „ Charles Martell, discharged Soldier.
1 „ Mr. Diber „
1 „ John Newman, Blacksmith.
1 „ Edward Haro, Tailor.
2 „ Mrs. Burton, a soldier's widow.
2 „ Lydia Thorpe.
2 „ Some French families.

On August 29, Mr. Francklyn wrote to Lord Hillsborough, stating that Mr. Cottnam, the chief magistrate, and such of the inhabitants as had any property, proposed to withdraw in consequence of the removal of the troops, as soon as their private concerns would permit, because 'the greatest part of those in the island are a composition of the dregs of the English and French garrisons, as also of Newfoundland and Nova Scotia, from whom every irregularity and disorder may be apprehended; and as it is necessary to have some officer of Government who also may collect intelligence of what passes in the island and in the neighbourhood of the islands of St. Peter's and Miquelon, as also to preserve as many of the houses from being destroyed as possible, I have, with the advice of His Majesty's Council, promised Mr. Cottnam a salary of 100*l.* per annum until His Majesty's pleasure be known.'

Looking at the above list of occupants of houses at Louisbourg in 1768, comprised mostly of persons who had been in the service of the Government, I cannot help thinking that Mr. Francklyn was, to say the least, rather hasty in stigmatising them as a 'composition of the dregs of the English and French garrisons.' Perhaps he may have referred to the petty traders, grog-sellers, and other loose characters, who had flocked to Louisbourg whilst the garrison remained there; but you may rely upon it, most of the people of that class left with the troops, and that there was no reason for apprehending any irregularities or disorders from the persons above mentioned.

Lord William Campbell, who returned to his government in September, writing to Lord Hillsborough soon after his arrival at Halifax, expressed some apprehension from the total removal of the troops, with reference to the coal mines. He says, 'The removal of the 59th Regiment from Louisbourg, without leaving even a sergeant's guard there, has been partly, and it is feared will be attended with a total, desertion of the inhabitants from that place, for want of the appearance of a military protection; and it must follow that the coal mines in that neighbourhood, which are particularly recommended from home not to be touched, may uninterruptedly be worked by any people who think proper to go there, as the prohibition before proceeded from a fixed guard of troops there.'

I will close this letter with a notice of a discovery made in 1768, which may perhaps stimulate you to try to prove its veracity:—'Some letters from Boston, New England, mention that an immense mine of rock salt had lately been discovered in the isle of Cape Breton, which alone would be sufficient to supply all the northern fisheries!!'[1]

[1] From *Scots Magazine* for June 1768.

LETTER XXII.

1768–1782.

As many of you have friends and relatives in the island of St. John (Prince Edward's Island), it may not be out of place to mention here that a survey of the island, made by Captain Holland, was completed in 1768, and that Michael Francklyn, the acting Governor of Nova Scotia, was instructed to issue grants to applicants. Francklyn not only carried out these instructions, but also proceeded to establish a regular government in the island, by appointing judges, magistrates, and other civil officers, and by erecting courts of common pleas and general sessions of the peace. This energetic action on the part of Francklyn soon attracted a number of settlers from Nova Scotia, New England, and Scotland; applications also were made to the Lords Commissioners of Trade and Plantations, by several noblemen in England, for grants of townships. Francklyn's conduct, however, was not approved by the British Ministry; on the return of Lord William Campbell, he therefore proceeded to England to make such explanations as he considered necessary for his own justification. Meanwhile, the tide of immigration which had set in from Scotland increased yearly in intensity, and the whole island was soon occupied by hardy, industrious Highlanders.

The great rush of applicants for lands in St. John's, probably again directed the attention of speculators to the island of Cape Breton, which, although inferior in point of fertility, possessed many superior advantages over St. John's. In the course of the year 1769, no less than forty-two memorials were sent to His Majesty by officers of the army and navy, lawyers, merchants, and private gentlemen, assigning various reasons for their applications. Almost every applicant asked for a lot or township of 20,000 acres; only four of the whole had the modesty to limit their claims to lots of 10,000 acres each. As a list of the names would occupy a considerable space and afford little interest, I will merely mention three who founded their claims upon the fact of their having been at the siege of Louisbourg in 1758—namely, Edmond Malone, Major in the 47th Regiment; Charles Basset, Lieutenant in the same regiment; and Thomas Timmins, of the Marines. The whole of the memorials were referred by His Majesty, on December 24, 1769, to the Lords Commissioners of Trade and Plantations, to report thereon; but there is not the slightest trace of the result in the Record Office. It is quite evident, nevertheless, that the report was unfavourable, as not one of the individuals who applied ever obtained a grant of land in Cape Breton. If they had obtained all they asked for—800,000 acres, about two-thirds of the whole of the land fit for cultivation in the island—very few of the present inhabitants of Cape Breton, probably, could have called your beautiful island their home.

Although Captain Holland's survey had been long completed, and grants of land had been issued in the neighbouring island of St. John's, the bonâ fide settlers at Louisbourg and other parts of the island, for no assignable reason that I could discover in the Records, were still denied the privilege, or rather right, of obtaining any other title than licences of occupation to the lands they had improved. They were therefore still disqualified to send representatives to the Assembly, not from any fault of their own, but simply because the Government would not give them grants. To remedy this grievance, the House passed a resolution on April 2, 1770, 'That no writ shall issue to the Isle of Breton, because of the want of freeholders to make an election, and that the said isle be deemed to be represented by the members for the county of Halifax, into which it has resolved and become a part thereof as heretofore.' This, you will observe, was no remedy whatever, as the inhabitants had no voice in choosing representatives for the county of Halifax. We may presume, however, that John Butler and Robert Campbell, who took their seats for the county of Halifax when the House met, on June 6, 1771, looked especially after the affairs of Cape Breton.

The coal mines of Cape Breton were at this period entirely in the hands of smugglers and unauthorised persons, who carried off large quantities of coal from the cliffs, and even took possession of the works at Cow Bay. In consequence of information received to this effect, the Governor brought the subject before the Council on May 4, 1770, and stated that, having applied to Lieutenant-Colonel Leslie, commanding His Majesty's troops in the province, and obtained a sufficient force to prevent trespassers on the King's rights for the future, he desired the opinion of the Council as to the measures proper to be taken. 'On which the Council advised that Mr. Cottnam, the chief magistrate at Louisbourg, should be directed to proceed to Cow Bay, and require all persons there to depart immediately, and that he should put the troops into the barracks or houses there belonging to the King, giving them orders to prevent any coals being dug or carried thence without the Governor's special order. Ordered also, that a Proclamation be issued, strictly forbidding all persons to dig or carry away any coals from the Isle of Breton.' In a letter of June 30, Governor Campbell informs Lord Hillsborough that Commodore Hood had provided a conveyance for the troops obtained from Colonel Leslie. He adds, that he had seized more than 500 chaldrons dug at one of the mines during the previous winter by the smugglers, and proposed to bring them to Halifax for the use of the troops.

There is nothing in the Records of the next three years worth transcribing, except perhaps the following entries in the Journals of the Council, which refer to a gentleman who long occupied a prominent and highly respectable position in Cape Breton:—

'At a Council held on November 29, 1773, the Governor submitted several charges taken on oath before George Dawson, Esquire, one of His Majesty's Justices of the Peace, against Lawrence Kavanagh, merchant at Louisbourg, setting forth that he had at several times pulled down the public buildings there and taken away boards, timber, iron, lead, and other materials, and carried them to his own dwelling and converted them to his own use. And he the said Lawrence Kavanagh having been called upon to answer the said charges, said that he had removed the several materials as set forth, but that he had converted them to the use of repairing several of the public buildings, which were then in a ruinous condition. Ordered that the aforesaid charges and informations be referred to the Attorney-General for his opinion thereon.'

'At a Council held on December 8, 1773, the Memorial of Lawrence Kavanagh, merchant and trader at Louisbourg, was submitted by the Governor, setting forth that Lieutenant Dawson of His Majesty's Navy, and commander of an armed vessel stationed at and about Louisbourg, had pressed seamen belonging to vessels in which he was concerned, and had at other times, under pretence of his power as a Custom House officer, stopped and detained his fishing vessels, and as a Justice of the Peace that he had lately solicited the depositions of several persons to the testimony of many false and scandalous assertions tending to calumniate the memorialist and hurt his reputation. And several papers in support of the said charge having been produced by the memorialist, it was ordered that the said Memorial and papers should be laid before Admiral Montague.'

From the next entry we learn that Mr. Kavanagh, about the time named removed from Louisbourg to St. Peter's, where he afterwards resided more than fifty years. November 7, 1774.—'At a Council held this day, on a complaint made by Mr. Cottnam, the chief magistrate at Louisbourg, that several building materials had been removed from Louisbourg to St. Peter's by Mr. Lawrence Kavanagh, also referring for further information to Mr. Hunter, commanding His Majesty's armed vessel, Gaspey, "together with a copy of a deposition to the fact." Ordered that the same be referred to the Attorney-General to report thereon.'

It is highly probable that these charges were brought by the officials named, in consequence of some feud with Mr. Kavanagh, for it was well known that the materials referred to were mere rubbish not worth looking after; this seems to have been the opinion of the Council, for it does not appear from the Records that any further notice was taken of such frivolous charges, and that they were suffered to sink into oblivion.

Lord William Campbell having been promoted to the office of Governor of South Carolina, was succeeded, in June 1774, by Major Francis Legge of the 46th Regiment. Being determined to make himself thoroughly acquainted with the state of the country entrusted to his charge, and of maintaining it in firm allegiance to his sovereign, 'as it was, in his opinion, the only settled province on the sea coast which had preserved itself from the madness and contagion which had overspread all the other of His Majesty's colonies,' Governor Legge ordered a census to be taken, for the purpose of ascertaining how many men were capable of bearing arms in its defence. The arrival of a number of Acadians from the French islands, who had 'squatted' at Isle Madame and St. John's Island at this critical period, caused him some apprehension, being afraid that, in case of a war with France, they would, regardless of the oath of allegiance which they had taken, unite with the Indians, supply them with arms and ammunition, and attack the English settlers. If there really was any just cause for apprehension, it is evident that, with slight external aid, the Island of Cape Breton might easily have been once more restored to France, as the French and Indians greatly outnumbered the English inhabitants. According to the returns sent in to the Governor, the population of the island on October 10, 1774, consisted of—

Persons of French origin	502
Indians	230
Persons of English origin	509
Total	1,241

Of these, 914, including the Indians, were Roman Catholics, and 327 Protestants. The numbers returned for each settlement were—

At Louisbourg	144	Nearly all English.
„ Mainadieu	131	
„ Labrador	30	
„ Baleine	39	
„ Miré	29	
„ Gabarus	47	
„ St. Peter's Bay	186	English and French.
„ Arichat	237	All French.
„ Petit de Grat	168	
	1,011	
Roving bands of Indians	230	
Total	1,241	

The live stock of the island at the same time consisted of 697 horned cattle, 222 sheep, and 553 swine.

The number of vessels owned in the island was 136, mostly small fishing shallops. Dry fish exported in the previous year, 26,020 quintals. Governor Legge's despatches do not give any account of the general trade of the island, but I have obtained from another source[1] the amount of exports from Cape Breton to England, and the imports from England during the ten years ending in 1780:—

	Exports.	Imports.
In 1770	197 0 0	Nil.
„ 1771	14 9 5	Nil.
„ 1772	255 8 7	Nil.
„ 1773	0 16 6	984 6 4
„ 1774	Nil.	321 18 9
„ 1775	Nil.	Nil.
„ 1776	Nil.	164 11 0
„ 1777	567 18 5	Nil.
„ 1778	Nil.	42 0 0
„ 1779	Nil.	22 8 0

This table merely gives a return of the direct trade with England, taken from the Custom House returns; it gives no idea of the general trade of the island, which then, as now, passed chiefly through the port of Halifax. The dry fish alone, as mentioned above, exported in 1773, was 26,020 quintals, worth at least 20,000*l.*

Governor Legge, like his predecessors, did not give a very favourable account of the character of the population of Cape

[1] McPherson's *Annals of Commerce*. London: 1805.

Breton in 1774; he says, 'They were a lawless rabble, and often interrupted the chief magistrate, Mr. Cottnam, in the execution of his duty; they had no grants [which was not their fault], and many of them even had not fishing licences.'

A few last words respecting Mr. Cottnam, who had for more than fifteen years occupied an important position at Louisbourg, will not be out of place here. In the early part of the year 1775, Governor Legge, finding that the Royal instructions, which required that strict accounts should be kept of all the receipts and payments of the public money, had not been carried out, instituted a searching inquiry into the financial affairs of the province. With this object he appointed Commissioners 'to make a full examination of all receipts and payments made in the Treasury, and to examine all persons employed as collectors.' Mr. Cottnam's accounts were duly examined; and the Commissioners, after a close investigation, reported that there was a balance of 272*l.* 6*s.* 6*d.* due to that officer. Mr. Cottnam continued to hold his various appointments at Louisbourg until his death, in 1780; but it seems his claims upon the Treasury had not then been settled, for his widow petitioned the House of Assembly, soon after his death, for payment of the sum of 280*l.* due by the province to her late husband. Nothing can more strikingly illustrate the rapid decline of Louisbourg after the removal of the Governor, in 1761, and the annexation of the island to Nova Scotia, in 1763, than the accumulation of so many offices in the hands of Mr. Cottnam. Owing to the gradual departure of such persons as could be entrusted with places of responsibility, Mr. Cottnam was appointed to the offices of—

Justice of the Peace	Jan. 24, 1764
Judge of Court of Common Pleas	June 15, „
Deputy to grant Passports	May 20, 1766
Custodian of Fortifications and Public Buildings	July 26, 1768
Stipendiary Magistrate	Aug. 10, „
Naval Officer and Collector of Excise	Sept. 14, „
Major-Commandant of Militia	Sept. 5, 1771
Commissioner for assessing taxes for support of Militia	Dec. 5, 1775

We have now arrived at a momentous epoch in the history of the British colonies—the breaking out of the American

Revolution. As all the events of the War of Independence must be quite familiar to you, I shall say nothing concerning them, except so far as they affected Cape Breton, which, happily, owing to its insignificance at that period, suffered less from the depredations and attacks of the enemy's privateers than the adjacent colonies. Energetic measures were of course taken by the Governor of Nova Scotia for the defence of the province, not only against external, but internal enemies also; for it was well known that there were many disaffected persons scattered through the country, who had originally come from New England, disposed to aid the revolted colonies.[1] On August 26, 1775, a Proclamation was issued, ordering light infantry companies to be raised throughout the province. The total number of men required was only 1,010, of which 'Cape Breton Isle and Isle Madame' were each ordered to raise 'two companies of Acadians and others well affected,' of 50 men each—200 in all. It cannot escape your notice that Cape Breton, including Isle Madame, was not fairly treated in this apportionment. The whole population of the island, exclusive of the Indians, according to Governor Legge's census in 1774, was only 1,011,[2] whilst that of Nova Scotia Proper was, at the lowest estimate, 20,000;[3] and yet the latter was called upon to furnish only 800 men, or 1 in every 25, whilst the former was required to supply 200 men, or 1 in every 5. On December 5 following, an Act was passed imposing a tax to be raised by assessment for the payment and support of the militia. The Commissioners appointed to make the assessment in Cape Breton were George Cottnam, William Russell, and —— Wheeler.

[1] 'Partisans of the American cause were more numerous in Nova Scotia than in Canada. They had formerly petitioned Congress, and had recently opened a communication with Washington. The distance, isolation, and weakness of Nova Scotia made assistance impracticable; but more than once, at subsequent periods, Massachusetts was solicited to aid in revolutionising that province.'—*Hildreth.*

[2] The Rev. I. Quinan, P.P. of Sydney, informs me that in 1775 or '76 fourteen Acadian families crossed over from St. John's Island to Chetican, and settled there. This accession, therefore, is not worth taking into the account of the population.

[3] The population of Nova Scotia is set down at 18,300 in 1772, in a Report sent to the Board of Trade. As many families left Boston for Halifax soon after the troubles began, and a great number after the battle of Bunker's Hill, on June 17, 1775, 20,000 must be greatly under the mark.

A great number of Loyalists left Boston on March 17, 1776, when it was evacuated by the British troops, and went to Nova Scotia, where they obtained free grants of land, but I cannot learn that any reached Cape Breton.

Not only was Cape Breton required to furnish five times as many men for the light infantry corps as the rest of the province, in proportion to its population, but she was called upon to supply fuel for the use of the troops at Halifax and the settlers on the western coast. As the digging of coal had been expressly forbidden by the King, the House of Assembly petitioned His Majesty, and obtained the permission required, as it is stated in Mr. Murdoch's recent 'History of Nova Scotia' that forty men belonging to Colonel Legge's regiment were employed digging coal at Spanish River in 1777. Yet, at the same time, will it be believed that the British Government refused to sanction an Act passed by the Legislature, permitting 'any persons inhabiting the island of Cape Breton, and such as are employed in the fishery, to cut down and use such wood as shall be necessary for fuel and the purposes of the fishery.' Certainly this was a strange proof of the 'tenderness' entertained by His Majesty for his subjects in Cape Breton! (See p. 367).

Although the coasts of Nova Scotia and Newfoundland were infested with rebel privateers, as they were then styled, the inhabitants of Cape Breton were not molested. St. John's Island, however, was not so fortunate, for the crews of two schooners belonging to Marblehead actually had the audacity to land at Charlotte Town and carry off Mr. Caldbeck, the Commandant, and some other officers of the Government. To guard against such outrages in future, a ship of war was stationed at Canceau.

The unsettled state of affairs, in consequence of the war, did not deter men of capital from embarking in promising speculations in the loyal colonies. In the year 1777, an association was organised in London, called the 'Acadia Company,' for settling and improving lands in Nova Scotia, and carrying on a large traffic between that colony and the mother country. Sir Herbert Mackworth, M.P., who was the prime mover in the speculation, in a Memorial to the Lords of Trade, dated December 16, stated that the Company had subscribed 20,000*l.*, with which they proposed to purchase the claims of other parties to 40,000 acres of land in Nova Scotia, and intended to carry on a fishery at Isle Madame, of which they asked for a grant, to enable them to carry their intentions into active operation. As the British Government had for some unknown reason refused to grant any land in Cape Breton, it is not likely that the application of the Acadia Company would have been successful, even if it had not been opposed by some Jersey merchants who had long before established fishing stations on the island. As soon as it became known that the Acadia Company was endeavouring to obtain a grant of Isle Madame, Mr. Robin, one of the parties concerned, wrote to Mr. George Lemprière in London, requesting him to do all in his power to stop the grant, stating that, 'he (Robin) was the first adventurer in the island, in 1764,' when only twelve families of Acadians were living there; that in the following year he formed an establishment upon the island, and in a short time other parties followed his example. He added, that thirteen vessels, navigated by 300 men, were employed in the preceding year in the fishery business; and that sixty families, owning fifty shallops of eight tons each, built by themselves, now lived upon the island, all occupied in the cod fishery. In conclusion, perhaps to alarm the Acadia Company, he stated that 'the people were in general industrious but keen enough to take in strangers who are not aware of them.' From a subsequent letter, of July 9, 1778, it appears the Jersey merchants had at that time fishing establishments at Chetican, on the north-west coast, and that the fishermen employed there were in the habit of bringing all their shallops and fishing gear to Arichat to lay them up for the winter. It is stated also, in the same letter, that the fishermen had been so much disturbed by the American privateers, that only two vessels had been sent out to Arichat in 1778, and that, if the troubles continued, their establishments there would probably be altogether abandoned. For these reasons the Acadia Company gave up their project; but the

Jersey merchants held their ground in spite of 'the troubles,' and, it is believed, have carried on a lucrative trade with the Cape Breton fishermen up to this day, but not upon such a large scale as in former times.

The English fishermen, or rather the merchants who furnished them with supplies, were no doubt greatly annoyed by the New England privateers, who were well acquainted with every harbour and creek in Nova Scotia and Newfoundland; but when France openly espoused the cause of the revolted colonies in 1777, and acknowledged the independence of the United States in the following year, their troubles were greatly increased. It is true, England had a sufficient naval force to cope with the French fleet under the Count d'Estaing, in American waters, but detached cruisers prowled about, keeping the fishermen in a constant state of alarm. You must not suppose that France espoused the cause of the Americans from disinterested motives only; she still looked forward with the hope of recovering Acadié and Cape Breton, as well as a larger share in the fisheries. When, therefore, the American Congress sent plenipotentiaries to the European Courts in 1778, with a proposal that Nova Scotia, Cape Breton, and half of Newfoundland should be annexed to the United States, and the other half of Newfoundland to France, excluding Great Britain from any share whatever in the fisheries,[1] the proposition does not seem to have been received with much favour, as France naturally supposed she was entitled to a larger share of the spoil. Nothing more seems to have been said about the matter, as no attempts were made by France and the United States to take Nova Scotia and Cape Breton. Cape Breton was rarely visited during the revolutionary war, by either the American or French cruisers, because it probably offered no temptation to the privateers. Its shores were, however, occasionally visited by French ships of war, but no attempt was made to establish a footing in the island. In the year 1781, a smart action was fought off the mouth of Spanish River, between two French frigates and a squadron of small English ships of war engaged in convoying

[1] McPherson's *Annals of Commerce*.

sixteen vessels to the mines to procure a supply of coal for the troops at Halifax. The English squadron, comprising the 'Charlestown' frigate, of 28 guns, Captain Evans; the sloops 'Allegiance' and 'Vulture,' of 16 guns each, Captains Phipps and George; the armed transport 'Vernon,' with some troops of the 70th Regiment on board, going to work at the coal-mines; and the cutter 'Little Jack,' of 6 guns, had nearly reached their destination on the evening of July 21, when they were discovered and chased by two large French frigates — 'L'Astrée,' Captain La Perouse, and 'L'Hermione,' Captain De la Touche, of 44 guns each. Finding that the enemy's ships were fast overhauling him, Captain Evans, having skilfully covered the merchant ships, to allow them to get into Spanish River in safety, formed his little squadron in line of battle and waited for the attack of the French frigates. The action commenced at 8 P.M. and was fought with little advantage to either side, until the 'Little Jack,' having been separated from her consorts, was obliged to strike; but the others maintained an incessant and well-directed fire until dark, when the French ships sheered off, taking their prize with them. Captain Evans was unfortunately killed by a cannon-shot early in the action, when Mr. Mackay, the officer next in rank on board the 'Charlestown,' continued the action with great skill and bravery. The British loss was rather severe; besides her Captain, the 'Charlestown' had seven men killed and twenty-nine wounded; the 'Allegiance,' one killed and five wounded; the 'Vulture,' one killed and two wounded; the 'Vernon,' seven killed and six wounded; and the 'Little Jack,' two killed and one wounded. The night being luckily very dark, and the English ships greatly shattered in the unequal contest, Captain Phipps made sail with his little squadron to the eastward. At daylight next morning, the enemy's ships not being in sight, the English squadron bore up for Halifax, where it arrived in safety, but in a crippled condition.[1] A recent French writer[2] gives a dif-

[1] Beatson's *Naval and Military History of Great Britain*, and other English authors.

[2] Hennequin's *Biographie maritime des Marins célèbres*. Paris: 1837.

ferent version of the affair; he says the English squadron was composed of six ships of war, 'dont une frégate de vingt-huit canons, le "Charlestown," à bord de laquelle était arboré le signe du commandement; les cinq autres étaient des corvettes de vingt-quatre, vingt et dix-huit canons. Les capitaines La Perouse[1] et La Touche-Treville n'hésitèrent point à les attaquer, malgré leur supériorité. Il était sept heures du soir lorsque le feu commença. Après une heure environ du combat le plus opiniâtré, le "Charlestown" et le "Jack" amenèrent leur pavillon, les quatre autres prennent la fuite, et le convoi fut dispersé.' This account, you will observe, is not correct; the armament of the English squadron consisted of only 75 guns instead of 150, and the 'Charlestown' was not captured, as therein stated. The cutter 'Little Jack' either escaped or was recaptured not very long after the action, for it is stated in Murdoch's 'History of Nova Scotia,' 'that the provincial armed cutter 'Little Jack,' 6 guns, commanded by R. P. Tonge, which had taken part in the action in which Captain Evans was killed, left Halifax on October 6 for Quebec, and on the 10th, as she was entering the Gut of Canceau, was met by two American privateers belonging to Marblehead. Tonge ran into Petit de Grat, where he anchored, and brought a spring upon his cable, and engaged them. He got one 9-pounder on shore on an eminence, and used it effectively. He captured one of them, and drove the other off. He then paroled all his prisoners but one, and on the 12th sailed for Quebec with his prize.'

The unhappy contest which had been raging in America by

[1] This was the same La Perouse who in 1785 had chief command of the frigates 'L'Astrolabe' and 'Boussole' on a voyage of discovery round the world. Nothing whatever was heard of the fate of the expedition, which left Botany Bay on February 5, 1788, until the year 1813, when some fragments of the wrecks were discovered by the captain of an English brig upon the Isle of Vanikoro, three degrees to the northward of the New Hebrides. It is a singular coincidence that the two celebrated navigators, Cook and La Perouse, one of whom was engaged in the destruction of the French ships in Louisbourg Harbour in 1758, and the other in the action off Spanish River in 1781, both perished on their voyages of discovery in the Pacific Ocean. The English Government supplied La Perouse with the nautical instruments which had been used by Cook on his voyages.

land and sea, for nearly seven years, was now drawing to a close, the great majority of the British nation being convinced that there was no chance of reducing the revolted colonies to subjection. A new ministry, strongly opposed to a continuation of the war, having been formed, negotiations for a peace were opened, and preliminary articles signed at Paris on November 30, 1782. Soon after the restoration of peace, several changes were made in the loyal colonies, of which the most important for our consideration was the separation of Cape Breton from the Government of Nova Scotia—a subject of too much importance to be discussed at the tail of this letter; I will therefore defer it to my next.

LETTER XXIII.

1783–1793.

IMMEDIATELY after the establishment of peace between Great Britain and the United States, a great number of Loyalists flocked to Nova Scotia, where the Governor was instructed to give them every encouragement. Free grants of land were offered to all, and in addition a daily allowance in the shape of money and provisions to the most needy; but, for reasons not stated, the Governor was strictly forbidden 'upon any pretence whatever to make any grants in the island of Cape Breton, or in any other island comprehended within his government, without express orders for that purpose.' In consequence of this order, many of the refugees, who were desirous of settling in Cape Breton, were obliged to remain in Nova Scotia. This policy, whatever may have been its object, was persevered in until 1784, when the Honourable Thomas Townshend, just raised to the peerage under the title of Lord Sydney, was appointed Secretary of State for the Colonies. On the accession of Lord Sydney to office, the new Ministry reversed the policy of its predecessors, and separated Cape Breton from the government of Nova Scotia. At the same time, the island of St. John's, and all that part of Nova Scotia lying to the northward of the Bay of Fundy, were erected into separate governments, the latter under the name of New Brunswick. Lieutenant-Governors were appointed to Cape Breton and St. John's islands, but the Governor of Nova Scotia was to continue Captain-General and Governor-in-Chief over the new colonies. To meet the requirements of the new Governments, a fresh set of instructions was issued by His Majesty to Governor Parr, on August 26, from which I will now give you the substance, in abbreviated paragraphs and extracts specially relating to Cape Breton. By these instructions, Governor Parr was directed: 1. To appoint nine members of Council. 2. To administer the usual oaths and declarations to the members of the Council, and to the judges or office-holders in the island. 3. To give copies of these instructions to the Council of Cape Breton, or of such parts as he might deem convenient for His Majesty's service. 4. To relieve Cape Breton from all interference of the Assembly of Nova Scotia, Parr was ordered 'not to assent to any law which shall be passed in our province of Nova Scotia, which shall extend, or be deemed or construed to extend, to our island of Cape Breton under colour or pretence that our said island is included in our commission to you, and is thereby part of your government of Nova Scotia.' 6. 'And whereas the situation and circumstances of our island of Cape Breton will not at present admit the calling of an Assembly, you, our Lieutenant-Governor of our said island shall, until it appears proper to call such Assembly, in the mean time make such rules and regulations, by the advice of our Council, for the said island, as shall appear to be necessary for the peace, order, and good government thereof, taking care that nothing may be passed or done that shall any way tend to affect the life, limb, or liberty of the subject, or to the imposing of any duties or taxes, and that all such rules and regulations be transmitted by the first opportunity, after they are passed and made, for our approbation or disallowance.' 7. It would appear that convicts were at that time occasionally sent out to the colonies, as it was ordered that 'you do not give any assent to, or pass any Act whatsoever for imposing duties on any importation of any felons from this kingdom in the province or islands under your government.' 8. Authorises the Governor of Nova Scotia to hear appeals from any of the Courts of Common Law in Cape Breton. 9. The order forbidding the passing of grants must have been revoked, as full instructions were sent respecting the conditions of all future grants, one being, that 'reservations shall be made to us, our heirs and successors, of all coals, and also all mines of gold, silver, copper and lead, which shall be discovered upon such lands. 10. Free grants are to be given to reduced officers of the army, and of provincial corps, who had served in the United States. And lastly, a strict friendship and correspondence should be cultivated and maintained with the Indians of Nova Scotia and Cape Breton, that they might be induced to become good subjects; and for this end interviews should be held from time to time with the heads of the tribes, promising them friendship and protection. Copies of these instructions, which may justly be styled the Royal Charter of Cape Breton and St. John's, were sent to the Lieutenant-Governors of those islands, who were at the same time informed that, in the case of the death of the Governor of Nova Scotia, the senior commanding in either of the islands should succeed him pro tempore; and in case of the death or absence of either of the Lieutenant-Governors, the eldest Councillor residing in the island should administer the government thereof.

On May 29, 1784, Governor Parr was notified by Lord Sydney that a 'Lieutenant-Governor with a suitable civil establishment would be placed upon the island of Cape Breton,' and on July 7 following, that Major Frederic Wallet Desbarres had been appointed by His Majesty to that office. The sum of 1,750*l.* was also voted by Parliament on August 5 of the same year, for 'defraying the charges of the Civil Establishment of His Majesty's island of Cape Breton.' Desbarres sailed from Portsmouth in September, in the ship 'Blenheim,' which had been chartered to carry out provisions and stores to Halifax, where he arrived on November 16, and immediately proceeded to Cape Breton. As Major Desbarres was the first civil governor of the island under the new régime, you will no doubt be glad to hear what were his claims to such a responsible situation. He has himself furnished us with a detailed account of his services, in a work which he published after his removal from Cape Breton, from which I have gleaned the following particulars:—

Mr. Desbarres first embarked for America in 1756, being then a lieutenant in the 60th Regiment, and was for some time employed in raising recruits in Pennsylvania and Maryland,

and in disciplining a corps of field artillery. In 1757, with a small detachment of volunteers he was sent in pursuit of a band of Indians which had plundered the village of Schenectady, on the frontier of New York, and scalped several of the inhabitants. Overtaking and coming upon them by surprise, in the night, he routed the Indians and made prisoners of some of their chiefs. He then established a post in the heart of the forest, where he remained three months, and kept the savages in subjection. During the remainder of the campaign of that year, he served under Lord Howe near Lake George, and was employed to reconnoitre and report upon the state of the French Works at Ticonderoga. In 1758 he distinguished himself at Louisbourg by seizing an entrenchment of the enemy, which greatly facilitated the debarkation of the army, and towards the close of the siege opened a sap at the foot of the glacis, with such judgment and promptitude that General Wolfe brought his conduct under the notice of the King, who ordered him to attend Wolfe as an engineer in the celebrated expedition against Quebec. On the field of battle, upon the Heights of Abraham, in 1759, Desbarres was in the act of reporting to General Wolfe an order he had just executed, when that gallant hero received his mortal wound. In 1760 and 1761 he served in Canada, and, after its conquest, was sent to Nova Scotia to make plans and estimates of fortifying the dockyard and harbour of Halifax. In 1762 he served in the capacities of Engineer and Quarter-master-General, in the expedition under Colonel Amherst for the recapture of St. John's, Newfoundland. During a period of ten years, commencing in 1763, Desbarres was employed in making surveys of the coasts and harbours of Nova Scotia and Cape Breton, and during the succeeding ten years in preparing and adapting these surveys for publication. As his promotion had been stopped whilst he was engaged upon these surveys, the Government, taking into consideration his long and valuable services, appointed him Lieutenant-Governor of Cape Breton—an appointment which in the end proved rather a punishment than reward, as it was intended to be.

The knowledge which Desbarres had acquired of the geography of Cape Breton, whilst engaged in making his survey of its coasts and harbours, enabled him to fix upon the most suitable place for the site of its future capital, immediately after his arrival there in November 1784. Louisbourg, it is true, possessed the advantage of an open harbour all the year round; but its situation was in other respects so objectionable, that there could be no question of the superior capabilities of the place chosen by Desbarres—the peninsula at the head of the south arm of Spanish River, one of the safest and most capacious harbours in British America. Here, accordingly, Desbarres determined to establish the seat of government, which he called Sydney, in honour of the Secretary of State, by whose advice, it was supposed, Cape Breton had been severed from Nova Scotia.

This decision gave the finishing blow to Louisbourg, which had been rapidly declining ever since the garrison was withdrawn, in 1768. The few respectable inhabitants who had clung to its falling fortunes in the hope of better days soon abandoned it, and Louisbourg dwindled down, in the course of a few years, into a mere fishing village of the smallest dimensions, such as you will find it at the present day. Its present condition has been well described by Montgomery Martin, in his 'History of the British Colonies':—'The ruins of the once formidable batteries, with wide broken gaps (blown up by gunpowder), present a melancholy picture of past energy. The strong and capacious magazine, once the deposit of immense quantities of munitions of war, is still nearly entire, but, hidden by the accumulation of earth and turf, now affords a commodious shelter for flocks of peaceful sheep, which feed around the burial ground where the remains of many a gallant Frenchman and patriotic Briton are deposited; while beneath the clear cold wave may be seen the vast sunken ships of war, whose very bulk indicates the power enjoyed by the Gallic nation, ere England became mistress of her colonies on the shores of the Western Atlantic. Desolation now sits with a ghastly smile around the once formidable bastions—all is silent except the loud reverberating ocean, as it rolls its tremendous surges along the rocky beach, or the bleating of the scattered sheep, as with tinkling bells they return in the dusky solitude of eve to their singular folds; while the descendant of some heroic Gaul, whose ancestors fought and bled in endeavouring to prevent the noble fortress of his sovereign being laid prostrate before the prowess of mightier Albion, may be observed wandering among these time-honoured ruins, and mentally exclaiming, in the language of the Bard of Erin:—

On Louisbourg's heights where the fisherman strays,
When the clear cold eve's declining,
He sees the war ships of other days
In the wave, beneath him, shining;
Thus shall memory often in dreams sublime,
Catch a glimpse of the days that are over,
And sighing look back through the vista of time,
For the long faded glories they cover!

As soon as it became known that a Lieutenant-Governor was to be sent to Cape Breton, and that grants of land would be issued, as in the other provinces, many persons directed their attention towards the island. One of the first was Abraham Cuyler, Esq., formerly Mayor of Albany, then residing in London, who laid before the King a memorial dated February 21, 1784, in which he stated that he himself and many other persons who had been deprived of their property on account of their loyalty, had removed to Canada in 1782, and were desirous of obtaining grants of land in Cape Breton, with the intention of settling there. This memorial having been favourably received, a number of persons, styling themselves the 'Associated Loyalists,' sailed in three vessels for Cape Breton, under the charge of Colonel Peters, Captain Jonathan Jones, and Mr. Robertson, late officers in the corps of Royal Rangers, and associates of Mr. Cuyler, where they arrived about October 28. About one hundred and forty persons came to Cape Breton by these vessels, furnished with clothing and provisions by the British Government, under the charge of Captain Jones and Mr. Alexander Haire. Some of these persons settled near St. Peter's, others at Baddeck, and the rest, who had gone direct to Louisbourg, were there met by Mr. Cuyler, lately arrived from England. As Lieutenant-

Governor Desbarres had not then reached Cape Breton, these last[1] were obliged to remain all winter at Louisbourg. The houses were in such a ruinous condition that Mr. Cuyler was obliged to send a vessel to Mirá to obtain wood to repair them, which was unfortunately lost in a snow-storm, when all on board perished. Some few of these immigrants settled at Louisbourg, but the greater part went with the Governor in the following spring to Sydney, where they were employed for some time in clearing the woods and erecting houses for themselves and the Government. As soon as the woods were cut down and burnt, the town was marked out by Mr. Tait, and barracks were commenced for the reception of six companies of the 33rd Regiment, which had arrived from Halifax under the command of Lieutenant-Colonel Yorke. The military staff comprised a Town Adjutant, Barrack Master, Commissary of Stores and Provisions, Chaplain, Surgeon, Assistant Surgeon, and Commissary of Musters, all of whom, together with the troops, had to camp out until winter. Houses were also begun for the officers of Government, but these, as well as the Governor himself, had long to reside in shanties of the meanest description.

About eight hundred persons arrived, and settled in various parts of the island in the early part of the summer. It is stated by Desbarres that an accession of 3,397 speedily followed the publication of his proclamation on September 1, describing the natural advantages of the island, and offering a liberal supply of provisions for three years to immigrants, with clothing for themselves and their families, lumber and materials for farm buildings, and tools and implements for clearing land. Many valuable settlers were induced in consequence to come to Cape Breton; but it is to be feared the very liberal terms offered in the proclamation also brought in a number of dissolute, idle characters, well satisfied to live upon the bounty of

[1] Amongst them was the ancestor of the Lorways, a family well and favourably known in Cape Breton. Mr. Cuyler says, in a letter addressed from Louisbourg to the Under Secretary of State, that 'Lorway and Grant, two Loyalists, refused to admit Richard Mandeville into their quarters, and that he consequently stopped their rations.' He adds, as there was no custom-house officer there, some of the inhabitants retailed spirituous liquors and caused disturbances.

the Government so long as they were not obliged to make any exertions for their own support.

The great rush of immigrants, and the bustling scene presented by so many people busily engaged in erecting barracks, storehouses and dwellings, seem quite to have turned the head of the Governor, and made him fancy that Cape Breton would soon eclipse all the neighbouring colonies. From the very first he appears to have imbibed an idea that the people of Nova Scotia were jealous of Cape Breton, and looked with dissatisfaction at its rising importance. Writing on August 17 to the Under Secretary of State he says, 'New settlers are coming in fast; the New England people do not like the settling of the island of Cape Breton at all; they know it will be the loss of every advantage they derive from the fishery. Nova Scotia is jealous, and don't wish with thorough sincerity the success of this Government, lest its growing importance and value should raise it to the first rank amongst His Majesty's and the national favourites.' Desbarres seems to have imagined that he possessed vice-regal powers, as he instructed Lieutenant Graham to hoist a pennant upon the armed brig 'St. Peter's,' employed in carrying coals to Halifax. This notion was, however, soon dispelled by Commodore Sawyer, who wrote to Desbarres on July 13, informing him that Captain Stanhope of H.M.S. 'Mercury' had seized the 'St. Peters,' and that he (Commodore Sawyer) being by virtue of his commission Chief Commander of H.M.'s ships in British America, could not permit any other person to commission vessels and appoint commanders.

Being required to appoint a Council to advise him on all important matters, the Lieutenant-Governor in the first instance named the following gentlemen, who were duly sworn in:—Richard Gibbons, Chief Justice, President; David Mathews, Attorney-General; William Smith, Military Surgeon; Thomas Moncreiff, Fort Adjutant; J. E. Boisseau, Deputy Commissary of Musters; Rev. Benjamin Lovell, Military Chaplain. Having subsequently quarrelled with Lieutenant-Colonel Yorke, the Commandant of the garrison, Desbarres then discovered that it was incompatible with the service of the

Crown for military officers to hold seats in the Council, and suggested that they had better resign. Only two of the officers acted upon this suggestion—Moncreiff and Lovell—whose places were filled up on December 20, by the appointment of Alexander Haire and George Rogers. At the same time, Thomas Uncle, William Brown, and John Wilkinson were sworn in councillors, which made the Council complete in number, according to the Royal instructions.

The officers of the civil establishment, all paid by the British Government, were—Richard Gibbons, Chief Justice, late Attorney-General of Nova Scotia; David Mathews, Attorney-General; Abraham Cuyler, Clerk of Council, Provincial Secretary and Registrar of Grants, &c.; Thomas Hurd, Surveyor-General; William Brown, Comptroller of Customs; George Moore, Naval Officer; Thomas Uncle, Postmaster; ———, Provost-Marshal. The coal mines on Spanish River were reopened under the directions of the Lieutenant-Governor, and worked on Government account. Nearly all the new settlers were of course employed chiefly in providing shelter against the coming winter; but, nevertheless, some enterprising individuals prosecuted the fisheries with success. The value of the exports from the ports of Sydney, Mainadieu, Louisbourg, St. Peter's, and Arichat, in the year 1785 exceeded 40,000*l.* sterling, the principal articles being

30,580 Quintals of Fish	255 Moose and Caribou Skins.
174 Barrels „	87 Beaver and Otter „
304 „ Oil.	163 Martin and Mink „
1,190 Chaldrons of Coal.	38 Fox and Wild Cat „

In addition to these, considerable quantities of fish were exported from L'Indienne (Lingan), St. Ann's, Port Hood, Gabarus, and L'Ardois, of which no returns were sent in.

The young colony was reduced to great straits during the first winter, for want of provisions. Finding that there was not a sufficient stock on hand, Desbarres says he applied to the Governor of Nova Scotia for a supply, and was refused, because the latter 'had an aversion to the measure of erecting Cape Breton, formerly included within the jurisdiction of his province, into a separate government, and, together with some of the officers of his civil establishment and mercantile men long used to enjoy a monopoly of trade in Nova Scotia, seemed hurt by its dismemberment, expecting that their perquisites and exclusive profits would be reduced. Accordingly, in order to frustrate the measure, they depreciated the natural advantages of the island, discouraged the accession of settlers, intercepted the supplies for its support, and predicted that the infant colony would be broken up the first winter.' He then goes on to say that it had been preconcerted at Halifax that Colonel Yorke, the Commandant at Sydney, should take possession of the supplies sent out from England in the ship 'President,' specially for the relief of the settlers in the autumn of 1785, and that Colonel Yorke had accordingly refused to allow the provisions to be taken out of the military storehouse, where they had been put for safe keeping.[1] Whoever was to blame, it is quite certain the colonists were reduced to such straits in the winter of 1785–86, that the Governor, with the advice of his Council, decided upon sending a party to seize a cargo of provisions on board a vessel from Quebec, ice-bound in Arichat harbour. Instructions were given to the party 'to obtain the cargo by purchase, impress, or any means possible;' but the master having agreed to sell both cargo and vessel, she was cut out of the ice and taken round to Louisbourg, from whence the provisions were carried on sledges to Sydney. This seasonable acquisition relieved the settlers for the winter, but did not allay the feud between the Governor and Commandant. A long correspondence ensued between the Governor and the authorities in England, and the bills drawn by the former for provisions were dishonoured, because it was alleged that he had given a large quantity of provisions to persons who were not entitled to them. The Governor therefore determined to send the Chief Justice—Mr. Gibbons—to England

[1] Lieutenant-Colonel Yorke acted upon orders received from Major-General Campbell at Halifax, who instructed him on November 17 to give no provisions out of the military stores, except to the troops, or such loyalists and disbanded soldiers as should have orders to receive them from him (Major-General Campbell). In consequence, the 40,000 rations sent out in the 'President,' and reshipped to Sydney by the brigantine 'Brandywine,' were taken possession of by Colonel Yorke.—*Records.*

in the following spring, to rebut the charges brought against him. On August 2, Mr. Gibbons addressed the Under-Secretary of State, asking for an interview for the purpose of showing that 'unparalleled oppositions, contempts, and violence had been given by the officers of His Majesty's 33rd Regiment to the laws of the land, the King's courts of justice, the magistracy and executive civil officers in the island of Cape Breton.' The mission of the Chief Justice was not successful; for we learn by a letter addressed by Lord Sydney to Desbarres, on November 30, 1786, that he had laid the despatches received by the Chief Justice before the King, and that 'His Majesty had in various instances observed a disposition in you to encourage a disunion of affection between his subjects residing on the island of Cape Breton and those in the province of Nova Scotia. From whatever your suspicion of the jealousy of the latter of the increasing importance of Cape Breton may have been entertained, your proceedings upon these occasions appear to me injudicious, and likely in their consequences to be productive of very mischievous effects.' Referring to the constant disputes with the military, and the complaints in consequence made against him, he says, 'Many doubts have been entertained of the rectitude of your conduct, or at least of your prudence and discretion, which neither the reasoning contained in your despatches, nor the information given by the Chief Justice, are sufficient to remove. Upon these accounts His Majesty has thought it fit that I should signify to you his Royal commands for your return to England as soon as possible, to give an account of your proceedings . . . leaving the island in the charge of the senior councillor until such time as you may return thither, or that His Majesty may determine upon naming a successor to you.' With respect to his accounts, he adds, 'that charges were inserted of a nature which, consistently with your duty to the public, you ought to have discountenanced instead of promoting, and that purchases of provisions and other supplies were made by you for the use of persons whose situations did not entitle them to such an indulgence, whereby a considerable expense has been unnecessarily incurred.'

Governor Desbarres, seeing clearly that his reign in Cape Breton would soon terminate, made good use of his time until his successor arrived in October 1787. His liberal gifts of rations to all comers, whether entitled or not to that indulgence, having made him popular with the people generally, an address dated March 1, 1786, signed by 140 inhabitants of Sydney, was presented to him, approving highly of his conduct and complaining of the treatment he had received from the military; and on the 8th of the same month seventy-eight Acadians, chiefly of the Isle Madame, thanked him for his attention to their spiritual wants, and asked for the remission of certain taxes upon their shallops, which he graciously conceded. Desirous of gratifying the settlers, a great number of grants, previously promised, were issued in various parts of the island to Loyalists, disbanded soldiers, and many other applicants, and one tract of 100,000 acres to Jotham White and 120 families of Loyalists from New Hampshire. As the greatest part of this grant, commonly known as the 'Mirá Grant,' was never settled, it was subsequently escheated.

The only incidents worthy of mention during the years 1786 and 1787, previous to Desbarres's departure from Cape Breton, were—the arrival of the 42nd Regiment, commanded by Lieutenant-Colonel Graham, in 1786, to replace the 33rd, removed to Halifax; the appointment of Archibald C. Dodd (who afterwards became Chief Justice) to the Clerkship of the Council; of Alexander Haire to the office of Surveyor-General, in the place of Thomas Hurd, suspended; of Patrick Rooney Nugent to be Deputy-Surveyor of the island; of Abraham Cuyler to be Comptroller of Customs, *vice* William Brown, deceased; and of the Reverend Ranna Cossit to the incumbency of St. George's Church, for the erection of which Parliament granted 500*l.* in addition to the sum of 2,050*l.* for the charges of the Civil Establishment of the island in 1786. Jonathan Jones, John Ley, —— Ferrers, and Hugh Watts, were appointed magistrates for the District of Louisbourg (which included Sydney and Baddeck); and Niel Robertson, Francis Murphy, and John Higgins, for the District of St. Peter's. Several ordinances were passed by the Governor and

Council, of which the most important was that for establishing a militia in the island. Some changes also were made in the composition of the Council from time to time, but it would occupy too much space to give them in detail.

Nothing of importance occurred during the remainder of Desbarres's adminstration until October 11, 1787, when Lieutenant-Colonel Macormick, who had been appointed to succeed him, arrived at Sydney. Desbarres immediately proceeded to England and demanded an investigation into his conduct, but this was never granted, though supported by Sir Herbert Mackworth and other influential persons. The Ministry having refused to pay the bills which he had drawn, he was obliged to retire for a time to Jersey to avoid being arrested by the parties who had furnished supplies of provisions ordered by him for the starving settlers. In wading through the voluminous documents relating to the transactions of many years subsequent to his removal from Cape Breton, I repeatedly came across letters from Desbarres to the Ministry, demanding redress for his losses, but I could not ascertain that his claims were ever satisfied. I cannot but think that Governor Desbarres received scant justice from the British Government of that day; he was wrong, perhaps, in giving rations indiscriminately to all the settlers, but surely he would have been much more blameable had he refused to supply them in their urgent necessity; if he erred at all, he erred in the cause of humanity. Colonel Desbarres subsequently removed to Halifax, where he died on October 27, 1824, in the 103rd year of his age.

The new Lieutenant-Governor, who was to have healed the dissensions of the little colony, had scarcely settled down at Sydney, when he found himself involved in a quarrel with the Chief Justice, Mr. Gibbons, whom he accused of having sided with some persons who were opposed to the enrolment of a militia for the defence of the island. A long and angry correspondence ensued, and the upshot was the suspension of Mr. Gibbons as Chief Justice until His Majesty's pleasure could be known.

One of the most notable events of the first year of Macormick's Government was the arrival, in September 1788, of His Royal Highness Prince William Henry (afterwards William IV.) at Sydney, in the frigate 'Andromeda,' of which he was commander. The Prince remained several days at Sydney and then returned to Halifax. To mark his sense of the honour conferred upon Sydney by this visit, the Governor gave the harbour the name of 'Prince William Henry's Sound;' but it was never used except in a few official documents of the time, and has been long forgotten.

Soon after the departure of the 'Andromeda' another ship arrived on the coast, bringing a number of less welcome visitors. This was the ship 'Providence,' Captain Devonham, which had left Cork with eighty convicts for Quebec, where they were to have been landed and sent up to the back settlements. Finding the season too far advanced to get up the St. Lawrence, Captain Devonham returned through the Gut of Canceau, ran along the coast to the eastward, and anchored his ship between Port Nova and Scatari on December 11. Here the brutal Captain hoisted out his yawl and landed all the convicts, after knocking off their irons, upon the shore two miles to the eastward of Mainadieu. The landing was not completed until 7 P.M. (more than two hours after dark), when the ship sailed for the westward, leaving the poor wretches without a morsel of food upon the beach. About seventy men, women, and boys, found their way during the night to Mainadieu, where they were kindly received by the few inhabitants residing there, but seven were found next morning, who had strayed into the woods and died from exposure to the weather at that inclement season. Those who reached Mainadieu in safety were sent to Sydney in a shallop belonging to one Luke Keegan, except twenty which the shallop could not take.[1] On their arrival at Sydney, the poor creatures were liberally supplied with provisions, and as the provincial brig 'Relief' was not large enough to carry them all to Halifax, and no other vessels could be hired for that purpose, arrangements were made for housing them for the winter at a short

[1] From an account sent by Charles Martell (a name familiar to many of you) to the authorities at Sydney.

distance from Sydney, as it was feared a contagious disease might break out in their abject condition. Owing to the severity of the winter, there were seldom less than fifteen patients in hospital from frost-bites, and several became permanently lame from the same cause. As no instructions were received in the spring relative to their disposal, the convicts were allowed to go wherever they pleased; some left the island altogether,[1] whilst others found employment with the settlers, where they were allowed to remain undisturbed by the Home Government, glad no doubt to get rid of them by paying the sum of *567l. 12s. 5d.* sterling, the cost of their maintenance during the winter. Governor Macormick was of opinion that the captain of the ship ought to be punished in an exemplary manner for his inhuman conduct; but Mr. Grenville, the Secretary of State, informed him that 'in the present state of the law he was afraid the captain could only be sued for the penalties of the bonds which had been forfeited. Measures would be taken to prevent the recurrence of such cases.' The most painful incident connected with this affair remains to be told; on the very night that they were landed on the coast, two of the convicts, Pendergast and McDonald, murdered an old man—one of their companions, in the woods, for the sake of a trifling sum of money he had about him; for which they were tried at Sydney, found guilty, and condemned to be hanged. Mr. Matthews, the Attorney-General, recommended that the sentence should be carried into effect, but the Governor, having some doubts of the legality of the trial, wrote to Mr. Grenville for advice; in the meantime, waiting for an answer, the Governor was relieved of the difficulty by the escape of Pendergast and McDonald from gaol, with the supposed connivance of the corporal of the guard and sentinel on duty, who were put under arrest by Major Lovell.

The case of the convicts was the cause of much trouble and annoyance to the Governor in another way. Mr. Cuyler stated in council that he had proposed a more effectual means of disposing of the convicts when they first arrived, that would

[1] 'Convicts had been landed in Cape Breton in the past winter, and suspected of lurking about Halifax.'—Murdoch's *Nova Scotia*.

have saved a great deal of expense, but that the Governor would not agree to it. This brought on a quarrel which occupied the attention of the Council for about six months. The various documents relating to this dispute cover nearly 300 folio pages in the 'Cape Breton Papers' in the Record Office. The upshot was the suspension of Cuyler on August 19, 1789, from his offices of Provincial Secretary, Registrar, and Clerk of Council, until the King's pleasure could be known. This prompt action of the Governor was not approved by the Ministry. Even his friend, Mr. Evan Nepean, the Under Secretary of State, thought the Governor was wrong, for he says in a private letter to him, of October 20, that 'he is sorry there is likely to be further suspensions of officers, which, except for atrocious proceedings, are not regarded with favour by the Ministry. . . . With a little temper and proper management things will always go on well, and measures of that sort may generally be avoided. It cannot be a pleasant thing to the King's servants, who have constantly enough upon their hands, to be troubled upon every little bickering in the colonies. I speak plainly and freely to you as a friend, and advise you to try what can be done with a view of keeping things quiet.' Not long after the receipt of this letter, the Governor had the mortification of receiving an Order in Council of March 23, 1790, restoring Cuyler to all his offices in Cape Breton. This Order, however, was revoked upon its coming to the ears of the Ministry that Cuyler had written and circulated in the colonies a pamphlet of a very violent and mischievous character. On October 20 he resigned all his offices at the suggestion of the Secretary of State. In connection with this subject, I may here mention some other changes in the staff of the Civil Establishment made previous to the year 1793—namely, the appointment of Thomas Uncle to the Collectorship, and William Plant to the Comptrollership, of Customs in 1788; of Archibald C. Dodd, Ingraham Ball, and Thomas Crawley to the Council; of Mr. Storey to the office of Postmaster, and David Tait to that of Provost-Marshal in 1789; and of William McKinnon, by Royal Mandamus, to the offices of Provincial Secretary and Clerk of the Council in 1792.

The garrison, consisting of the 42nd Highlanders, having left Sydney direct for England in 1789, was replaced by two companies of the 21st Regiment, under the command of Major Lovell. The reduction of the strength of the garrison from six to two companies in 1789, and the orders received by Major Lovell on May 31 following, from Brigadier-General Ogilvie, the commanding officer at Halifax, to hold the troops in readiness to move at the shortest notice, created great uneasiness at Sydney. As the presence of the troops was considered necessary occasionally to act as a police, or to enforce the revenue laws, and to protect the settlers from the savages, who had threatened acts of violence against them, and boasted of the powerful help they could procure, the Governor, by advice of the Council, petitioned Brigadier-General Ogilvie to take measures for the security of the island. It is stated in an anonymous letter in the Record Office, that in consequence of the expected departure of the troops, 'the inhabitants were leaving the island daily, and so many houses were unoccupied that rents had fallen from 30*l.* to 10*l.* per annum.' Beyond all doubt the presence of a small body of troops was absolutely necessary, as the following incident will show:—At this time there were large herds of moose and caribou in the northern parts of the island, which afforded sustenance to the settlers in the remote districts, and even furnished the people of Sydney with an abundant supply of fresh venison at the moderate price of 2*d.* or 3*d.* per lb. Thousands of these valuable animals were killed by persons who came from Newfoundland and the other colonies, merely for the sake of their skins, which were worth about 10*s.* each. It is said that nearly 9,000 were killed during the winter of 1789 alone, and that the stench arising from their decaying carcases was sensibly perceived by the crews of vessels passing along the coast between St. Ann's and Cape North. Ordinances were passed by the Governor and Council to stop this wholesale destruction; but as they did not produce much effect, the Governor sent Thomas Crawley and George Moore, magistrates, supported by a subaltern and thirty men of the 21st Regiment, in the spring of 1790, to Cape North and Ingonish, to endeavour to put an end to the slaughter of the moose. A number of men were found assembled at both of these places, where they had built huts and collected a considerable quantity of skins. These men, advised of the approach of the troops, had effectually concealed the skins in the woods, but all their huts were destroyed, and themselves dispersed by the troops. Without the aid of the troops, the civil power, armed only with ordinances of the Council, could never have dispersed the offenders.

The commerce of the island, during the five years ending in 1793, did not show much increase. The documents in the Record Office do not contain regular returns of the exports, but they nevertheless afford sufficient information to enable me to say, that during the above period the Sydney district (exclusive of coal) exported only a few thousand quintals of dry fish, small quantities of mackerel and salmon, and a considerable number of moose skins; whilst the Arichat district sent to market about 35,000 quintals of dry fish and 500 barrels of mackerel annually. One of Macormick's first measures, on assuming the Government, was to lease the coal mines at Sydney to Thomas Moxley, who held them until his death, in 1791, when they were let to Messrs. Tremain and Stout, 'the only respectable merchants in the place,'[1] for a term of seven years, at a royalty of five shillings Halifax currency per chaldron. From a letter written on October 6, 1792, by Governor Macormick to Mr. Dundas, we learn that the mines at Cow Bay and Sydney were the only ones worked in Cape Breton, and that the former, which were let under contract by Governor Desbarres, had been abandoned by the contractor, who had absconded without paying the duties; also, that the mines at Spanish River, before the town of Sydney was founded, 'were apportioned to the commanding officer of the troops stationed there,' who was paid half-a-guinea per chaldron for all coal raised for the use of the garrison at Halifax, being furnished with tools, implements and materials by the Government. Any coal which could be raised beyond the quantity required by the garrison, formed a perquisite of the commanding officer,

[1] Governor Macormick's letter of October 6, 1792, to Mr. Dundas, Secretary of State.—*Records.*

who sold them to merchants and traders at the rate of 19*s.* 6*d.* per chaldron. The troops having been withdrawn from the mines in 1784, Governor Desbarres worked them on Government account, selling the coal at 16*s.* per chaldron. In 1788 the price was reduced to 13*s.* 6*d.* per chaldron, a price which could have left no profit to the Government; for out of this price, '5*s.* per chaldron was reserved as the perquisite of the Governor,' leaving only 8*s.* 6*d.* per chaldron to cover all charges. In the same letter Macormick says that the total sales of coal, from the date of his arrival at Sydney, on October 11, 1787, up to October 6, 1792, were 9,147 chaldrons, or an average of 1,829 per annum. The old practice of stealing coals from the cliffs on the coast was still prosecuted to a large extent, as Macormick states that at least 500 chaldrons were taken from Cow Bay to St. Pierre and other places in 1789, and that it would occupy at least three vessels to guard the coast properly, whereas he had only one—a schooner chartered for the service of the Government, commanded by Captain Prichard, 'who had been very active lately, and had seized three vessels loading at Cow Bay. Three more escaped.'

A number of grants were passed in the earlier years of Macormick's administration, in various parts of the island, but chiefly in the vicinity of Sydney Harbour, the Louisbourg Road (which had been just opened), the Little Bras d'Or, Baddeck, Margaree, Judique, Chetican, Arichat, Port Hood, the River Inhabitants, and on the Gut of Canceau, where, in 1787, there was not a single settler on the Cape Breton side of the strait.[1] According to a return made by Macormick to the Secretary of State, on March 17, 1793, 179 grants had been issued in the island since 1784, of which thirty-one were to loyalists, and seven to disbanded soldiers. This return gives us no idea of the number of persons who had settled in the island, because the issuing of grants had been discontinued since the month of June 1790, when instructions were received from the Secretary of State 'to restrain further grants except completing those for which warrants had been issued.' It was at this period the Indians built their chapel at the Indian

[1] Paterson's *Life of the Rev. J. McGregor, D.D.*

Islands, near St. Peter's, which they still occupy, Francis Bask and Michael Tomma, two chiefs of the Micmacs, having obtained leave on November 28, 1792, 'upon their personal application, to build a chapel on the island St. Villemai in the Bras d'Or Lake, near to the portage of Mount Grenville, for the exercise of divine worship agreeable to the rites and ceremonies of the Roman Catholic religion, and to possess the same during His Majesty's pleasure.'

I ought to have mentioned before, that Governor Parr, who died at Halifax in 1791, was succeeded by Sir John Wentworth in the government of Nova Scotia. In his capacity of Royal Commissioner of Woods and Forests in America, before the revolution, Sir John Wentworth had made himself well acquainted with the resources of Cape Breton, which he turned to good account on his appointment to the office of Governor-in-Chief, by suggesting some changes which were adopted by the Government at home, of which more anon in my next letter.

LETTER XXIV.

1793–1800.

THE young colony of Cape Breton, from its establishment in 1784 up to 1792, had been distracted only by internal discord; but in the beginning of 1793, when war was declared against England by the French National Convention, it had every reason to fear that, having so lately been a French possession, the island would be attacked by the vessels of that nation and its coasts ravaged by privateers.

When I tell you that the whole of the garrison, except one subaltern and twenty men, had been withdrawn for the defence of Halifax, and that even these were under notice to leave in the spring, you will not be surprised to hear that great alarm prevailed, and that many of the inhabitants left the island and went to the other colonies, where they hoped to find better protection. In this emergency the Governor and Council, after remonstrating against the removal of this handful of men, which at best would hardly have been sufficient to keep the Indians in subjection, ordered the militia to be enrolled without delay, for the defence of the island. The total number of inhabitants liable to serve in the militia was only 423, scattered over wide and remote districts, as will appear by the following return, made out on April 16, 1793:[1]—

At the town of Sydney	41
On the south-west branch of Sydney Harbour . .	10
,, north-west ,, ,, . .	22
,, south-east ,, ,, . .	27

[1] It is stated in a return sent by the Governor to the Secretary of State, on July 26, that there were 611 male inhabitants from fourteen to sixty years of age; 1,766 black cattle, 565 sheep, 95 horses, and 167 shallops, in the island.

At the Coal Mines, or Spanish River	33
„ Harbour of St. Ann's and Baddeck	10
„ Gut of Canceau	20
„ Port Hood	20
„ Chetican	30
„ Louisbourg, Gabarus, and Mainadieu	37
On Isle Madame and adjacent to it	173
Total	423 men

It is quite evident that, with such an inadequate force, even if mustered at one point, a successful resistance could not have been made against a single well-armed privateer; but it was hoped that an enemy might be deceived by the mere appearance of preparations for defence, and be deterred from making an attack. With this object in view, the militia were supplied with 300 stand of arms sent down from Halifax, two large boats carrying two guns each were stationed outside the bars for the protection of the coal-mines and the mouth of the harbour; and night watches, consisting of a corporal and four men each, were established at the town of Sydney and the coal-mines, under the command of Lieutenant-Colonel McKinnon, the Commanding Officer of the Eastern District. Lieutenant-Colonel Moore, the Commanding Officer of the Southern District, was despatched to occupy a redoubt at 'the important post of Mount Grenville,' near St. Peter's, armed with eight guns. The remains of this redoubt, which commanded the isthmus of St. Peter's and access to the Bras d'Or Lakes, may still be seen. If the intelligence of the declaration of war produced so much alarm, you may easily conceive the consternation of the inhabitants when they learned, from the deposition of Captain Gorham of the schooner 'Greyhound,' which was read at the Council, on August 30, 'that a French ship of forty-four guns was lying in Boston, expected to sail in a few days for Cape Breton;' and that a privateer of ten guns was lying at Tusket Harbour in Nova Scotia. However, there was no cause for apprehension; France had so much to do in other quarters, that she could not even protect her fishing stations in Newfoundland against an expedition despatched from Halifax, composed of only 310 men of the 4th and 65th Regiments, and a few artillerymen, under the command of Brigadier-General Ogilvie. The islands of St. Pierre and Miquelon fell into the hands of the English, and were held by a small garrison of the 4th Regiment, under the command of Major Thorne. There was more real cause for alarm towards the autumn, when news arrived that a French squadron of five ships of the line and several frigates were on the coast of Newfoundland, which had destroyed all the fishing stations in Fortune Bay, and was about to detach some ships to Cape Breton to lay waste the town of Sydney. It turned out afterwards that several vessels were actually detached from the squadron for that purpose, but, having been dispersed in a heavy gale, they were not able to reach their destination.

Some uneasiness was caused during this summer (1793) by the return of the Acadians who left Cape Breton in 1765 for Miquelon and the Magdalen Islands. Finding their situation in these islands not so agreeable as they could wish, these people decided upon going to Cape Breton, where they had friends and relations, and upon their arrival offered to take the oath of allegiance to His Majesty's Government. To guard against any deception, the Lieutenant-Governor sent an express to the naval commander on the Halifax station, requesting him to send down an armed vessel 'in case they should prove refractory.' During this and the following summer about 360 of these people came from Miquelon and the Magdalen Islands, and settled in various parts of Cape Breton, but principally on Isle Madame and the Little Bras d'Or. Amongst them were some who had come out to St. Pierre on the breaking out of the French Revolution, who were regarded with some suspicion, as it was feared their minds were embued with the democratic principles then prevalent in France, but they never caused any trouble; their descendants may now be ranked among the most peaceable and industrious portion of the inhabitants of the island.

In the year 1794 the defence of the island was improved by the arrival of a detachment of fifty men of the Royal Nova Scotia Regiment (a local corps raised in that province), and by the erection of a battery of four guns upon the commanding position called Peck's Head, near Indian Cove. A guard-house and magazine were also constructed during the winter upon the South Bar (in some of the documents of that period called Guion's Bar) by the crew of the armed schooner 'Lady Apsley,' then employed in the service of the Government. Any person ignorant of the facts might suppose, from an inspection of a plan sent to England by Governor Macormick, that the harbour of Sydney was well defended, the insignificant works at the town of Sydney, on the South Bar, and on Peck's Head, being distinguished by the titles of Forts Ogilvie, Edward, and Dundas, respectively.

I regret to say that, although the tranquillity of the island was not disturbed by foreign enemies, the later years of Macormick's reign were perplexed by most unseemly quarrels between himself and some members of his Council, to the great annoyance and discouragement of the well-disposed inhabitants. The Council, after many changes which I need not specify, was composed on April 8, 1794, of the following members:—Richard Gibbons, David Mathews, William Smith, Archibald C. Dodd, Ingraham Ball, Thomas Crawley, George Moore, and William McKinnon, who all held their seats until Macormick's departure, in 1795, except Chief Justice Gibbons, who was captured in the Channel on his way from Falmouth to Halifax in the brig 'Rashleigh,' on March 25, 1794, by the French frigate 'Tribune,' and carried into Nantz. Mr. Gibbons, with his wife and son, were thrown into prison, where he died of fever on August 3, 1794. His widow and son were released and sent to England in April 1795.

Macormick, who had now been seven years Lieutenant-Governor of Cape Breton, finding that his conduct was not approved by the Secretary of State, applied for leave of absence to go to England, professedly to give his vote as a Member of the Corporation of Truro, at the approaching election of a Member of Parliament for that borough, but in reality to escape quietly from a position which had become very uncomfortable. Leave of absence was readily granted, and Macormick left Sydney on May 27, 1795, in the Government schooner 'Hope,' for Halifax, from whence he sailed for England, leaving David Mathews, Attorney-General and Senior Councillor, to administer the government in his absence, or until a successor should be appointed.

The condition of the island at this time, according to an account sent by Mr. Miller, the Government Superintendent of the Mines and Member of Council, to the Duke of Portland, was by no means satisfactory. Mr. Miller sent a plan and view of the town of Sydney, showing here and there detached houses separated by wide intervals of vacant ground. You may form some idea of the place when I tell you that the whole of the peninsula now occupied by the town of Sydney then contained only eighty-five houses, many of them of a very poor description, and about one-third of them in ruins. Mr. Miller says there were only—

27	Private dwelling-houses inhabited.		
17	"	"	uninhabited
27	"	"	in ruins.
14	Public buildings.		

He adds, that the total number of inhabitants was 121, of whom about 26 were preparing to emigrate, and that when these should have left, there would not be a single person in the town except those who had salaries to subsist upon—not a tailor, shoemaker, smith, butcher—not even a washer-woman.

President Mathews took a more hopeful view of the state of affairs in Cape Breton. In a letter addressed to the Duke of Portland, on May, 6, 1796, he says, the persons who had left Sydney were chiefly dealers in spirituous liquors (no great loss to any country), who were following the same traffic in Halifax, and that, if a regiment were sent down, they would all come back. He adds, 'The condition of the country is now more satisfactory than heretofore, being based upon agriculture, which is progressing.' He reported again, in the month of August, that all was quiet, and that the rumour of two French privateers being upon the coast had caused no uneasiness, as a block-house (which is still standing) had been erected at the mines.'

I ought to have mentioned in its proper place that in the

autumn of 1795 three transports arrived at Sydney from England with 400 men of the 2nd battalion of the Royal Fusiliers on their way to Halifax, afflicted with scurvy, having been fifteen weeks at sea. They remained five weeks at Sydney, where several men died, and then sailed for Halifax under the convoy of the Government armed schooner 'Hope,' as privateers were reported on the coast.

The elevation of Mr. Mathews to the Presidency of the Council, though strictly in accordance with the Royal instructions of August 26, 1784, was not calculated to allay the dissensions which had so long prevailed in Cape Breton, as he was the leader of one of the contending parties. His first measure was to appoint his son—a very young man—Attorney-General, which gave great offence to others who considered they had better claims to that office; and the next, to appoint Mr. A. C. Dodd *pro tempore* to the office of Chief Justice, vacant by the death of Mr. Gibbons, without the advice of his Council. This last measure, of course, was anything but agreeable to the principal competitors for that office, Mr. Ingraham Ball, the acting Judge, and Mr. William Smith. The latter, who was in England at the time, offered, provided he were made Chief Justice, to perform the duty of Lieutenant-Governor also, without any additional remuneration. In the month of May, 1797, Richard Stout was appointed Councillor in the place of William McKinnon, suspended for having, as alleged by Mathews, 'manifested an open and avowed determination to transgress the laws,' in sending a challenge to the acting Chief Justice; and William Plant to the clerkship of the Council *vice* McKinnon, who refused to act in that capacity after he was deprived of his seat at the Board. Several other changes of minor importance were made by Mathews, which, with those already mentioned, caused such discontent with his administration, that a number of persons, including several officials,[1] memoralised the Duke of Portland

[1] Ingraham Ball, Assistant-Judge; James Miller, Superintendent of the Mines; William McKinnon, Provincial Secretary; Ranna Cossit, Parochial Minister; William Baker, Coroner; William Hill, Comptroller of Customs; and Thomas S. Bursey, Surveyor and Searcher.

on June 27, 1797, upon the state of affairs at Sydney, and urgently represented, 'that the unfortunate divisions and jealousies which predominated in Cape Breton could not be effectually removed unless a Governor was sent out.' This memorial seems to have produced the desired effect upon the Duke of Portland, who addressed a long despatch, on December 13, to Brigadier-General Ogilvie, the Commandant at Halifax, stating among other matters, 'that whereas the King's service in Cape Breton required that effectual measures should be taken for putting an end to the disputes and differences which prevailed there among His Majesty's servants, in the exercise of their respective functions, His Majesty had been pleased with that view, and for the further and more immediate security of that island, to place you, by the within instruction, at the head of the Council of Cape Breton, and thereby, in the absence of the Governor or Lieutenant-Governor, to put the administration of the affairs of that Government in your hands.' He was specially desired 'to settle those differences which have so unhappily disturbed that colony, no less to the injury of the public interest than to the discredit of His Majesty's Government in that quarter.' Being furnished with copies of all the correspondence with President Mathews, he was required to investigate the causes of the disputes, and especially why Mr. McKinnon was deprived of his seat in the Council, 'who was reinstated by this instruction in order that the charge against him might be investigated by the Board.' He was also directed to examine the returns of the superintendent of the coal-mines, and all matters of dispute, which His Majesty authorised him to settle 'upon his own discretion.' Finally, General Ogilvie was told, 'His Majesty considered his appointment, in a military point of view, would give security to this important outpost of his North American possessions, and that His Royal Highness Prince Edward had been instructed to send a force under his command, for the protection and defence of the island.'

Having been wrecked near Scatari, on June 23, in H.M.S. 'Rover,' General Ogilvie, did not reach Sydney until the

29th, where he found Mr. McKinnon in prison for debt. To investigate the charges against McKinnon, he was therefore obliged to pitch his marquee within the precincts of the gaol, for the accommodation of the Council and the examination of witnesses.[1] After a long and searching investigation, the result was transmitted to the Duke ot Portland on October 24, together with copies of the examinations of the witnesses. As might have been expected, Ogilvie found much to blame on both sides, but acquitted McKinnon of the most serious charges brought against him by Mathews—that of having attempted to defraud an individual in regard to a grant of land, which turned out to be merely a mistake in transcribing the patent; and, though he considered McKinnon had acted improperly in sending a challenge to Mr. Dodd, Mathews was not justified in suspending the former as a Councillor. The other matters treated of in the Report were mostly of a trifling nature and not worth repeating.

During his short stay at Sydney, General Ogilvie made particular enquiries concerning the military defences of the island. It appears, from a Report sent by him to the Duke of Portland in September, that the militia of the whole island was composed of 1 colonel, 2 lieutenant-colonels, 24 lieutenants, 13 clerks, 28 sergeants, and 526 privates. There were besides, 150 men of the Royal Nova Scotia Regiment stationed at Sydney, under the command of Lieutenant-Colonel Kearney; several batteries all in ruins; and a block-house at the mines in good repair. General Ogilvie strongly recommended that the seat of Government should be removed from Sydney to the North Bar. His mission to Cape Breton in the character of a peacemaker was not very successful, for his successor, Brigadier-General Murray, on his arrival at Sydney on June 21, 1799, as President of the Council, found all the old animosities subsisting in full force. His first duty was, of course, to report to the Secretary of State upon the condition of the colony, which he did at great length, pointing out

[1] There was no Court House at this time. The sum of 500*l.* was granted by Parliament for that purpose in 1796; 40*l.* a-year also was granted to pay a schoolmaster.

very fairly the difficulties of his position, and the measures he had adopted to restore peace and order to the distracted colony. In reply to this communication, the Duke of Portland wrote on October 11, that, 'as it was absolutely necessary to take effectual means to put an end to these disorders, and more particularly to re-establish the due administration of justice within the island,' by His Majesty's command, William Smith [1] was appointed Chief Justice, Mr. Ball was dismissed from the office of Acting Judge, and Mr. Mathews from that of Attorney-General. These prompt measures, however, having failed to secure the object in view, and General Murray, having found that he could not hold a neutral position between the contending parties, determined to form a Council composed in a great measure of military men, whom he expected to make subservient to his purpose; accordingly he nominated the Reverend Ranna Cossit the Military Chaplain; Doctor Stafford Staff Surgeon; his Secretary, Major Murray; and John Martyr, Collector of Customs, to seats in the Council. At the same time he dismissed Tryon Mathews, son of the late President, from the situation of Provost-Marshal; Mr. Plant from that of Superintendent of the Shipment of Coals; and Mr. McKinnon from the office of Provincial Secretary. These energetic measures did not produce the designed effect; on the contrary, they brought upon the General a sharp reproof from the Duke of Kent, the Commander-in-Chief at Halifax, who directed his Military Secretary, Mr. Gordon, to inform General Murray, February 15, that he had no right to employ military gentlemen under his command in duties committed by the British Constitution to the civil power exclusively; and that the military pay of Major Murray, the Reverend Ranna Cossit, and Doctor Stafford, would be suspended until His Majesty's pleasure could be known. Whatever were General Murray's faults, he was certainly justified by precedent, Lieutenant-Colonel Graham, the Reverend R. Lovell, and William Smith—all military men—having occupied seats in the Council under previous administrations.

[1] Mr. Smith was Surgeon of the 33rd Regiment, when stationed at Sydney in 1784, and held a seat in the Council under Governor Desbarres.

The last year of the eighteenth century brought General Murray's administration to a close. Before I enter upon that of his successor, I must give you a short account of the coal trade of Cape Breton at that period—a subject of much more importance than the petty personal squabbles which have, I fear, occupied too many of my pages. I gave you in my last letter a return of the coal exported up to October 6, 1792; I will now endeavour to complete the return up to the end of the century, and to lay before you such information as I have been able to collect relative to the mines at that period. Sir John Wentworth having suggested to the Secretary of State, on December 13, 1792, that if a stone pier were built at the mines for the more convenient shipment of coals, and the mines leased upon liberal terms, and worked under the inspection of a competent engineer, the trade would increase and yield a considerable revenue which might be very beneficially appropriated to the construction of roads in the island, which were very much needed, the Ministry, in compliance with this suggestion, sent out Mr. Miller to Sydney to survey and report upon the state of the mines. Instructions were at the same time sent to the Lieutenant-Governor to devote the whole of the revenue derived from the mines to public purposes, 'as neither the commanding officer nor the Lieutenant-Governor had any authority to reserve to themselves any portion of that revenue,' as they had hitherto been in the habit of doing (p. 403). Having completed his survey, Mr. Miller returned to England in December 1793, and submitted a long report to the Secretary of State, in which he recommended that a stone pier should be erected in Indian Cove, 280 yards in length, at an estimated cost of 2,822*l.* 7*s.* 5*d.*; but the Ministry did not sanction this measure, considering that the coal business was not of sufficient importance to warrant such an outlay. Mr. Miller returned to Sydney in 1794, to superintend the working of the mines on behalf of the Government, at a salary of 200*l.* per annum. He held the office until his death, in 1799 [1] when Mr. William Campbell,

[1] I am disposed to think Mr. Miller was the first person who noticed the fossil trees in the coal measures of Cape Breton. He says in a private letter to Mr. King,

Member of Assembly for the county of Sydney, in Nova Scotia, was appointed Superintendent of the Mines, and Attorney-General of Cape Breton, by His Majesty's Mandamus.

The mines were during this period worked by Messrs. Tremain and Stout, under a lease commencing on October 1, 1792. Upon the termination of their lease, on October 1, 1799, it was renewed for an uncertain time, subject to six months' notice. On February 5, 1800, Tremain and Stout surrendered the mines, which were then worked under the superintendence of Mr. Campbell, on account of the Government, until they were again leased in 1801.

Owing either to the limited extent of the workings, or the imperfect manner in which they were conducted, Messrs. Tremain and Stout were not able to supply the demand, small as it was, from the Sydney mines; they were, consequently, allowed to dig coals from the cliffs between the mines and Point Aconi, to make up the deficiency, under the inspection of Mathew Stubberts, Deputy-Superintendent. The inability of the lessees to supply the demand of course encouraged the smuggling of coal from the cliffs to the eastward of Sydney, to such an extent, that it was found necessary in 1794 to employ two vessels—the schooner 'Lady Apsley' and shallop 'Hope,' to watch the coast. In the following year an Ordinance was passed by the Council, making all vessels captured in this traffic liable to forfeiture. The following table shows the quantities of coal exported since the date of the return submitted in my last letter (p. 404) up to the close of the year 1800, excepting for 1793, which I could not find in the Records:—

	Chaldrons.		Chaldrons.
In 1794	3,147	In 1798	4,249
" 1795	3,144	" 1799	6,391
" 1796	3,039	" 1800	6,001
" 1797	4,314		

the Under Secretary of State, 'I had some thoughts of sending a cask of petrified branches of trees, in part converted into coal, to my Lord Duke, if I was assured it would be acceptable to His Grace. This phenomenon favours the opinion that coal strata are no other than decayed forests compressed, indurated, and petrified. I could also send a trunk of a large tree petrified.'

In addition to the above, 651 chaldrons were shipped from the Bras d'Or in 1795, and 711 in 1796. The principal markets were Halifax and Newfoundland; the former, including a small quantity sent to the town of Sydney and two or three other places, took about three fourths; the latter, the remaining fourth of the whole quantity exported.

The Records occasionally furnish us with voluminous details of the exports and the imports of the island, but not with sufficient regularity to enable me to make out a complete table for the seven years ending in 1800. To givė you a tolerable idea of the general trade of the island at the close of the eighteenth century, I may state, that from July 1, 1797, to July 1, 1798,

	At Sydney.		At Arichat.	
	No. of Vessels.	Tonnage.	No. of Vessels.	Tonnage.
Clearances were . .	195	8,588	54	2,154
Entries were . . .	135	6,470	64	2,548

Giving a total of 448 vessels and 19,770 tons.

Bearing in mind the fact, that during a period of fifteen years the Lieutenant-Governors had appropriated to their own benefit the sum of five shillings per chaldron out of the Coal Mines Revenue—the only revenue the island possessed, you will not be surprised to hear that little progress was made in opening roads from the capital to the outlying settlements. In the year 1800 there were barely half-a-dozen miles of passable road in the whole island; even those which had been made by the French were nearly obliterated by the rapid growth of underwood. Nothing can give you a better idea of the means of communication in Cape Breton at this time, than a condensed narrative of a journey made by the Rev. James McGregor, D. D. from Pictou to Sydney, in 1799. Dr. McGregor, who was a Presbyterian minister on the East River of Pictou, received an invitation from some persons of that denomination to visit Sydney, and started from the former place in the autumn of 1799, in an open boat with a crew of three men. Proceeding down the Gulf of St. Lawrence they reached the Gut of Canceau, from whence they sailed up Lennox's Passage to St. Peter's, where they were hospitably entertained by the late Lawrence Kavanagh, Esq., whose house was always open to travellers of the highest and lowest degree, without distinction. Having dragged their boat, with the aid of Mr. Kavanagh's oxen, across the narrow isthmus which separates St. Peter's Bay from the Bras d'Or Lake, the worthy Doctor and his adventurous crew embarked upon the waters of the lake, which was then surrounded by an unbroken forest, unrelieved by the hut of a solitary settler, to the head of the East Bay, where, after hauling up their boat upon the beach, and 'concealing the sails and oars in the bushes from thieves' (a very unnecessary precaution at that period), they composed themselves to sleep in the open air. Next morning, rightly judging that they were only twelve miles from Sydney, they set out in different directions in search of a road, but found only a narrow pathway, which they followed about three miles through the woods, when they discovered that it came to an abrupt termination at a brook, with no traces of a continuation on the opposite bank. The pathway they had followed was, as they concluded, the portage or carrying place used by the Indians in transporting their canoes from the lake to the head waters of Sydney River; but, as their own boat was too heavy to be carried such a distance, they again set out in search of a road, simply believing that a noted place like the capital of Cape Breton must surely be approached by good roads. They were, however, again disappointed, after a weary tramp over fallen trees and through swamps, in which the Doctor sunk so deep that 'he was struck with a sudden fright lest he should sink irrecoverably, or be bitten by snakes, or unheard of creatures (water kelpies);[1] for the long grass concealed danger.' Beating a hasty retreat from these imaginary dangers, the Doctor and his crew returned to their boat, embarked once more on the

[1] The good Doctor surely did not believe in the kelpies mentioned by Sir Walter Scott in the *Monastery*:—

> Merrily swim we, the moon shines bright;
> Downward we drift through shadow and light.
> Under yon rock the eddies sleep,
> Calm and silent, dark and deep;
> The Kelpy has risen from the fathomless pool,
> He has lighted his candle of death and of dool;
> Look, father, look, and you'll laugh to see
> How he gapes and he glares with his eyes on thee.

waters of the lake, and proceeded through the Great Narrows, thence down the Little Bras d'Or to the open sea, and round Cranberry Head to Sydney, a distance of eighty miles.[1] So you see, the only route from the East Bay to Sydney, a distance of only twelve miles, was by a circuitous voyage of eighty miles, some sixty or seventy years ago.

Having now brought my story down to the beginning of a new century—a century destined to witness great and important changes in your island, I will close this letter, and endeavour in my next to give you a brief exposition of the causes which first led to the great influx of Highland immigrants between the years 1800 and 1828.

[1] I recommend you to read Mr. Paterson's *Memoir of Dr. McGregor*, in which you will find much valuable information respecting the state of Nova Scotia and St. John's Island at the close of the eighteenth century.

I may here remark, while speaking of St. John's Island, that its name was changed to that of Prince Edward's Island in 1799, in honour of His Royal Highness the Duke of Kent, at that time Commander-in-Chief in Nova Scotia.

LETTER XXV.

1800–1817.

MAJOR-GENERAL DESPARD, the successor of Brigadier-General Murray, arrived at Sydney on June 17, 1800, but did not enter upon his duties as President of the Council until September 16, Murray having refused to surrender the Civil Government, asserting that Despard was sent by the Duke of Kent to take command of the troops only. Murray remained at Sydney until June 1801, in the expectation of being reinstated in his office by the Secretary of State, to whom he had despatched Mr. Baker on November 4, to lay his case before that functionary.

General Despard, in a letter dated December 18, to the Duke of Portland, charges Murray with remaining at Sydney for the purpose of causing trouble among the inhabitants and embarrassing his government: he adds, 'I have the satisfaction of stating that these futile attempts to disturb the peace of the settlement have not succeeded in the smallest degree, and I can venture to say that this island never enjoyed more tranquillity and content than at this present time.' Murray's administration does not seem to have been very popular with any party; two days after the accession of Despard, an address was forwarded to the King, signed by the principal inhabitants, officers of Government, and nearly all the members of Council, thanking His Majesty for removing Murray.

One of Despard's first measures was to take into favour all those who had been inimical to his predecessor; Mr. McKinnon was restored to his offices of Registrar and Clerk of the Council; David Tait was appointed to the Council in the place of Chief Justice Smith, who had left in September without leave, with the connivance, it was supposed, of General Murray; and several other changes were made not worth recording. Mr. Smith, on his arrival in England, having signified to the Duke of Portland that he did not intend to return to Cape Breton, Mr. Gambier was appointed to succeed him. Mr. Gambier held the appointment until February 1803 (though I believe he never went out to Cape Breton), when he sent in his resignation, having been made Surveyor-General of Canada.

The most important events of this year (1801) were the establishment of an ordinance, at the suggestion of General Despard, imposing a small duty on rum, 'as a measure tending to the preservation of the health and morals of the island, whilst it would provide a fund for its internal improvements;' the erection of a Court of Escheats, of which Archibald C. Dodd was named Commissioner; and the receipt of intelligence from Lord Hobart (who had succeeded the Duke of Portland), that preliminaries of peace had been agreed upon with France, and it was no longer necessary to keep any armed vessels in the service of the Government. The restoration of peace relieved the colony from one great cause of anxiety, but in other respects it was not acceptable to the people of Sydney, being followed by the removal of all the troops[1] in 1802, except a sergeant and nine men of the Royal Artillery.

It will be seen, by the following statement of the population, live stock, &c., of the island, sent by General Despard to Lord Hobart on December 24, 1801, what small progress had been made since the first establishment of a separate government in 1784:—

	Inhabitants.	Black Cattle.	Sheep.	Horses.	Vessels.
In the Sydney district . .	801	1,083	576	58	18
" Louisbourg district . .	192	201	113	13	7
" Arichat district, including N.W. shore . . .	1,520	1,647	1,988	83	192

There is no reason to doubt the accuracy of this return. If it be correct, you cannot avoid noticing that Desbarres's statement, of 800 persons having arrived in the island in 1784,

[1] The Royal Nova Scotia Regiment, of which the garrison at Sydney was composed, was disbanded in 1802.

which 'were speedily followed by an accession of 3,397 more,' must have been erroneous. We are told that a number of families left in Macormick's time, but taking into consideration the natural increase in a healthy climate like Cape Breton, the population of the Sydney district could never have fallen from 4,190 to 801 souls in the course of seventeen years. We have therefore, comparing this return with the statement of the number of persons liable to serve in the Militia in 1793, every reason to conclude that Desbarres's account of the arrivals in 1784 was greatly exaggerated. The population being so small, there was ample room for the hordes of hardy Highlanders, who first began to arrive in considerable numbers in 1802, to establish themselves in Cape Breton. Before I give you an account of the arrival of the first cargo of immigrants, I must endeavour to show what first directed them to your island. Many of the Highland chieftains, as you are aware, were very averse to the Union of England and Scotland in 1707, and rose twice in rebellion—in 1715 and 1745, for the purpose of restoring their ancient monarchs—the Stuarts—to the throne of Scotland. After the suppression of the rebellion of 1745, the Highlands were occupied by English soldiers, stationed at various commanding points, to keep the clans in subjection. The officers, one of whom was Major Wolfe, better known afterwards as 'the Hero of Louisbourg,' observing the restless character and bravery of the Highlanders, and experiencing the difficulty of keeping them in subjection, recommended that their young men should be enlisted in the British army and formed into regiments possessing all the distinctive characters of the several clans in regard to dress, equipment, &c. The Government wisely adopted these suggestions; several Highland regiments were raised, which relieved the country of a great number of restless discontented subjects, and added at the same time to the national army some 10,000 brave hardy soldiers, who distinguished themselves in many a hard-fought battle in the French wars, and nowhere more than at the siege of Louisbourg, in 1758, and the conquest of Canada. On the return of peace, in 1763, a great number of troops were disbanded, amongst the rest some of the Highland regiments. Many of the Highlanders, with that prudence and foresight peculiar to their countrymen, who had noted with observant eyes the fertility of the provinces in which they had served, in every respect so much superior to the bleak and barren hills of their native land, determined to make them their future home. Those who settled in Canada, Nova Scotia, and St. John's Island, sent home to their friends such glowing accounts of their new homes, about the year 1773, that the latter prepared to join them as soon as possible. It so happened, that just at the time these accounts reached Scotland from the colonies, many of the Highland chieftains, who had discovered that the raising of cattle and sheep afforded greater profits than the letting of their lands to miserable tenants, were dispossessing the latter of their farms and holdings; this harsh treatment of course gave a great impetus to the emigration, and thousands left almost every district in the Highlands to join their friends in the colonies. In the course of the twenty or thirty years following 1773, whole baronies were turned into sheep farms, and hundreds of families were driven across the Atlantic to look for a home in the backwoods of America. Many of these who had friends in the colonies, and knew what they had to expect, emigrated with great alacrity; but thousands, who had no such desire, on the contrary, the greatest repugnance to leave the land of their fathers, the familiar hills and 'the green slopes of Lochaber,' were heart-broken at the idea of being separated from them by a thousand leagues of raging sea. Many, it is true, especially the young men, gladly embraced the offers of their landlords to assist them in emigrating to a country where labour was abundant and the remuneration ample, and where they could with common industry soon acquire a comfortable subsistence; but the old people, who had passed all their lives in their native glens, clung to their birthplaces with a tenacity known only to the Celts. To these it was painful enough to leave home and friends and the haunts of their childhood, even voluntarily—how much more so, as was often the fact, at the whim of some powerful landlord, governed only by his own selfish views. It is all well enough to say now, that the Duke of Sutherland

and the other great Scottish landlords, who banished men from their estates to form deer forests, have conferred a lasting benefit upon their tenants by driving them across the Atlantic, where they have found more comfortable homes than they ever possessed in their native land; but the banished had little consolation in reflecting 'that their houses were unroofed before their eyes, and they were made to go on board a ship bound for Canada, even although the passage money was paid. An obscure sense of wrong was kindled in heart and brain. It is just possible that what was for the landlord's interest might be theirs also in the long-run, but they felt that the landlord had looked after his own interest in the first place. He wished them away, and he got them away; whether they would succeed in Canada was a matter of dubiety.'[1]

The first Scotch settlers who came to St. John's Island, in 1769, were a number of officers and men of Colonel Fraser's Highland regiment, from whence they sent such glowing accounts of the fertility and resources of the island, that a regular tide of immigration set in, which continued for several years, spreading over not only St. John's Island but also the opposite shore of Nova Scotia. The 'Hector,' the first ship that arrived at Pictou with immigrants, in 1773, was followed by others in such rapid succession, that in the course of eight or ten years, not only the country bordering on the harbour and rivers of Pictou, but also the coast to the eastward as far as Merigomish, was taken up and occupied. So far, all the immigrants who had arrived at Pictou were Presbyterians, but two ships having arrived there in 1791, with Roman Catholics from the Western Islands, they were persuaded by the Rev. —— McEachern of St. John's Island to leave Pictou and settle along the Gulf shore towards Antigonishe. Some of these, dissatisfied probably with the poverty of the soil, crossed over to Cape Breton, and settled upon the north-west shore at several places between the Gut of Canceau and Margarie, where they found a more congenial soil and greater facilities for prosecuting the sea fisheries, in which they had been engaged in the Western Islands. The favourable accounts of

[1] *A Summer in Skye.* By Alexander Smith.

the country, sent home by these wanderers, induced many of their countrymen to find a passage to the western shores of the island (by the way of Pictou), where they settled, chiefly about Judique and Mabou. There were of course no roads, not even a blazed track through the forests, from the sea-coast to the Bras d'Or Lakes, at that time; nevertheless, some stragglers were not long in finding their way to the fruitful sheltered shores of the lakes, whose innumerable bays, arms, and creeks offered such desirable places for settlement, that the emigration agents who had furnished ships for conveying the people hitherto to Pictou or Canceau, were induced to send their vessels direct to the Bras d'Or Lakes. The pioneer ship on this route arrived at Sydney on August 16, 1802, with 299 passengers, of whom 104 were heads of families, the remainder children. As it was too late to plant seed, the Council voted a sum of money to enable them to subsist until they could be provided for, by way of loan payable in twelve months.[1] From this time (1802) the tide of immigration gathered strength as it advanced, until it reached its highest point in 1817, when it began gradually to decline. The last immigrant ship arrived in 1828. All the best lands fronting on the lakes, rivers, and sea-coast, were taken up previous to the year 1820; since that period the lands in the rear of front lots have been occupied by the later immigrants, who are in consequence distinguished by the name of 'Backlanders.'

The great influx of Scottish immigrants (said by some authorities to have exceeded 25,000 souls), gave quite a new complexion to the population of Cape Breton, if it can with propriety be said that it was, before their arrival, distinguished by any complexion whatever, being composed only of a few hundred Micmacs, Acadians, and English and Irish settlers. The island is now decidedly 'Scotch,' with every probability of its continuing so to the end of time. Although many of the first settlers came to Cape Breton sorely against their will, none, I believe, have had reason to regret the change from the wretched abodes they left to the comfortable homes they now

[1] Three pounds ten shillings to a man and his wife; one pound to each child over, and fifteen shillings to each child under, twelve years of age.

occupy. Even the log hut, in the depths of the forest, is a palace compared with some of the turf cabins of Sutherland or the Hebrides.

Leaving the Scotch immigrants to their own resources, let us now return to Sydney, the seat of Government, which was again disquieted by the receipt of a despatch of May 16, 1803, from Lord Hobart, announcing the renewal of hostilities with France, and instructing General Despard to detain all French vessels in ports of Cape Breton—an instruction not easily carried out, if there had been any occasion to do so, as the whole garrison consisted only of a subaltern and twenty men of the 5th battalion of the 60th Regiment. The most important occurrences, from this time to the close of Despard's administration, in 1807, were:—The appointment of Mr. Woodfall to the office of Chief Justice, in 1804, and his death, in 1806, when he was succeeded by Mr. Archibald C. Dodd, by instructions from the Secretary of State, 'directing that Letters Patent should pass the Great Seal of the Island, constituting and appointing him to be Chief Justice;' the appointment of Thomas Crawley, in 1803, to the office of Surveyor-General; and of J. B. Clarke and Thomas Crawley to seats in the Council, in 1805, by command of His Majesty. After these changes, the Council, on February 1, 1807, consisted of the following members, under the Presidency of General Despard:—George Moore, A. C. Dodd, R. Stout, William Cox, William Campbell, David Tait, Thomas Crawley and J. B. Clarke. In the year 1803 the sum of 300*l.* was expended by order of Lord Hobart in completing the church at Sydney; the Miré Grant was escheated; and Commissioners appointed to manage the expenditure of the revenue derived from the tax upon rum, in making roads, building mills and other works of public benefit.[1] The want of light houses was severely felt, wrecks being of frequent occurrence. In the year 1804, the ship 'Sovereign,' with a valuable

[1] The revenue from this source, during the five years ending with 1806, averaged 242*l.* per annum; the expenditure upon roads, bridges, mills, &c., 156*l.* per annum. The Commissioners were A. C. Dodd, R. Stout, William Campbell, and J. B Clarke.

cargo, including presents for the Indians in Canada, was wrecked upon Low Point, where the lighthouse now stands; and a transport bound to Quebec with detachments of the 41st, 49th, and 100th Regiments, was wrecked near Louisbourg. Ensign Evylyn was drowned in landing; all the rest got safely on shore, and were sent round to Sydney, where they remained all winter. On their voyage from Sydney to Quebec in the spring, they were again wrecked, having been driven on shore by the drift ice. His Majesty's sloop 'Champion' was then sent down to Sydney to convey them to Quebec; while at Sydney, she lost a midshipman and eight men by the upsetting of a boat in a squall.

Before I enter upon the administration of the Government by Brigadier-General Nepean, who succeeded General Despard in 1807, I must say a few words about the commerce of the island, which seems to have retrograded during the seven years ending in 1807. The coal-mines—the chief source of revenue—which were in the hands of the Government in 1800, were leased on November 17, 1801, to William Campbell, the Attorney-General, for a term of seven years, at 7*s.* per chaldron royalty. On March 2, 1803, Campbell, finding he could make no profit by his lease, being bound to sell the coal at no higher rate than 18*s.* per chaldron, applied for a reduction of the royalty, which General Despard would not agree to; the mines then fell into the hands of the Government, Campbell having surrendered his lease on May 1, 1804, being unable to comply with its conditions. The returns of coal shipped from 1801 to 1807, both inclusive, are not quite perfect; as nearly as I could make out, the total quantity was 33,055 chaldrons, giving an average of 4,722 per annum. The commerce of the Arichat district, during the same period, seems to have made some progress, the clearances in 1804 having amounted to eighty-six vessels against fifty-four in 1797. The exports from Arichat for 1804 consisted of 22,200 quintals and 1,533 barrels of fish, 20,730 gallons of oil, and a small quantity of lumber.

Brigadier-General Nepean, who arrived at Sydney on July 6, 1807, had scarcely entered upon his duties as President of

Council, when he found that certain persons 'had,' as he tells the Secretary of State, 'manifested a disposition to oppose him in the Government by forming parties, and that, being determined to strike at the root of all opposition to His Majesty's Government,' he had deprived Mr. Campbell of the office of Attorney-General and his seat in the Council. I will not weary you with a detail of the various reasons given by Nepean for the dismissals and appointments which occurred during his tenure of office; I will merely state that Mr. Dodd, who had been suspended by General Despard, was restored to his seat in the Council in October 1808; Mr. Gibbons, who was appointed to be acting Attorney-General in 1809, was dismissed from that office as well as his seat in the Council, in 1810; Benjamin Smyth was appointed Clerk of the Council in 1811, vacant by the death of Mr. McKinnon;[1] Mr. Dodd was suspended from his office of Chief Justice in 1812; and some other changes made, not worthy of notice. After all these 'ups and downs,' I find that, on May 4, 1812, the Council was composed of Brigadier-General Nepean, President; A. C. Dodd, Thomas Crawley, C. E. Leonard, Rev. William Twining, William Bown, junior, P. H. Clarke, and Ranna Cossit.[2]

One of the most serious drawbacks to the advancement of Cape Breton, whilst it had a Government of its own, was the maintenance of a host of officials beyond all measure too costly for a small colony. All the revenues of the island, together with an annual sum of about 2,000*l.* voted by Parliament, were swallowed up in the payment of the salaries of officers whose duties were in many cases purely imaginary, leaving nothing for the construction of roads and other necessary works. Lord Castlereagh, when Secretary of State, seems to have had some idea of reducing the Civil Establishment, as he ordered General Nepean to send home a list of all the officers

[1] Mr. McKinnon died on April 13, 1811, from the effects of a wound received on board the 'Bristol,' in the attack of Sullivan's Island, near Charlestown, under Sir Peter Parker.

[2] In the year 1808, a company of the New Brunswick Fencibles was sent by the Commander-in-Chief to Cape Breton. Part of the company was stationed at Sydney, the remainder at the mines.

employed in the island, with a particular account of their emoluments. This list, which was sent to England in 1809, gives a full and explicit account of the various offices, the names, services, and ages of the occupants, and their emoluments. I beg to submit the following abstract, believing that it possesses sufficient interest to entitle it to a place here :—

Occupants.	Offices.	Total Annual Emolument.		
		£	s.	d.
A. C. Dodd	Chief Justice, 500*l.* per annum			
Do.	Deputy-Surveyor of Woods, 12*l.* per annum, in Fees	512	0	0
Richard Gibbons	Attorney-General, 85*l.* per annum	85	0	0
Do.	Solicitor-General, no Fees			
Wm. McKinnon	Provincial Secretary, Registrar, and Clerk of Council, Salary and Fees	240	0	0
James Hill	Clerk of the Crown, 86*l.* in Fees			
Do.	Clerk of the Pleas, Fees not stated			
Do.	Clerk of the Peace, ditto	131	0	0
Do.	Public Schoolmaster, 45*l.* per annum			
William Cox	Provost-Marshal	120	0	0
Richard Stout	Surrogate and Judge of Probate, Fees	10	0	0
Do.	Acting Auditor	22	10	0
William Day	Messenger to Council, and Gaoler	52	10	0
Philp. Dumaresq	Collector of Customs, Salary and Fees	350	0	0
George Moore	Ditto at Arichat, per annum	120	0	0
Ranna Cossit	Comptroller of Customs, Salary and Fees, 151*l.*			
Do.	Receiver of Seamen's Duty, Fees 1*l.* 4*s.* 6*d.*	151	4	6
Do.	Deputy-Treasurer, Greenwich Hospital, Nil			
Samuel Plant	Surveyor and Searcher, Salary and Fees 141*l.*			
Do.	Collector Prov. Revenue 10 per cent. Commission 25*l.*	171	0	0
Do.	Coroner, Fees 2*l.* 10*s.*			
Do.	Clerk of Licences, Fees 2*l.* 10*s.*			
C. Hubert	Col. Prov. Revenue, Western District, 10 per cent.	30	0	0
P. H. Clarke	Treasurer of Prov. Revenue } 5 per cent. Commission, about 300*l.*			
Do.	Do. Mines do. }	391	5	0
Do.	Private Secretary to Governor, 91*l.* 5*s.* per ann.			
Wm. Twining	Parochial Minister, 144*l.* per annum	189	12	6
Do.	Garrison Chaplain, 45*l.* 12*s.* 6*d.*			
Thomas Crawley	Surveyor of Lands, 140*l.* per annum	240	3	0
Do.	Superintendent of Mines, 100*l.* per annum			
J. W. Clarke	Medical Officer at Mines	150	0	0
J. C. Ritchie	Agent of Government at Mines, 225*l.* per ann.	450	0	0
Do.	Allowed to supply men with Goods, 225*l.* more			
George Bown	Harbour Master	50	0	0
Phillip Elly	Clerk of Market, Fees	9	0	0
		3475	2	0

This statement requires no comment. It is no wonder the island made such little progress when the expenses of the Government amounted to 3,475*l.*, exclusive of the Governor's salary, which, I believe, was 800*l.* per annum; and this too, you must bear in mind, at a period when the whole population of the island did not exceed 4,000 or 5,000 souls.

Before I close my sketch of General Nepean's administration, I must notice an incident of a very painful character which occurred at Sydney in 1812, the murder of a man of the name of William Harris, by the Captain of His Majesty's sloop of war 'Recruit.' The 'Recruit,' it appears, was sent down by Sir John Sherbrooke, to convoy a number of vessels loading with coal at Sydney for the Halifax garrison; while she was lying at anchor before the town one Sunday morning, the commander, Captain Evans, went on shore and insulted a female, which led to a disturbance in the street. The officers of the 'Recruit,' supposing their Captain was in danger, sent a corporal of marines and a file of men on shore to protect him. On their appearing, Captain Evans, who, according to all accounts, was the aggressing party, ordered the marines to fire, when Harris, who had merely stepped out of his house to see what was going on, was shot in the forehead and killed; the Rev. William Twining and two constables were also wounded in the affray. The main guard having meanwhile been called out, Evans and the marines were secured and lodged in gaol, where they were kept until the month of October 1813, when they were brought to trial, but owing to some irregularity in the proceedings, escaped the punishment they justly deserved. While Evans was in gaol, he appealed to the Lords of the Admiralty for protection,[1] but they refused to interfere, and left him to be dealt with by the civil power. The 'Recruit' left Sydney under the command of Lieutenant Bannister, with her convoy, in the beginning of January, but was obliged by stress of weather to put back to Sydney on the 21st, where she was frozen in and did not get out until May 22 following.

The coal-mines were worked during Nepean's administration by the Government, but apparently with little advantage,

[1] Captain Evans was, beyond all doubt, not in his right mind. On June 15, 1813, he wrote a most intemperate letter to the Lords of the Admiralty, in which he said, 'The inflexible inhuman brute, Brigadier-General Hugh Swayne, continues me confined, both legs in iron, with a chain attached to them.' He added that his trial was postponed by Swayne, to try to destroy his constitution!

the profit, according to a report sent to the Secretary of State on July 5 1811, being only 1*s.* 8*d.* per chaldron. As nearly as I can ascertain, the sales, including a small quantity obtained from the cliffs, averaged about 6,000 chaldrons per annum.

The practice of granting land to *bonâ fide* settlers was, for some reason not stated, discontinued in 1811, and Crown leases terminable at will substituted. This, of course, caused much dissatisfaction generally, and induced the Council to consider the 'propriety and expediency of convening a General Assembly, agreeably to the 15th Article of the Royal Instructions.' (See p. 387.) It was finally decided to issue a proclamation to the people of the island, requesting them to communicate their sentiments through the medium of the magistrates. A petition asking for a General Assembly was accordingly adopted and forwarded to the King in 1812.

Brigadier-General Swayne, who arrived at Sydney on January 1, 1813, had scarcely been a week in office when he forwarded a long despatch to Lord Bathurst, the Secretary of State for the Colonies, in which he gave a most deplorable account of the condition of the island:—'I found,' he says, 'this colony in a most unpleasant state—the Chief Justice has been suspended, and the most violent animosities prevail amongst some of the officers of the Government as well as between many of the principal inhabitants. The magistrates of the country have been suspended for these some months past, from an opinion which has been industriously circulated that they had not been duly qualified. It also appears that the finances of the country have been reduced to the lowest ebb, the Treasury drained, and a debt against it. In addition to which, I find that the coal-mines, which were the only source of revenue since the Provincial Revenue ceased to operate, are in a state of bankruptcy.' In a subsequent despatch of the same year, he informs Lord Bathurst that he had dissolved the Council, but does not give the names of the new Members; that he had appointed Richard I. Uniacke, Attorney-General, in the place of R. Gibbons, suspended by General Nepean; and Charles E. Leonard, naval officer, *vice* George Moore, deceased; that the Council had renewed the ordinance imposing a tax upon rum; and that a road had been opened from Sydney to the Great Bras d'Or Lake. He also complains that, owing to the remissness of his predecessor, the country during the previous year was so unprotected, that the enemy's privateers landed their crews and established signal stations between Spanish River and Cape North, to the great injury of the Quebec trade.

Great preparations were made throughout the colonies at this time to resist the depredations of the American privateers which swarmed on their coasts. General Swayne did all in his power, with the limited means at his command, to provide for the security of Cape Breton, by organising the militia of the island, consisting only of 1,468 men,[1] and by repairing the batteries on both shores of Sydney Harbour. The only regular troops in the island—a company of the 104th Regiment, stationed at Sydney—were sometimes called upon to oppose the imaginary attacks of the dreaded privateers, but, fortunately, there was no real cause for alarm, as neither the French nor the Americans visited Sydney.

General Swayne had been scarcely three years at Sydney, when he applied for leave to return to England on account of his health—more probably to escape from the unpleasant position he occupied, having become embroiled in quarrels with some of the other officers of his Government. The Cape Breton documents in the Public Record Office contain hundreds of pages of correspondence relating to the suspension of the Chief Justice and the Attorney-General, and similar affairs, but as they would afford you neither pleasure nor profit, I will say no more about them. The only additional appointment that I noticed, worthy of mention, was that of James Crowdy, on September 13, 1814, to the offices of Provincial Secretary and Registrar.

If the General had paid more attention to the material interests of the island, and less to the jealousies and feuds which disgraced his administration, the Records would have

[1] The population of the island is stated in a letter to Lord Bathurst, of June 1, 1813, to be 5,909.

furnished us with more satisfactory evidence of the progress of the coal trade than the only entry they contain—the following:—

	£	s.	d.
Cash received for Coals sold in 1813 . . .	8,006	1	4
Paid Salaries, Charges, &c. . . .	6,008	3	1¼

On the departure of General Swayne, Lieutenant-Colonel Fitzherbert of the 98th Regiment was sent from Halifax by Sir John Sherbrooke to act as President of Council until the arrival of Major-General Ainslie, who had been appointed Lieutenant-Governor of the Island. Under Colonel Fitzherbert's rule, from February 5 to November 4, 1816, the island enjoyed comparative tranquillity, and all branches of trade made some progress. The Returns sent to England for the year ending December 31, 1816, show that the value of the merchandise entered at the ports of Sydney, Arichat, and Ship Harbour, amounted to 83,724*l.* 7*s.*, and the exports to 53,880*l.* 16*s.* 9*d.* The amount of articles exported—the actual produce of the island—did not exceed 38,783*l.* 8*s.* 3*d.*, consisting of the following items:—

			£	s.	d.
6,157	Chaldrons of Coal	at 23/	7,080	11	0
34,039	Quintals of Cod Fish	„ 14/6	24,678	5	6
4,191½	Barrels Pickled Fish	„ 20/	4,191	10	0
6,341	Gallons Fish Oil	„ 1/9	554	16	9
129	Head of Cattle	„ 180/	1,161	0	0
4	Thousand Oak Staves	„ 200/	40	0	0
200	Barrels Potatoes	„ 7/	70	0	0
34	Bundles Hoops	„ 10/	17	0	0
32	Do. Shooks	„ 10/	16	0	0
260	Bushels Oats	„ 3/	39	0	0
70	Barrels Salmon	„ 50/	175	0	0
2,000	Lbs. Butter	„ 1/3	125	0	0
19	Cords Firewood	„ 20/	19	0	0
1	Puncheon Furs		63	0	0
102	Furs and Skins		25	0	0
40	Head of Sheep	„ 25/	50	0	0
217	Barrels Pickled Fish	„ 25/	271	5	0
552	Tons Plaister of Paris	„ 7/6	207	0	0
		Total	38,783	8	3

For many years previous to the arrival of General Ainslie, a duty of 1*s.* per gallon upon rum, imposed by an Ordinance of Council, had produced an annual revenue, which, together with that raised from the coal-mines, was sufficient to cover all the expenses of the Government; but the payment of this duty having been resisted in the summer of 1816 by Messrs. Leaver and Ritchie, the lessees of the coal-mines, upon the ground of its illegality, His Majesty, they asserted, having given up his prerogative of making laws in Cape Breton imposing a tax upon the inhabitants, by virtue of the Proclamation of October 7, 1763, when the island was annexed to Nova Scotia; and again, on August 26, 1784, by the 15th Article of his instructions to Governor Parr, when Cape Breton was erected into a separate Government, which ordered, 'that nothing be passed or done that should any way tend to affect the life, limb, or liberty of the subject, *or the imposing of any duties or taxes*,' an action was brought against Messrs. Ritchie and Leaver to recover the duty. The case was tried before Chief Justice Dodd (who had been reinstated in his office by order of the Home Government in the month of April preceding), and a verdict given, by his direction, in favour of the defendants. This decision proved very embarrassing to the Lieutenant-Governor, as it was the opinion of the Attorney-General, 'that as His Majesty, according to the Chief Justice's decision, had relinquished his prerogative over the island, all the ordinances then in force were illegal, and the situation of the island was in a disorganised state regarding the public revenue and the execution of the provincial laws, which called for the immediate interference of His Majesty's Government.' In this dilemma, General Ainslie, in reporting to the Secretary of State on November 25, on the state of the island, said, that in consequence of the decision of the Court, every ordinance that had been passed for a great length of time was illegal; that no impost could be laid in future; no statute labour enforced; no militia called out; no prisoner put in gaol; nor any other regulations most necessary in an infant colony could be made. He added, in conclusion, that the decision had met with the execration of the whole of the inhabitants except a few rum sellers, and that the tax, which was of great service in opening roads and other needful works, was cheerfully paid by all. If the petition of the inhabitants, mentioned at page 431, asking for a General Assembly, had been complied with, such a serious difficulty could never have arisen; but strange to say, no notice whatever seems to have been paid to their request until the year 1817, when Lord Bathurst informed General Ainslie that he fully coincided with him in opinion, 'that a House of Assembly would be destructive of the prosperity the island then enjoyed, limited as it was, and that there was not a sufficient number of persons in easy circumstances to attend an Assembly.'

Lord Bathurst having applied to Messrs. Shepherd and Gifford, the legal advisers of the Crown, for their opinion upon the decision of the Supreme Court at Sydney, received in reply the following answer on April 11: 'We think it right to submit to your Lordship our doubts as to the legality of the imposition of the duty for which the action is brought. If the extract from the King's Commission and Instruction to the Governor be correct, the Governor and Council of the island are not authorised to impose any duties or taxes, inasmuch as such power is expressly excepted.' This opinion of the law officers of the Crown settled the question. As the island could not be allowed to remain without a regular government, the only method of overcoming the difficulty was, either to convene a House of Assembly, or to reannex it to the Government of Nova Scotia. The Ministry, as you are aware, decided upon the latter course. In my next I will tell you how the proposed measure was received by the people of Cape Breton, and the manner in which it was carried into effect.

LETTER XXVI.

1817-1846.

BEFORE I enter upon the important question of the re-annexation of Cape Breton to Nova Scotia, I must give you a short account of what occurred during the last two or three years of the existence of its separate government. In the year 1817 an overland postal communication was established with Halifax, by despatching an Indian once a month during the winter, when the harbour of Sydney was closed by ice. Also at the urgent solicitation of General Ainslie, who represented that in consequence of the vacillating policy of the Ministry respecting the issuing of land grants, many valuable settlers had left the island for the United States, orders were received to issue grants to bonâ fide settlers as usual. These orders, however, for reasons not stated, were revoked in 1818, when instructions were sent out by Lord Bathurst 'to suspend passing grants until further commands.' The garrison of Sydney, consisting of a company of the 7th battalion of the 60th Rifles, under the command of Captain Barrington, was relieved in 1817 by a company of the 3rd battalion of the same regiment, under the command of Captain Imthurn, which was in its turn relieved in 1818 by a company of the 74th Regiment, commanded by Captain Stewart. Large quantities of gypsum having been carried off clandestinely by American vessels from the Gut of Canceau, General Ainslie advised the Ministry to close that strait against foreign vessels, but was informed that it could not be done according to the late treaty with the United States. To stop this traffic the hired Government schooner was employed to watch the coast and drive off any vessels attempting to take in cargoes. In the execution of this duty an American vessel was seized, loading with gypsum at the port of St. Ann's, and taken round to Sydney. In the year 1818 the first cargo of timber ever shipped direct from the Bras d'Or Lakes was loaded on board a vessel which had brought out immigrants in St. George's Channel. In the same year the Rev. Hibbert Binney, father of the present Bishop of Nova Scotia, was appointed to the mission of Sydney by the Society for Propagating the Gospel in Foreign Parts; and Messrs. Ritchie and F. Leaver relinquished their lease of the coal-mines, which were transferred to Messrs. Bown and John Leaver, who held possession of them until January 1, 1821. The sales of coal in 1818 amounted to 5,300, and in 1819 to 6,209 chaldrons. There are no returns in the Cape Breton papers in the Record Office for 1817 and 1820.

I should gladly have here closed my brief summary of events; but however disagreeable the task, I must not omit to inform you that General Ainslie's reign, like that of all his predecessors, was from first to last disgraced by continual quarrels and disputes, alike dishonourable to all the parties concerned. If I were to give you a detailed account of all those transactions, it would fill many hundred pages with very unprofitable matter, and undoubtedly give great offence to many persons now residing in Cape Breton; I will therefore merely enumerate the changes made by General Ainslie in the Council and the public offices during his administration. In 1817 Captain Imthurn and Captain Weekes were appointed to seats in the Council in place of Mr. Bruce and Mr. Dumaresq, and Mr. Stout was dismissed from the office of Judge of Probate, but immediately afterwards reinstated by the order of Lord Bathurst. In 1818 Mr. Ranna Cossit was suspended from his office of Comptroller of Customs, and Mr. Pooley forbidden to practise as a barrister in the Court of Chancery. One of his last acts—perhaps the only unobjectionable one—was the appointment of Captain Stewart to a seat in the Council. Having quarrelled with the Chief Justice, the Provincial Secretary, the Surveyor-General, the Provost-Marshal, and the Naval Officer, and made enemies of almost every person of respectability in Sydney, Ainslie closed his career in 1820 with a scurrillous, intemperate letter to the Under Secretary of State, denouncing the inhabitants generally as a set of deceitful unprincipled aliens, 'embued with the Yankee qualities of the refuse of the three kingdoms.' We cannot be surprised, under these circumstances, that the British Ministry, harassed with complaints from all parties of the conduct of the rulers which had been set over them, decided to annex the island to the Government of Nova Scotia, as the only means of relieving it from the baneful influences to which it had been subjected ever since its separation from that province in 1784.

The first intelligence of the intention of the British Government to re-annex Cape Breton to Nova Scotia reached Sydney in the month of August, only three months after a petition had been forwarded to the Prince Regent, praying him to order a General Assembly to be convened, as the only constitutional remedy, in their opinion, for the evils under which they had so long laboured. As no answer was sent to their petition, the inhabitants of Sydney immediately addressed a strong remonstrance to Lord Bathurst, in which they expressed their grief and astonishment at the proposed measure of annexation, stating that the island would be swamped by the Legislature of Nova Scotia, that its interests would be neglected, and that the distance of the island from Halifax—the seat of government—would cause great inconvenience to the inhabitants. They further stated, that as the island now contained a population of 8,000 or 9,000 souls, which was rapidly increasing by immigration, and was capable of raising a sufficient revenue, the time had arrived for calling together an Assembly, as promised in the instructions sent out to Governor Parr in 1784, when Cape Breton was erected into a separate government. Finally, they prayed that his Lordship would adopt such measures as would secure to them the blessings to which, as loyal British subjects, they were entitled. This address was signed by men of all parties in Sydney and the north-eastern districts, but it was not heeded by the Colonial Secretary, who instructed Sir James Kempt, then about to sail to Halifax to assume the government of Nova Scotia, to carry the annexation into effect immediately upon his arrival in that colony. Sir James Kempt reached Halifax on June 1, 1820, and having notified General Ainslie of his arrival and the purport of his instructions relative to Cape Breton, the latter, on the 20th of the same month wrote to Mr. Crowdy, the Provincial Secretary of the island, announcing his immediate departure. On the 22nd a council[1] was held, at which it was decided that the senior military officer, Captain David Stewart, was the proper person to take upon himself the administration of the Government[2] until Sir James Kempt had completed his arrangements for annexing the island to the Government of Nova Scotia.

As everything connected with the important subject of the annexation of your island to Nova Scotia must be highly interesting, I will now give you a copy of the despatch sent by Lord Bathurst to Sir James Kempt, for his guidance:—

'*Downing Street, August 15, 1820.*

'SIR,—I had the honour of intimating to you, previous to your departure from this country, the decision to which His Majesty had come, of re-annexing the island of Cape Breton to the Government of Nova Scotia; and you must have observed the alteration which had in consequence been made in your commission and instructions.

'His Majesty considers it most desirable that this arrangement should be no longer delayed, and has commanded me to instruct you to take into your immediate consideration the measures which may be necessary to give effect to His Majesty's instructions. For this purpose it will be necessary that you should in the first place direct the issue of writs for the election of two members from the county of Cape Breton, to sit in the Legislative Assembly of Nova Scotia; and in this you will follow the course adopted in 1765, when two members were actually so returned.

[1] The Councillors present at this meeting were Archibald C. Dodd, President; David Taitt, Thomas Crawley, Joshua W. Weeks, Frederick Imthurn, David Stewart, and Charles R. Ward.

[2] General Ainslie left Sydney on June 24, in the brig 'Hannah,' direct for London, where he arrived on August 3.

'Upon this, you will dissolve the Council at Cape Breton, appointing, however, to seats in the Council of Nova Scotia, any one or more members whose knowledge of the local interests of the island, or whose merits in other respects, entitle them to that distinction.

'The object being to make the island in every respect an integral part of Nova Scotia, it will be your duty to consider of the measures which it will be necessary for the Legislature of Nova Scotia to adopt, in order to give effect to this intention.

'You will at once see the necessity of either applying to Cape Breton the laws actually applicable to other parts of Nova Scotia, or of giving, by some legislative Act, legal validity for the future to the several ordinances passed since by the Governor and Council of Cape Breton, and under which that colony has hitherto been administered.

'It will be for the Legislature to decide upon which of these two courses it may be most convenient to adopt; but I cannot withhold my opinion, that it would be far more advisable to follow that which would place the whole of the province under one and the same system of law.

'With respect to the administration of justice, it will only be necessary to provide that the judges of Nova Scotia should extend their regular circuits to Cape Breton, in order to secure to the inhabitants every facility which they have any title to expect.

'I shall be most anxious to receive from you, as early as possible, a report as to those officers whom you may consider it necessary, either permanently or for a time, to retain at Cape Breton after its annexation to Nova Scotia. Among the latter, it appears to me expedient that the Officer of the Customs, the Naval Officer, the Surveyor-General, and the Superintendent of the Mines—who have all duties independent of any question of union or separation of the Government—should remain as heretofore, with the difference only of reporting to you, through the Superintendent, who is to be appointed resident within the island, instead of the Lieutenant-Governor; but as this part of the question will in no degree fall under the regulation of the Assembly, it is a point of less immediate attention, and it will be a proper subject for the future consideration of His Majesty's Government.

'It is clear that the services of the judges, and it is probable also that those of the greater part of the subordinate officers of justice, may be altogether dispensed with; but with respect to all these, it will be necessary that I should receive from you a specification of the length of their several services, in order to judge how far they may be entitled to a continuance of the whole or a portion of their respective emoluments, or to be transferred to some other situation.

'Parliament has already made provision for the payment of their several annual salaries for the present year, and it will therefore be proper that the new arrangement, though completed, should not actually take place until January 1, 1821.

'I have the honour to be, Sir,
Your obedient humble Servant,
'BATHURST.

'Lieut.-General Sir James Kempt, G.C.B.,
&c., &c., &c.'

Immediately after the receipt of this despatch, Sir James Kempt sailed for Sydney in the Government hired brig 'Chebucto,' where he issued the following proclamation on October 16, 1820:—

'J. KEMPT.

'A Proclamation by His Excellency Lieutenant-General Sir James Kempt, G.C.B., Lieutenant-Governor and Commander-in-Chief in and over His Majesty's Province of Nova Scotia and its Dependencies, &c.

'Whereas His Majesty, with a view to promote the welfare of his faithful and loyal subjects of Nova Scotia and Cape Breton, hath been graciously pleased to direct that the island of Cape Breton should be re-annexed to the Government of Nova Scotia, and the same island should from henceforth be and remain an integral part of the Government of Nova Scotia—

'I do therefore, in pursuance of His Majesty's instructions and by and with the advice of His Majesty's Council, declare that the island of Cape Breton is, and from henceforth shall be and remain, a several and distinct county of the Province of Nova Scotia, to be called and known by the name of the County of Cape Breton, and to be represented, and the Civil Government thereof to be administered, in like manner as the other counties of the province are administered and governed.

'And in pursuance of His Majesty's instructions, I have caused a writ, in the usual form, to be immediately issued, directed to the Provost-Marshal or his Deputy, resident in the island, for the election of two Members to serve in the General Assembly of Nova Scotia, being the number directed to be summoned to such Assembly before the time when the said island was first separated from the province of Nova Scotia.

'And I do hereby, in obedience to His Majesty's commands, dissolve the Council of the said Island of Cape Breton.

'And that the peace and good order of the said island may be preserved, and justice duly administered therein, until more effectual provision shall be made by the Legislature of Nova Scotia, or until further order shall be duly made therein, I do hereby authorise and require that all Judges, Justices of the Peace, Constables, and other Civil Officers in commission in the said island, do continue in the execution of their respective offices, agreeably to the several ordinances passed by the Governor and Council of Cape Breton, and under which that Colony, since its separation, has been hitherto administered.

'Given under my hand and Seal at Arms, at Halifax, this ninth day of October, 1820, in the first year of His Majesty's reign,
By His Excellency's Command,

'RUPERT D. GEORGE.

'God save the King.'

Soon after the promulgation of this proclamation, writs were issued for the election of two members for the County of Cape Breton, when Richard John Uniacke, junior, and Lawrence Kavanagh, were duly elected. Mr. Uniacke took his seat on the opening of the first Session of the twelfth General Assembly of Nova Scotia on November 12, 1820, but Mr. Kavanagh, who was a Roman Catholic, did not present himself for admission, as he could not conscientiously subscribe the declaration against popery and transubstantiation. Sir James Kempt, supposing that he might claim his seat at the next Session, applied on November 15, 1821, to the Under Secretary of State for instructions for his guidance, representing that, as a large proportion of the inhabitants were Roman Catholics, it appeared but just and fair that they should have a representative of their own persuasion, especially as Mr. Kavanagh was one of the most loyal and respectable men in the whole community. In reply to this, Lord Bathurst said, 'If Mr. Kavanagh should present himself, and on his objecting to the oath required by the instructions, the Council should be of opinion that it should be dispensed with, you will consent to submit their wishes to His Majesty's Government and wait His Majesty's pleasure. I should not recommend so much encouragement to be given to this proposition, if I were not prepared to advise His Majesty (on the receipt of such application) to dispense with the oath in the instance of Mr. Kavanagh, on condition of his taking the oath prescribed by the Act of 1783.'[1] Sir James Kempt having submitted the substance of this letter to the House, by message on April 2, it was, after some discussion, resolved on the 3rd, 'That His Majesty, having been graciously pleased to give his consent that Lawrence Kavanagh, Esquire, elected to represent the County of Cape Breton, a gentleman professing the Roman Catholic religion, should be permitted to take a seat in the House without making the declaration against popery and transubstantiation, That this House, grateful

[1] The oath here referred to was a modification of that against popery and transubstantiation, usually administered to magistrates and other public functionaries of the Roman Catholic persuasion.

to His Majesty for relieving his Roman Catholic subjects from the disability they were heretofore under, from sitting in the House, do admit the said Lawrence Kavanagh to take his seat, and will in future permit Roman Catholics who may be duly elected, and shall be qualified to hold a seat in the House, to take such seat without making declaration against popery and transubstantiation; and that a committee be appointed to wait upon His Excellency the Lieutenant-Governor, and communicate to him this determination of the House.' Whereupon Mr. Kavanagh took the State oaths and his seat in the House on the same day (April 3, 1823.)

Having, for the purpose of disposing of Mr. Kavanagh's case, gone rather too fast ahead, we must now go back to the year 1820, when an Act was passed by the Legislature on December 22, extending the laws of Nova Scotia to Cape Breton, agreeably to His Majesty's instructions. At the same time, according to the same instructions, provision was made for the principal officers of the late Government of Cape Breton. The Chief Justice was allowed a pension of 500*l.* per annum, and the Provincial Secretary, Naval Officer, and Provost-Marshal, retiring allowances equal to one half the amount of their salaries. The officers of Customs, the Surveyor-General, and some subordinate officers of the Courts of Justice, were continued in office.

The visit of Sir James Kempt to Sydney, Louisbourg, and Arichat, in October 1820, enabled him to collect much valuable information concerning the wants of the people, and especially with regard to the system of granting lands, which had long been a source of much dissatisfaction. One of his first acts was to issue a code of instructions to the Surveyor-General, to lay off lands in lots of 100 acres to single, and of 200 acres to married men, with permission to occupy them under tickets of location until they were prepared to pay for grants, with the proviso, that no absolute title should be given except to bonâ fide settlers who had actually made improvements. To encourage poor settlers, several persons were allowed to acquire titles to their respective lots in one grant, which saved much expense. It appears from a return prepared by the Surveyor-General, which Sir James Kempt laid before the Council at Halifax in 1821, that the quantity of land taken up in Cape Breton up to that time was 685,640 acres, held under the following titles:—

	Acres.
Under Grants in Fee Simple	229,220
„ Crown Leases	98,600
„ Tickets of Location, or Licences . . .	15,000
„ Warrants of Survey, Petitions, and by Squatters .	342,820
Total .	685,640

On March 26, 1821, Sir James reported to Lord Bathurst that a weekly post had been established between Halifax and Sydney; that 1,000*l.* had been voted by the Legislature for roads and bridges; that 250*l.* (authorised by the Lords of the Treasury) had been appropriated out of the Coal Mines Revenue to the repairs of the church at Sydney; and that the people, though generally poor, were represented to him as being contented, thriving, and happy, with the exception of a few individuals about Sydney.[1]

Sir James took a great interest in the affairs of Cape Breton, and did everything in his power to reconcile the inhabitants to the new order of things. He visited the island again in August 1821, and reported to the Sècretary of State, on October 19, that the people of Cape Breton expressed the highest satisfaction at their re-annexation to Nova Scotia, and appeared already to feel the advantages resulting from it. He added, 'A very strong address to this effect was presented to me at Arichat by the principal inhabitants of that district, by far the most populous and important in the island.'

On May 10, 1823, he again reported to Lord Bathurst, that two of the judges had gone to Sydney and Arichat annually, to hold the Supreme Court, and that he had appointed four of the most respectable magistrates in the island to be Justices of

[1] This agrees with General Ainslie's statement to Mr. Goulburn on February 12, 1820:—'I can conscientiously declare re-annexation to be the wisest plan Lord Bathurst could have adopted, and the only one capable of doing justice to its vast resources. This is the universal opinion of the Colony, a few jobbers in Sydney only excepted, whose petty importance will be lessened and swallowed up by their elder brethren of Nova Scotia.'

the Inferior Court of Common Pleas. Also, that the magistrates and people of Cape Breton being less intelligent and less accustomed to regular government than those of Nova Scotia, he had found it necessary to appoint a professional judge to reside there, as a legal adviser to the magistrates in all cases of difficulty, and to preside at the Inferior Courts of Common Pleas. The person selected for this office was Mr. J. G. Marshall, a Master of Chancery and a Member of the Assembly. The Legislature voted 500*l.* per annum to pay the salary of this officer. This appointment gave great satisfaction to the people of the island generally. The magistrates and the principal inhabitants of the district of Sydney sent an address in consequence to Sir James, thanking His Excellency for his solicitude and attention to the interests of the island, especially in appointing a Chief Justice of Common Pleas.

You must not conclude, because the people of Sydney very justly thanked His Excellency for his solicitude and attention to the interests of the island, that they all approved of its annexation to Nova Scotia; on the contrary, from the very first many of them expressed a strong aversion to the measure, and in the month of December 1820 sent a petition to the House of Commons, praying that a Bill might not be allowed to pass the House confirming the union of Cape Breton with Nova Scotia. But the Government of that day had no idea of asking the assent of the Commons to a measure of that kind; the Ministry decided that Cape Breton was to be annexed to Nova Scotia, and it was annexed accordingly. Though their petition was unheeded, the matter was not allowed to drop altogether. It was again brought forward in the month of October 1823, when the inhabitants of Sydney and its vicinity were assembled for the purpose of voting money for the support of the poor. Mr. Justice Marshall, who was residing at Sydney at the time, sent Sir James Kempt a report of the proceedings on November 8, in which he stated, that after the business for which the inhabitants had met was over they (forty or fifty in number) were harangued by Mr. Gibbons upon the subject of annexation, and several resolutions were proposed and adopted,[1] denouncing that measure and censuring General Ainslie; also, that a committee was appointed to prepare a petition to Parliament, and to take measures for carrying their object of a separation into effect. He added, 'From all which has come to my knowledge since I have been here, I must candidly declare my belief that most of the principal people in this place, and chiefly the merchants, are in a greater or lesser degree dissatisfied with annexation, and desirous of the change proposed. . . . The great body of the people, I am fully persuaded, are well enough satisfied with the present government and laws, and if it were not for the restless and dissatisfied disposition of the gentleman before named as the chief actor at the late meeting, I am well convinced that no such measures as I have mentioned would have occurred.' And again, in a subsequent letter, of January 22, 1824, Mr. Marshall told Sir James that the petition which was forwarded to England in December, 'was said to have about 500 signatures to it, but he had heard the greater number were made by a gentleman here, and that many of the persons whose names were subscribed never saw the petition, particularly those about Mainadieu and other places on the coast.'

Mr. Gibbons, who was sent to England with the petition, placed it in the hands of Mr. Hume, by whom it was presented to the House of Commons on June 18, 1824. The following is the entry in the Journals of the House:—

'A Petition of the Freeholders and Inhabitants of the Island of Cape Breton was presented and read; setting forth, That the Petitioners are urgently impelled to state to the House the sentiments of apprehension and anxiety with which they are inspired, by a view of the circumstances in which the country is at present placed by the unjust and ruinous attempt of His Majesty's Government to unite the Colony of Cape Breton to that of Nova Scotia, in violation of all law, humanity, and good faith—an attempt involving every constitutional

[1] Mr. Leonard stated in a letter to the Hon. Michael Wallace, on January 6, 1824, 'that there were only about half a dozen respectable persons and a few mechanics present, and that the resolutions were passed by about forty Irishmen and labourers of the lowest class.

right to liberty, property, and security, ever considered as irrevocably possessed by British subjects residing in the colonies, and deprived of which they must be degraded below the subjects of the most despotic States; and praying the House to adopt such measures as to them shall appear expedient, to restore to the petitioners their former legal government and laws; or otherwise, that the House will be pleased to grant them a full indemnity for the damage their property has sustained by a revocation of those conditions, on which they were influenced to become settlers in Cape Breton.

'Ordered, that the said Petition do lie upon the table, and be printed.'

In presenting this petition, Mr. Hume made use of such intemperate language—going so far as to say, if relief were not granted, the island would at the first opportunity throw off its allegiance to Great Britain—that many, who probably would have supported the prayer of the petitioners, were deterred from doing so. The Under Secretary of State, Mr. Wilmot Horton, stated in reply, that the petition, like one presented on a former occasion, was a tissue of falsehoods, and that there was no general feeling in favour of its sentiments in the island. Mr. Hume, nevertheless, contended that if he had an opportunity at the next Session, he would again bring the subject before the House, and pledged himself to retire from Parliament if he did not satisfactorily prove that the re-annexation was illegal. As Parliament was prorogued on June 25, no further action was taken in the matter; but Mr. Wilmot Horton, who seems to have had some misgivings of the legality of the measure, applied in the month of July to Mr. Stephens, the law adviser of the Crown, for his opinion upon the subject. Mr. Stephens, in reply, after recapitulating and explaining the nature of the several documents bearing upon the question, and pointing out their inconsistency, stated, 'Whatever may have been the origin and inconsistency of the measures formerly pursued, I am of opinion that His Majesty's Government could not do otherwise than revert to the principle established by the Proclamation of 1763, and that Mr. Gibbons's "Case," when collated with the documents to which it refers, does not suggest any sufficient reason for changing the system under which the island of Cape Breton has been governed since the year 1820.'

It does not appear from the Journals of the House of Commons that Mr. Hume again brought forward the subject at the next Session, as he had promised. The people of Cape Breton, like good and loyal subjects, submitted to the decision of the Imperial Government, but nevertheless did not abandon the hope of obtaining a restoration of their constitution at some future day. The question was often agitated by a party in Sydney, but no decisive action was taken until 1843, when a committee was appointed at a public meeting to prepare a petition to the Queen upon the subject. In this document, the petitioners stated that, after the conquest of Canada and Cape Breton, His Majesty George III., by proclamation on October 7, 1763, annexed the island to the *government* of the Captain-General and Governor in Chief of Nova Scotia, and *not to that province* as an integral part thereof; and that, although no Lieutenant-Governor was sent to Cape Breton at that time, a Commission to that effect was addressed in 1784 to Joseph F. W. Desbarres, who immediately proceeded to the island and organised a Government; and that it continued to be governed by a succession of Lieutenant-Governors or Presidents of Council for a period of thirty-five years, independent of the Council and Assembly of Nova Scotia. Also, that the Governor of Nova Scotia was required by his Commission of September 11, 1784, to summon an Assembly to be elected by freeholders in the island, but in a subsequent instruction informed that, whereas the situation of Cape Breton did not then admit of calling an Assembly, he was in the meantime to make such rules and regulations, 'by the advice of our Council of the said island, as shall appear necessary for the peace, order, and good government thereof;' and in a later instruction was ordered 'to take due care that in all laws, statutes, and ordinances passed in our province of Nova Scotia, that the same do not extend, or be deemed or construed to extend, to our islands of Prince Edward's and Cape Breton, under colour or pretence that our said islands are included in this our Commission to you and parts of our Government of Nova Scotia.' In conclusion, the petitioners submitted, that a constitution once granted by the Crown could not be revoked except by the consent of the people, or by an Act of the Imperial Parliament; in proof of which the case of Grenada was cited, in which it was decided by Lord Mansfield, that 'the King was bound from the date of his Commission to call an Assembly; and that, though not convened, yet that His Majesty could not after the date of the Grant or Commission to call an Assembly, by his sole act annul the same.' After some delay, the petition was by Her Majesty's commands submitted to the Judicial Committee of the Privy Council, and the result was communicated to Lord Falkland, the Governor of Nova Scotia, in the following letter of June 2, 1846, from Mr. Gladstone, the Under Secretary of State:—

'Downing Street, June 2, 1846.

'My Lord,

'With reference to your Lordship's despatch of the 16th May, with its enclosure, on the question of the legality of the annexation in 1820 of the island of Cape Breton to Nova Scotia, and to previous despatches on the same subject, I have now to inform your Lordship that the petition addressed to the Queen in Council by certain inhabitants of Cape Breton, praying for the separation of that island from Nova Scotia, having by Her Majesty's commands been referred to the Judicial Committee of the Privy Council, the hearing was brought on on the 1st April, and was continued to the 2nd, 6th, and 7th of that month, when Counsel were heard on behalf of the petitioners; and the Attorney and Solicitor-General were likewise heard on behalf of the Crown. A Report has since been made, which Her Majesty was pleased to approve on the 19th May, by and with the advice of the Privy Council, stating that "the inhabitants of Cape Breton are not by law entitled to the constitution purported to be granted to them by the Letters Patent of 1784, mentioned in the above Petition." I have to request that you should make known this decision to the inhabitants of the colony under your charge.

'I have the, &c., &c.,

'W. E. GLADSTONE.

'Lt. Governor Viscount Falkland.'

This despatch settled the question. Nothing has since been heard about a repeal of the union.

I might properly have brought my story to a conclusion at the period of the annexation in 1820, but I thought it would not be complete without some account of the attempts made by a portion of the people to recover their former separate government; though in doing so I may be accused of trespassing upon the domain of Mr. Murdoch, who has already brought his history of Nova Scotia down to the year 1827, and leads us to hope that he will continue it to a later period. I will not venture to give an opinion upon the legality of the union of Cape Breton and Nova Scotia, which, notwithstanding the decision of the Privy Council, was considered unconstitutional by several eminent lawyers of that day; but I may remark that, if Cape Breton was legally annexed to Nova Scotia by a simple Order in Council, in opposition to the remonstrances of the people, Nova Scotia herself (which is said to have regarded the measure with much favour) has now no reason to complain that she has been annexed to Canada *with* the consent of her House of Assembly, and the approbation of the Imperial Parliament. Whatever may be your opinion of the legality of the annexation, I think you will all admit that the island has made great and rapid progress in wealth and population since that event. You are, of course, so well acquainted with your own country, that it may appear needless on my part to refer to the state of the island here; but as these letters may, perchance, fall into the hands of strangers desirous of obtaining information upon the subject, I will give you in my next and concluding letter a short account of its present condition, compiled from the Census Returns of 1861 and other authentic sources.

LETTER XXVII.

1846–1867.

I CANNOT pretend to give you a full account of the present condition of your island within the limits of a single letter, but I shall be able to show, by reference to the Census of 1861, that great progress has been made since the annexation, in the three most important branches of its industrial resources—its mines, agriculture, and fisheries. The coal mines, as I have already told you, during the existence of the separate government of the island, from 1784 to 1820, were worked either by the Government on its own account, or by private individuals, to whom they were leased at royalties varying from five to seven shillings per chaldron. Under these arrangements, the annual sales increased very slowly, having advanced from 1,190 chaldrons in 1784 to only 6,000 in 1820. At the latter period they were held by Messrs. Bown and Leaver, but were leased on January 1, 1822, for a term of five years, to Messrs. T. S. and W. R. Bown, at a royalty of seven shillings and sixpence per chaldron. At the expiration of Messrs. Bown's lease, on January 1, 1827, the General Mining Association of London obtained possession of the mines, and made preparations for opening an extensive trade with the United States and the neighbouring colonies. I must now tell you how the General Mining Association came into possession of the Sydney mines. You are, of course, aware that in all grants of land the Crown reserved a right to the mines and minerals, and that in the year 1826 these reservations were leased to the late Duke of York, by whom they were transferred to Messrs. Rundell, Bridge, and Rundell, who organised a company, styled 'The General Mining Association,' for the purpose of working the mines of Nova Scotia and Cape Breton. It was at that time reported that there were valuable mines of copper in the province, which the Association proposed to work upon an extensive scale; but these reports having proved, upon careful examination, to be inaccurate, the Association directed their attention chiefly to the coal mines. Here, however, they were met by another disappointment. The best coal mines in the province were already leased, and one condition of the Duke of York's lease was, that it should not contain any mines let to other parties at the date of its passing. As the Messrs. Bowns did not feel disposed to renew their lease of the Sydney mines, which expired on December 31, 1826, upon the old terms, Sir James Kempt, the Governor of Nova Scotia, made an arrangement with the Association to work them for one year at the royalty paid by their predecessors. Before the year expired, another arrangement was made with the British Government, by which the Association obtained a lease for a term coeval with that of the Duke of York, at a much lower rate of royalty. As nearly all the coal above sea-level had been exhausted by former lessees, the General Mining Association were obliged to erect steam engines, sink deeper shafts, and construct a railway to a safe and commodious place of shipment. Every needful requisite was provided for carrying on a large business, but no corresponding profit was derived for many years, chiefly for want of a market for the produce of the mines. This difficulty was, however, in time overcome by the exertions of the agents of the Association in the United States, and the proprietors began to derive some returns for their great outlay in opening mines at Sydney, Bridgeport, Pictou, and other places. The first operations of the Association were regarded with much favour by all parties, as it was naturally expected that the introduction of English capital would confer great advantages upon the province; but as soon as it was found that the Association were receiving a moderate interest on the vast sums expended in the country, a cry of monopoly was raised, and the legality of the Association's right to the mines was questioned. The subject was discussed year after year with much acrimony in the House of Assembly, until the session of 1857, when, finding they could not annul the just claims of the Association, it was decided to send delegates to England to confer with the Directors of the General Mining Association, for the purpose of effecting, if possible, an amicable arrangement. Two leading members of the Assembly were accordingly sent to London in the summer of 1857, when the Directors of the Association agreed to give up all their claims to the unopened mines in the province, upon condition of receiving an undisputed title to certain areas in the coal-fields of Cape Breton, Pictou, and Cumberland. As this is a matter of very recent date, and within your own knowledge, I need not say any more on the subject.

During the thirty years which the General Mining Association held the exclusive possession of the Cape Breton mines, the sales of coal gradually advanced from 12,000 tons in 1827, to 120,000 tons per annum in 1856, but as soon as they surrendered their claim to the unopened mines in 1857, several new companies obtained leases of coal areas[1] from the Government, and the sales increased rapidly. This increase, however, was not wholly due to the operations of the new companies, but in a great measure to the establishment of the Reciprocity Treaty with the United States, which allowed coal, that had hitherto been burdened with a heavy duty, to be admitted entirely free of any impost. According to the latest official returns, the total shipments of coal from Cape Breton, for the year ending on September 30, 1867, were 339,649 tons, of which 145,728 were supplied by the General Mining Association, and 193,921 by the new Companies. The sales would undoubtedly have been much larger in 1867 had not the Reciprocity Treaty been abrogated in the preceding year. If the Treaty be renewed, as generally expected, all the mines of Cape Breton will, I trust, find ready markets for their produce in the cities of the great Republic.

When I first began to write these letters, it was my intention to have given you a short sketch of the geological structure of the island, particularly of its coal fields, but I have been obliged, from want of space, to give up the idea. The

[1] You will find the situations of all the collieries marked upon the map of the island at the end of the book.

subject has been so ably handled by my friend Dr. Dawson, in his valuable work on 'Acadian Geology,' that I have less reason to regret my inability to carry out my intention.

Cape Breton, beyond all doubt, contains many valuable mineral products besides coal, which will be discovered in due time. Gold has been found in the alluvial lands bordering on the Middle River of Baddeck, and copper ore in the hills near Cheticamp, but not in sufficient quantities to induce capitalists to embark in them. It has often been asserted that the existence of the precious metals was known to the French when they held possession of the island;[1] if this be true, I am inclined to believe that a careful examination of the metamorphic regions between St. Ann's and Cape North will be found to be the most likely locality to prove the assertion.

The following Tables, compiled from the Census Returns of 1861, will, when compared with the meagre information given in my previous letters, furnish you at a glance with a correct view of the state of the fisheries and agriculture of the island, and the progress made in these branches since the annexation.

1. CLEARED AND CULTIVATED LAND IN 1861:—

Intervale	11,209	acres.
Upland	184,044	"
Dyked Marsh	2,233	"
Salt Marsh	1,064	"
Total	198,550	"

[1] Soon after my first arrival in Cape Breton, the late Chief Justice Dodd, who was then living, gave me the following memorandum:—

'When I was in London in 1805, a gentleman of the name of Smith, who was of some celebrity as a mineralogist, was introduced to me. On understanding that I came from Cape Breton he expressed a marked satisfaction, and assured me that he was well acquainted with many local circumstances of the island, although he had never been out of England. Of the truth of this he fully convinced me by describing several objects and places in the island which I knew to be correct. He showed me a piece of silver ore, very richly loaded, which he had from a priest who had resided in Cape Breton from the year 1729 to 1755, and was contemporary and associate with the learned Charlevoix. This ore, he also assured me, was found in Cape North Bay, and gave me the marks and signs of its local state, which I will endeavour to find; but I am afraid that I may have parted with it from some irritation I formerly received in my pursuits and researches in attempting to explore the riches of this island.'

2. Agricultural Produce in 1860:—

Hay Cut	43,067 tons.
Wheat Raised	26,252 bushels.
Barley	7,274 ,,
Rye	2,323 ,,
Oats	600,625 ,,
Buckwheat	3,684 ,,
Indian Corn	170 ,,
Peas and Beans	1,183 ,,
Timothy Seed	1,317 ,,
Potatoes	548,075 ,,
Turnips	32,851 ,,
Other Roots	1,886 ,,
Apples	6,226 ,,
Plums	955 ,,
Butter	946,187 lbs.
Cheese	151,460 ,,

3. Farming Stock in 1861:—

Neat Cattle	27,472 head.
Milch Cows	26,801 ,,
Horses	9,921 ,,
Sheep	84,131 ,,
Pigs	13,714 ,,

4. Fisheries in 1860:—

Vessels employed	173
Men in Vessels employed	952
Boats employed	2,300
Men employed	2,754
Nets and Seines employed	11,512
Dry Fish cured	111,213 quintals.
Mackerel do.	16,369 barrels.
Herring do.	23,387 ,,
Do. do.	109 boxes.
Alewives do.	2,483 barrels.
Salmon do.	794 ,,
Fish Oils made	58,284 gallons.

The following Tables will furnish you with some interesting information relating to the wealth and population of the island:—

5. Vessels:—

Launched in 1860	27
Their Tonnage	1,655
Building in 1861	40
Their Tonnage	3,013
Registered	345
Their Tonnage	20,609
Boats built in 1860	564

6. BUILDINGS, SCHOOLS, AND PLACES OF WORSHIP:—

Inhabited Houses	9,313
Vacant do.	353
New Houses building	530
Stores and Shops	663
Barns and Outhouses	10,845
Schoolhouses	212
Temperance Halls	6
Places of Worship belonging to the Church of England	11
Ditto ditto ditto Rome	39
Ditto ditto ditto Scotland	2
Presbyterians of Lower Provinces	32
Baptist Chapels	8
Wesleyan do.	10
Congregationalist do.	1
Other do.	1

7. MILLS AND MANUFACTORIES IN 1861:—

Water Grist Mills	83
Steam do.	1
Water Saw Mills	72
Steam do.	1
Carding Mills	4
Shingle do	9
Fulling do	2
Tanneries	3
Iron Foundries	1
Engine Factories	1

8. LUMBER MANUFACTURED IN 1860:—

Sawn deals	297,000	superficial feet.
Spruce and Hemlock Boards	1,164,000	„
Pine Boards	1,958,000	„
Staves	499,000	„
Squared Timber	3,088	tons.

9. ASSESSED VALUE OF PROPERTY IN 1861:—

Real Estate	2,332,642	dollars.
Personal Property	1,226,012	„
	3,558,654	„
Add one-third of the above for Inverness County, not returned	1,186,218	„
Total	4,744,872	„

10. POPULATION IN 1861:—

Natives, including 8,200 Acadians and 600 Indians	52,310
Born in England	179
„ Scotland	9,160
„ Ireland	669
„ all other Countries	765
Total	63,083

11. RELIGION:—

Church of England	3,162
" Rome	33,386
" Scotland	3,332
" Presbyterians of Lower Provinces	19,982
Baptists	1,349
Wesleyans	1,476
Other Denominations	396
Total	63,083

These tabular statements are well worthy of your serious attention. You will learn from them that the people of Cape Breton can not only raise a sufficiency of the necessaries of life for their subsistence, and of materials for making many articles of clothing, but also a surplus for exportation to Newfoundland and other places, to enable them to purchase the products of tropical climates and the manufactures of the mother country. The fisheries, it must be admitted, have not reached that pitch of prosperity which they enjoyed under French domination; but you must bear in mind that in 1758 the French, when driven from their best fishing-grounds on the coast of Newfoundland, had at that time flocked in great numbers to Cape Breton, and formed large establishments at various places in the island. Besides, the French fishermen were encouraged by heavy bounties, almost equal to the value of the fish, which enabled their merchants to undersell the English in the markets of the Mediterranean, the West Indies, and South America.

You will observe from Table 10 that, exclusive of Acadians and Indians, there were more than 40,000 persons born in the island, of British descent, and only 9,000 of the Scottish immigrants then living. It is no disparagement to the immigrants to say that they were in many respects inferior to their descendants. Few of the former had ever seen in their native hills and isles any agricultural implement save a hoe or a spade, or any domestic animal larger than a sheep; while the latter have gradually become skilled in the arts and handicrafts so essential to settlers in a new country. There is therefore every reason to conclude that agriculture—the foundation of national wealth and progress—will be much better understood during the next generation, and gradually improve with the increasing population.

The condition of the Acadian population has improved greatly since the annexation. From poor fishermen they have become owners of vessels, some of considerable burthen, which are engaged in coasting and foreign voyages. In the Isle of Madame and its vicinity they own 264 vessels, of a burthen of 16,031 tons. The Acadian builds and rigs his own vessel, and mans it with members of his own family and near relatives. Industrious and thrifty in their habits, the Acadians engross a large proportion of the coal freights from Sydney and Pictou to Halifax and the United States. Some few are still fishermen as their forefathers were; nearly all possess small farms in Isle Madame, Lennox's Passage, and L'Ardois.

Even the Micmac Indians, who have been rapidly dying out in Nova Scotia Proper, hold their ground in Cape Breton. Some of them till the ground upon the tracts wisely reserved for them by Government, but the majority are employed in making barrels for the fishermen, or butter firkins for the farmers. The squaws find ready markets for their baskets, moccasins, and quill work, on board the steamers which touch at Sydney for coal. A few families reside in snug log huts upon their farms, but the greater number in wigwams of birch bark, which they can remove from place to place in their canoes whenever they please. The rapid extension of cleared lands has driven most of the game into the interior, where the Indians occasionally make hunting excursions, but none of them now look to that source as a means of subsistence.

Finally, considering the relative situation of Cape Breton to the principal cities of the surrounding colonies, and its vast industrial resources, I think I am fully justified in predicting that it will ere long assume the prominent position to which it is justly entitled in the new dominion. Much will of course depend upon you and your descendants; but I feel convinced that you will not be wanting either in the energy or industry displayed by your forefathers, who in the short space of forty years have converted its dreary and trackless forests into the thriving farms and happy homesteads which you now occupy.

Having now told you all I had to say about Cape Breton, I might here take my leave and say good bye; but I feel that my work would not be quite complete if I did not give you a short account of an event which will ever be memorable in the annals of Cape Breton—the visit of the heir-apparent to the British throne to Sydney, on July 28, 1860. I am aware that this subject belongs to the domain of future historians, and may by some be considered out of place in these letters, which profess to bring down the history of the island to the year 1820; but as many of you, together with myself, had the honour of receiving His Royal Highness when he landed upon your shores, and I may never have another opportunity of referring to it in print, I hope you will not consider that I am trespassing upon your patience, or laying myself open to the charge of unpardonable vanity, in introducing it here. The 'Hero' and 'Ariadne,' bearing His Royal Highness and suite, left St. John's, Newfoundland, on July 26, with the intention of proceeding direct to Halifax, where great preparations were in progress to receive His Royal Highness upon an appointed day; but the ships having made a more rapid passage across the Gulf than was expected, it was deemed advisable to fill up the spare time by calling at Sydney for the purpose, as the Prince expressly stated, of inspecting the Sydney Mines Volunteers.[1] The 'Hero' and 'Ariadne' were first descried rounding the Lighthouse Point at 9 A. M. on the morning of July 28, when, as many of you can testify, their unexpected appearance created a scene of bustle and excitement amongst the employés of the General Mining Association and their families, which will not soon be forgotten. About 10 A. M., the ships having anchored in the mid-channel abreast of the mines, orders were immediately issued to the volunteers, most of whom were at their usual occupations a hundred fathoms below the surface and nearly a mile from the shaft, to muster as quickly as possible. In the meantime, the lieutenant-colonel and captains proceeded to the beach with the intention of going on board

[1] The Sydney Mines Volunteers, which I had the honour of commanding, was one of the first corps organised in the province, having come forward with great alacrity when called upon by the Lieutenant-Governor in 1859.

the 'Hero' to receive His Royal Highness's commands, where they were met by Captain Orlebar, R.N., who brought a message from the Duke of Newcastle, signifying that the Prince would land at Indian Cove at 12 o'clock, for the purpose of seeing as many of the volunteers as could be assembled at so short a notice. Notwithstanding the shortness of this notice, all the officers and about two-thirds of the men were ready to receive the Prince with due honour when his barge reached the landing-place, accompanied by some half-dozen boats with His Royal Highness's suite and the principal officers of the ships.

His Royal Highness, after inspecting the volunteers, having expressed a desire to see some of the aborigines of the island, was taken, together with his suite [1] to the Indian encampment at the North Bar, but unfortunately all the inmates were absent at their great annual festival of St. Anne, at Chapel Island, in the Bras d'Or Lake, except two or three squaws and a group of young children. The squaws, with a natural politeness for which many of them are distinguished, expressed their pleasure at seeing the Prince, in very appropriate terms, and had the satisfaction of disposing of some trifling articles of their own making at fabulous prices. The party drove through the village at the North Bar, where they received a hearty welcome from the inhabitants, and then returned towards the mines. As the Prince's visit was quite unexpected, there were of course few persons present at his landing, except the volunteers and the people of the mines and the immediate vicinity; but the news of his arrival having by this time spread through the neighbouring settlements, the Prince was followed by scores of country waggons, whose owners kindly accommodated the officers of the 'Hero' and 'Ariadne' with seats, on their return to the mines. The long procession of waggons—many of the spider-shaped American build—others of a less pretentious character, of Cape Breton manufacture, all crammed with persons of every rank, 'from the prince to the peasant,' some dressed in naval uniform, and others in native homespun,

[1] The Prince's suite consisted of the Duke of Newcastle, the Earl of St. Germains, Major-General Bruce, Major Teesdale, Captain Grey, Dr. Acland, and Mr. Engleheart.

Lightning Source UK Ltd.
Milton Keynes UK
UKHW022202030221
378202UK00003B/160

9 780343 875275